D1062010

On the Edge of the Bush

THE ANTHROPOLOGY
OF FORM AND MEANING

ON THE EDGE OF THE BUSH

Anthropology as Experience

Victor Turner

Edith L. B. Turner, Editor

The University of Arizona Press
Tucson, Arizona

About the Author

Victor Turner (1920 – 1983) is recognized worldwide for his work as an anthropologist and comparative symbologist. His research of ritual and symbolism took him initially to Africa, where he studied amongst the Ndembu, and then to India, Israel, Mexico, Ireland, and Japan as well. In 1963, he left a post at the University of Manchester to come to the United States, where he joined the faculty of Cornell University. During the next years he published *The Forest of Symbols, The Drums of Affliction,* and *The Ritual Process.* In 1977, he moved to the University of Virginia where until his death he was William R. Kenan Professor of Anthropology and Religion. In these last half dozen years, his interest shifted increasingly from ritual to theatre (where his formal studies had begun), from social processes to cultural performances, and from the "liminal" phase of tribal ritual to the "liminoid" of complex, post-industrial society. His most recent book, *From Ritual to Theatre: The Human Seriousness of Play,* was published in 1982.

About the Editor

Edith L. B. Turner, anthropologist, author, and poet, edited this volume of her late husband's essays from the perspective of a co-fieldworker. From the time of their first research venture to Northern Rhodesia, she worked alongside Victor Turner, pursuing her own special interest in the women of the various cultures in which they lived. Since 1983, she has been director of Comparative Symbology, Inc., and a lecturer in anthropology at the University of Virginia since 1984. In late 1985, she returned to Africa to do further research.

THE UNIVERSITY OF ARIZONA PRESS

This book was set in 10/12 Compugraphic 8400 Bembo.
Manufactured in the U.S.A.

Library of Congress Cataloging in Publication Data
Turner, Victor Witter.
On the edge of the bush.

Bibliography: p.
Includes index.
1. Symbolism—Addresses, essays, lectures.
2. Rites and ceremonies—Addresses, essays, lectures.
3. Ethnology—Addresses, essays, lectures. I. Turner, Edith L. B., 1921– . II. Title.
GN452.5.T86 1985 306 85-20885

ISBN 0-8165-0949-2

To Daniel, Benjamin, John, and Rose

Contents

PART TWO
Performance and Experience

PART THREE
The Brain

PART FOUR
Reference Material

Prologue: From the Ndembu to Broadway

When Victor Turner died in 1983 he was in the full swing of a productive life. Our days had become so full for both of us that although it was my role to collect his papers for publication, I had not been able to work on them for some time. Now we are able to present the first of two volumes of selected essays, chosen to represent the development of his ideas on process theory. The first six chapters are based on ethnography: it was from fieldwork that Vic drew theory, from the grassroots that he respected so much.

As his principal collaborator in every field that Vic explored, I recall our life together at one level as a series of stories about the events that were steps in his development. For his readers it was a series of ideas; for me it was a life.

It was just after World War II in Britain. Vic and I were living in a gypsy caravan, for a proper home was unobtainable due to the German bombing. However, we were determined not to be without books, so we would walk four miles to Rugby Town to visit the public library, wheeling a pram containing two little boys, Freddie and Bobbie. Vic had been in the army in the lowly rank of a conscientious objector, digging up unexploded bombs. He continually worked with laborers and liked their type of interaction. He even searched through books to find more on such real life interaction. At the library he found *Coming of Age in Samoa* by Margaret Mead and *The Andaman Islanders* by A. R. Radcliffe-Brown; and he realized that tribal life was even more down to earth, certainly more socially integrated, than that of the British private soldier. I remember Vic as he read *The Andaman Islanders* suddenly resolving: "I'm going to be an anthropologist."

So it was decided. First, he went back to school at University College, London, for his B.A. in anthropology. At this time Vic began to read Karl Marx and think about the dialectic—the essence of process. It so happened that Max Gluckman, professor of social anthropology at Manchester University, also used Marxism, especially in *The Economy of the Central Barotse Plain* (1941), which Vic read aloud to me while I was sewing the children's clothes. I saw the sense of this kind of anthropology and began to look forward to fieldwork. It was Max, on one of his preambulations in search of good graduate students for his new department at Manchester, who spotted Vic and offered to arrange a grant with the Rhodes-Livingstone Institute, Zambia, for fieldwork in an African tribe. Vic agreed gladly. He would be able to avoid static formalism by working out of Manchester. He was assigned the Mambwe tribe, a people in the midst of change, to study economics; but it so happened that Vic never arrived at the Mambwe homeland. While he was at the Institute he received a telegram from Max: "Suggest you change to Ndembu tribe Northwestern Province much malaria yellow fever plenty of ritual." Vic consulted me. "Of course," I said. I knew the side of Vic that loved the world of symbols—but how did Max know? "We'll manage," I said, "We'll get shots and take quinine." And I arranged an interview with a doctor, who gave me the drugs and plenty of good advice.

So here we were in Mukanza Village, making hut counts, village and garden maps, genealogies, researching personal budgets, and most important, learning the Ndembu language. This was the "out trail," sung in poetry by Kipling; we both thrilled to the experience. We used to mutter to each other in Aldershot accents, whenever there was a ritual in the village: "The drums, Carstairs, the drums!" I would reply, blocking my ears dramatically, "By gad, Fotheringay, the drums! They're driving me mad!" Then we'd go out and join them.

During the years of fieldwork, Vic's training and background came into play. He had been exposed to the work of Bronislaw Malinowski and Radcliffe-Brown, and had learned that Radcliffe-Brown was a pioneer in his time, for he had broken away from pure ethnography to found a true social anthropology. And now that we were in the field we appreciated even more Max's dynamic diachronic approach, process anthropology in fact. Max had begun to outline some of the details supporting his theory, such as the presence of cross-cutting ties between divided sections of a social group, and the countervailing tendencies that corrected otherwise harsh or dysfunctional systems. Vic was looking for just this. He was interested in the events of life, processes he could watch unrolling. Thus we aimed in the field for an extremely close-up view of process, a view informed by Vic's growing knowledge of Ndembu social structure and regularities. The striving of the Ndembu—their consciousness, their activity—seemed to ramify into innumerable complexities at whatever level of affairs they were engaged in, whether it was disputes over matrilineal descent and succession, problems of slavery, social change, marriage, chieftainship, or ritual. The organic interconnections of human life were visible in motion, in operation. Vic did not only watch like a theater goer. He loved sitting in the men's hut with the calabashes; he knew that the "plays" he observed were serious—and that we ourselves in Western society should be more intimately concerned with our fellows, as the Ndembu were.

In the second year of fieldwork, once we had started to focus on ritual, on rites of passage, on Ndembu awareness about their own rituals and about the spirit world, the theory of functionalism, that these rituals were designed as some kind of all-purpose social glue and reflected structural patterns, began to look inadequate. We had been reading Meyer Fortes and his work on the Tallensi, which indeed portrayed a dynamic system, but as Fortes showed it, one entirely revolving around social structural requirements. One day—the scene is imprinted on my mind—we were walking across an old village site where Mukanza Village used to be (for the Ndembu move their villages every five or six years). No vestige of walls or house timbers remained, just a wide stretch of sand where grew little wild round cucumbers and mossy flowers. Vic started to talk. How could the ritual we were studying (it was Chihamba, in which we were being initiated as novices) be an expression of social structure? If expression were all that was needed, why did such complex cults of affliction as Chihamba spring into existence? There was no call for such extraordinary phenomena in the existing social system. Social glue may be needed, but not this cultural marvel. Radcliffe-Brown's theory was not enough. He saw culture merely as a derivative of social structure. Ralph Linton, the American anthropologist (1936), was right, for he considered the social system to be part of the total culture. It was something new for Vic to digest, and it became for him a shift in emphasis. He need not explain the riddling talk of the demigod in Chihamba, and the curious way artifice was mingled with belief, even in the very making of the contraption that represented the god, as an expression of the social structure. He could now extend his field into psychology and religion. He would study ritual symbols in their own right—but of course he would not neglect to recognize them as factors in social action, "a positive force in an activity field" (1967:20).

Fieldwork became our delight. Arriving at a distant village we would be greeted by the whole population, shaking hands and thumbs with us and clapping. I would find the women's kitchens, while Vic sat in the meeting hut with the men. If you listened you could hear the warm deep buzz of voices over the beer calabashes. They liked Vic. The women took me to visit their girl initiate in her seclusion hut, while our own three children played around the cooking fires. On the way home Vic and I discussed the going-into-seclusion ceremony of the previous week. "What's interesting," said Vic, "is the name of the spot where she was laid down under the milk tree. 'The Place of Death.' Then she becomes a 'baby,' and is carried backwards into her seclusion hut. She's sacred, and mustn't touch the earth." "The hut's sacred too. Her white beads—her 'children'—are in the roof. She mustn't look up." And so we would go on, testing out ideas and listening for clues to help interpretation.

When we returned from the field, we entered the theoretical environment of the Manchester School, functionalism. Max took Vic aside and warned him that his dissertation had to be on the social organization of the Ndembu (which appeared as *Schism and Continuity* in 1957). "Until you've mastered that, you're in no position to analyze ritual." Max had a very intense relationship with his students, a rewarding but sometimes uncomfortable one for those that felt his tensions. For preference he gathered around him those who changed him and pushed him on a course of theory that he was about to adopt anyway. That course was the further development of process theory. It was A. L. Epstein (Bill) who gave Max the idea of law as process, hence Max's book *The Judicial Process* (1955)—an idea for which he was ready. Social process was in the air continually from Max himself, who was a follower of Marx and the dialectic rather than Radcliffe-Brown's structuralism. Most strongly of all, process emerged from Vic's work. Vic by temperament was opposed to formalism and structure, whether British or French. He enjoyed what was earthy, what was fecund, growing, seminal. Many were the conversations between Bill Epstein, Max, and Vic. Max was a South African, a colonial, not wedded to tradition, fresh with ideas, not seeking after the prestige of the double-barreled Radcliffe-Brown. One night in 1955, when I was nursing a sick child, Vic and Bill went off to the Victoria Arms. They both had been struggling with their dissertations. We had amassed heaps of facts, figures, maps, and genealogies, but they were getting stale on us. Was this the right soil to produce a living account? Vic and Bill drank their beer and from what I can gather cursed away at the impossibility of grafting the quantitive method onto Malinowski's "living tale" method. Vic did not want to submit tables of regularities illustrated by apt little stories. He saw the Ndembu system for what it was: full of anomalies, the fault lines that bred conflict. On his desk lay many field reports of conflict, recorded under

Max's instructions. These occasions of conflict had troubled the Ndembu bitterly—long, complex, repeated, reverberating conflicts, not little stories. The term "extended case" was an understatement. At some point along the developing process of conflict, the ideals that the Ndembu truly sought were often revealed.

To explain Vic's ear for social life as a play, it would help to go back to his childhood. His mother was an actress, and used to rehearse her lines in front of his high chair. His head was full of lines and verses of poetry. Once when his mother took him to the dairy for milk, where a crowd of respectable Glasgow matrons in coal scuttle hats were waiting to be served, wee Victor suddenly shrilled out: "For *lust* of knowing what should not be known, we take the golden road to Samarkand!" All the coal scuttle hats turned around. "Lust? Wha's the wee laddie talkin' aboot? Lust?" His mother got him out of there pretty quick.

Drama was in his blood. He was reared on Shakespeare, Aeschylus, Shaw, Flecker, Ibsen. Ibsen's plays were like Ndembu trouble cases; out of each of them shone some emerging truth, that the courage of Nora was a good in itself, that the pious Brand was possessed by a demon, not God as he thought. Vic was preoccupied with the character of his old friend, the sorcerer Sandombu, and with the odd personality of Kamahasanyi, both marginal characters made suddenly central as the focus of conflict. Their stories and the rituals involved in them were fascinating to the Ndembu—these events were their great product. A new term was needed. Vic and Bill with their beer mugs before them wrestled with the problem. "Social drama," said Vic. "Of course." Returning home he wrote out his paper for Max's seminar next day, introducing the new concept. Next morning he made the wearisome journey south by bus to the mid city, then a change of buses and two miles south in the rush hour to the dusty seminar room. With controlled excitement he read the story of Sandombu: and he analyzed its stages—breach, crisis, redress, reintegration—the social drama as the window into Ndembu social organization and values. Now you see the living heart. Max sat, his hands folded on top of his bowed bald head. When it was over he raised his head, his eyes burning. "You've got it! That's it."

Vic came home radiant. He had brought his dissertation to life after all. He quickly finished it, and then very rapidly it was put into press production, for Max recognized its value and had no trouble at all convincing Manchester University Press of the same. I was conscripted to draw up the tables, to correct them endlessly, to put together satisfyingly complex genealogies—while all the time both of us felt impatient to write the girl's initiation, Chihamba, and other ritual processes of the Ndembu.

At last the time came for Vic to return to his previous insight at the old site of Mukanza Village, his resolve to study ritual symbols in their own right, then an almost untouched sphere. Both of us worked on the symbolic system until we understood it as one understands a language, though this was a language of things, of relationships, of patterns, never quite translatable into words. Vic began to write and deliver a number of papers explaining the analytic tools we were developing for dealing with symbols. These included the concept of the dominant and instrumental symbol, the condensation of meanings and multivalence of a symbol (derived from Edward Sapir, 1934), the unification of disparate significata within a symbol, its polarization into ideological and orectic poles (derived from Freud), and the manifest, latent, and hidden senses of a symbol. In "*Chihamba,* the White Spirit: A Ritual Drama of the Ndembu" (first published in 1962) he wrote, "At one time I employed a method of analysis essentially derived from Durkheim via Radcliffe-Brown. I considered the social function of *Chihamba* with reference to the structural form of Ndembu society. But this method did not enable me to handle the complexity, asymmetry, and antinomy which characterize real social processes, of which ritual performances may be said to constitute phases or stages. I found that ritual action tended thereby to be reduced to a mere species of social action, and the qualitative distinctions between religion and secular custom and behavior came to be obliterated. The ritual symbol, I found, has its own formal principle. It could be no more reduced to, or explained by, any particular category of secular behavior or be regarded as the resultant of many kinds of secular behavior, than an amino-acid molecular chain could be explained by the properties of the atoms interlinked by it. The symbol, particularly the nuclear symbol, and also the plot of a ritual, had somehow to be grasped in their specific essences. In other words, the central approach to the problem of ritual has to be intuitive, although the initial intuition may then be developed in a logical series of concepts.... *Chihamba* is the local expression of a universal human problem, that of expressing what cannot be thought of, in view of thought's subjugation to essences" (1975a [1962]: 186–87). This statement looks forward in a striking way to Vic's much later essay on brain research, included in "Body, Brain, and Culture" (p. 249). That which "has to be intuitive" and which "may then be developed in a logical series of concepts" clearly arises in the intuitive but inarticulate right hemisphere of the neocortex. It seems as if the spirit figure in *Chihamba* is a right brain manifestation. He must not be named, he is wayward and purposely hard to conceptualize.

Much of *Chihamba* struck a chord in Vic's character. With his theater background he had a built-in attraction towards ritual just as the Ndembu had. Here was a tribe with clearly marked rites of passage—and here was the man who could genuinely understand them. It is hard to imagine how it would have gone if Vic had not done his fieldwork among the Ndembu.

When Vic first wrote "*Chihamba,* the White Spirit" the reaction was not entirely positive. It was felt that he was getting into uncharted waters, dangerous ones, he was being too daring. Even Max was nervous about it. Max was very much the strong head of the department, and his self image—and my own ambivalence about him—was shown by a certain incident. He had summoned, as was his custom, a number of graduate students to his backyard for a work bee. His bushes needed trimming and the lawn aerating with a large spiked roller. We were in good humor, kidding around whilst working. Max grew tired of pulling the spiked roller, so I, the ever practical, went up to him and took the handle from him, saying "Speak hands for me." I had forgotten where I had heard that tag, but when I looked at Max I remembered, for his face had gone white. Of course, it was Brutus's speech as he stabbed Julius Caesar. Max tried to joke it off, saying "Look, they want to murder me—kill the king. It's the Oedipus complex." Vic, however, was always loyal to Max and never attacked him in print.

At about this time, in the middle of 1963, Vic received an offer of a professorship at Cornell University, which he accepted. There followed for Vic a time of change on many levels, which caused him to turn toward the study of rites of passage—the most important change of all. To begin with, he and I and the children were held up with visa trouble, before our long-awaited new life in America. We had sold our house at Manchester and were staying at Hastings on the English Channel. There was something about our stay in Hastings. We were in a state of suspense. The place of our waiting was on the margin of the sea, roughly at the spot where William the Conqueror first penetrated Britain—which was an event known to the English as a changing point in history; while Hastings itself was felt to be a threshold, a gateway. For us hopefully it was to be a gateway out. And what was strange, Vic found as he worked at the public library in Hastings that he was attended by the same kindly lady librarian who had helped him in 1947, when he was studying for his B.A. sixteen years before. Meeting this woman made us realize how peripatetic our lives had been in contrast with hers, how marginal we were. Lastly, news of the assassination of John F. Kennedy reached Vic while he was on a trip back to Manchester, and reached me in our rented home. Terribly shocked, we felt the world would never be the same again. And what were we reading? None other than Arnold van Gennep's *Rites of Passage* (1960 [1909]) in which the importance of the liminal, marginal, inner phase of rites of passage was first recognized. Our own immediate predicament began to resonate with everything to do with "passage." The world was full of flux. We were uncertain whether our future was to be in England or America. The liminal phase in rites of passage struck an echo in our own experience. We, too, were neither here nor there, just as a boy novice in initiation is neither a boy nor a man. So it was that in the public library Vic wrote "Betwixt and Between: The Liminal Period in Rites of Passage" (1967:93–111), the first of his explorations into liminality. He was able to present it in America, at the American Ethnological Society's Annual Meetings in March 1964. The "liminal" is now well understood, but at that time hardly anyone had considered its nature, except for van Gennep himself and Henri Junod (1913). Max Gluckman (1962:3) makes one solitary reference to liminality in his article on van Gennep.

"Betwixt and Between" was the precursor to a considerable new development in the study of ritual from 1965 to 1974, including the publication of *The Ritual Process* (1969) which clearly belongs to the domain of process studies. Vic's further exploration of liminality in the historical dimension and his search for it in the modern world led to his later use of the word "liminoid" to represent leisure-time, nonreligious genres of art and performance.

Let us return to Vic's first period at Cornell. The year 1964 began an era of political anthropology for him. From my unique vantage point I could see a curious process going on, for it became clear that he had two main directions of interest: symbols and social or political anthropology. It was as if, as his thought progressed, there would come a stage when it was time for him to take a new tack, like a sailboat beating upwind. Quite quickly he would reverse direction. Here he had gone far enough for the time being on the tack of symbols. Now back to his insight at the Victoria Arms, the idea of the social drama. Vic, Marc Swartz, and Arthur Tuden met at a panel on political anthropology at the 1964 Annual Meetings of the American Anthropological Association, and the interest of the three of them in political anthropology caught fire. Alex Morin of the Aldine Press was caught up in it too. He it was who published the symposium, *Political Anthropology* (eds. M. Swartz, V. Turner, and A. Tuden, 1966). The theory derived fully from the Manchester School, dealing with dynamic phenomena, becoming, conflict, faction, and process. New concepts were now developed, "field" and "arena"—for Vic had been reading Kurt Lewin's *Field Theory in Social Science* (1951). In "Ritual Aspects of Conflict Control in African Micropolitics" and "Mukanda, Boys' Circumcision: The Politics of a Non-Political Ritual," both included in this book, we find a way of handling what appear to be vague and ephemeral factional tendencies spread through a wide social group. These tendencies constituted the field, "an abstract cultural domain where rules are formulated, established, and come into conflict, rules from which many kinds of sequences of social action may be generated.... Arenas are the concrete settings in which...power is mobilized and in which there is a trial of strength between those with influence" (Turner 1974:17). An arena could be a village meeting house, a courtroom, the polls, or even the pages of a newspaper.

Political anthropology and process can be seen working continually in Vic's thought. He would return constantly to the grassroots, that is, to the use of detailed field material to give strength to his progress. He was fond of a maxim of Karl Marx's about the giant Anteus who could never be beaten if he kept his feet on the earth. The earth was the people and actual events.

In 1972 at the Toronto Meetings of the American Anthropological Association, in a panel on symbolic inversion, Vic met Brian Sutton-Smith, who introduced him to the fascinating world of play as a field of study. "What interests me about Sutton-Smith's formulation is that he sees liminal and liminoid situations as the settings in which new symbols, models, and paradigms arise—as the seedbeds of cultural creativity in fact. These new symbols and constructions then feed back into the central economic and politico-legal domains and arenas, supplying them with goals, aspirations, incentives, structural models, and *raisons d'etre*" (Turner 1982:28). This idea of feedback was to become the basis of Vic's idea of the way social drama and stage drama are linked (p. 300). A new phase in his research was in the making. He loved acting, as we have seen, and poetry, art forms, and all aspects of performance. This side of him was echoed when he met Richard Schechner, the Off-Off Broadway theater director. Vic began to be involved in New York theater, focusing on another aspect, life as performance. The theater world of his youth became material for anthropology. A series of Wenner-Gren conferences commenced. Their director, Lita Osmundsen, well understood the possibilities inherent in the new kind of research that was being pioneered by Vic and Richard. With the generous support of the Wenner-Gren Foundation for Anthropological Research, master performers of theater and ritual from all over the world were brought together to enact their work and to compare notes, along with theoreticians to analyze the data. The result was a pooling of ideas never before experienced in anthropology or theater. During this stage of our research, in various contexts and countries, Vic and I witnessed or participated in the Yaqui Deer Dance, Suzuki's Japanese postmodern theater, a Brooklyn gospel-singing healing service, the Manhattan Pentecostals, Japanese Noh plays, and other performances such as Kabuki, Bunraku puppet theater, the Kagura dance of divinity, and popular festivals, Indian Kutiyattam, and Kathakali temple theater, Wole Soyinka's Yoruba theater, Korean shamanism, Eskimo dance, Indonesian Wayang and Topeng, postmodern Off-Off Broadway theater, Carnaval, Umbanda, and the Kardecism spirit cult in Brazil, the Jewish Purim and Passover, the Samaritan paschal sacrifice, Easter at the Holy Sepulchre,

Indian tribal marriage, the Indian Sariswati celebration, the *Ik* theater production in the U.S.A., and *Chorus Line*—the list could go on.

There was a thread of continuity in these perfomances that interested Vic, a thread he worked over and dealt with. He could fly from one performance to another finding the thread. His conclusions found expression in several essays on performance and experience. About theater, he quoted Constantin Stanislavski when he applied the subjunctive "if" to theater: " 'If' acts as a lever to lift us out of the world of actuality into the realm of the imagination" (1936:43). "The realm of the imagination," Vic said, "corresponds to the realm where images of heterogeneous pasts jostle with images of heterogeneous presents and are worked into alternative patterns by the shaping wills of authors, directors, actors, and onlookers, one of which will finally emerge as the most satisfactory 'as if' expression for assigning meaning in the contemporary relation between social dynamics and its interpretative double, the theater.... The theater is a kind of living, constantly changing ritual, which is congruent with the nature of a turbulent society which can be characterized more by becoming than being" (unpublished manuscript). Here we see the connecting thread of process theory coming through his work on performance. He speaks of performers as "explorers of our future—we should take note of the messages that they give us" (unpublished ms).

It may seem a long leap from the Ndembu to Broadway, but Vic delighted in finding the thread that connected them together. He did not regard the ritual of the Ndembu as show; rather, their mode of performance suggested to him that he should look at the performance of other societies. He traced the performance process: "In the past we began with an initiation to our social dramas, and a consummation, not merely a beginning and an end, because will and emotion are involved as well as mere sequences or even cognitive processes.... But now... theater and cultural performances are the exploring antennae by which we move forward" (unpublished manuscript). The theater and other performance arenas have taken over the liminal space that belonged to ritual; they free the community of performance from its mundane bonds, so that a level of symbolic power can be generated, effective in its own right, which feeds back into the social body.

While in the thick of the study of theater and ritual Vic came across the philosophy of Wilhelm Dilthey. It was typical of him that he reached out unexpectedly to a philosopher to draw in a new strand of thought. He needed Dilthey, because at the basis of Dilthey's world view was "experience," the atom, as it were, of the human process. From experience arise value and meaning, all the meanings in the symbols that Vic had so closely analyzed. Dilthey's philosophy complemented Vic's lifelong approach, that it was in human action, human process, that the roots of meaning, of ritual, performance, and all of culture originated. Competence, he realized, could be established by the work of generalization. The study of performance and experience was like catching the electron in motion, by no means an unfitting task for the scientific anthropologist.

In 1980, Vic and Edward Bruner organized a panel on the Anthropology of Experience at the American Anthropological Association meetings at Washington; the essay in this book on experience (chapter 9) is based on the results of that conference. I attended it myself, and it was partly because of an act of mine that Vic took up an even more intriguing field. I was strolling among the book displays at the Hilton when my eyes lit on a title, *The Spectrum of Ritual,* and looking closer I saw the subtitle, *A Biogenetic Structural Analysis* (1979). I picked it up. It was more concerned with neurobiology than with genetics—the neurobiology of ritual. This was an unfamiliar field to us. We obtained a copy and came to understand that an extensive biology had developed around ritualization. What was interesting was the work on the function of the cerebral hemispheres of the neocortex, the left and right brain. The left was the rational, verbalizing side, the side that structured experience. The right was the side that comprehended the metaphor, the symbol, and was capable of the holistic view. What were these but the two aspects of society that Vic had been looking at, structure and liminality? The interaction of the two at the height of ritual, producing the "flash," was beginning to be understood. Other facts about brain function also corresponded to Vic's analyses, such as the existence of brain levels, resembling the ideological and orectic poles of a symbol. The two essays at the end of this book give Vic's argument. They were responses he made to overtures from Philip Hefner of the journal *Zygon* and the Institute for Religion in an Age of Science, of which R. Sperry, the Nobel Prize winner, is a member. Links were also forming with Eugene d'Aquili, one of the editors of *The Spectrum of Ritual.* Vic was asked to speak at the Institute conference at Chicago University in the fall of 1982. When we arrived at the conference hall, it was packed; Vic read his paper, "Body, Brain, and Culture," (Chapter 11 in this book) and received a standing ovation.

Now Vic and Phil Hefner worked for an even broader conference, planned in the summer of 1984. But sadly, only our son Rory and I were able to attend, for Vic had come to the end of his life's journey.

The implications of this last area of research seem to be that religion is not, after all, the opiate of the people, but that it has healthy genetic foundations. The details of our neurobiological heritage—lateralization and the spillover effect, inhibition and disinhibition control, brain operators, the archetypal bundles with their endowment of preparedness for social action and social relationships—are certain to have implications for anthropology.

The Essays

The essays appearing in this volume have been selected from those of Vic's writings that have not yet been collected under one cover. When reviewing the scores of articles available for this purpose I saw clearly that he began to teach his fieldwork method right at the beginning of his career—always concerned with human relationships on the ground, at the grassroots. His understanding of the human process was there from the start. In many of these essays he takes some basic sequence of human behavior and sets it in motion within its own field of social relationships. Thus he could watch process. The first six essays in Part One illustrate this method. I follow them with a theoretical piece on process, entitled "Process, System, and Symbol." This group of seven corresponds to Vic's ideas about social drama which started in Manchester, and also covers his later interest in Kurt Lewin's field theory.

As we have seen, there intervened contrasting stages in which Vic was occupied with rites of passage and the issues related to ritual and symbolism. Essays deriving from those periods will be presented in volume II. Here we will be able to concentrate on the aspect of human behavior. In Part Two of this volume, Vic links the spontaneous behavior evinced in a social drama to staged performances of various kinds. Human beings are conscious of both kinds of drama, and they consciously relate them. Vic makes it clear that no formalistic philosophy will work for him—for he is studying man alive, woman alive.

Later still, in the course of his investigations inwards into the more subtle regions of human consciousness, Vic discovered that many of the intimate workings of the human brain were already known, for the neurobiologists had made a step forward. The two essays in Part Three show how Vic related his framework for process and ritual to the new neuroscience, a science whose richness is fully worth the attention of anthropologists.

Thus the essays presented here will lead the reader along the route of Vic's work on process, stopping at various centers on the way that he researched in detail to prepare for the next advance.

In Part One, the essay "Aspects of Saora Ritual and Shamanism: An Approach to the Data of Ritual" originally appeared in 1956 as a review of Verrier Elwin's *The Religion of an Indian Tribe.* It still carries a salutary warning to those who record a ritual system without tracing the relationships between members of cults, or relating something of their life histories and the events leading up to the ritual, or shamanic, episodes. Even though ritual is autonomous and powerful in its own right, it still does not operate in a vacuum, but in a certain setting, one that is moving and dynamic.

In the next two essays, "Ritual Aspects of Conflict Control in African Micropolitics," first read at the 1964 Annual Meetings of the American Anthropological Association, and "*Mukanda,* Boys' Circumcision: The Politics of a Non-Political Ritual," first read at a Wenner-Gren conference in 1966, may be found detailed demonstrations of how to perform the task demanded in the first essay. Here Vic maps out the field of tension in the villages participating in the boys' circumcision and runs the drama through the text in live motion. In *The Forests of Symbols* (1967) appears an account of the ritual proceedings of the boys' circumcision; "Three Symbols of Passage" (1962: 124–279) is a close analysis of the main symbols of the ceremony, and the two essays presented here complete the theoretical framework for analyzing the social processes of the ritual. Thus there are four essays covering different aspects of the rite. Vic provided not merely a detailed record of this ritual but has scored it in many different ways enabling the full flavor to be appreciated. Rarely has a ritual received such thorough handling. The texts constitute a bank of material that can be reanalyzed by future anthropologists.

In writing "An Anthropological Approach to the Icelandic Saga" and "The Icelandic Family Saga as a Genre of Meaning-Assignment"—dealing with a form of literature in which the texts themselves describe the social and kinship background in meticulous detail—Vic acknowledged his debt as an anthropologist to the early training in Old Icelandic and the sagas which he received at University College London before World War II. Was his consciousness of social process, social drama, field, and arena rooted in the study of these sagas? Vic often claimed that it was. "An Anthropological Approach to the Icelandic Saga," written for Evans-Pritchard's festschrift, *The Translation of Culture* (1971), discusses *Njal's Saga,* the greatest of the sagas; and "The Icelandic Family Saga as a Genre of Meaning-Assignment," which Vic wrote for his seminar in 1980, and which is now published for the first time, deals with the processes implicit in *The Eyrbyggya Saga,* another saga masterpiece. Vic's latter essay is preceded by an explanation of his term "epic relation," a relation that consists of the "heroic time" of the narrated events; "narrative time," when the epic was first composed; and "documentary time," the period in which emerged manuscripts of the epic in their various recensions. He also discusses the merits of the theories for and against the written origin of the sagas, as opposed to the oral. These passages constituted a paper read to the Chicago Interdisciplinary Faculty Seminar on epic in 1969.

The last essay in the group that deals with a particular culture area was read in 1980 as the Ethel Weigert Lecture at the Forum on Psychiatry and the Humanities at the Washington School of Psychiatry and is newly published here. It was the first fruits of a field tour in Brazil and is entitled "Conflict in Social Anthropological and Psychoanalytical Theory:

Umbanda in Rio de Janeiro." The Umbanda cults came as a welcome challenge to Vic: their very peculiarity was to help prove his contention that one must consider ritual in its social setting. Yvonne Velho of the Department of Social Anthropology at the Federal University, Rio de Janeiro, took us to a cult center in Rio where we were able to participate in the ritual. Yvonne herself had produced a fine analysis of the events in two cult centers, including some of the life histories of the members. In the present essay Vic uses part of her material as well as our own observations in his discussion of this new ritual process, not neglecting the fascinating problems of factionalism and the impact of modern life upon the trancers.

The theoretical essay, entitled "Process, System, and Symbol: A New Anthropological Synthesis," was first published in *Daedalus* (1977). Here Vic analyzes "the processes, involving shared symbols, gestures, and language, by which social interaction generates an emergent social reality distinct from and external to that of the individuals who produce it" (p. 154). And it is through often discrepant norms, through the indeterminacies of actual social life, that the true picture emerges. He discusses liminality as the means of generating variability and the free play of humanity's cognitive and imaginative capacities.

Part Two breaks open the world of performance. The essay "The Anthropology of Performance," written for his seminar in 1980, now published for the first time, lays out the new development, in which he integrates his concept of the social drama with the processual reflexive character of postmodern drama. He leads on to the richness and subtleties of contemporary social performances, where communitas, though "intrinsically dynamic, is never quite realized" (p. 190). It is through Dilthey's dynamic view of "Weltanschauung" and of "lived experience" that Vic shows us the next step, which takes us to the anthropology of experience.

In the essay "Experience and Performance: Towards a New Processual Anthropology," written for the panel on experience at the 1980 Annual Meetings of the American Anthropological Association at Washington, D.C., first published here, Vic sees processual analysis not as the mere marking of movement, of events, in society, nor of the social drama as event only, but as the analysis of "the lived experience of some whole unit of meaning" in Dilthey's words. The essay contains a useful bibliographical commentary on Dilthey's works and those of his exponents, also a postscript on the meaning of the word "experience."

"Images of Anti-Temporality: An Essay in the Anthropology of Experience" was a paper given in the Ingersoll Lecture Series at the Harvard Divinity School in 1981. In it Vic takes the reader by various earthy stages in the world of anti-temporality. Going right back to the beginning, he shows how human beings are "prepositional entities" by nature (p. 229), relating positively or negatively to others—there is a hint here that this is a genetic endowment. Then he leads on through the social drama, the activity of that prepositional entity, to the situation of redress, to ritual, which contains both the sacred and the sacrilegious, thus to the Clown in the sacred sphere. His Clown here is the Kutiyattam Clown in temple theater in South India, whose performance is in timeless time, whose person is invulnerable, immune, whatever treasonable things he says. Here is Vic's key to anti-temporality.

Part Three was Vic's last venture into the unknown, his meeting with the neurobiologists. In "Body, Brain, and Culture," published in *Zygon* (1983) he courageously looked back at his former stance when he believed that human behavior was basically bred from culture, and found he had to revise it. The essay probes the secrets of culturetype and genotype, hemispherical lateralization, play, religion and archetypes, and dreaming. "The New Neurosociology," part of the fourth William Allen Neilson Lecture at Smith College in 1982 and first published here, looks at Carl Jung's psychology and its concept of the whole "self," now seen as the unification of the whole brain, left and right, upper and lower. Freud's "ego" seems to be the domination of the left hemisphere, the rational mind alone. Vic uses William Blake's *Four Zoas* as a literary allegory of the unification of brain's neuropsychical levels.

In the concluding essay, "Are There Universals of Performance in Myth, Ritual, and Drama?" given in the Neilson Lecture Series at Smith College (1982), and first published here, Vic draws together with the use of diagrams the threads of the argument of this book. Social drama and stage drama are linked in the "Turner-Schechner Loop" (p. 300), and social drama's progeny right down to our own modern culture and arts is traced in a continuous "genealogy" of performance.

Acknowledgments

Victor Turner's colleagues in the Department of Anthropology at the University of Virginia have been generous with their time and help in the production of this book. I particularly acknowledge the valuable assistance of David Sapir and Peter Metcalf in the writing of the Prologue. Peter Metcalf supplied the title of the book, while Mary Gelber aided in typing, preparation, and general encouragement. My thanks are due to all.

EDITH TURNER

PART I

Processual Analysis

1

Aspects of Saora Ritual and Shamanism

An Approach to the Data of Ritual

Some time ago I was asked to write a review of Verrier Elwin's book, *The Religion of an Indian Tribe* (1955), a descriptive account of the religious beliefs and practices of the Hill Saora of Orissa. I jumped at the chance, for I had collected comparable field data in a Central African society, the Ndembu of Zambia. Elwin's book, I hoped, would shed light on some of my own problems, particularly on the relationship between ritual and social structure. But, in this respect, I was disappointed. For Elwin does not write as a social anthropologist, but as an eclectic ethnographer, and where he interprets, he uses the language of a theologian. He gives exhaustive lists of the names and kinds of mystical entities believed in by the Saora, describes in cultural detail many sorts of ritual to propitiate or exorcise them, and contributes a most valuable section on shamanism. From all this he concludes that "the whole structure of Saora theology and mythology may be regarded as an attempt to make the mystery and horror of the unseen more bearable." The burden of the "wholly other" was too great for them to bear, and so they produced

---

Reprinted with permission of Tavistock Publications, Ltd., from *The Craft of Social Anthropology,* edited by A. L. Epstein, Copyright 1957.

ghosts, who were related to them, deities who had the same desires and passions as themselves. Such ghosts and gods might still be alarming and dangerous, but they were not overwhelming; rationalization, of however simple a sort, had drawn their sting. This formulation may well meet with the approval of the theologian or the psychologist of religion, but the social anthropologist would, I think, examine the same sets of data in a different conceptual framework and require additionally a fuller treatment of the social background of Saora religion than Elwin has given us. For religion, particularly in tribal societies, bears the imprint of many features of the social structure. Crucial religious symbols, for example, may represent a society's articulating principles of social organization. The dominant symbol of the girl's puberty ritual among the Ndembu, for instance, is a tree which exudes a white latex when cut. As a religious symbol this tree ranges in meaning from "mother's milk" (primary sense) to "matriliny" (a much more abstract significance). Other symbols may represent social *groups, categories,* or social *positions* (in a perduring system).

Furthermore, performance of rituals may make visible specific structural aspects of the situation to which they refer, as, for example, the local or tribal hierarchy of authority or patterned opposition between the sexes. And to obtain an adequate understanding of a given performance, the investigator must take account of the idiosyncratic relations obtaining between particular groups at that time. Relations between village pressure groups may, for example, influence the allocation of roles in a particular performance of ritual. These considerations entail the collection of systematic data about the *social field* in which ritual is observed. (Although I write as an Africanist about Indian data, I would like to stress that we have many common problems and must find common methods of tackling them if social anthropology is to develop a genuinely scientific basis.)

The methods I shall use to interpret certain features of Saora ritual have been fruitfully applied by anthropologists to the study of societies with widely differing ethnic and cultural backgrounds. I hope that this will serve as an adequate excuse for my presumption in analyzing Indian data although I have never done fieldwork in India.

Let me try to show with the help of three examples how Elwin might have clarified certain features of Saora ritual if he had made a prior analysis of the social system. On p. 411, he cites the case of two brothers who lived together with their father, until his death, when each set up a separate establishment. Shortly after one of the brothers had built his new house, he became very ill. He summoned a diviner-shaman, who ascribed his illness to the affliction of three gods. These gods had been regularly worshipped by his father, and his brother had painted an ikon (i.e., a sacred drawing, on an inner house-wall, dedicated to gods and spirits) in their honor. The shaman, impersonating the three gods, declared to the sick man that "this man's father used to worship us, and so did his brother. So long as he lived with them he joined in the worship, but now that he has separated from them, he neglects us. If he wishes to recover he must honor us in his house also." The patient begged the shaman to paint an ikon to the gods, sacrificed a goat before it, and we are told that he recovered from his illness.

In this case, reference is made to no less than five categories of social relationship: father-son, brother-brother, shaman-patient, shaman-god, moral offender-god. Indeed, the shaman performed two roles that in Saora society are often undertaken by different individuals, those of diviner and doctor. Does Elwin supply us with sufficient background material to enable us to put these relationships in their relevant structural context? Unfortunately he does not, for his main interest in this case is in Saora iconography. We do learn, however, from the introduction to the book, that the "one essential unit of the Saoras is the extended family descended from a common male ancestor." But it is impossible to discover whether "the extended family," called *birinda,* is really a paternal extended *family* or a *patrilineage* with internal segmentation, or whether the same term covers both meanings. Again, Elwin says next to nothing about the modes of succession and inheritance, whether these are dominantly adelphic (along a line of brothers) or filial (from father to son). He does indeed mention that a man's "paddy fields are divided among the sons," but on the other hand he cites a murder case (on p. 539) in which "a youth named Turku killed his paternal uncle Mangra in a dispute over a field." On the following page he mentions how quarrels over the inheritance of a palm tree from which wine is made "often lead to tragedy, for these trees are the most cherished of a Saora's possessions." An uncle killed his nephew in one such dispute and in another a nephew killed his uncle. I presume that the term "uncle" in these cases refers to "father's brother," although Elwin does not make this clear. From these cases, it would appear that there was no clear rule of inheritance, and that the death of any man with property was the prelude to sharp disputes between persons belonging to several categories of his close paternal kin. In the ritual case mentioned earlier, one may not be far off the mark in inferring that the brothers had quarrelled, since the shaman states that the patient had "separated" both from his father and from the brother who had continued to worship his father's domestic gods. It may very well have been that the brothers had disputed over their share of the inheritance, and that the brother with the superior share had continued to worship his father's gods. But Elwin does not tell us this, nor does he tell us whether the patient was the elder or the younger brother.

In view of the widespread belief in tribal societies that spirits and gods frequently afflict the living with illness and misfortune to punish them, whether for quarrelling openly with their kin or for harboring malignant wishes against them, it seems feasible in this instance that the shaman, using the idiom of mystical affliction, was in fact redressing a breach of the customary norms governing behavior between seminal brothers. At the same time, the ritual he performed would seem to have had the effect of restating and reanimating the value set on patriliny. For the patient's recovery was made dependent on his consenting to worship his father's gods. After the ritual both brothers worshipped the same gods, and were presumably reconciled.

One learns further that it is believed that the gods actively intervene to punish breaches between living kin and to maintain the continuity through time of patrilineal ties. The shaman mediates between gods and men and makes the wishes of gods known to men. One is led immediately to inquire whether the shaman may not perform a structural role of great importance in the day-to-day adjustment or adaptation of Saora society, since it would appear that one of his tasks is to reestablish the social order after disputes have led to the breaking of certain of its relationships. For example, in the case cited, patriliny is asserted as an axiomatic value. Now, patriliny is a principle that apparently governs a number of quite distinct sets of relationships in Saora society. It appears to govern domestic relationships in the household. But it also seems to articulate households that are spatially distinct and may even belong to different quarters and villages. In ritual, *patriliny* is asserted as a unitary value that transcends the different kinds of relationships governed by patrilineal descent, and also transcends the conflicts of interests and purpose that in practice arise between paternal kin. This case also leads one to inquire whether the position of shaman may not be structurally *located* outside the local or kinship subdivisions of the Saora social system. The shaman may well have no structural links to either of the parties in a dispute. It is also possible that he has the permanent status of an "outsider" or "stranger" who has little stake as an individual in any of the ordered arrangements of secular society. He appears to mediate *between* persons or groups as well as between gods and ancestors, on the one hand, and the living, on the other. And as he mediates he mends not only the idiosyncratic tie that has been broken, but also adjusts a far wider set of relationships that have been disturbed by the quarrel. Let me give another illustration of the redressive role of one of these functionaries, this time of a female shaman, or *shamanin,* to use Elwin's term. Incidentally, it is worth noting in connection with this concept of the shaman as an outsider that shaminins outnumber shamans, although in secular political and social life women rarely occupy positions of authority or prestige.

This second case is dominantly concerned with affinal relationships, although the patrilineal basis of Saora society is an important factor in the events described. A man's wife died and a year afterwards a girl came "of her own accord" to live with the widower. She fell ill, and her illness was attributed by a diviner-shamanin to the first wife's spirit. It would seem, although Elwin does not mention this, that the husband had *married* the girl before she became ill. The shamanin, reputedly possessed by the spirit, declared to her, "What are you doing in the house I made? I was there first, and you have entered it of your own accord, and have never given me a thing."

On the shamanin's advice the husband instituted a ceremony of friendship (*gadding*) to bring his two wives, the living and the dead, together. Another shamanin acted as officiant, and said to the husband speaking as the spirit, "Why did you bring this woman into my house? I had a little sister; she was the girl you should have married. She would have looked after me properly." The husband replied, "But that was the very girl I wanted to marry. I went to her father's house for her. But the old man made such a fuss that we quarrelled. Then this girl came. She works well; you ought to be pleased with her." The shamanin, acting in the character of the dead wife, agreed to make friends with the new wife, and gave the latter a cloth and bracelets (supplied by the husband) in token of ritual friendship. Two funerary priests, dressed up to represent the two wives and carrying bows and arrows, then mimed the antagonism of the two wives, while bystanders threw ashes over them. In Africa the throwing of ashes might have represented in some tribes a symbolic "cooling" of the anger, but Elwin does not explain the significance of this act for the Saora. In the end the funerary priests drank together, embraced and fondled one another, thus dramatically portraying the end of the dispute.

From these events we may infer that the Saora practice the sororate. Indeed, Elwin states elsewhere that they do, and also that sororal polygyny is not uncommon. In this respect the Saora resemble many other patrilineal peoples. The data also show that the bond between seminal sisters is highly valued. It would also appear that most marriages are arranged, for the second wife is blamed for coming to live with the widower *of her own accord.* Her action, it is implied, disregarded the values attached to the sororate (a form of marriage that maintains the structural relations between patrilineal groups), to the relationship between sisters, and to the custom of arranging marriages. The husband tries to defend the new wife by claiming that he had tried to fulfill Saora norms by marrying his deceased wife's sister. Her father was in the wrong, he suggested, for "making such a fuss" that they quarrelled. If Elwin had been interested in sociological problems he would have inquired more closely into the content of this alleged quarrel, which might conceivably have thrown light on the nature and functions of bridewealth among the Saora. One would like to know, for example, whether a woman's father has to return her widower's bridewealth, if the widower does not marry her younger sister. In the case we are discussing the husband might have claimed the return of his bridewealth, rather than marry a little girl. Or the father might have wanted to marry his younger daughter to another, perhaps wealthier husband, and this may have occasioned the "fuss" he made. It appears probable that neither the husband nor the father desired a radical breach in their relationship, for the symbolism of ritual friendship between dead and living wives seems to signify that the new marriage was accepted by the kin of the dead wife. In this connection, it would have been interesting to know the social composition of the ritual gathering, whether representatives of the dead wife's paternal extended family (*birinda*) were present or not, and whether they partook of the sacrificial meal with the husband. Again, since each *birinda* has its hereditary funerary priest, one would like to know whether the two funerary priests who mimed conflict and reconciliation between the dead and living wives represented the *birindas* of the women. Elwin does not give us this kind of information.

What we can say, however, is that both the diviner-shamanin and the doctor-shamanin who performed the friendship ritual reaffirmed a number of Saora norms and values in a situation following their breach or neglect. The doctor-shamanin fulfilled the further task of reconciling the various parties to the quarrel. Through her mediation their relationships were realigned, so as to take into account the fact of the new marriage.

In the case just mentioned the agent of affliction was a spirit, not a god. It is possible that different kinds of mystical beings are invoked to explain misfortune in connection with different kinds of social relations. It may be merely that gods and spirits are invoked haphazardly according to the caprice of diviners. At any rate, the difference in the afflicting agency does not seem to depend upon the severity of affliction, for both gods and spirits are believed to have power to *kill* the living. My own guess is that gods are regarded as agents of affliction where emphasis is laid on the general interests and values of Saora society, or when general disasters, like plagues, strike the people, while spirits are brought into account for misfortunes arising from open quarrels and concealed hostilities within its component subgroups. The point I wish to make is that if the investigator had been concerned with the sociology of Saora religion, awareness of such problems would have influenced his selection of data.

My last example of the interdependence of aspects of ritual and social structure is a fragment of a genealogy. It is a very odd genealogy indeed, for it portrays marital and blood ties between human beings and spirits. The human beings are Saora shamans and shamanins. The spirits are not ancestor-spirits but a special class of mystical beings called tutelaries by Elwin, who are believed to marry diviner-shamans and shamanins, to possess them in trances, and to assist them in divining into the causes of misfortune and illness. The genealogy is extracted from an autobiographical text recorded by Elwin from a famous shaman, who was both diviner and doctor (p. 258). This shaman's father, who was also a shaman, was said by his son to have had four children by his tutelary spirit, two boys and two girls. One of the spirit-sons became the tutelary husband of a shamanin, in a village about three miles to the north, and one of the spirit-daughters became the tutelary wife of a shaman in another village. It would appear from this and similar texts that shamans and shamanins are in the habit of linking themselves to one another by collaborating in the manufacture of fictitious or, rather, fantasy genealogies of this sort. The Saora, in real life, attach a political significance to intervillage ties of affinity, perhaps because they have no indigenous centralized political authority, but live in autonomous villages, each largely self-supporting and self-contained. Shaman-diviners express their professional unity in the idiom of affinity and kinship, and fabricate genealogies in which the significant links are unseen, fictitious beings.

There is another curious feature about these fictitious genealogies. Many of the marriages between diviners and their tutelary spouses would be reckoned incestuous if they were between living Saora. Thus, on p. 435, Elwin describes how a shaman married the tutelary daughter of his father's father, in other words his father's spirit-sister. On p. 149, a shamanin is recorded as having married her deceased mother's tutelary, i.e., her spirit stepfather. Another shaman married his spirit-cross-cousin, and cross-cousin marriage is forbidden in real life. Moreover, irregular forms of marriage are practiced between humans and tutelaries. One shaman and a male spirit lived in polyandrous marriage with a female tutelary in the Under World, where ancestor spirits and tutelaries live, and whither the shaman believed he went in dream and trance (p. 436). Another shamanin was married to two tutelaries simultaneously (p. 138).

These examples suggest that at least some of the fictitious genealogical interconnections between living shamans and shamanins arise from fantasies of incestuous matings and irregular forms of marriage. Once again, in another aspect of his social personality, the shaman is placed outside the rules that govern ordinary secular life. The genealogies also express his privileged position as well as his estrangement, for he enjoys considerable prestige and may become a wealthy practitioner. For he is privileged to transgress rules that others must obey. When we come to consider what sorts of persons become shamans and shamanins we may also feel justified in saying that the strong elements of fantasy in these genealogies may arise from the fact that many shamans feel dissatisfied with their real kinship connections and with their positions on real genealogies. In other words the complicated syndrome of the fantasy genealogy may contain an aspect of *psychological compensation.* Such compensation may be related to a number of characteristics of the typical shaman, some of which we will consider later, such as physical inadequacy or low secular status. The shaman or shamanin seems to be a person who is in some way extruded from the structured subgroupings of his society, or who voluntarily disaffiliates himself from them, and who compensates by becoming a representative of the total system, regarded as a simple homogeneous unit. He is at once within and outside his society. Another aspect of compensation for personal inadequacy or structural inferiority may be expressed in the fact that tutelary spirits are often supposed to be Hindu or Christian Doms, not Pagan Saora. These groups, who oppress the Saora in secular life, are wealthier, and more powerful than they are. And like shamans themselves, Dom and Paik tutelaries have the further attribute of *externality* to the structural order of Saora society. But I shall return to this topic when I have made an attempt from Elwin's somewhat sketchy material on Saora social organization to determine just what are the major subunits of Saora society and how they are interconnected and subdivided.

The Hill Saora inhabit the Agency Tracts of the Ganjam and Koraput Districts of the modern state of Orissa. Saora are mainly distinguished from other peoples by linguistic and cultural criteria, and by the occupation of a given territory. The most typical of these Saora live in the Gumma and Serango *Muttas* or subdivisions of the Ganjam District, and in the villages within ten miles of Pottasingi in Koraput. Not all Saora living in this area are Hill Saora though most of them are. Hill Saora live in long streets, in which they build little shrines; they erect menhirs (stone memorials) to the dead, whom they cremate; they sacrifice buffalos to the dead; shamanism is the most conspicuous feature of their religion; they engage in both terraced and shifting cultivation; they have a peculiar form of dress. Other Saora are becoming assimilated into the surrounding populations, and are losing their language; and they have begun to worship Hindu gods, to adopt Hindu food taboos, and to wear different clothes and ornaments from the Hill Saora. The Hill Saora have no overall centralized political organization of their own. The Koraput Saora have no overlords or landlords, and pay taxes directly to the State. But the Ganjam Hill Saora territory is divided into tracts of land under the rule of feudal overlords called Patros or Bissoyis. Each of these overlords has a small army of "home guards" called Paiks. The "environment" of the Hill Saora includes, therefore, Hindu Bissoyis and their Paik retainers, who live in their own villages. It also includes Christian Doms, who inhabit separate hamlets, sell cloth to the Saora, and have in recent times become moneylenders who despoil the latter of cash and produce.

There are three main branches of Hill Saora: Jatis, who do not eat beef, and claim that they are pure in blood, custom, and religion; Arsis, from the term for monkey, who wear a long-tailed cloth and eat beef; and Jadus, from a word meaning "wild," who live on the tops of hills and in the wilder tracts north of Serango. There are also a few occupational groups, whose members live with the other Saora and "resemble them in every respect except in the special craft they have adopted." These include basketmakers, potters, brass-workers, and blacksmiths. Different groups are what Elwin describes as "vaguely endogamous." A Jati may marry an Arsi or a Jadu without eliciting much comment. The barriers are, however, a little stronger between the cultivating and occupational groups, yet an elopement between a potter and a Jadu cultivator is not taken very seriously and is forgiven after the payment of a small fine. But a Jati hereditary priest or *Buyya* cannot marry an Arsi *Buyya* or Jadu *Buyya.* Members of all these groups look, dress, and behave alike. Even blacksmiths and potters have their fields and cattle. Different groups often live in the same street. A most significant feature of Hill Saora society is the high degree of political autonomy enjoyed by the most important residential unit, the village. It may be said without exaggeration that a sociological analysis of the structural relationships within and between Saora villages would provide an indispensable introduction to Elwin's study of Saora ritual. But his data on village organization and on the demographic aspects of village residence are thin and fragmentary.

Several of the ritual case-histories cited by Elwin refer to quarrels within and between *villages.* Elwin also mentions (p. 57) "the acrid disputes that occasionally disfigure a Saora *village.*" Before performing a ritual a shaman usually makes an invocation to the unseen beings and powers, which includes the following phrase: "Let no one in the following *villages,* a, b, c, etc., work evil (i.e., sorcery) against us" (p. 235).

These data suggest that there are stabilized conflicts between villages, perhaps over rights to scarce tracts of fertile land, perhaps as the vestigial traces of feuds forbidden now by the Central Government. We cannot tell from Elwin's account. And it would be important to know the motives for intervillage conflict and the customary mechanisms for restoring order *between* villages from the point of view of our analysis of shamanism—for shamans practice outside as well as inside their own village.

What, then, are we entitled to say about Saora village structure? In the first place we can quote Elwin as saying that Saora villages are, for the most part, "large," long-established in their present sites, and "built in the most difficult and inaccessible sites that can be imagined." But Elwin gives us little indication as to precisely *how* large these villages are. He has made no attempt to discuss in quantitative terms such factors as the magnitude and mobility of villages, and the residential mobility of individuals through villages. We can obtain no information about the *average* magnitude of a Saora village or of the *range* of village size. He does mention tantalizingly that "shifting cultivation means that some Saora villages are very small, with only three or four houses, high in the hills, lonely and remote, but convenient for the swiddens"—by which term he means ash-gardens. But he has just previously written that "Saora villages in fact resemble established Gond or Santal settlements rather than the rough and ready camps of Baigas and Konds, for whom shifting cultivation means shifting homes" (p. 39). He does mention that in three of the Ganjam political subdivisions called *Muttas* there are 104 villages. Now there are, according to Elwin, about 60,000 Hill Saora in Ganjam, living in eight *Muttas.* Putting these figures together, and making the admittedly risky assumption that three-eighths of the Ganjam Hill Saora do in fact live in the *three Muttas* he mentions, we may guess that the average village population in these *Muttas* is about 216. In a later chapter entitled, "The Cost of Religion," Elwin mentions that in one Koraput Hill Saora village there were eighty households, in another seventy-four, and in a third twenty-five. This information is not entirely helpful, since he nowhere discusses the social composition or the average size of a household. But we are able to infer from some of his case histories that certain households—a household may own several houses, for each wife has her own—contain three generations of kin. He also mentions here and there that the Saora practice polygyny and widow-inheritance. "Polygyny," says Elwin, "is fairly common. In Dokripanga I found every married man had at least two wives" (p. 56). Now let us suppose that an average elementary family contains four members. Then let us suppose that various accretions from polygynous marriage, temporary coresidence of adult brothers (Saora are patrilocal), widow-inheritance, and such account on the average for another four members. The first village would then contain approximately 640 inhabitants, the second 592, and the third 200. The first village he mentions, Boramsingi, he refers to several times as "large" and divided into "widely separated hamlets" (p. 51). I think that we would not be too much in error if we assumed that the average size of a Hill Saora village was between 200 and 300 inhabitants, with a range of from about 30 to 800.

I have laid stress on this question of village size since there may well be a functional relationship of some importance between the *size* and the *structure* of an important residential unit in a society like the Saora, which emphasizes kinship as a significant principle of residential organization. Limitations on village magnitude may, for example, impose limits on the number of groups of unilineal kin who can dwell together, and on the size of each group. Such limitations can also control the extent of differentiation of the village into occupational and subterritorial groups. Village size may significantly influence the relationship between lineal and familial modes of organization. If patrilineal descent is an important principle governing residential affiliation, as it appears to be among the Saora, and if in small villages patrilineages are stunted, it is probable that the social mechanisms for promoting cohesion and reducing conflict in the residential unit will differ from those found in patrilineal societies where a larger village is typical or in social systems, such as the Zulu, where emergent new settlements can move out to found new small villages. Again, the average magnitude of villages may be connected with ecological factors. Above a given population threshold a village may have to split to avoid pressure on resources. And indeed Elwin writes that in the Western Ganjam District "there is considerable pressure on land" (p. 36). On p. 536, he quotes from the report of a Forestry Office that already in 1907, in Ganjam, "denudation of the hills by axe-cultivation had seriously affected the water-supply, and that the pressure of population had already resulted in far too short a rotation in the use of clearings." In larger-than-average villages one might expect to find tensions between subgroups and factions. Elwin, indeed, gives cases of quarrels over gardens in such villages. The small villages that he mentions may well result from the fission of villages that have exceeded a certain optimum size. And it is in just such over-large, quarrel-ridden villages that I would have expected to find many performances of curative ritual, a type of ritual that writers on Central African ritual have found to have the latent function often of redressing disturbed social relationships. It may be more than coincidence that many of Elwin's examples of ritual are drawn from villages he describes as "large," such as Boramsingi, mentioned above.

Since Elwin has emphasized that most Saora villages are long-established and "have nothing of the nomad about them," and since most are difficult of access, and were formerly "forts" for defense against the raids of other Saora, we may infer that such villages are social entities with a high measure of cohesion and continuity, towards which their members feel strong sentiments of loyalty. Yet at the same time Elwin shows us that each village is internally divided into a number of local and kinship subdivisions. In the first place, most Saora villages are divided into a number of groups of houses called *sahis* which Elwin translates as "quarters" or "hamlets." Often these are named after their most important residents. In Saora villages, there are a number of political officials. Each has a quarter named after his office. Thus the *Gamang* or Chief, the *Karji,* and the *Dhol-behera,* other political functionaries, have quarters. So has the village priest or *Buyya,* who has political as well as ritual functions. The nuclear group in each quarter consists of the paternal extended family of the quarter-head. Not infrequently, however, quarters are named by some geographical or occupational term, and not after a political or ritual office.

What is the social composition of a quarter? Here as elsewhere in his introductory section Elwin is extremely vague. He points out that in contrast to all the neighboring tribes the Hill Saora have no exogamous totemic clans, no phratries, no moieties. "The one essential unit," he writes, "is the extended family descended from a common male ancestor." This extended family, the *birinda,* is the main exogamous unit of Saora society. It has no name and no totem. It is possible, as I suggested earlier, that the term *birinda* refers to two distinct kinds of grouping—a patrilineage and an extended family. If both senses are present in *birinda,* there may be conflict between the organizing principles of these two kinds of grouping. Members of two or more *birindas* may live together in one quarter or hamlet, or members of one *birinda* may be divided between two or more quarters. But nearly every *birinda* is to be found within a single village. A woman does not change her *birinda* membership after marriage, and it appears from several of Elwin's texts that a person's mother's *birinda* plays an important part in his or her affairs. There does not appear to be any clear rule of postmarital residence and we hear of married sisters living in the same quarter as their seminal brothers, that is, brothers by the same father. I suspect that one of the basic conflicts of Saora society is between a woman's husband and father or brother for control over her and over her children's residential allegiance. In other words, the conflict would lie between her husband's *birinda* and her own. Furthermore, this indeterminacy with regard to postmarital residence would appear *prima facie* to inhibit the development of deep local patrilineages, for a man has the choice of residing with either his father's or his mother's *birinda.* Residential affiliation would seem in fact to be "ambilateral," in the sense in which Professor Firth (1957) has defined this term. This view receives support from Elwin's remark that "if a man migrates to another village and settles there, he can—provided that someone in the relationship of mother's brother, father's sister, or their sons is living there—be admitted to a sort of honorary membership of their family" (p. 361). As Elwin always translates *birinda* as "family," one has now the impression that the local *birinda* is a composite group containing a nuclear membership of patrilineal kin of both sexes, with men preponderating, descended from an apical ancestor, perhaps not many generations back from the oldest living members, with a fringe of sisters' children and their children. The fact that cross-cousins are forbidden to marry is also consistent with the view that sisters' children are regarded as "honorary members" of the *birinda.* One might infer from this feature of residential structure that there is incompatibility between the principles of patrilineal and matrilateral affiliation. Since Elwin points out that there is considerable intermarriage between separate villages, it is possible that this conflict of loyalties underlies the hostility between villages expressed in sorcery accusations. One might also postulate that disappointed claimants for village office and men who have failed to obtain what they considered to be a fair share of their patrimony express their discontent by going to reside with their matrilateral kin in the villages of the latter. They might bring up their children in those villages. Such children might be unable to succeed to office or inherit *birinda* property—for it would appear that the *birinda* owns the permanent terraced rice-fields supplying the staple crop. If this conception of the structure of the *birinda* is correct, it may help to clarify features of the shaman's role. For three shamans, mentioned by Elwin, said that their tutelary wives were brought to them by the tutelaries of their mothers, and one by his mother's brother's tutelary, in other words, from tutelaries associated with their mother's *birindas*. In complementary fashion many shamanins acquire their tutelary husbands from their fathers' sisters' tutelaries, that is, from members of their fathers' *birinda*. Shamans of one sex stress ritual loyalties to the *birindas* of their parents of the opposite sex. In the case of shamanins, ritual loyalties coincide with their secular loyalties and strengthen an attachment which conflicts with that of marriage. Thus many shamanins emphasize the ritual importance of principles other than those which ought to govern their dominant loyalties in secular life; a significant proportion of shamans in Saora society stress matrilateral ties against patriliny and women stress a reinforced patrilaterality against the marriage bond. In this connection it is interesting to note that funerary shamanins (*Guarkumbois*), who are "usually trained and initiated by their fathers' sisters, ought not to marry and have children" (p. 146). The patrilateral tie is reinforced in a ritual context at the expense of the secular marriage tie. Such shamanins are "outsiders" to the customarily expected role of women. Both shamanins and shamans use ritual links with the *birindas* of their parents of opposite sex to place themselves outside their customarily expected group allegiance and emphasize their personal independence from customary claims made upon their loyalties. Freudian analysts might postulate that the shaman's marriage with a matrilateral tutelary spouse represents a barely disguised wish for incest with his mother and that the shamanin's patrilateral spirit-husband is really her father. But this interpretation would have to reckon with the fact that religious beliefs are customs, collective representations, social stereotypes, not private fantasies. It might be argued, however, that the operative residential group among the Saora is not, as it ideally ought to be, strictly patrilineal, but consists of brothers and sisters and their adult children who stand to one another in the relationships of cross-cousin. This bilateral group resists the loss of its women by virilocal marriage. And although in social reality it must recognize the force of exogamy, in the powerful wish-world of ritual, men and women mate in fantasy within forbidden degrees of kinship, or with surrogate parents, and thus assert the omnipotence of the primary group against the structured, differentiated order, based on exogamy, of adult society. It would seem that some women prefer celibacy as shamanins to relinquishing full participant membership in their father's groups. We can only speculate because Elwin's material is thin on this point, but I suggest that Saora shamanistic beliefs are related to the universal human problem of the basic contradiction in exogamy—the primary kin group wants to *keep* its own members and at the same time to win members from other groups.

Because Elwin was preoccupied with religious custom and belief *sui generis,* he failed to collect the data that would have enabled him to make a prior analysis of the Saora social system, and this has given his book a curiously invertebrate appearance. For the same reason he has been unable to interpret adequately those items of religious custom itself which are directly linked to the social structure. For, as Simmel once wrote (1950, p. 15): "religious behavior does not exclusively depend on religious contexts, but it is a generally human form of behavior which is realized under the stimulus not only of transcendental objects but of other motivations....Even in its autonomy, religious life contains elements that are not specifically religious but social...only when (these elements) are isolated by means of sociological method, will they show what within the whole complex of religious behavior may legitimately be considered purely religious, that is, independent of anything social." What kinds of data, then, do we need to collect, in order to understand the Saora rituals in their social context, and even to understand their significance for the individuals concerned with them? What I am about to say may seem elementary, indeed naïve, but the omission of the data I shall list has seriously reduced the value of many otherwise excellent compilations of ritual customs by leading modern anthropologists.

We need census surveys of several complete villages both in Ganjam and Koraput. We need information about the amount of bridewealth paid or received at every marriage recorded, the amount of compensation paid for adultery or divorce, the number and ages of children of village members, the natal villages and villages of rearing village members, the quarters of those villages in which they formerly resided, the village, quarter, and *birinda* affiliation of their parents, their own occupation and status, and similar situationally relevant information. We also require full genealogical data from *birinda*-heads and elders, so that we can attempt to link together all members of a *birinda* on a single genealogy. We need records of all the affinal ties interlinking different *birindas* in the same village, and the affinal ties connecting members of census villages with other villages. We should also have hut diagrams of a considerable number of villages, relating the hut-ownership pattern to our village and *birinda* genealogies. From our numerical analysis of census and genealogical data we would then be in a position to infer the effective principles determining village structure. We would then have been able to compare this analysis of "the situation on the ground" with the ideal pattern as it is stated by Saora informants. Collaterally, we require village histories giving actual cases of succession to various kinds of political and ritual positions. From these we may infer not only the mode of succession but also whether struggles for office follow a definite pattern, so that we may ask, for example, whether the factional groupings that support the main claimants tend mainly to be their patrilineal kin, members of their village quarters, or other categories of persons. We would also like to know the class and occupational attributes of such groupings. It would be reasonable to collect data on the mode of inheritance of movable and immovable property and on the system of land-tenure. It would be important to have case histories of disputes over inheritance of property and rights to different categories of land, for quarrels over land are mentioned in Elwin's cases of sorcery-accusation. I consider that information of these sorts, properly analyzed and succinctly presented in a couple of introductory chapters, would have enormously enhanced the value of Elwin's *ritual* data. Furthermore, if he had collected systematic information about a series of rituals performed in a single village, or in a neighborhood cluster of villages over a period of months or even years, he might have greatly illuminated our understanding of the role of ritual in Saora group dynamics. In other words, if he had given us first a general model of Saora social structure, followed by an analysis of actual social processes in significant sectors of Hill Saora society, he would have been able to show us to what extent principles, values, norms, and interests, and the relationships they govern and establish in secular contexts, are represented in ritual, both in its social and in its symbolic aspects. He would then have been in a better position to detach from the whole complex of ritual behavior and ideas what was "purely religious," in Simmel's words, and "independent of anything social."

Systematic collection of these kinds of data, then, would have given us a firmer foundation for analyzing village structure than the morsels of sociological information that Elwin interpolates in his descriptions of religious customs. But let us nevertheless try to construct a model of the Saora village from these scanty bits of information. The village, as we have seen, is divided into quarters or hamlets. The nucleus of each quarter is a *birinda,* which itself has a core of patrilineal kin and a fringe of matrilaterally attached kin, cognates, and affines. Cutting across these groupings is a division between aristocrats and commoners. In most Saora villages, there are titled political functionaries, and in Ganjam there is additionally a village priest or *Buyya.* Each of these functionaries, of whom the most important is the village chief, has his own quarter, named after his title. Elwin does not tell us whether the *birindas* of these functionaries, each member of which may call himself by the title of their head, tend to dominate their quarters or hamlets numerically. The *birindas* of political functionaries and village priests together constitute the aristocracy. It is possible that villages are spatially divided between preponderantly aristocratic and preponderantly commoner sections, each section consisting of several quarters. Each quarter also would appear to have its internal divisions between patrilineal kin and its "honorary" members. Again, each *birinda* contains separate households, and a household may be divided between the matricentric families of a polygynous household head, or between the families of brothers who live together. Beyond these divisions there is the gradation in descending order of prestige between the three branches of Hill Saora, Jatis, Arsis, and Jadu. Members of all three branches may live in one village. Then there is the distinction in status between cultivators, both aristocratic and commoner, and occupational groups, such as basketmakers and potters. In summary, the Saora village is by no means a homogeneous, undifferentiated unit. It is governed by a number of distinct, and even discrepant principles of organization.

Professor Srinivas, in his book *Religion and Society among the Coorgs of South India* (1952), isolates the various subunits of Coorg society, village, caste, joint family, domestic family, and lineage, and refers to each of these in different contexts as *the* basic unit of the Coorg social system. If he had said that each of these subunits was *a* basic unit, he would have resolved the discrepancy in his analysis by affirming the existence of discrepancy in social reality. For the structural principles to which he refers in some situations may come into conflict with one another, in others again may operate in isolation from one another. From the point of view of social dynamics a social system is not a harmonious configuration governed by mutually compatible and logically interrelated principles. It is rather a set of loosely integrated processes, with some patterned aspects, some persistencies of form, but controlled by discrepant principles of action expressed in rules of custom that are often situationally incompatible with one another. Similarly in Saora society, we may expect to find conflicts, under varying circumstances, between its different articulating principles: village affiliation, quarter, *birinda,* household, elementary family, social class, and occupation. Within the individual these would take the form of conflicts of loyalty to different social groups.

It is primarily in ritual that discrepancies between structural principles are overlaid or feigned not to exist. One way in which the Saora do this is by ritualizing each crucial principle in isolation from the others. Thus we find periodic rituals each of which celebrates the importance of a different principle of grouping. These rituals are performed at different periods in the annual cycle. Each of them asserts the paramountcy of a particular principle of grouping in connection with a specific set of activities and motivations. The functionaries at the periodic, prescribed rituals that celebrate these structured groupings of Saora society are not, like the shamans, outsiders, but rather insiders to the groups they concern, although shamans also have a role in some of these rituals, as representatives of the most inclusive Saora community.

I have no time to do more than point up the contrast between calendrical rituals of this type, associated with the fixed structure of the Saora system, and curative rituals, associated with the reestablishment of that structure, after breaches have occurred in its critical relationships. Here is an abbreviated list of these regular rituals, the groups they typically involve, and the principal ritual officiants at each.

Most of the Harvest Festivals, which ostensibly celebrate the harvesting of different kinds of crop, involve the whole membership of the village. In that part of Saora country where the institution of village priest exists, this priest or *Buyya* presides over the ritual. His special function is to offer sacrifice for the whole village in the culminating phase of the ritual at one of the public *sadru*-shrines, which are located *outside* the village. These shrines are for the gods; shrines made within the village are for the ancestors of particular households, and for the gods worshipped in private cults.

The *Buyya* priest, who has political and jural, as well as ritual, functions, has the further task of guarding the village lands from the interference of hostile sorcerers, spirits, and gods connected with other localities of Saora-land. He is not usually invited, as the shaman is, to visit other villages to perform ritual. It would seem that his office has to do with maintaining the unity and continuity of the village. A new priest is selected by a shaman in state of trance from among the patrilineal kin of his predecessor. This mode of succession to office conforms to the general Saora pattern, and contrasts with that followed by many shamans. In the Harvest Festivals, presided over by the *Buyya* priests, the principle of the unity of the village is stressed over and above its internal divisions. The emphasis here is on the maintenance of the social order, not, as in curative ritual, on its reestablishment after breaches have occurred. But in the secular interstices of the ritual, as it were, in the intervals between sacred events, and on the margins of sacralized sites, behavior indicative of conflict in other ranges of behavior may be observed. To quote Elwin (p. 325): "A father may choose this moment for the dedication of his daughter as a shamanin; sick people may decide to consult the already excited shamans for diagnosis of their maladies; the ancestors are always breaking in, and their coming affords a convenient opportunity to consult them about domestic and other matters." Quarrels that have been situationally suppressed by ritual prescription here obtain indirect representation in the idiom of Saora ritual. Both priest and shaman uphold the order of Saora society: the one by positively affirming it, the other by redressing natural misfortune and the consequence of human error or malice. Each has a different social personality and employs different means; but both are devoted to the same ends, social peace and natural prosperity, which Saora, like most preindustrial societies, regard as interdependent or complementary aspects of a single order. The interdependence of priest and shaman is recognized in the fact that a new priest is selected by a shaman.

Again, the priest worships the same gods in their fertility bestowing aspect that the shaman propitiates or exorcises in their punitive capacity.

Elwin gives little detailed information about ritual associated with the village-quarter, but writes that "many ceremonies take place within the quarter for its own members who owe a special loyalty to their particular leader."

The *birinda,* or paternal extended family, has its special ritual autonomy, for it controls certain sacrifices, as well as the ceremonial eating of food in public rituals. The *Doripur* and *Ajorapur* ceremonies, to propitiate respectively the fever-giving god of cattle grazers and the snake god who causes miscarriages, are performed only for and by members of the afflicted person's *birinda,* although I suspect that doctor-shamans initiated into the cults of these gods may also take part regardless of their *birinda* affiliation. Each *birinda* has its own hereditary funerary priests and priestesses, who succeed patrilineally; these cannot function for other *birindas.* At the great funerary rites of the *Guar, Karja,* and *Lajap,* at which members of several villages attend, members of the *birinda* of the dead person eat their share of the ritual food in their own homes and obtain more than strangers, who eat out in the fields and obtain less. At the actual cremation of the dead only members of the *birinda* may attend, and each *birinda* has its separate burning-grounds and separate cluster of stone memorials for its dead. But these funerary rituals interlink neighboring villages, as well as emphasizing the value set on patriliny. For at the *Guar* ritual, which transforms a dangerous wandering shade into a reputable ancestor with a home in the Under World, certain physical remains of patrilineal *birinda* members who have been residing with matrilateral kin or who have married out in other villages are brought back by their kin. Members of both villages perform roles in the *Guar* ritual cycle. And there is a special class of shamans and shamanins, the *Guarkumbois* (including many celibate women), who officiate at these interconnecting funerary rites.

Some occupational groups are recognized as distinct units in some rituals. For example, at *Karja* ceremonies the Kindal basketmakers ceremonially exchange mats and baskets for a share in the rice and meat of the feast.

The household, in some ritual situations, becomes the effective unit, for the rites of the threshing-floor are performed by each householder separately.

We see how, in these different kinds of rituals, the validity of certain crucial principles of organization is insisted on, outside the specific contexts in which they produce conflicts. These rituals, as it were, feign that the principles are never in conflict, and that there are no antagonisms of interest or purpose between persons and groups organized under each principle. But in social reality, there is much antagonism of principle and purpose. And it is at this point, I think, that we should reconsider the outsider position of the shaman.

For the shaman, as I have said, does not represent a particular group, but, as Elwin says, "may go wherever he is summoned (p. 131)....He is regarded with respect and often with affection, as a man given to the public service, a true friend in time of affliction." Helped by his tutelary spouse, he has access to the gods, ancestors, and shades who punish the living for sinning, quarrelling, bearing grudges, and failing to remember particular gods and spirits when making invocations during ritual. These mystical agencies afflict with misfortune and illness, and the shaman cures the afflicted. Such afflictions are the common lot of mankind, and ritual directed towards their removal seems to possess in Saora culture a politically integrative function. The widest Saora community is a community of suffering; there is no Saora state with centralized administrative and military institutions. Nor are there great national rituals attended by the whole Saora people. The concept of pan-Saora unity, transcending all the divisions of the secular system, and expressed in beliefs and symbols shared by all Saora, is rather the product of innumerable, fitfully performed occasions of localized ritual, each couched in the idiom of unity through common misfortune. The shamans and shamanins maintain this widest unity, mainly because they are structurally located outside the local and kinship units of their society.

Men and women become diviner-shamans as the result of an experience that Elwin calls "conversion." The person who will become a diviner often dreams about a parent's tutelary who comes with a young tutelary, who may or may not be a relative of the latter, to arrange for the intended diviner to marry the spirit. At first he or she refuses and becomes very ill, sometimes to the point of madness. There exists, in fact, the implicit assumption that psychic conflict in the individual prepares him for the later task of divining into the conflicts in society. Such psychic conflict itself may be related, as we have speculated, to the social fact of exogamy. The diviner-elect wanders about the village and out into the woods dancing and singing. This may be said to represent his disaffiliation from the ordered life of village society. Dreams and illnesses of these sorts typically occur during adolescence for diviners-elect of both sexes. When the afflicted person consents to marry his tutelary, he recovers his health and poise and enters on his vocation as a diviner. He then receives additional training from accredited diviners, who are frequently his close paternal or maternal kin.

Through conversion the diviner achieves a socially recognized status as a sacred outsider. But the question remains: was he or she in any sense, social or psychobiological, an outsider before conversion? Are shamans and shamanins recruited from categories of persons who have either some inherent deficiencies or a low ascribed social status? In the first place, many, but by no means all, diviner-shamans and -shamanins possess some physical or psychical abnormality. For example, Elwin mentions a male eunuch who practiced as a shamanin with a male tutelary. This tutelary had formerly been the eunuch's mother's tutelary husband, according to the diviner's account. Another shaman was born "with a great head that caused his mother much pain." Another was impotent, "for all his seed was in his head," as he told Elwin. One shamanin was a leper, another said that "because she had a child in the other world she did not think she would have one here," and yet another had lived naked from birth, doing a man's work, "even sowing seed," among the Saora a typically masculine task. But before saying that abnormalities of these kinds mark men and women out to be shamans and shamanins, we should like to know how many abnormal people did not become diviners. For shamanism is a phenomenon of culture and society, not of bodily or psychic abnormality, and sociocultural phenomena are associated with a plurality of motivations and interests. Thus many apparently normal Saora become diviners, and it is possible that many abnormal Saora do not. Again, it looks as though social factors are involved.

Elwin has said that both male and female commoners, as well as aristocrats, can become shamans and shamanins. Village priests, on the other hand, and political functionaries are drawn exclusively from the aristocracy. But he does not tell us what is the ratio of commoner to aristocratic shamans. He writes (p. 449) that "some shamans come from very poor homes" and mentions "two Arsi Saora (shamans) in largely Jati villages." One wonders whether there are significant structural differences between the domestic and *birinda* arrangements of the two social classes and also between the three different branches of the Hill Saora. For Elwin stresses (p. 52) that the aristocrats marry commoners hypergamously. He has also said that polygyny is fairly common, and we have noticed above that he mentions a village where "every married man had at least two wives" (p. 56). The question arises, where do the Saora obtain the women to enable them to do this? By raiding other tribes? Clearly, no, for tribal warfare is forbidden by the Central Government. Alternatively, there may be a very early marriage-age for girls (and this is indeed the case), and a late marriage-age for men. But Elwin states explicitly (p. 54) that Saora boys commonly marry "at sixteen or seventeen." This paradox might be resolved if *male aristocrats* married early, and *male commoners* late. The village with many polygynists might be a village of Jati aristocrats. But this situation would produce numerical imbalance between the married and unmarried of both sexes in the different social classes. For example, under hypergamy, some aristocratic women might not be able to find husbands.

Perhaps it is from these women that the celibate funerary shamanins are mainly recruited? It might also mean that there would be a shortage of marriageable commoner women, with corresponding male competition for them. If, in addition, commoner men married fairly late, there might well be sharp tensions between the older and the younger men who might tend to commit adultery with the older men's wives.

We have no information on these important points. Indeed, Elwin regards the "conversion" of a shaman or shamanin as a general phenomenon of adolescence, instead of considering differences in adolescent reactions between members of different groups and sections of Saora society. It is not a universally human psychological problem but the problem of a specific social system. I have already mentioned earlier that there appears to be a conflict between patrilineal and matrilateral affiliation, and that a certain proportion of patrilineal members of each *birinda* live with their mothers' patrilineal kin. This linking-political role must impose a strain on those who perform it, and so I suggest that a significant proportion of shamans may be recruited from avunculocally resident young men, especially from those who have already a constitutional tendency to psychic abnormality.

All one can safely say is that many shamans may be recruited from groups and categories of persons whose social position debars them from obtaining political or priestly office, substantial wealth, or high secular prestige. Their only path of upward mobility may be through shamanism. As individuals, shamans of this sort may be psychobiologically normal, and may even inherit their shamanistic status patrilineally. On the other hand, some of the shamans who exhibit aberrant psychic or physical characteristics may not be structural outsiders, but may belong to office-holding classes and families. Elwin has introduced a certain amount of confusion by classing under the rubrics of "shaman" and "shamanin" the roles of diviner and doctor. Doctors are specialists who do not have tutelaries, and who learn the medicines and practices of particular curative rituals, such as the *Doripur* and *Ajorapur*, from other experts. I would guess, by analogy with African studies, that such doctors were formerly patients themselves in those rituals. Then, when they were successfully treated, they became doctor-adepts in a curative cult to propitiate the god who had afflicted them. Certainly, those who are believed to have been killed by a particular god are thought by Saora to "become" that god themselves, either by becoming merged in him, or by becoming one of his assistants in afflicting the living. If curative cults do in fact exist, this would mean that cult-ties cut across other forms of affiliation and provide links between villages and *birindas*.

There remains the problem of how shamanism is made respectable, in view of the fact that many of its exponents withdraw themselves to a considerable extent from the obligations of ordinary group life. In the first place, it is an imperative of Saora culture that the diviner-shaman has to be *coerced* by his tutelary into accepting his vocation. He affects to resist the forces that prevent him from occupying the social position that would have been his in the normal course of social maturation. Everyone believes that the diviner has had little or no choice in the matter, that he is not a diviner by free will but by mystical election. He cannot then be held personally responsible for seeking an exceptional (and indeed often lucrative) status at the expense of many of his normal secular commitments. In the second place, his fantasies of sexual intercourse with his tutelary are legitimized by the belief that he must marry the latter. The value set on marriage in secular society is upheld by the cultural stereotype of spiritual marriage. The tutelary is not an incubus or succubus, a "demon lover," but a spouse. Yet the illicit nature of a diviner's sexual strivings is sometimes betrayed by his choice of a spirit-mate. For, as we have seen, Elwin mentions several cases of marriage to the child of a parent's tutelary, in other words, to a spiritual half-brother or half- sister. Other Saora shamans married their spiritual cross-cousins, although cross-cousin marriage is prohibited in reality. Diviners' fantasies may thus offer a legitimate outlet for incestuous wishes. They constitute further aspects of the shamanistic syndrome, that is, compromise-formations between social norms and illicit wishes. A social factor may also be present here: for commoners may have only a few available mates and there may be a high polygyny rate among elders. This situation may encourage sexual relations between forbidden categories of kin in this group.

Several features of the behavior of a diviner-elect during the period before conversion are consistent with the view that a diviner-shaman is outside and in a sense *opposed to* the structural arrangements of the social order. It is significant, I think, that conversion occurs on the threshold of adult life. I have found no evidence in Elwin's book that the Saora have life-crisis ritual, initiating juniors into adult tribal status. Rather it would seem that most Saora gradually attain social maturity, and that men achieve social and economic independence rather late in life—often after their fathers have died. But for the diviner-shaman there is an abrupt break between his childhood and his adult life as a ritual practitioner. His conversion and spiritual marriage is a life-crisis that sets him outside the normal life-cycle. During the limited period between childhood and divinerhood, he is culturally conditioned to behave as though he were mad. Now, madness in many societies seems to symbolize the negation of all order. In more than one African society, for example, the Nyakyusa, either the simulation of madness as ritual behavior, or madness as a sanction against breach of ritual taboos, is a feature of several kinds of life-crisis ritual, especially of funerary ritual (Wilson, M. 1957:46–54).

Funerary ritual constitutes a passage from one set of ordered relations to another. During the interim period the old order has not yet been obliterated and the new order has not yet come into being. The effect is analogous to the attempt to photograph two successive family groups on the same negative. Many events of a typical funerary ritual are concerned with the careful disengagement of past from present, and with the systematic reordering of social relations, so that the dead person is converted from a dangerous ghost into a helpful ancestor, while the relationships of the living are reorientated so as to take account of the changes in status and mutual positioning brought about by death. Madness in such a situation may represent the breakdown of a former order or the confusion of two orders. Similarly, the disordered, disorientated behavior of the shaman-elect is the appropriate accompaniment of his transference from an ascribed position in a local subsystem of social relations to a new position where he will perform a role concerned with the maintenance of Saora tribal values transcending those of household, *birinda*, quarter, and village.

It must, however, be stated that not all diviners completely separate themselves from secular life. Some marry and have children by earthly as well as spiritual spouses. Elwin claims that there is less conflict between a person's role as diviner and as ordinary citizen than might have been expected, yet he gives examples of sharp conflict. One man, whose mother had been a shamanin, treated his shamanin wife with great brutality (pp. 169 – 70) and felt "a passionate jealousy and suspicion of his wife whenever she went anywhere to fulfil her duties as a shamanin." Another (p. 168) "felt greatly cut off from his wife's inner life. There was always something going on; she had a range of interests into which he could not enter. She had a baby from her tutelary and a lot of her heart was wrapped up in the boy whom she saw only in dreams, but who was as real to her as any human child. Once she wandered out into the jungle and stayed there three days, living entirely on palm wine. She said that she had been with her tutelary and had enjoyed the experience." "No wonder," comments Elwin, "that some husbands regard their shamanin wives with suspicion." The earthly wife of a shaman was asked by her husband's tutelary, speaking through his mouth, "Tell me, will you honour me or no, or are you going to quarrel with me?" (p. 137). These cases indicate, to my mind at any rate, the existence of conflict in the role of a shaman or shamanin who is not a celibate.

To sum up both the section on shamanism and the essay as a whole: Simmel's point that "even in its autonomy, religious life contains elements that are not specifically religious, but social" would appear to have some justification in the case of Saora shamanism. Conversion and spiritual marriage are better understood not as religious phenomena *sui generis*, but in relation to Saora social structure and to the social maturation of individuals occupying ascribed positions in that structure. It is also possible that investigators trained in psychology and psychoanalysis would have been able to throw further light on those elements of Saora shamanism that appear to be "independent of anything social." Only after the sociological and psychological factors influencing religious behavior have been closely examined, is it justifiable to speak, as Elwin does, following Rudolph Otto, of a "numinous" element in religion, of "the recognition of something entirely different from ourselves." Finally, I would suggest that the notion that the abnormal person and/or the structural outsider is in Saora society allocated the role of representing and maintaining the transcendental, unifying values of the widest social system, might be fruitfully tested out in other ranges of data. It might help to explain, for example, some of the phenomena of mysticism, asceticism, conversion, and holy mendicancy in the higher religions.

2

Ritual Aspects of Conflict Control in African Micropolitics

Extended case histories of disputes in African villages, neighborhoods, and chiefdoms reveal that each dispute tends to have a life cycle with distinct phases (see Mitchell 1955; Middleton 1960; and Turner 1957). Since relationships in these small face-to-face communities tend to be multiplex, with total personality involvement in activities of all types, whether these may be defined as primarily domestic, jural, economic, political, or religious, the consequences of interaction in one type tend to affect the premises of interaction in the immediately succeeding activities of another (see Gluckman 1955a: 19–20). This tendency can best be described, and later analyzed, if we adopt Dorothy Emmet's view, the result of a cogent but complex argument in her book *Function, Purpose and Powers* (1958:293), that a society is "a *process* with some systematic characteristics, rather than a closely integrated system, like an organism or a machine."

A dispute, then, has a life cycle that is systematized by routines, procedures, and symbols that establish the character of its successive

---

Reprinted with permission of Aldine Publishing Co., Chicago, from *Political Anthropology*, edited by Marc J. Swartz, Copyright 1966.

phases or "situations" as primarily "political," "ritual," "economic," and so on. Some of these situations may be prescribed and predetermined by custom; for example, religious performances that occur at fixed points in the annual cycle, or regularly reformed initiations into age-sets. Other situations have a contingent, ad hoc character, sometimes developing out of the dispute itself, sometimes representing a response or adjustment to events originating outside the community.

A dispute runs its course through a series of situations of different types, but two kinds of sequences are involved. The first is purely chronological: situations, of whatever type, are temporally juxtaposed. The second is typological: situations of the same type follow one another, but at a remove. Between one political situation and the next a number of different types of situations is interposed: perhaps a ceremony, perhaps a collective hunt, perhaps a fiesta. Chronological sequences are continuous; typological sequences are discontinuous; at least this is the case in on-going interactions, regardless of their qualities.

But there is another sense in which chronological sequences are discontinuous and typological sequences are continuous, for certain kinds of issues are thought to be appropriately confined to certain types of situations. It is widely held, for example, that in legal and political situations conflicts of interest, opinion, and purpose may be ventilated, discussed, underscored, or resolved. On the other hand, many kinds of ritual situations are concerned with social unity and solidarity, and with the suppression of overt expression of disputatious actions and sentiments. Thus, when a ritual situation immediately succeeds a political situation, the contentious issues raised in the former are kept in abeyance in the latter; but, at a later phase in the social process, the dispute may again attain public status in a new political situation.

The point I wish to make here is that the intervening situations will have left their imprint on the subsequent patterns of behavior. The second political situation will have been influenced by the ritual and economic situations that separate it from the first, because one and the same set of persons moves, in ever changing patterns of relations, through all of them. For example, a dispute between two village factions may threaten, in the first political situation, to become violent. At that point the obligation of all members to participate in ancestor worship or in a life-crisis ceremony may supervene; and their enjoined cooperation in ritual may then have a curbing effect on their political rivalry, so that—when next their roles are politically defined—their differences may be composed peacefully and rationally instead of disrupting community life. On the other hand, political rivalries may carry over into ritual situations and markedly affect their behavioral patterns.

It must not be thought that a community's social life is entirely constructed out of "situations." A social situation is a critical point or complication in the history of a group, and most groups are subdivided into parts that possess varying degrees of autonomy; and a considerable proportion of an individual's social participation is in the purposive activities of these subgroups, such as the nuclear family, the ward, the lineage segment, the age-set, and so on, rather than in those of the wider group, such as the village or the chiefdom.

Situations that involve groups of large span and great range and scope are relatively few. When they occur, however, the roles, interactions, and behavioral style that constitute them tend to be more formalized than those of subgroup behavior. The gradient of formality may extend from the mere display of etiquette and propriety, through ceremonial action, to the full-blown ritualization of behavior. Even when situations develop spontaneously, out of quarrels or celebrations, they rapidly acquire a formalized or structural character. Most anthropologists have observed that in the course of village quarrels, the contending factions draw apart, consolidate their ranks, and develop spokesmen who present their cases in terms of a rhetoric that is culturally standardized. Situations, too, have rather clearly defined termini: the investigator can observe when they begin and end.

Thus a society is a process that is punctuated by situations, but with intervals between them. Much behavior that is intersituational from the perspective of the widest effective group may, however, be situational from the perspective of its subgroups. Thus a nuclear family may have its own situational series, its family councils, its acts of worship devoted to its "Lares atque Penates," its gardening bees, and so on, and these may have little to do with the functioning of the total community. Yet, especially in regard to its disputes, the family may not be able to control divergencies from its inbuilt behavioral norms by its traditional machinery and these become a matter for the community. They may then precipitate community-wide social situations.

Doing fieldwork among the Ndembu of Zambia, I collected a fair amount of data in the form of extended case histories, and thus was able to follow the vicissitudes of a social group over time. In several publications I have, in a preliminary way, indicated how I think such diachronic studies should be made in the context of village organization; but here I would like to recount a series of situations I observed, over a short period of time, that involved the social group I have called a "vicinage."

An Ndembu vicinage is a cluster of villages with matrilineal cores; it has a changeable territorial span, and is fluid and unstable in its social composition. It has no recognized internal organization that endures beyond the changes in the identity of its villages making it up; but it is not just a neighborhood around *any* village. The vicinage becomes visible as a discrete social entity in certain types of situations, and a particular headman within it usually exercises moral and ritual leadership.

Villages in a vicinage do not move as a compact bloc; each moves in its own time and to its own chosen site—either within the same, or to another, vicinage. The frequency with which Ndembu villages change their sites—as a result of shifting cultivation, of quarrels with neighbors, or in search of economic advantage—means that the composition of vicinages is constantly changing: new villages move in from other areas and old villages move out. It also means that each vicinage is sociologically heterogeneous; few of its component villages have mutual ties of matrilineal descent, or even originate in the same chiefdom.

What, then, are the types of situations in which the vicinage emerges as a significant social group? These situations are dominantly ritual, but they have political implications.

The vicinage I want to consider here contained in 1953 eleven villages within an area of twelve square miles. Nyaluhana Village was founded by the sister of the senior chief about 1880. Wukeng'i Village split away from Nyaluhana (a few years before my investigation) and built a new village a quarter of a mile away. One mile from Nyaluhana was Wadyang'amafu, which came in the nineteenth century from another Lunda chiefdom in the Congo. Two miles from Nyaluhana was Kafumbu Village, inhabited by the autochthonous Kawiku people who inhabited the area before the Ndembu arrived (more than two centuries ago); Kafumbu broke away from a larger Kawiku village in another vicinage twenty-five years earlier. A mile and half on the other side of Nyaluhana was Sampasa, which arrived from another Ndembu chief's area fifty years earlier; its headman was related to that chief (the senior chief's institutionalized successor) and of the same matrilineal dynasty.

Four miles from Nyaluhana, in yet another direction, was Machamba, whose headman was descended from a son of the first Ndembu senior chief, and who considered himself the "owner of the land" (though the British authorities had abolished his chieftainship while retaining its title, Mwinilunga, as the name of their administrative district). Near Kafumbu, the autochthonous village, were Sawiyembi and Mukoma, which came thirty-five years before from an Ndembu chief's area in Angola; the matrilineal core of Mukoma consisted of descendants of the former slaves of Sawiyembi. Near them was Nyampasa Village, founded by a woman who split away from the village of the senior headman of all the Kawiku autochthones in yet another vicinage.

In addition to these villages were three small, modern, residential units—called "farms" by the Ndembu—that were based on the nuclear family and were not recognized by the British administration as tax-registered villages: Wukeng'i farm, originally from Nyaluhana but located near Wadyang'amafu, and Salad Farm and Towel Farm, within a short distance of Machamba.

The series of situations I want to describe embraced the membership of all these residential units and was concerned with the decision to hold, and the successive stages of, a boys' circumcision ceremony (*mukanda*). These rites are held approximately every ten years, boys between six and sixteen years are circumcised, and the social group from which initiands is drawn is the vicinage (with a few exceptions that need not concern us here). The ceremony is complex in character, rich in symbolism, lasts throughout much of the dry season (from May to August or September), and involves several of the vicinage's senior men as officiants.

To act as an officiant is an index of status. The process of selecting ritual officiants is, in the sense employed by such scholars as Levy (1952), Easton (1959), and Fallers (1965), political, for it is concerned with "making and carrying out decisions regarding public policy, by . . . institutional means." The public recognition of status thus acquired has further political implications in that these officiants may later be called by the territorial chief—whose area is a multiple of vicinages—to act as counselors and assessors in his court.

The four major ritual functionaries are: (1) the "sponsor," the headman of the village near which the camp of initiands' parents and close kin is built; (2) the "setter-up of circumcision," the male member of the village that contributes most sons (and other junior male kin) to the group of initiands; (3) the "senior circumciser," the leader of a group of circumcisers, who undertakes the task of circumcising the senior initiand (usually the oldest son of the "setter-up of circumcision"); (4) the "lodge instructor," who is responsible for the teaching and discipline of the initiands during the long period of bush seclusion in a ritual lodge. (There are several other important ritual roles, but these four are the major objects of competitive importance.)

In the vicinage I am speaking about, the decision to hold *mukanda* began with a decision of the people of Machamba, Salad Farm and Towel Farm to call a meeting of all the villages to discuss the desirability of committing the vicinage to this exacting task. In their private council they planned that the headman of Machamba should be sponsor, that the head of Salad Farm should be the setter-up, and that the headman of Sampasa should be the senior circumciser. Their case was to rest on the fact that Machamba was traditionally "owner of the land," that the sister's son of Headman Salad had four uncircumcised sons to be initiated, and that

Sampasa was the most efficient circumciser in the vicinage. At the vicinage council, however, Nyaluhana strongly opposed this "slate" when its composition was hinted at; fear of Nyaluhana's prestige and sorcery restrained the Machamba bloc from advancing it openly.

Nyaluhana's prestige was the product of several factors. First, the headman was a close relative of the senior chief and lived in that chief's realm. He was, moreover, in the line of direct matrilineal descent from several former senior chiefs, one of whom founded his village. He was a councillor in the senior chief's court and could be regarded as his representative in the vicinage, although he had no institutionalized political authority over its members. Second, he had already acted as sponsor of two previous *mukanda* ceremonies in the village. Third, he had acted as senior circumciser, as well as sponsor, in these and in other performances of *mukanda* in various Ndembu vicinages.

With such a formidable area of qualifications for senior ritual roles, why was it that Machamba and his coterie ventured to aspire to usurp Nyaluhana's position? These "young Turks" had several points in their favor. I have said that where relationships are multiplex the consequences of one set of interactions influence the premises of the next; and there had been many signs that Nyaluhana's prestige was in decline. Wukeng'i, for example, had split away from his village, taking more than half of its original population with him. Gossip about Nyaluhana's sorcery had helped to precipitate this schism; Nyaluhana had been rigidly opposed to modern changes of all types, and was regarded as a master of traditional expertise, including malevolent magic. He had, moreover, insisted on being paid the deference due to a chief. In short, he represented the *ancien régime*.

Many others in the vicinage no longer adhered to its norms and values, and some of them—including Machamba, Salad, Towel, and Wukeng'i—had worked as labor migrants in the towns of the then Northern Rhodesian copperbelt. Wukeng'i had left Nyaluhana's village partly to emancipate himself from the latter's traditionalism, and others saw this successful breakaway as a sign that the old man had become a "has-been." Furthermore, the Machamba cluster had always resented the deposition of their headman from the position of "government chief," holding that he was the first Ndembu chief to be so installed and that his fall was due to the machinations of the senior chief and his close matrikin, including Nyaluhana.

Thus a mixture of modern and traditional considerations impelled them to use the occasion of *mukanda* as a bid to restructure the vicinage prestige system. Also, they opposed Nyaluhana's claim to be senior circumciser on the grounds that old age had made his hands unsteady and he might harm the initiands. This was another aspect of the attitude that he was "over the hill."

In situation 1 (sponsorship), which had a political character, Nyaluhana managed to obtain the support of Wukeng'i with the argument that the rites should be sponsored by senior members of the royal matrilineage and by proposing that Wukeng'i should be the setter-up, since he had three sons ready to be initiated. The village cleavage between Nyaluhana and Wukeng'i was thus put in abeyance by the need to unite against the Machamba faction.

The villages of Nyaluhana, Wukeng'i, Wadyang'amafu, Kafumbu, and Nyampasa, moreover, constituted a connubium with a relatively dense network of affinal interconnections. Nyaluhana and Wukeng'i, between them, managed to secure the support of the heads of Wadyang'amafu, Kafumbu, and Nyampasa. It was therefore decided that Nyaluhana should sponsor the rites, and Wukeng'i should be the setter-up.

During the interval between this meeting and the day appointed for the beginning of the rites, the Machamba faction began a series of intrigues to bar Nyaluhana from acting as a circumciser. They spread much gossip to the effect that not only was Nyaluhana too old to operate properly but that he would use his ritual power and medicines to bewitch the boys.

On the opening day of the rites, after many intervening events (in which both sides tried to enlist my support as an influential stranger), the role of senior circumciser was still unfilled. The Machamba faction still supported Sampasa, and it imported another autochthonous headman from the next vicinage, with whose village they were linked by marriage, to circumcise beside Sampasa. In addition, they had played so hard on the fears of Wukeng'i for the safety of his three sons, the eldest of whom would be circumcised by Nyaluhana, that he secretly supported Sampasa against his mother's brother.

The afternoon and night before circumcision (which occurs some hours after dawn) constitute an important ritual situation for Ndembu. The circumcisers set up a shrine and display their lodge medicine baskets; the initiands' parents' camp is ceremonially erected; and a night-long dance with traditional songs and drum rhythms is held. Traditional symbolisms and rites, with the observance of traditional food and sex prohibitions, dominate the scene; for a time, the old Lunda culture is paramount.

In this situational context (situation 2), headman Nyaluhana made an impassioned speech in which he stressed the danger to the initiands of mystical powers that might become active if people were to cherish grudges in their hearts against one another, if taboos were broken, and especially if open quarreling were to break out. He emphasized that the ritual officiants must cooperate with one another if "our children" were to pass safely through the mystical dangers of *mukanda*.

I heard much grumbling against Nyaluhana around the beer pots of the Machamba faction during the night, and expressions of fears of his sorcery if they should offend him; it seemed he was getting the upper hand. The dramatic moment came next morning (situation 3), when the boys were ritually snatched by a lodge officiant from their mothers, taken beneath a symbolic gateway out of the domestic realm of their childhood, and borne crying to the secret site of circumcision in the bush.

Litters of leaves had been prepared for the boys, each litter attended by a circumciser and two assistants. The senior initiand was borne to the site, and quick as thought, Nyaluhana rushed to the *mudyi* tree beneath which this initiand was to be circumcised, inaugurating the rite. He beckoned with his hand and croaked: *Kud'ami* ("Take him to me"). (Actually his work was neat and effective, and the boys he operated on all recovered well.)

This terminated the situation in Nyaluhana's favor. Sociologically, he had succeeded in reasserting his status, and not only his status but the "Ndembu way of life," in face of the opposition of the "modernists." He had also vindicated the claim of the royal matrilineage to moral authority over the vicinage. The fact that no one challenged his claim to act as senior circumciser indicated that traditional Ndembu values, at least in this type of situation, were collective representations that still had considerable power to compel assent. Furthermore, only three circumcisers operated: Nyaluhana, Sampasa, and yet another member of the senior chief's matrilineage, who resided in another chiefdom. The defeat of Machamba faction was complete.

Only a brief analysis is needed to put this case in its theoretical perspective. The dispute between Nyaluhana and Machamba may best be understood not in terms of synchronic structure but in terms of the dynamic properties of the vicinage social field and in terms of the situational series.

When the situation was defined politically, it seemed that Machamba's faction might succeed in at least nominating the senior circumciser, since they were numerically superior and better organized and could appeal to those elements most sensitive to modern changes. But when the situation was defined ritually, and when several ritual situations followed one another immediately, traditional values became paramount, and Nyaluhana played on the relative conservatism of Ndembu to maintain and even enhance a status that had political implications.

The outcome of this particular dispute process was also an index of the degree to which Ndembu were still committed to pre-European values. This conservative bias was with the Ndembu, for, at least until 1964, in Central African national politics, most of the Ndembu supported Nkumbula's African National Congress rather than the more radical United National Independence Party of Kaunda; and they were staunch partisans of the policies of their fellow Lunda, Moise Tshombe in the Congo.

Finally, we may venture, as a tentative proposition, that if a person occupies political and religious positions of some importance, his *political* power is reinforced at those points in the seasonal cycle or group's developmental cycle when his *ritual* office gives him enhanced authority.

3

Mukanda, Boys' Circumcision

The Politics of a Non-Political Ritual

When I came to examine the data I had collected on a single performance of the *Mukanda*, or boys' circumcision rites of the Ndembu of Zambia, I found myself in a quandary about the most fruitful mode of presentation. For the mode of presentation depends on the mode of analysis. I had brought into the field with me two distinct theoretical orientations, and these determined the kinds of data I collected, and to some extent predetermined the sorts of analysis I expected to make. On the one hand, following in the tradition of Rhodes-Livingstone Institute research, I collected the kind of data that would have enabled me to analyze the structure of the social system in which Mukanda occurred. I recorded genealogies, made hut diagrams, discovered political ties and cleavages between groups and subgroups, and noted the social characteristics of the ritual participants. On the other hand, I recorded ritual details, their interpretation by experts and laymen, and those items of secular behavior directly related to the servicing and maintenance of the ritual complex.

Reprinted with permission of Aldine Publishing Co., Chicago, from *Local-Level Politics: Social and Cultural Perspectives*, edited by Marc J. Swartz, Copyright 1968.

From the first set of data, I was able to abstract a system of social relationships among the participants, and to relate this specific system to what I already knew about the general principles underlying Ndembu social structure. From the second set of data, I was able to exhibit Mukanda as a system of customs governed by the same principles that I had already isolated in the analysis of many kinds of Ndembu ritual. I was then left with two virtually autonomous spheres of study, one of the social, the other of the cultural structure of Mukanda.

And yet, during the period of Mukanda, I had felt keenly that most of the events I had observed, not only at sacred sites and during sacred phases but also at other places and times in the sociogeographical area primarily concerned with its performance, were significantly interconnected with one another. Such events exhibited a dynamic interdependence, and I felt that it was incumbent upon me to expose the grounds of this interdependence. A simile that occurred to me likened the cultural structure of Mukanda to a musical score, and its performers to an orchestra. I wanted to find some way of expressing and analyzing the dynamic interdependence of score and orchestra manifested in the unique performance. Furthermore, I wanted to find a theoretical framework which would enable me to understand why it was that certain persons and sections of the orchestra were obviously out of sympathy with the conductor or with one another, though all were obviously skilled musicians, and well rehearsed in the details of the score. Neither the properties of the orchestra *qua* social group, nor the properties of the score, taken in isolation from one another, seemed able to account fully for the observed behavior, the hesitancies in certain passages, the lapses in rapport between conductor and strings, or the exchanged grimaces and sympathetic smiles between performers. Similarly, it became clear to me that the events both in and out of a ritual context that I observed at Mukanda were influenced by the structure of a field which included both "ritual" and "social" components.

When I first read Kurt Lewin's *Field Theory in Social Science* (1951), I realized that an important advance had been made in the analysis of social life. Lewin found it possible to link in a definite manner, by means of his "field theoretical" approach, a variety of facts of individual and social psychology, which, from a classificatory point of view, seem to have little in common. He was able to do so by regarding the barrier between individual and environment as indefinite and unstable. His approach requires the consideration of an organism-environment field whose properties are studied as field properties, and not as the properties of either organism or environment, taken separately. The flow of events within the field always is directed to some extent by the relations between the outer and inner structures.

According to Lewin, "a basic tool for the analysis of *group* life is the representation of the group and its setting as a 'social field.'" Any event or happening in this field he views as "occurring in, and being the result of, a totality of coexisting social entities, such as groups, sub-groups, members, barriers, channels of communication, etc." This totality has "structure," which he regards as "the relative position of the entities, which are parts of the field."

I realized after reading Lewin that the behavior I had been observing during Mukanda became, to a large extent, intelligible if it was regarded as occurring in a social field made up, on the one hand, of the generic beliefs and practices of Mukanda and, on the other, of its specific social setting. In practice these major sets of determinants could not be clearly demarcated from one another. Since the predominant activity within this field was the performance of a protracted ritual it seemed appropriate to call it the "ritual field" of Mukanda. What, then, were the major properties and relationships of that ritual field?

First, the spatial limits of the ritual field had to be considered. These were fluid, varying from situation to situation, but corresponding approximately to the boundaries of a vicinage, which I have defined elsewhere as a discrete cluster of villages. All the boys to be circumcised came from the vicinage, and the majority of the officiants. At the great public ceremonies that preceded and terminated Mukanda proper, however, people from several vicinages, and even chiefdoms, attended, and during one phase of the seclusion period, masked dancers from the lodge visited villages in adjacent vicinages. The boundary of the ritual field was therefore vague and variable. Nevertheless, for most of the ritual the effective boundary of the ritual field tended to overlap the perimeter of the vicinage.

Now the Ndembu vicinage has certain general properties which crucially affect the structure of the ritual field of any performance of Mukanda. It consists, as we have said, of a number of villages—anything from two to over a dozen, separated from one another by variable distances of fifty yards to a couple of miles. Few of these villages are interlinked by matrilineal ties, that is, by the dominant principle of descent. Most of them have only short histories of local settlement and have come from other vicinages or chiefdoms. Such villages soon become interlinked by a complex network of marriages, and affinity assumes a political significance. Since marriage is virilocal, and most marriages occur within the vicinage, most villages rear as their seminal "children" the junior matrilineal members of the other villages. I mention this because it is an important feature of Mukanda that fathers protect and tend their sons during circumcision and seclusion. The father-son link which is crucial for the integration of the vicinage is also stressed in the ritual custom.

As I have shown in *Schism and Continuity in an African Society* (1957), vicinages are unstable groupings, for villages frequently split through time and wander overland. The split-off section or migrant village often changes its vicinage affiliation. These characteristics of the vicinage, its instability and transience, render impossible political control by any one headman over the others. No clearly dominant criterion exists to validate such authority. As in other sets of Ndembu social relations, we find rather the coexistence and situational competition of several principles which confer prestige but not control. Thus in each vicinage there are usually two or more villages who claim moral preeminence over the others, each advancing its claim by virtue of a single criterion. One village, for example, might claim seniority on the grounds that it has resided for a longer time in the territory occupied by the contemporary vicinage than any other village. Its claim may be countered by a later-arriving village whose lineage core is closely related to the Ndembu senior chief or to the government subchief of the area (which includes several vicinages). The conflict between them is pertinent to the analysis of Mukanda, for the headman sponsoring this ritual thereby obtains general recognition in and outside his vicinage as its moral leader, if not as its political head. Thus, every Mukanda is preceded by faction struggles for the right to sponsor it. Each important headman tries to exploit his ties of kinship, affinity, and friendship with members of other villages to strengthen his following. He may also attempt to win the favor of his local chief, who must ritually inaugurate Mukanda. On the outcome of this struggle depends the specific allocation of ritual roles, for the most important fall to members of the victor's faction.

In delimiting the ritual field, the structure of the village and the pattern of intervillage relationships have also to be considered. Villages are the major local subdivisions of the vicinage, and must be considered both in terms of their interdependence with that wider grouping, and with regard to their degree of autonomy within it. Furthermore, they must be examined from the standpoint both of their interdependence with and independence from each other, that is, of their relationship with structurally equivalent groups.

Membership of villages helps to shape the composition of the ritual assembly at Mukanda and is an important factor in the disputes that arise in the secular intervals between sacred phases and episodes. Indeed, what is more important than the general characteristics of village structure in this kind of ritual is the specific content of intravillage and intervillage relationships during the period of Mukanda. This content includes the contemporary interests, ambitions, desires, and goals of the individuals and groupings who participate in such relationships. It also includes patterns of interaction inherited from the immediate past: personal grudges, memories of situations of blood vengeance, and corporate rivalries over property or over the allegiance of individuals. In other words, when we analyze the structure of a social field we must regard as crucial properties of that field not only spatial relations and the framework of persisting relationships which anthropologists call "structural," but also the "directed entities" at any given time operative in that field, the purposive activities of individuals and groups, in pursuit of their contemporary and long-term interests and aims.

One aspect of the enduring structure of Ndembu society assumes heightened significance in this kind of ritual field. I refer to *categorical* relationships which stress likeness rather than interdependence as the basis for classification. Mukanda has the prominent characteristic of expressing in its symbolism and role-pattern not the unity, exclusiveness, and constancy of corporate groups but rather such widespread classes as "men," "women," "elders," "children," "the married," "the unmarried," "circumcised and uncircumcised," and so on. Such categories cut across and interlink the memberships of corporate groups. In a sense they represent, when ritualized, the unity and continuity of the widest society, since they tend to represent the universal constants and differentiae of human society, age, sex, and somatic features. By emphasizing these in the sacred context of a great public ritual, the divisions and oppositions between corporate groups, and between the total social system, viewed as a configuration of groups, and all or any of its component groups, are "played down" and forced out of the center of ritual attention. On the other hand, the categorical relationships are ritualized in opposed pairs (men and women, old and young, circumcised and uncircumcised, etc.), and in this way a transference is made from struggles between corporate groups to the polarization of social categories. But it must be emphasized that Mukanda is dominantly a repressive ritual, not a ritual of rebellion or an acting out of socially illicit impulses. On the whole, conflict is excluded from the stereotyped behavior exhibited in ritual events. On the one hand, the severe physical danger to the novices and, on the other, the danger of fights breaking out between corporate groupings in the secular interstices of the ritual situation are partially countered by a strong stress on the need for social categories to cooperate. Harsh penalties are exacted upon those who disobey ritual officiants, and dreadful supernatural sanctions are believed to punish taboo breaking. By these means the opposition between social categories is confined within narrow limits, and in the ritual situation their interdependence, rather than their mutual antagonism, is emphasized.

Although specific corporate groups do not receive direct expression in the ritual customs of Mukanda, certain typical kinship relationships are vividly represented. These are the parent-child relationships. One of the aims of Mukanda, as we shall see, is to modify the relationship between mother and son, and between father and son, in the sense that after

Mukanda the relationships between occupants of these three social positions are guided by different values and directed toward different goals than those which prevailed before that ritual. Boys, from being "unclean" children, partially feminized by constant contact with their mothers and other women, are converted by the mystical efficacy of ritual into purified members of a male moral community, able to begin to take their part in the jural, political, and ritual affairs of Ndembu society. This change has repercussions within their relationships to their parents. These repercussions not only reshape the structure of the elementary family, that is, the modes of interlinkage between sons and parents, but also reshape extra-familial links of matrilineal descent and patrilateral affiliation. For a boy is linked through each of his parents to different kinds of corporate groups: through his mother to the matrilineal nucleus of a village, and through his father not only to another village, but also, by extension, to units of the wider society, vicinage, chiefdom, tribe. Mukanda strengthens the wider and reduces the narrower loyalties. Matriliny is the principle governing the persistence of narrow local units through time. It is a principle of cardinal importance in Ndembu society and is ritualized in a great number of contexts. But in Mukanda, emphasis is laid on the unity of males, irrespective of their matrilineal interconnections. The father-son tie assumes special prominence and is almost regarded as representative of the values and norms governing the relationships of the widest Ndembu community. It is a ligament binding together local groups into a tribal community. The separation of men and women in Mukanda is not only a ritualized expression, indeed an exaggeration, of the physical and psychological differences between men and women, but it also utilizes the idiom of sexuality to represent the difference between opposed modes of ordering social relations, which in Ndembu culture have become associated with descent through parents of opposite sex. The mother-son and father-son relationships have, in Mukanda, become symbols of wider and more complex relationships.

I have stated some of the major spatial and structural properties of the ritual field of the Mukanda I studied, and indicated that the general characteristics of Ndembu social structure were here combined in an idiosyncratic way, consonant with the interests and purposes of members of the contemporary community. The previous essay (chapter 2) shows how the actually existing social relationships were specifically aligned in a single performance of Mukanda. Now I would like to point out that from the standpoint of our analysis these spatial and structural properties really relate to what Lewin would call a "power field," rather than "force field." The concept of "power" refers to "a possibility of inducing forces" of a certain magnitude on another person or group. It does not mean that Nyaluhana's group actually exerts pressure on Machamba's group. I have described a power field, the boundaries of which were roughly coterminous with an Ndembu vicinage, containing villages of various sizes, some of which claimed moral leadership of the vicinage by various criteria, and which were interlinked with one another by ties of kinship and affinity of variable number and efficacy. I have discussed other groupings and relationships in the structure of this power field. (See also Turner 1967:151 – 279.)

Now the decision to perform Mukanda converted this power field into a "force field." (Here, of course, I am not using the terms "power" and "force" as political scientists normally use them. Rather they correspond roughly to "potency" and "act".) Lewin defines force as a "tendency to locomotion" where locomotion refers to a "relation of positions at different times." What does this mean for us in analyzing Mukanda? It means, on the one hand, that the various component groupings put their "power" to the test, in competition for the leading ritual roles. Forces are goal-directed, and goals determine the structure of particular force fields. In this situation, the participants in Mukanda, individually or in sections and factions, competed for common goals, i.e. major ritual roles, in order to obtain prestige. But the concept of "force field" implies more than this at Mukanda. More than the teleology of struggle for short-term benefits is meant here. For the complex sequence of ritual events which makes up Mukanda is associated with other than particularistic ends. In an important respect, Mukanda is a cybernetic custom-directed "mechanism" for restoring a state of dynamic equilibrium between crucial structural components of a region of Ndembu society which has been disturbed by the growing up of a large number of boys. Too many "unclean" (*anabulakutooka*) boys are "hanging around" the women's kitchens. Not enough youths are sitting in the village forum (*chota*) and participating in its adult goings-on. It is in the general interest of many villages to bring these boys into the adult fold and thus to correct the obstructions in the course of regular social life brought about by their presence. Given the belief that uncircumcised Ndembu males are both unclean and immature, the natural increase of such persons must lead to a numerical imbalance, and also to an imbalance in social influence, between men and women. For uncircumcised boys belong to the women's sphere of activities and their attachment to this sphere becomes greater as time passes. At any given time the nuclear constellation of social relationships in a village is between male kin, matrilineally or patrilaterally attached to its headman. But relationships of authority-respect and superordination-subordination concern only the circumcised. If "structural relationships" may be defined as social relationships that are given a high degree of constancy and consistency by norms sanctioned by organized force and/or by mystical agencies, it may be said that only circumcised men participate in such relationships. Men do not normally order about or chastise uncircumcised children. Ancestral spirits are not believed to afflict uncircumcised boys with illness or misfortune for their own misdemeanors, since they are not regarded as responsible persons. Children are not *entitled* to suffer. Such boys may, however, be afflicted for the misdemeanors of their mothers, since they are regarded as part of the social personality of their mothers. But after the boys have been purified and rendered "men" by Mukanda they must obey their elders, fulfill the norms governing each category of kinship relationship, and may be punished for disobedience by any male senior to them. They can also be afflicted by the spirits as independent persons or as representatives of structured subgroupings of Ndembu society. If there is an undue preponderance of uncircumcised boys, therefore, in a village or in a vicinage, there may not be enough initiated boys to perform routine tasks of village maintenance, and there may exist a tendency for uncircumcised boys to become increasingly less amenable to the discipline whereby structural relationships are maintained. Prolonged attachment to mother and to the women's sphere is symbolized in the fact that the foreskin is compared to the *labia majora*. When the foreskin is removed by circumcision the effeminacy of the child is symbolically removed with it. The physical operation itself is symbolic of a change of social status.

Thus there are two main categories of forces in the ritual field of Mukanda, associated with two types of goals. One type of goal is concerned with the maintenance of the traditional structure of Ndembu society. The means employed is a bounded sequence of ritual customs directed to the correction of a deviationary drift toward numerical imbalance between socially recognized categories of Ndembu. Ndembu themselves do not formulate the situation at this level of abstraction. They say that "there are many children (*atwansi*) in the villages who have not been cut (*ku-ketula*) or circumcised (*kwalama* or *kwadika*), and so the elders of the vicinage feel that it would be good to circumcise them." Pressed a little further Ndembu admit that it is inconvenient if there are many uncircumcised boys in a village, for circumcised men may not eat food cooked on a fire used for cooking such boys' meals nor use a platter on which they have eaten. Again they will say that the boys in a village get sharply divided into circumcised and uncircumised, and that the former mock the latter. This division cuts across groups of siblings, and it is felt to be inappropriate that brothers should revile brothers. Uterine brothers and the male children of sisters form the principal unit in founding a new village, and in other contexts also the principle of the unity of brothers is strongly stressed. We have seen that older brothers or parallel cousins frequently act as guardians (*ayilombweji*) for their younger brothers or cousins in the seclusion period following circumcision. In this way they are brought into a close, helpful relationship with their junior siblings, which to some extent helps to overcome their earlier cleavage.

Customary beliefs about the function of Mukanda, then, give rise to a situation of both moral and physical discomfort when there are many uncircumcised boys in a vicinage. It is this feeling of discomfort, associated no doubt with anxiety on the part of their fathers about whether the boys are becoming too closely attached to their mothers, and with irritation among the men generally that there are so many undisciplined youngsters around, that sets the prevailing tone of vicinage life. In such an atmosphere the suggestion by a responsible adult that Mukanda should be performed is received with a certain amount of relief, although this is tempered by the knowledge that Mukanda is a difficult and dangerous ritual to undertake, and that it involves the participation over several months of almost everyone in the vicinage in some capacity or other. Human beings everywhere like to feel secure about the functioning of certain dominant social relationships. If these work smoothly and, so to speak, unobtrusively, they are the better able to pursue their personal and sectional aims. If they feel that custom is, on the whole, being upheld and observed, they are better able to predict the outcome of activities set in train to achieve their particular goals. They may well feel that the totality of social interactions in which they participate in overlapping time cycles has a "framework." Certain actions and transactions are obligatory, however onerous they may seem to the individuals who perform them. If these are left undone or are done inadequately, the framework can no longer be relied upon as a safeguard and standard of general social intercourse. Insecurity and instability result when the interactions through which crucial structural customs are maintained and expressed fail repeatedly to be performed. Now Mukanda, as stated above, is a mechanism built into the system of customs which give a measure of form and repetitiveness to Ndembu social interactions. It is a mechanism which temporarily abolishes or minimizes errors and deflections from normatively expected behavior. Such errors are not here to be regarded as overt, dramatic breaches of norm or challenges to values but rather as drift away from a state of ideal complacency or equilibrium. Other kinds of mechanism than Mukanda, both jural and ritual, are indeed available in Ndembu culture for redressing breaches of norms. Mukanda, like rituals in many other societies which are connected with the sociobiological maturation of broad categories of individuals, is a corrective rather than a redressive mechanism, a response to cumulative mass pressures, and not to specific emergencies.

The other set of goal-directed forces in the ritual field of Mukanda is constituted by the carrying forward into that field of all kinds of private pursuits of scarce values from the preexisting state of the vicinage field. Individuals and groups see in Mukanda not only a means of correcting and adjusting the wider framework of their social relationships but also of augmenting their own prestige or establishing their claim to certain rights in subsequent secular and ritual situations. They also see in it an opportunity to reduce the prestige and damage the future claims of rivals.

In dynamic terms the ritual field of the Mukanda I am discussing represents the overlapping of two force fields, each orientated toward different and contradictory sets of goals. I say "contradictory" for the same persons were at one and the same time motivated to act for the general good of the vicinage and to compete with one another for scarce values. If one were in a position to examine every item of public behavior during the period and in the site of Mukanda, one would undoubtedly find that one class of actions was guided by the aims and values of Mukanda, another class by private and sectional strivings, while yet another represented a series of compromises between these "altruistic" and "selfish" tendencies. And if one could have access to the private opinions of the participants, it could probably be inferred that ideals and selfish motives confronted one another in each psyche before almost every act. My own observations and records of a few confidential conversations would lend support to this point of view.

It must be clearly understood that I am not positing a simple dichotomy between "ideals," as embodied in the customs of Mukanda, and "selfish or partisan interests," as expressed in certain kinds of behavior. For the principles themselves, consciously recognized or implicitly obeyed, which govern social interaction are never, in any society, so interrelated that the kind of behavior each instigates falls harmoniously into place with behavior according to other principles. Even where each principle controls a separate field of activity, nevertheless activity fields are intercalated by individuals pursuing their life-goals. Wherever a principle leaks into an, as it were, alien activity field, it modifies the behavior of persons who pursue their aims in that field. It often happens that in practice the intruding principle, highly valued in its original activity field, exercises a stronger influence on behavior than the principle normally dominant. Thus the principle of matriliny, which should govern only relationships arising from *descent* in the case of married Ndembu women, sometimes ousts the principle of virilocality as a determinant of *residence*. I write as though I have personified principles, but this is merely a convenient device for expressing a very complex interrelation of variables. In reality, tensions within individuals and between groups generate behavior which renders already established principles operative or inoperative. But even where behavior is principled and is not entirely self-seeking, the principles that support it may be discrepant and induce the actors to pursue mutually inconsistent or even contradictory aims at the same time and with regard to the same people. It is arguable that without a certain looseness of fit or discrepancy between its principles of organization there would not be such a thing as a "society." A society is essentially a whole hierarchy of corrective and adaptive activities, in which each more inclusive activity corrects or redresses the deflections or breaches of the activity below it in the hierarchy. But there is never in this hierarchy such a thing as the radical correction of deviation or the complete restoration of breach. Biopsychological needs and drives on the one hand, and external sociocultural stimuli on the other, ensure the immortality of disturbance in each society. But the activities that make up a society are patterned by custom, and pattern only emerges in corrective and adjustive situations. Society is a process, a process of adaptation that can never be completely consummated since it involves as many specialized adaptations as there are specialized influences in the environment to be met, as Herbert Spencer wrote a century ago. An essential feature of the process that is society is the discrepancy among its structuring principles. The struggles between persons and groups that are provoked by such discrepancy continually call into play the corrective and adaptive activities whose hierarchy summates human social life.

The ritual field of Mukanda, then, exhibits certain relatively constant properties and relationships, such as its spatial coordinates and customary principles of social organization. It also exhibits, as we have seen, dynamic properties in the form of aim-directed chains of activities. These aim-directed activities can be envisaged as force fields which overlap and interpenetrate. The circumcision ritual itself, with its aims of purifying and conferring social manhood on uncircumcised boys, establishes one such force field. The kinds of relationships which are handled by this ritual tend to be categorical relationships, and the overt expression of corporate relationships is concomitantly suppressed. Private and sectional aims set up an antithetical force field. In this field the units of structure and struggle tend to be just those units and relationships which are suppressed by the ritual, that is, those of a corporate character. This means that since there can be no licit admission of the tensions between corporate groups, behavior indicative of such tensions was on the whole excluded from the sacred episodes of Mukanda. But it could be clearly observed in the secular intervals between such episodes, and in those regions of the ritual field which had not been sacralized. It is perhaps hardly correct to speak of "secular" and "sacred" behavior in the ritual field of Mukanda. All behavior I observed in the neighborhood of the main ritual sites and between rites was directed by the relations between the structural and dynamic components of the total field. Behavior characteristic of the social relationships suppressed by ritual custom flourished outside the jurisdiction of such custom. And ritual custom itself was modified and even distorted from the ideal pattern which one could elicit from the accounts of ritual specialists under placid interview conditions. It was modified by the purposive activities of persons and groups organized according to the very principles repressed by overt ritual custom. Shifts in the balance of power between structural components of the power field of the vicinage are referrable to the force field of interests which exerted pressure on the structure of forces directed toward the end of the ritual proper. There were regions of the total field where the structures of the two major force fields tended to coincide, but there were also regions of stress and discrepancy between them. The methods of analysis which have become established in anthropology cannot provide adequate constructs to explain the relationships between the interacting factors which determine successive and simultaneous events in a behavioral field of this type. If, on the one hand, one abstracts that behavior which can clearly be classified as ritualistic, that is, prescribed formal behavior not given over to technological routine but having reference to beliefs in mystical agencies, one gains possession of a set of data useful primarily in comparative cultural analysis. One can compare the observed ritual behavior with other observations of the same kind of ritual, and with informants' accounts of that kind of ritual. From these observations and accounts one can construct two types of models. From repeated observations of the same kind of ritual one can make tentative statements about its real pattern at a given time, the accuracy of this model varying with the number of observed instances. From informants' statements one can make a similar model of the ideal pattern. Then, if one wishes, one can estimate the degree and kind of deviance between the specific instance and both types of models.

If, on the other hand, one abstracts the kind of data that one can label as structural, that is, reasonably related to the constant and consistent relationships between persons, groups, and categories, one gains possession of data pertinent to the construction of two similar models at a different level of abstraction from the pair of cultural models.

From the first pair of models one can demonstrate that deviation exists between specific instance and real and ideal normative patterns, and show where precisely it occurs, but one cannot show *why* it occurs, what are the causative factors behind it. From the second pair of models one can exhibit which features of the structure of the total social system receive expression in the given kind of ritual. Where deviation exists between ideal and real patterns, one can speculate whether this is due to the intrinsic nature of ritual, which perhaps always allows in its symbolic pattern a high degree of leeway to accommodate local and situational variations in the structure of the groups performing it, or whether social change is the factor responsible for marked divergence. It is of the very essence of structural analysis that it regards as irrelevant items of behavior which are never or seldom repeated, the unique events of which social life is full. Yet it may be just such items of behavior which have the highest significance for the study of society regarded as a *process*. A further objection to the kind of abstracting activity which leads to the framing of models, often on assumptions borrowed from the study of two dimensional figures, is that the structural and cultural models cannot be compared with one another, for they belong to different planes of analysis.

It is doubtful whether fruitful problems can still be posed in terms of the culture-structure dichotomy. If society is conceived as a hierarchy of activities, or as a process of adaptation to innumerable and ever renewed stimuli from the environment, then "culture" becomes a property of a single important class of activities, and "structure" becomes a term signifying a certain constancy in the positions of active individuals relative to one another over a period of time. To conceive society thus as the motion of entities under the influence of forces is to allow scope for the systematic treatment of modes of motion which are not directly determined by culture. The idiosyncratic behavior of individuals can now be handled within the analytical context of activity field, for the consequences and implications of this kind of behavior are related to the constant and dynamic properties of such a field.

The sorts of constructs or, to use Lewin's term, "elements of construction" I have in mind are not general concepts based on abstraction from individual differences in such a way that there is no logical path back from the taxonomic abstraction to the individual case. Rather, like Lewin, I believe that the individual case, the unique event, the particular relationship, may be represented by the aid of a few constructive elements or their properties. Such elements and properties refer to activity fields as dynamic wholes. A total activity field or *situation* must first be characterized, not as an aggregate of isolated elements, but in terms of the kinds of interdependences, spatial and temporal, which express its operative unity. Only when this has been done is it possible fruitfully to examine aspects and phases of the situation. Each individual instance may then be represented as a specific spatio-temporal nexus of "field" constructs. For Mukanda what are the constructs and their properties?

The period of Mukanda, including preparations for it and its immediate *sequelae*, corresponds to the *time* of the situation. The vicinage in which it is performed locates it in *space*. Both its time and space have *limits* or *boundaries*. These have their *conditions*. Among these conditions are their degree of *permeability* or *impermeability*. Mukanda, for example, has its aspect of temporal uniqueness, insofar as it involves the suspension of many activities hitherto performed, but it also constitutes a *phase* in a social process of greater inclusiveness, and many of its distinctive activities have reference to activities typical of that wider process. The *initial* limits of Mukanda, therefore, terminate certain series of activities and mark the commencement of other series. The *final* limits of Mukanda reverse this order. During the time of Mukanda, there are also *mediate* limits, at which certain activities characteristic of preritual time are resumed and ritual activities discontinued. These mediate limits are concerned with the relation between ritual time and nonritual time, and not with the phases of ritual time itself. Mukanda, moreover, has its aspect of spatial autonomy, as we have seen above. Its effective boundary with the environing society coincides with that of the vicinage. But since Mukanda is, in *principle*, a tribal ritual, several members of its *personnel* came from outside the vicinage, and during one phase of its performance, Mukanda was taken to adjoining vicinages. Within the situation of Mukanda, too, there are boundaries that demarcate areas of ritual space. Some of these boundaries also delimit Mukanda from the environing sociogeographical region, in that they allow selective entry into esoteric areas of specific categories of persons from that region, that is, entry to circumcised males.

Having established the temporal limits and spatial boundaries of the Mukanda situation, and their conditions, the next step is to consider what are its *constructional elements*. Priority must be given, I think, to those elements which organize behavior in a ritual setting. What might be called the *esemplastic* elements, or the unifying factors, of Mukanda, are the goals of the ritual behavior. These may be divided into *explicit* and *implicit*. The explicit goals are those which can be verbalized by the majority of participants. The implicit goals may be further divided into *unavowed* and *unconscious*. Unavowed goals can be verbalized by a minority of intelligent informants and are concerned with the readjustment of social relationships in the field. Unconscious goals cannot be verbalized but betray themselves in the *form* of ritual symbolism and in the comparative study of discrepancies in the meanings of symbols given by informants in different ritual contexts. Such goals are concerned with the adaptation of the psychobiological disposition of the individual to the general conditions of human social existence, for example, with adapting that disposition to the exigencies of the incest taboo which it seems, on the evidence of depth psychology, to find innately uncongenial.

"Goals" are distributed through the duration of Mukanda, in such a way that persons, resources, and activities are mobilized to attain instrumental goals, which, when attained, are seen as means to further goals. Thus one of the first explicit goals of Mukanda is to circumcise the boys without mishap. Once reached, the next aim is to see that the boys are properly healed. When this has been done, the next aim is to see that the boys are properly instructed, and so on, until the final goal, that of returning the boys to society as purified and socially mature tribesmen, has been effected. Each aim or goal focuses a force field of specific structure, and there is a logical progression from mediate goals to final goal. The goal-structure of Mukanda may then be likened to a many-step rocket, each step of which increases velocity in order to build up a momentum adequate to reach a target.

Interpenetrating the gradient of explicit goals are implicit goals of both categories. Thus, those who circumcise aim explicitly at bringing the boys to life as men. Unconsciously, however, as songs and symbolism indicate, the older men go as near as they dare to castrating or killing the boys. Infantile and archaic impulses seek gratification in the ritual situation in directions and by means clean opposite to those prescribed by the explicit goal-structure. Indeed, I would argue that the symbol-form which is characteristic of ritual represents a conjunction of opposite tendencies. Contrary goals are represented by the same form, which owes much of its apparent obscurity to this antilogical property. In most kinds of ritual the sequence of explicit goals is logical, if their premises are accepted. But the symbolism of the same rituals must remain enigmatic unless one postulates the existence of implicit goals which often run counter to the explicit ones.

The goals of the ritual itself, expressed in words or buried in symbols, structure relationships for a determinate period of time. Preexistent forms of groupings and relationships are realigned in a new structure of relationships established in goal-directed behavior. A force field is superimposed on the network of intervillage interactions within a vicinage. This force field is characterized by a specific role-structure of officials, novices, and other participants. But each ritual role itself becomes a goal to be attained, and when attained, a part to be played *competitively* in relation to other roles, and *successfully*—to demonstrate the importance of the actor. In other words the ritual force field supplies what Lewin would call a set of "positive valences" for members of the vicinage field. A positive valence is "a region (which may represent an activity, a social position, an object, or any other possible goal) which is attractive to (a given) person (or group)." Thus the same set of goal-directed activity patterns which make up the ritual proper both covers up and *activates* the antecedent power field of vicinage interrelations. The system of vicinage interrelations becomes a vicinage force field or rather a set of interpenetrating force fields. But this set of interpenetrating force fields is subordinated to the "esemplastic" goals of the ritual force field. The ritual force field is characterized by a cooperative atmosphere; the vicinage force fields are typified by a competitive atmosphere. But values held in common by all Ndembu determine that the attainment of the ritual goals has priority over the attainment of prestige in the ritual situation by specific groups and persons. Individuals and factions have to accept the frustration of their ambitious strivings in the interests of what is regarded as the general welfare of the widest community.

The subjacent force fields with their competitive goals are not merely arbitrary features of the total ritual field, but integral parts of it. Many kinds of ritual contain observances which express conflict and struggle. Such stereotyped forms may well induce the feelings they portray in the psyches of the participants. Gluckman has analyzed such "rituals of rebellion" in *Custom and Conflict in Africa* (1955b) and in *Order and Rebellion in Tribal Africa* (1963). But where rituals exclude the expression of certain kinds of conflict and competition from their overt and licit structure, I would postulate that their cultural environment is full of just those kinds of conflict and competition which are excluded. The extreme case is found in puritanical Protestantism which in its ritual structure suppressed parent-child and sibling competition and enjoined dependence and collaboration in these relationships. In the environing secular life, however, fierce competition reigned, the classical *bellum omnium contra omnes* of nascent capitalism. This competition existed between entrepreneurs and their surrogate parents or brothers in the national economic system.

Among the elements of construction of the ritual field of Mukanda are various kinds of social grouping. If we regard the vicinage just before Mukanda was performed as a power field, that is, a set of possibilities of inducing forces of various sorts and magnitudes, we must examine the power units and their interrelations. The dominant power units in an Ndembu vicinage field are villages, and so we must say something about their general structure and the characteristic form of their interdependence. But since we are considering a specific activity field, we must also discuss the content of the actually existing relationships between the villages in *this* field. We must deal with *general* form, with *patterned* interdependence, and also with *idiosyncratic* content and with *specific* properties.

I began the analysis by setting out general and specific features of village relationships in the vicinage where the Mukanda I discussed took place. I called this set of relationships a power field—after Lewin—rather than a social system in order to bring out the point that this is a study in social dynamics, and not in social statics. Although power field does not have the same conceptual dimension as that of force field, it still implies the possibility of motion. Nevertheless, to investigate the state of the vicinage as it was just before and during the preparations for Mukanda was to make something closely resembling a structuralist analysis. The major difference between this and an orthodox structuralist analysis is that I discussed the contemporary state of power relations among the real groups in the field, as well as examining the traditional principles of organization which govern the relatively constant interdependencies of person and groups. Since I have made my abstraction from reality with reference to a particular place and time, I could not exhibit the vicinage power field as a balance of power, but rather as an imbalance of power, an unsteady state, which the process of Mukanda ritual would shortly transform into overlapping and interpenetrating force fields, rife with struggles between individuals and groups. "Power equilibria" and "steady states" refer to ideal models of a certain type and seldom to social reality which at any given time may well exhibit disequilibrium and deviation from norm. Karl Deutsch (1966, pp. 89–91) has argued, in a way I find convincing, that the traditional equilibrium analysis must be replaced by a cybernetic model as a tool in the social sciences for studying social units over time. Equilibrium analysis, he points out, assumes that a system will return to a particular state when "disturbed"; that the disturbance is imagined to come from outside the system; that the system "will return with greater force to its original state the greater has been the disturbance"; that "the high or low speed with which the system reacts or with which its parts act on each other is somehow irrelevant (and we term this quality 'friction' to denote that it is a sort of imperfection or blemish that has no proper place in the 'ideal' equilibrium)"; and finally, equilibrium analysis suggests that "no catastrophes can happen within the limits of the system, but that, once an equilibrium breaks down, next to nothing can be said about the future of the system from then on."

This is not the place to consider the implications of the cybernetics model for the study of political systems and fields, with its related concepts of feedback, lag, input, and gain. But it seems that this model, which makes both order and change, equilibrium and disequilibrium problematical and "normal," has distinct advantages over a model which predicts one direction of change only—that which restores the system to a steady state. Clearly, the nascent discipline of political anthropology must find concepts which take fully into account changes of the state of fields, disequilibria, and uncertainties of systemic survival.

4

An Anthropological Approach to the Icelandic Saga

This article is essentially a tribute to the greatest living British anthropologist, Professor Evans-Pritchard of Oxford University, who in 1950 had the temerity to declare in his Marett Lecture, in face of the structural-functionalist orthodoxy of most of his colleagues, that he regarded "social anthropology as being closer to certain kinds of history than to the natural sciences" (Evans-Pritchard 1950: 198). This view provoked a storm of protest from the majority of British anthropologists, who held to the position formulated by the late Professor Radcliffe-Brown and his followers, including Evans-Pritchard in his earlier days, that the behavior and interpersonal relationships observed during fieldwork by anthropologists should be "abstracted in the form of structural relationships between social positions and groups and these structural relationships (should) further be abstracted in the form of separate systems: economic, political, kinship, etc." (van Velsen 1967: 130). Comparison between such timeless and abstract structures elicited from the rich variety of cultures in different parts of the primitive world was

---

Reprinted with permission of Tavistock Publications, Ltd., from *The Translation of Culture*, edited by T. O. Beidelman, Copyright 1971.

thought to be in thorough accordance with scientific method. History, according to Radcliffe-Brown, in societies without written records or about which written documents by alien investigators were not available, could never be anything but "conjectural history." Such guesses were almost worthless and much time and energy could be saved, as both Radcliffe-Brown and Bronislaw Malinowski asserted, if stress were laid on exposing the functional interconnections between social positions and institutions as they existed in the "ethnographic present," in the here-and-now of anthropological investigation, or even, as we have seen, in a timeless milieu of structural relationships. Indigenous tales about the past were considered pseudo-history or "myth," and, at least in Malinowski's view, had the main social function of providing a charter and justification for *contemporary* institutions and relationships between positions and groups. Much understanding of the nature and functioning of certain kinds of social system was undoubtedly obtained by the use of this so-called "synchronic method." But it led to a widespread devaluation of historical research by British anthropologists, even where an abundance of written documents was available, as in West Africa and India, for example. Since Evans-Pritchard's Marett Lecture in 1950, and even more pronouncedly since his Simon Lecture at Manchester University in 1960, the trend has been in considerable measure reversed. A stream of historical studies by anthropologists, particularly in African tribal history, has rushed from the presses in the past few years. Professor Jan Vansina, now at Wisconsin University, has even been able to show us how the formerly despised oral tradition can be handled as reliable historical evidence, if it is critically assessed in relation to other sources of knowledge about the past; as he writes (1965:7 – 8),

> [Oral tradition] . . . has to be related to the social and political structure of the peoples who preserve it, compared with the traditions of neighboring peoples, and linked with the chronological indications of genealogies and age-set cycles, of documented contacts with literate peoples, of dated natural phenomena such as famines and eclipses, and of archaeological finds.

He also recommends the comparative use of linguistic evidence (ibid.: 180 – 81). Vansina, whose fieldwork was conducted from 1952 to 1960, was undoubtedly influenced by Evans-Pritchard's 1950 Marett Lecture and by the controversy that followed it, and perhaps even more powerfully by Evans-Pritchard's historical study, published in 1949, *The Sanusi of Cyrenaica*. A recent British example of Evans-Pritchard's pervasive influence is the publication of a volume of historical studies by anthropologists entitled *History and Social Anthropology* (Lewis 1968). In the United States the great Californian anthropologist, A. L. Kroeber, also stressed, even before

Evans-Pritchard, the importance for anthropology of the historical approach (Kroeber 1935:558), and the recent book *An Anthropologist Looks at History* (Singer 1966) is a testimony to his sustained interest in the matter.

When I heard Professor Evans-Pritchard deliver his Simon Lecture, "Anthropology and History" (1961), at the University of Manchester in 1960 I remember being deeply impressed, and oddly moved, when he said (ibid.:13):

> An anthropological training, including fieldwork, would be especially valuable in the investigation of earlier periods of history in which institutions and modes of thought resemble in many respects those of the simpler peoples we study. For such periods the historian struggles to determine a people's mentality from a few texts, and anthropologists cannot help wondering whether the conclusions he draws from them truly represent their thought.

For example, "Can an Oxford don work himself into the mind of a serf of Louis the Pious?" (ibid.:14). I was impressed by this because it was largely through studying an early period of history that I had become addicted to anthropology. This period was the Icelandic Commonwealth, from Ingolf's settlement at Reykjavik in A.C. 874 to A.D. 1262 when the Icelanders of their own free will in solemn parliament made a treaty of union with the King of Norway in which they accepted, at last, his supremacy. I had come green to these white pastures as an undergraduate just before World War II when I studied under Professor Chambers, Dr. Batho, and Dr. Hitchcock, all of whom had been students of W. P. Ker, author of *Epic and Romance* (1967) and *The Dark Ages*, whose ruling passion was Icelandic literature. I was moved by Evans-Pritchard's words because they revived for me and made suddenly palpable not only my years of fieldwork among the Ndembu tribesmen of Central Africa, but also nights in the British Army when I had read E. V. Gordon's *An Introduction to Old Norse*—full of potent extracts from the Icelandic sagas—by torchlight under my blankets to evade the sergeant's baleful eye. On my return to civilian life, it was partly a desire to work in a live society not too dissimilar to ancient Iceland that made me switch from English to anthropology. But Evans-Pritchard vividly revealed to me the possibility of applying my anthropological experience and thinking to the very literature that had sent me indirectly to Africa.

Indeed, in this case it was not at all a matter of "determining a people's mentality from a *few* texts" (my emphasis). The texts here are many and rich and full of the very materials that anthropologists rejoice in when vouchsafed to them by informants in the field. I shall say something about the nature and reliability of these texts in a moment, but would first like to make clear why they are of theoretical concern to me. In my

African work I had proposed to analyze some important events which arose in village life, and which I called "social dramas," as possessing a regularly recurring "processional form" or "diachronic profile"—in other words crisis situations tended to have a regular series of phases. They usually began with a breach of rule or norm and led, typically, to a rapidly ramifying cleavage, bringing about opposition between the largest groups that may be involved in the dispute, it may be between sections of a village or segments of a chiefdom. In Ndembu society, the small tribal group in Zambia I lived among for two and a half years, cleavage is accompanied by a set of adjustive and redressive procedures, ranging from informal arbitration to elaborate rituals, that result either in healing the breach or in public recognition of its irremediable character. I had derived the "processional form" of the "social drama" from data I had collected during fieldwork among the Ndembu of Zambia (formerly N. Rhodesia). These data, if not 'historical' in type, were at least "microhistorical," in that they related to chains and sequences of events over a time, however limited, rather than to events coexisting at a given time. A large part of my data consisted of direct reporting, but I was forced at times to rely on accounts by informants of happenings in the village past. I made a virtue of necessity by placing in an analytical central position the very bias of my informants. For the main "aim of the 'social drama' is not to present a reputedly objective recital of a series of events; it is concerned, rather, with the different interpretations put upon these events, and the way in which these express nuanced shifts or switches in the balance of power or ventilate divergent interests within common concerns" (Epstein 1967:228). My intention was that if "facts" were examined from different points of view, and discussed with different informants, the extended case would take on a multidimensional aspect: the individual parties would be more than mere names but become characters in the round whose motives would become intelligible not only in terms of personality or temperament, but also in terms of the multiple roles they occupy simultaneously or at different times in the social structure or in transient factional groupings. In all this there was the notion that social events are spun into complex patterns over time by custom and will, and especially by conflicts of customs and wills and collective wishes and needs to resolve those conflicts. It was not long before I began to look for comparable data in other societies, for I was convinced that each society had its own variant of the social drama form. Each society's social drama could be expected to have its own "style," too, its aesthetic of conflict and redress, and one might also expect that the principal actors would give verbal or behavioral expression to the values composing or embellishing that style. I was not in favor of "abstracting separate structural systems, economic, political, kinship, legal, etc." from the unitary yet phased movement of the social drama. A distinct aim of this study was to compare the profiles of dramas in different societies, taking into account such aspects as their degree of open-endedness, their propensity to regression, the efficiency of their redressive procedures, the absence of such procedures, the degree to which violence or guile were present in crises, and many more besides. Yet when I wrote my book there was a dearth of such information except in the works of some of my colleagues in the Central African field—and even there it was not systematically presented or related to relatively constant features of the social context. But if cross-cultural studies appeared to be "out," cross-temporal studies were feasible. The writings of historians are bulging with "social dramas," narratives of successive events that can be fitted without Procrustean violence into the schemas outlined earlier. But I was not sufficiently temerarious to tackle the data presented and handled by professional historians. Then I suddenly remembered my early predilection for Icelandic literature—indeed, it could well have served as the unconscious, or, at any rate, preconscious model for the "social drama." I had read most of the sagas available in English translation and had once had a smattering of Old Norse that could be revived, if necessary. And the sagas were nothing but connected sequences of social dramas. From them could also be inferred, so I thought, many features of ancient Icelandic social structure and economics—enough to provide a preliminary frame for the "phase developments."

The more I thought about using the sagas as collections of data comparable to my African extended cases, the better I liked the notion. It seemed to me, too, that since there was an abundance of "native writings relating to the settlement and early history of Iceland" (as Vigfusson and Powell partly subtitle their *Origines Islandicae*) it might even be possible by examining the sagas in proper time-sequence to plot the successive stages of the development of effective adjustive and redressive procedures and this from the very foundation of Icelandic society. Icelandic scholars will readily perceive how naïve I was and how little I then knew of the jagged and treacherous terrain of Icelandic saga origins and datings. Nevertheless, I am still confident that, with due precaution, anthropologists can make a positive contribution to Icelandic studies, and in doing so sharpen their own understanding of social processes—for through the saga medium Icelandic society is portrayed as in constant change and development, though with certain repetitive and cyclical aspects.

Before examining a saga as a set of social dramas, which may be regarded as both indices and vehicles of changes in the structure and personnel of the social arenas to which they refer, let me sketch in briefly something of the salient Icelandic settings in space and time. Iceland itself contains about 40,000 square miles—one-fifth as large again as Ireland—but except for the narrow strip of coast "between fell and foreshore" and along several river valleys there are few places suitable for settlement. Huge jökulls or ice mountains back most of the coast. Iceland contains over a hundred volcanoes, a quarter of which have been active in historical times; fields of lava cover hundreds of square miles and hot springs or geysers are numerous. In brief, about six-sevenths of Iceland's area is unproductive, wild, and inhospitable; barren cold rock intermittently laced with inner fire. Owing to the position of the Gulf Stream, however, the climate, considering the latitude (63° – 67° N.), is quite mild and humid. The weather seems to have been rather better during the saga period, for there is no mention of floating ice to the south at the time of the first settlement. There appear, too, to have been richer natural resources in wood and pasture. Shortage of wood was, nevertheless, a constant problem in the sagas. Men would voyage to Norway or Britain to load up with building-timber, and some of the bitterest feuds, such as Njal's Saga, began with quarrels between thralls over the precise boundaries of woodlands. Today, apart from small stands of mountain ash and birch, there is hardly any woodland to speak of in Iceland.

The early settlers took land around the coast, sailing without haste from one creek or bay to another to find good unoccupied land. Many sagas mention quarrels over land only a few generations after this original "land-taking." It has been calculated that about 5000 such settlements were recorded in the so-called colonizing period between A.D. 870 and 930. Many of these records appear in the *Landnámabók*, an early masterpiece of historical scholarship, by Ari Thorgilson the Wise, a cleric who wrote in the first half of the twelfth century. Since the settlers often came with married children and servants, it is likely that by A.D. 930 something like 30,000 – 50,000 people (the larger figure is Sir George Dasent's estimate) were living on about 6,000 square miles of utilizable land, much of which was sheep and cattle pasture. Three hundred years later, during the so-called Sturlung Age, it has been estimated by Einar O. Sveinsson that the total population was "about 70,000 – 80,000" (Sveinsson 1953: 72). By that time there was much vagrancy, and mention is made of large numbers of itinerant seasonal or day-laborers. It seems likely that the carrying capacity of the land, or critical population density, had been exceeded, in relation to the means of subsistence and cultivable percentage of land then available. The present Icelandic population of about 200,000, about half of which lives in Reykjavik, depends largely upon commercial fishing for sale in the international market, and could not survive on farming and small-scale fishing alone. But it would seem that during the main saga period, around the turn of the first millennium, there was already pressure on land, or at any rate on certain categories of scarce resources, such as woodland and pasture, and that this pressure was one major source of the conflicts described in the sagas in terms of personalities, and such values as honor and shame.

Why did the settlers come to this bleak island in the first place and where did they come from? The answers to these questions shed much light on the form of the social dramas in the saga literature. The emigration from Norway, where many of the earliest settlers came from (though some came indirectly, stopping for a while in Scotland, Ireland, the Orkneys or Shetlands before moving on) was undertaken by many chieftains and kinglings to escape the over-rule of King Harald Fairhair, who sought to impose centralized monarchical rule on all Norway. As W. P. Ker had said (1967:58): "Iceland was colonized by a picked lot of Norwegians; by precisely those Norwegians who had . . . strength of will in the highest degree." He points out that "political progress in the Middle Ages was by way of monarchy; but strong monarchy was contrary to the traditions of Germania, and in Norway, a country of great extent and great difficulties of communication, the ambition of Harald Fairhair was resisted by numbers of chieftains who had their own local following and their own family dignity to maintain in their firths and dales." The first Icelanders, in fact, were intractable, "reactionary" aristocrats who refused to make themselves tenants or vassals of any king. This political and spatial disengagement made them a highly self-conscious group, who, as Ker says, began their heroic age "in a commonwealth founded by a social contract" (ibid.:59). Individuals came together to invent a set of laws and to try to set up jural procedures to make them work; it was not the movement of a group already possessed of a joint polity. The result was that, again in Ker's words, "this reactionary commonwealth, this fanatical representative of early Germanic use and wont, is possessed of a clearness of self-consciouness, a hard and positive clearness of understanding, such as is to be found nowhere else in the Middle Ages and very rarely at all in any polity" (ibid.). From the anthropological point of view this self-recognizant clarity that Ker calls "dry light" makes them excellent informants about the growth of their institutions—as set off from those of Norway—and about their cumulating relations with one another.

As A. Margaret Arent has well expressed it (1964:xvi):

> in the founding days, the sovereign power lay in the hands of the *goðar*, chieftain-priests who fulfilled both political and religious functions. A *goði's* authority extended over those who paid dues and worshipped at his temple. In exchange for this privilege and the *goði's* protection, these followers pledged him their allegiance and support. These quite naturally were the farmers and neighbors in his immediate vicinity. The number of *goðar* was limited and the title was generally hereditary. The farmers reserved the right to choose the *goði* whom they wished to follow, but loyalty to a certain one usually became more or less habitual. The relationship was thus one of mutual trust and agreement—the old Germanic code of loyalty between chieftain and followers. The years of the Commonwealth saw the establishment of the *Althing* (A.D. 930), a democratic parliament with a

> strong aristocratic base. The *goðar* automatically became members of the ruling bodies of parliament (the legislature and the judicature) and a Lawspeaker was elected to recite the laws at the meeting of the *Althing* which took place once a year on the plains of Thingvellir in the southwest of the country. As time went on, the *goði's* obligations became more political than religious, his power territorial.

There was no centralized authority over and above the *goðar*. The *Althing*, and the local *Things* for each of the Quarters into which Iceland was divided, had no punitive sanctions behind them; men met there to seek compensation for wrong or homicide, but there was no organized state to back their claims with force even when plaintiffs were awarded compensation *consensu omnium*—indeed, as we shall see, much depended on how many supporters a plaintiff could get to "ride with him" to Thingvellir or recruit on that spot, if he were to have a hope of even obtaining a hearing.* This weakness in the politico-legal structure—due to the self-conscious independence of *emigré* aristocrats who had fled centralized monarchy—left much leeway for internal and localized feuds, and, in the Sturlung Age particularly, led to power politics on a large scale and personal aggrandizement by the rich at the expense of the small farmers. It may well have been directly due to the lack of centralized political authority that Icelanders put so much stress on personal dignity, honor, and loyalty, and especially on the obligations of kinship. Since the courts had no mandate to carry out sentence, one had to take the law into one's own hands. One result was that even fancied slights might lead to bloodshed and homicide, for this sector of the culture became, as it were, overloaded with value emphases to compensate for the lack of sanctioned legal procedures. It was left to the plaintiff himself to enforce outlawry, fines, and settlements, and a good deal of the saga literature is taken up by accounts of how these things were done. There one can clearly see that if too much is left to personal honor, dishonorable deeds often result. The tragedy of the Commonwealth is the gradual corruption into oligarchy of its own principle of honorable, aristocratic independence from supreme overlordship—and doubtless the terrain with its natural barriers to easy communication was a factor here, though it must be said that Norway was equally rugged yet generated a kingship.

How far may the sagas be regarded as recorded history rather than historical fiction, as works of creative imagination inspired by the past?

---

*In practice the system worked out as a balance of power between districts and landholders; a majority decision of the *Thing* could only be enforced if you had power on the winning side. If you had not, the decision was unrealistic and probably some excuse was found to alter it.

The problem is a real one, for though the sagas purport to tell of the ninth, tenth, and eleventh centuries, they were actually composed in the thirteenth century, the turbulent Age of the Sturlungs. Anthropologists may well suspect that several important social and political aspects of that age have been foisted by the sagamen upon the earlier events. Sveinsson (1953:2) has eloquently described the Sturlung period (named after an important lineage):

> By this time the power of the individual chieftains has multiplied; one man may rule entire districts or quarters . . . Some of the chieftains are possessed of greater wealth than their grandfathers dreamed of, others must provide for their initial establishment by forcible means. A considerable number of the common people are destitute . . . . All is restless motion. In earlier days . . . a man might send to the nearest farms for help in a fight with others of the same district or hostile visitors from a neighboring one. Now forces are levied from whole quarters for expeditions into other sections of the country. Instead of skirmishes there are pitched battles.

One might comment on this that *Njal's Saga,* which professes to describe events around A.D. 1000, also tells of "forces . . . levied from whole quarters," for example, the followers of Flosi who came to burn down Njal's homestead and household were drawn from the southern and eastern quarters. On the other hand, virtues are extolled in the sagas about early times which appear to have grown tarnished in the Sturlung Age, personal integrity among them. Here, again, anthropologists might suspect that, as in Roman accounts written in the Empire about the Republic, a process of idealizing the past was going on. Thus both present reality and idealization may have distorted the picture presented by the sagas of the early Commonwealth. On the other hand, the Sturlung history itself, written by Sturla almost contemporaneously with its events, has the form and vividness of the sagas about earlier times. As W. P. Ker has said (1967:252):

> The present life in Sturla's time was, like the life of the heroic age, a perpetual conflict of private wills, with occasional and provisional reconciliations. The mode of narrative that was suitable for the heroic stories could hardly fail to be the proper mode for the contemporary factions of chiefs, heroic more or less, and so it was proved by Sturla.

My own view is that there were so many major continuities between the earlier and later years of the Commonwealth, at the basic levels of kinship and territorial organization, mode of subsistence, forms of adjudication and arbitration, and norms governing relations between individuals and groups, that sagas treating of both the earlier and later periods can be regarded equally as models of and for Icelandic social life as it lasted over several centuries. I do not think we have as anthropologists to concern ourselves too much with the problem of whether there was a highly developed oral art of saga-telling before the sagas were written down (the so-called Freeprose theory), or whether the sagas were from the outset deliberate works of art, making considerable use of written sources (such as Ari's *Landnámabók*) as well as oral traditions (the so-called Bookprose theory). The written sagas are clearly master-products of Icelandic society, which from the beginning contained a relatively high proportion of literate men, and we can thus regard them as authentic expressions of Icelandic culture. In many ways, too, early Icelanders are the best anthropologists of their own culture; they have the sober, objective clarity about men and events that seems to belong to the Age of Reason rather than the Age of Faith. When they show, in saga form, how institutions came into being and disputes were settled, I am inclined to believe that they were reporting facts. Nevertheless, the sagamen are not sociologically conscious of the contradictions and discrepancies in their own principles of organization, and regard the conflicts and struggles resulting from them as the effects of either Fate or personal malice. And, as in today's Africa, though to a lesser extent, witchcraft is sometimes invoked to explain mischance. It should also be said that though the sagas were written well within the Christian era in Iceland, many were about pre-Christian times and customs. Moreover, in the thirteenth century most sagas were written not by learned clerics but by laymen. Ari Thorgilsson, whose "exact history . . . precedes the freer and more imaginative stories, and supplies some of them with their matter, which they work up in their own (less strict) way" (Ker 1967:248), was indeed a priest, but he wrote in the twelfth century, which intervenes between the times portrayed in the sagas and the time of their writing. Other priests wrote sagas and histories after Ari and in his sober manner in the twelfth century. By the thirteenth century it is evident that some crucial change had occurred in the relationships between Churchmen and laity. To understand this change we must go back to the beginning of the Christian era in Iceland. Iceland's conversion to Christianity was characteristically pragmatic. As narrated in *Njal's Saga* and Ari's *Íslendingabók*, it resolves into a collective decision taken at the Althing in A.D. 1000 to accept Christianity in order to prevent a radical cleavage in Iceland itself between Christians and pagans, and to facilitate trade and avoid conflict with the peoples of Europe, most of whom by that date had been converted. Individuals might continue to sacrifice to the Norse gods in private—and this was stated in A.D. 1000 by the Lawspeaker Thorgeirr at the Althing—as long as their public worship was Christian. One consequence of this was that, although "organized paganism never revived," as Professor Turville-Petre points out (1953:68), neither were pagan ideas excoriated as diabolic. The nobler pagan standards of conduct, which gave the feuds moral stature, continued to be effective—such as *dreng-skapr*, manly excellence, or a sense of honor. Such ethics, of course, did little to make peace, and, as Sveinsson has said (1953:129), "one saga could outweigh a hundred sermons." Many of the *goðar*, or chieftain-priests, were ordained as Christian priests, and continued to exercise both sacred and secular functions, though sacredness was now interpreted in Christian terms. Priests, and even bishops, could and did marry and raise families. It took quite a while for Rome to exercise effective centralized authority over the isolated Icelandic Church "out there" in Ultima Thule. In the permissive twelfth century, according to Einar Sveinsson (ibid.:116 – 17),

> men in holy orders, the ordained chieftains not least, were the leaders in the intellectual life of the country, and they combined, in one way or another, a native and foreign way of thinking; these learned men naturally were the first to employ writing. But . . . there were also at this time a number of laymen who were but little affected by ecclesiastical influences and lived and moved in native learning. By 1200 knowledge of reading and writing had become not uncommon, at least among the chieftain class . . . (and, also, apparently among some gifted commoners) . . . There is no reason to suppose that literacy had declined by 1200, in the very springtime of the saga-writing of the laity, and . . . was far more widespread in Iceland than abroad. But just at that time, around 1200, the ecclesiastical and the secular separate.

The Church orders priests to give up chiefly powers, enjoins celibacy on them, and in general raises them above other men as sacrificing priests in terms of the definitions of the Lateran Council of 1215.

> The Church thrusts away the laity, as it were, and the spirit and taste of the secular chieftains prevail. The laity now use their knowledge of writing to express that spirit. They inherit the critical spirit of the twelfth century (exemplified by Ari), and it becomes one of the principal forces in the intellectual life of many of them, whereas about the same time the Church encourages veneration of saints and belief in miracles and thus becomes the main pillar of belief in the marvellous. The literature of the nation undergoes great changes in the turn-of-the-century generation. The antique style, the style of the twelfth century, which has a certain very agreeable clerical flavour, is now replaced by the pure and limpid classical saga-style, which thus belongs to the Sturlung Age, while in the hands of monks and zealous clerics the clerical style moves towards what was fashionable abroad: long-winded rhetoric and sentimental prolixity are its characteristics from now on.

Despite a clearly detectable anticlerical and chauvinistic note in Einar Sveinsson's work generally, I think that he here makes the point well that the prose sagas are mainly the product of laymen of the "chieftain class."

This structural perspective may partly account for the interest in and knowledge of pagan matters shown in the sagas and for their almost purely pagan attitudes to conduct—I say "almost" because in *Njal's Saga* particularly there are clear marks of Christian, even hagiographical, influences.

The major sagas, then, are the products of Sturlunga lay and chieftainly literate thought, reflecting on the written deposit of traditions about the early generations of the Commonwealth and, no doubt, on the oral traditions of great families as well. Such thought, kindled by creative fire and endeavoring to give meaning to an age full of outrage, has given us a series of peerless social dramas which yield us insight into the inner dynamics of Icelandic society before its "disastrous submission" to the Norwegian Crown.

The saga I wish to examine in anthropological terms is *The Story of Burnt Njal*, recently described by Professor Turville-Petre of Oxford University, in his Introduction to the Everyman Library edition of Sir George Dasent's classical translation, as "the finest of Icelandic sagas, and . . . one of the great prose works of the world" (1957:v). Its author seems to have lived in the late thirteenth century and to have been a learned man who had read not only most of the known sagas but many lost ones as well. Turville-Petre (1957:vii) believes that the outline of the story is "undoubtedly founded on fact, and the chief events described took place in the last years of the tenth century and the first of the eleventh." The author clearly lived much of his life in southern Iceland, for his knowledge of its features is intimate. *Njal's Saga* is preserved in some fifty or sixty manuscripts, the oldest of which date from the first years of the fourteenth century. It may be said to be the *fine fleur* of the saga age and the culmination of Icelandic literature. It is also the paradigmatic social drama of the Icelandic Commonwealth, containing if not resolving all its contradictions.

Njal's Saga

Njal's Saga is an anthropological paradise. Its very liabilities in the eyes of most Icelandic scholars, who tend to be literary historians or critics, are anthropological virtues. W. P. Ker, for example (1967:185) points out that "the local history, the pedigrees of notable families, are felt as a hindrance, in a greater or less degree, by all readers of the Sagas; as a preliminary obstacle to clear comprehension." But he is ready to admit, superb scholar that he was, that "the best Sagas are not always those that give the least of their space to historical matters, to the genealogies and family memoirs" (ibid.:185). Of course, anthropologists, with their practical immersion in small-scale societies with "multiplex" social relationships, that is, where "people interact with the same sets of fellows to achieve several purposes, familial, productive, educational, religious, organizing" (Gluckman 1965:256), attach great importance *precisely* to genealogical connections, for kinship as such, in societies of this type, is often the spine or main trunk of articulation of many kinds of social relationships, economic, domestic, political, and so on. Social relationships are otherwise undifferentiated, for there is little scope for specialization; and kinship, as Gluckman says (ibid.:54) involves a general obligation on people to help and sustain one another, whatever may be the precise field of activity. Kin, of course, fall into different categories of relationships by birth, marriage, and even fosterage, which entail varying obligations. With this peculiarity of the anthropological approach in mind, it will surprise no one that the Norse sagas have never been comprehensively studied in terms of the kinship systems so completely deployed in the so-called "family sagas," such as the *Laxdaela Saga* (which follows a set of linked and contiguous localized lineages over many generations from the first settlement, and in which types and degrees of kinship and affinity crucially influence behavior), *Haward's Saga, Vatzdaela Saga,* and *Njal's Saga* (to cite but a few). For few who read tales primarily for literary enjoyment would undertake such hardy work!

It has often been pointed out how in the sagas great heed is paid to particular individuals and how the mysteries of individual life are hinted at. This stress should be complemented by a study of the social positions occupied by individuals in kinship, territorial, and political structures, and in the roles played by them in what anthropologists call "action-sets"—quasi-groups that emerge in response to the pursuit of particular and limited goals—in the Icelandic case, for example, in feuds and litigations. From this point of view intuition and personal sensibility should be buttressed by a cool consideration of the genealogies and social geographies so richly supplied us by the sagamen. I am, of course, in no way arguing that the behavior of the saga actors is *determined by*, or is the *effect of*, social factors such as genealogical position, systems of values, institutionalized political roles, and the like. I am only saying that these actors enter into relations with one another in "social fields" that are in important ways structured *inter alia* by such factors. Their importance is such that it seems that quite often kinship obligations compel personal friends to fight one another.

I have mentioned the term "field." Let me now try to define it more precisely, throw in yet another term from political anthropology, "arena," relate these to "social drama," and then look at some of the rich data of *Njal's Saga* in terms of these concepts and their interrelations. A "field" is composed of the actors directly involved in the social processes under examination. Its social and territorial scope and the areas of behavior it implicates change as additional actors enter and former ones withdraw, and as they bring new types of activities into their interaction and/or abandon old types. It is often convenient initially to characterize a field when its actors are more or less at peace with one another or when the processes in which they are engaged are leading back to some previously established state. An arena may be described as "a social and cultural space around those who are directly involved with the field participants but are not themselves directly implicated in the processes that define the field" (Swartz 1968:11). Thus in *Njal's Saga* there are a number of fields, each being defined by a process, or set of linked processes, such as seeking vengeance and/or going to law to obtain compensation. There are several arenas also, the largest being geographically coterminous with the southern and much of the eastern quarters of Iceland and sociologically with their local political leadership patterns. In this sociogeographical arena there are a number of persons and groups that do not directly take part in field activities yet still exert a powerful influence on field behavior. It is perhaps useful, too, to talk about field and arena *contents*. Field contents include the values, meanings, resources, and relationships used, generated, and articulated by the actors. Arena contents refer to values, meanings, and resources possessed by the actors but not directly employed by them in the purposive processes which activate the field.

"Social dramas" represent, so to speak, the time axes of fields. More than this, they open up the psychological dimension because they throw into relief the feelings, attitudes, and choices of individuals, as well as the relatively constant and consistent, or "structural," aspects of arena and field. They also indicate where principles of organization are likely to be situationally inconsistent, discrepant or opposed, or even radically contradictory (as in the Icelandic case of pagan and Christian attitudes to revenge-killing in the *Sturlunga Saga*). The social drama, in short, shows how people actually live in arenas of a particular type, how they pursue their ambitious or altruistic ends in them, and how, through significant choices made by important individuals or groups, the arena structure may itself be changed.

Njal's Saga, as it has come down to us, quite naturally leaves the structure and properties of field and arena implicit—clearly, its intended audience is expected to have knowledge through personal experience of the institutionalized background and the kinds of values and motives that influence and appraise deeds. But, for the anthropological investigator, "field-arena" is more than a mere background; it is a theoretical construct, developed out of the study of many societies possessing widely divergent cultures. For the audience and actors Icelandic, or even Nordic culture is a "natural" background, Icelandic society merely "the way men live." Anthropologists know that other men live in quite other ways, and their task is to show how this particular Icelandic arena is constructed in terms that would allow for comparative study with the arenas of other cultures. I have said that kinship was an important, almost "irreducible" principle of Icelandic social organization, but this does not tell us what the specific rules of Icelandic kinship are, or how kinship is connected with other structural principles.

Anthropologists who try to study process and history without accounting for structural considerations are just as one-sided as the traditional structuralists who neglected process and history. Thus we can learn much about the Icelandic saga from Radcliffe-Brown, whom we earlier noted as one of the fathers of British structuralism. In the Introduction to *African Systems of Kinship and Marriage* (Radcliffe-Brown & Forde 1950), he has pertinent things to say about Teutonic kinship which bear on *Njal's Saga* (which he mentions but misspells! though his reference is almost the only one in anthropological literature to Iceland). He points out how in some Teutonic societies at least, "there existed large house-communities under the control of a house-father or house-lord, of the type of what it is usual to call the patriarchal family. Sons continued to live with their father under his rule and daughters usually joined their husbands elsewhere [a form known as 'virilocal marriage' V.T.]. But although the patrilineal principle was general or usual, it was not always strictly adhered to. Thus in . . . *Nyal's Saga* [sic] the house-community of old Nyal included not only his wife Bergthora and his three married sons but also a daughter's husband, and, with children, men-servants, and others, the household numbered some fifty persons" (ibid.:17–18). But while the core of the local group was a group of patrilineal kin, in matters concerning blood vengeance and *wergild*, which is the indemnity that is required when one person kills another, a wider range of kinsmen was involved. This was what the Anglo-Saxons called the *sib*, defined by Radcliffe-Brown as "computable cognatic relationship for definite social purposes." One's *sib* in Anglo-Saxon England, or in Iceland, was not a group but a range of persons focused on oneself. If one was killed the *sib* would receive the *wergild* or indemnity.

Commonly, the inner circle of an individual's *sib* included his father and mother, his brother and sister, and his son and daughter. Beyond that various degrees of kin were recognized. Anglo-Saxons appear to have included within the *sib* all the descendants of the eight great-grandparents. The situation in *Njal's Saga* is fairly flexible. Much seems to depend in this society of individualists on whether the principal kinsman of a victim of homicide, on receiving *wergild*, makes a personal decision to divide it among other members of the deceased man's *sib* or not. A big man will get his own way. Those who seek vengeance for a slaying, however, form a varied band, hardly equivalent to a *sib*, but united by diverse ties of kinship, affinity, neighborhood, political affiliation and friendship. Here politics, or better, politicking, rather than kinship duties alone, seems to play the major role. One musters support from any quarter where it may be had. But the fact that a wide range of kin, on both the killer's and the victim's side, are made visible at each homicide, is an important "arena-characteristic" of old Icelandic society. How many actually enter the field of purposive *wergild* or vengeance action depends on many other factors, political, economic, and psychological. Such factors become apparent as the "social dramas" succeed one another to make up at last the total "saga."

Other arena characteristics I should mention are territorial and political organization. Since we have from Ari information about the first "land-taking," we can plot the process of territorial settlement. The first settlers sought out the will of the gods by throwing into the sea just off Iceland the sacred pillars of the high seat (*öndvegi*), brought from Norway and watching where they drifted ashore. Next they viewed or "kenned" the land by climbing the nearest point of high ground. After that the land was ritually "hallowed" by surrounding it with a ring of bonfires. Hallowed land became the settler's own and its boundaries were then marked by natural or artificial landmarks or beacons. The next step was to demarcate house and farm buildings, and "town" or home fields. The chieflings who were first settlers built a *Hof* or temple for the gods, where blood sacrifices were made at important rituals and festivals. These priest-chiefs were the first *goðar*, whom we mentioned earlier. Their first step, after settlement, was to allot portions of land to kinsmen, followers, and friends—as is told at length in Ari's *Landnámabók* and the *Laxdaela Saga*. The first tracts were so huge that plenty was left for followers of the priest-chieftains. As time went on and land became occupied, the power of the *goðar* was often much reduced, since their followers were free to stay or go. As in New Guinea today among the so-called "big men," a *goði's* influence depended on such things as physical strength, personal fame, and skill at arms, just as much as on birth and inherited wealth. A man's power might wane with age, feuds would take toll of his children and kin, while younger *goðar* might wax in power and influence around him. The very attribute which gave him most fame, generosity in providing feasts for his own people and other neighbors, and helping them to pay debts and *wergild*, might be that which impoverished him most decisively. Giving to win and keep followers depletes wealth and loses followers. Thus much depended on a man's present achievements and less on his past glories or family fame. The main sanction against his abusing his powers was that his Thingmen might leave his temple and join another *goði's*.

The *goði* had the right to call together the *Things*, or meetings of the people, at stated times, to discuss public business and where suits at law might be taken up. As priest he hallowed the *Thing*, and proclaimed peace while it was in session, he was chief magistrate presiding over the meeting, he named judges and superintended the proceedings. In summary, he was leader of the district of his *goði*-ship, giving protection in return for allegiance. But another man, if strong enough, could build a new temple in his district and subvert his followers. The possession of a temple and personal power, based on numbers, organization, and resources, were all he needed as a title to his office. One even reads of *goði*-ships being bought and sold.

The picture we have at about the end of the first few generations of occupation is of a number of little priest-chiefdoms all round the coast of the island, under the influence, rather than the power, of *goðar*, who at stated times convened their adherents and retainers to meetings for the settlement of matters of common concern. Alongside the *goðar* were important secular household heads, some of whom aspired to *goði*-hood. Each *Thing* or meeting was independent of the others, and quarrels between them could only be settled by treaty or battle—as between sovereign powers. Here the local *goði* represented the community in what may be termed its "foreign relations" and tried to come to a settlement with his fellow *goðar*. But even when Ulfljot made a code of laws for Iceland, and Grim Goatbeard his brother found a southern site at Thingvellir for an *Althing* or general assembly of Icelanders in A.D. 929 – 930, one cannot assert that an Icelandic *state* had come into existence. Even at the *Althing* almost everything depended not on the law code—though this was manipulated in litigation to give a gloss of legitimacy to the acts of powerful men and to enlist support from the uncommitted—but on how much force a man could muster when it came to a showdown. Issues and grievances could be ventilated at the *Althing* but the settlement of issues was left effectually to the parties concerned and men continued to "seek their rights by point and edge" (*med odde ok eggjo*), as Njal once lamented.

Njal's Saga is mainly a matter of "point and edge" despite Njal's own creation of a Fifth Court, to be held at the *Althing* "to steer the law and set men at peace." I have counted the killings in *Njal*—they amount to 94 in the 330 pages of the Everyman Edition. Some take place out of Iceland, but most are intimately connected with the chain of feuds that compose the saga. One wonders how reliable this figure is when one considers Sveinsson's comment (1953:72) that the number of men killed in battle or executed between 1208 and 1260 (in the so-called "turbulent" Sturlung Age) has been computed at around 350 or about 7 per year—in a total population of 70,000 or 80,000. Quite possibly, the more sanguinary sagas had as one function that of the cautionary tale—they warned against what might happen if people did not respect the rules of kinship and neighborhood relations. In reality, many more feuds may have been settled peacefully than bloodily. But the extremism of Njal's saga throws into high relief the normal and fitting. There is in the case of Njal's household what might be called an almost unnatural stress on, or overevaluation of the father-son bond, at the expense of other *sib* and affinal ties, which are radically undervalued, as where Njal's sons kill their almost "saintly" foster-brother Hauskuld, the *goði*, whom Njal himself had set up in his office. Njal's sons, even after marriage, continue to reside not only on their father's land but in his very homestead. This solidarity was one cause of their deaths—had they not lived together and fought together they would not have been burned together. (The family that yearns together, burns together.)

The plot of *Njal's Saga* may be divided into three parts, each a separate narrative, yet interlinked like the phases of a great ritual. The first describes the heroic deeds at home and abroad of Gunnar of Lithend, and how his wife Hallgerda and Njal's wife Bergthora nearly set their households against one another, by "egging on" their thralls and servants to kill one another. Bergthora even involves her sons in the killings at last. But Njal and Gunnar remain firm friends and settle the homicides by *wergild* not retaliation. The first part ends with the killing of Gunnar in his home after having been exiled for a series of killings in self-defense. The second section begins when Njal's oldest son helps Gunnar's son avenge his father's death, and continues, through a chain of killings, counter-killings and attempts at settlement and reconciliation, to the burning of Njal, his wife, children, a grandchild, and many servants in their homestead, by Flosi, who has taken up the task of avenging Hauskuld the *Goði's* death. Flosi is accompanied by many who seek vengeance on Njal's sons for kinsmen slain by them. The final part narrates the retribution exacted on the Burners by Kari, Njal's son-in-law, whose wife perished in the flames. Kari harries the Burners over Iceland and even pursues them over the sea; he slays Gunnar Lambisson, a Burner, at the very feast-board of Jarl Sigurd of the Orkneys. The saga virtually ends with the reconciliation of Flosi and Kari, who goes on to marry Flosi's brother's daughter, and has a son by her whom he calls Flosi.

W. P. Ker remarks (1967:190) of *Njala*: "It carries an even greater burden of particulars than *Eyrbyggja* (another family saga); it has taken up into itself the whole history of the south country of Iceland in the heroic age." The "south country" mentioned is the arena for the field of social relations formed by the ultimate confrontation between the Burners and Njal's faction at the slaying of Hauskuld. Indeed, since Njal's burning raised suits in two Quarter Courts and then in the Fifth Court of the *Althing* it could be said to have had all Iceland as arena. Strangely, although it deals primarily with killings between the patrilineal residential cores of "house-communities," the saga's main sequence of events begins with a quarrel between unrelated women, Bergthora and Hallgerda, and ends with reconciliation between unrelated men, Kari and Flosi.

Kari, though unrelated by birth to Njal and his blood-kin, indeed, not even an Icelander but an Orkneyman, is linked by marriage to them, as is Bergthora, Njal's wife. Hallgerda is linked by affinity to the opposite faction, as is Flosi. Thus connections by marriage may serve as either disruptive or unitive factors in the relations between house-communities and sets of linked house-communities. In the case of the women who are incorporated into patrilineal core-groups by viri-local marriage and spend most of their post-marital lives in their husbands' communities, rising to the status of matriarchs, concern for the honor of these local, particularistic groups becomes a ruling passion. They are not concerned with the wider groupings, such as District, Quarter, or Iceland, but foment local conflicts with their sharp taunting tongues. But men, through their participation in juridical and legislative action on a wider scale than the local, may exert their influence as in-laws to reconcile disputing house-communities rather than exacerbate their enmities. Even when they are inimical to both parties to a dispute, like the sinister Mord Valgardsson, who provokes Njal's sons to kill Hauskuld by deceitful words, ill-wishing men have to couch their mischievous intentions in the honeyed language of the common good. But the women have no such inhibitions. When Hallgerda hires Brynjolf the Unruly to cause trouble among Bergthora's servants, early in the saga, she says to him (referring to Atli, one of Bergthora's men): "I have been told that Atli is not at home, and he must be winning work on Thorofsfell." [He was cutting wood there.]

> "What thinkest thou likeliest he is working at?" says Brynjolf.
> "At something in the wood," she says.
> "What shall I do to him?" he asks.
> "Thou shall kill him," says she.

Nevertheless the killings of servants for which these women are responsible are relatively small beer. The bulk of the saga is made up of long social dramas. As social drama the first phase, that of "breach" of regular norm-governed relationships is usually a killing, the next phase, "crisis," sees the mobilization of factions, either to take revenge and defend against it, or to seek compensation; if the drama continues to the phase of bringing in "redressive procedures," these may either be of an informal kind, as when Njal and Gunnar privately decide to offer one another compensation for the slain thralls, or involve formal measures ranging from "self-doom," where a plaintiff is conceded the right by his opponents to name the kind and extent of damages he thinks fair, through recourse to local and District *Things* to the *Althing* of Iceland and the "Fifth

Court" in it. *Njal's Saga* begins with simple breaches of order, minor crises, and informal redress, mainly at the level of relations between household-communities in a small region of the South Quarter, which cumulate, despite temporary settlement and redress, until finally the breach is the killing of a *goði* who is also a good man, the crisis involves a major cleavage between factions consisting of the major lineages and *sibs* in southern and south-eastern Iceland, and the parties seek redress at the *Althing* and Fifth Court. *Njal's Saga* shows pitilessly how Iceland just could not produce the machinery to handle major crises, for inevitably the *Althing* negotiations break down and there is regression to crisis again, sharpened crisis, moreover, that can only be resolved now by the total defeat of one party, even its attempted annihilation. The art of the literary genius who took the oral and written traditions and wove them into the saga we now have reveals for us how the bitterness of the early household feuds, which Njal and Gunnar had the authority to keep formally within local bounds, nevertheless trickled through the rivulets of many small crises into what might have been a national crisis had there been a nation. The fact that there was no nation was represented by the absence of national laws with teeth in them, the teeth of punitive sanctions jointly applied by the leading men. Thus local feuds which could be only transiently contained by enlightened individuals generated forces over time which sundered Iceland and revealed the weakness of her uncentralized, "acephalous" polity. Strong individualism can only be kept in bounds by strong centralized institutions. It seems, however, that *Njal's Saga* was written after Iceland had accepted Norwegian overlordship and Norway's king, and it may have been partly written to show how the traditional Commonwealth had no means of keeping the peace. Patently, *Njal's Saga* reflects the experience of the Sturlung Era. The saga relates, in terms of personalities, the story of a society. Njal succeeds in keeping local peace for a while but cannot curb his own sons, who disobey him in order to carry out their mother's will. Yet the greatest men of Iceland hang upon his words when he proposes to establish general legal machinery, such as the Fifth Court, and give him support. The irony of the saga is that it is through the continual disobedience of his own sons, who undertake revenge killings against his will, that the final disasters come about, exposing the impotence of Icelandic redressive institutions. Njal is shown as a man who always seeks peace and is forever trying to set up social devices for keeping it. For example he fosters Hauskuld, whose father Thrain has been slain by Njal's grim and blackly humorous son Skarphedinn, precisely to reconcile the lad and his kin *with* Skarphedinn, and Njal's other sons, Helgi and Grim. For a time this seemed to work and, as the saga says, "Njal's sons took Hauskuld about with them and did him honour in every way." Njal later had the Fifth Court make him a *goði*. But in the end Skarphedinn slew Hauskuld, and thus made the burning almost inevitable. For a time it seemed that Njal and Flosi, who took up the suit for Hauskuld's slaying, would come to terms about compensation but at the last moment Skarphedinn offered Flosi an unforgivable insult that could only be wiped out in blood. A society organized at its only effectual level, the local level, on kinship, and especially on patrilineal kinship, cannot cope with larger, more impersonal, national relationships and issues. Thus the very power of agnation, of the paternal bond, compelled Njal to stand by his sons and indeed suffer death with them, although they had willfully brought that death about by flouting his advice and ruining his efforts to create peace-maintaining machinery above the local level.

With the hindsight of the post-Sturlung period *Njala's* author is portraying for us the fate of a social order, of the old Germania transported to an inhospitable island where Teutonic nomadism was slowed down and halted by lack of adequate cultivable or pastoral land—save for the ultimate adventurers like Eirik the Red and Leif Erikson who discovered the New World. All the structural contradictions were left in the "laboratory experimental" conditions of Icelandic isolation to shake the polity to pieces. The settlers were aristocrats of the ancient breed, who fled to a "ruined land of sphagnum moss" to continue the old ways, even the old verse forms, in terms of the old attitudes which had elsewhere vanished before Christendom and chivalry. The sagas, especially *Njal's Saga*, chronicle, step by step, the suicidal character of that last stand.

Yet it was perhaps, by another paradox, the very fact of Germania's projection into the new literate age by four centuries that made Icelandic literature possible. The contrast between the new polities abroad, observed by vigilant and highly intelligent Icelandic travelers and vikings, and their own ancient acephalous polities, based on kinship and local organization of a small-scale character, made for an almost self-mocking self-awareness, and for W. P. Ker's "dry light." Yet aristocratic prideful obduracy kept the old order—or was it disorder?—going, and let us remember that some of the results were major literature as well as a high homicide rate.

I will have to conclude where I would like to have begun by pointing out that the sagas read like exceptionally well-filled ethnographic records and diaries, written by an incomparable literary artist. I would have liked to have begun by making a technical analysis in anthropological terms of the details of *Njal's Saga*, relating its copious genealogical materials to the siting of homestead owners on the map and pointing out how the meticulous descriptions of such things as seating order at wedding feasts reflect the social structure also visible in the patternings of genealogies and settlements. At the wedding of Gunnar and Hallgerda, for example, not only were the different kinds of kinship, affinal, and territorial relationships in which the guests stood to Gunnar represented in their placing round the festal table, but the shape of things to come was simultaneously represented by Njal's party's placement on one side of Gunnar and the foremost Burners' on the other—a clear indication of the importance of structural links and divisions for the development of the feud. Literary critics would assent to W. P. Ker's words that in Njal "the essence of the tragic situation lies in this, that the good man is in the wrong, and his adversary in the right" (1967:190 – 92). The anthropologist would see the situation less in ethical terms. The Icelander compelled by structural ties to take up a vengeance suit has a similar role to that of a mature man in an Ndembu village in Central Africa (Turner 1957:94). Such a senior villager is compelled sooner or later to take a stand on the question of succession to the headmanship. A person who tries to avoid pressing the claim for that office vested in his very membership in the village kinship structure, when the old headman dies is subjected to intense pressure from his close kin and children to put it forward. If he should still fail to do so, there occurs a displacement of the locus of conflict, not a resolution or bypassing of conflict. Instead of leading a group of kin against the representatives of other pressure groups or factions, he becomes the target of criticism and even scorn from members of his own group. At some point in the social process arising from succession he is compelled to turn and defend himself, whatever his temperament or character, however "good" or "bad" he may be. As I wrote, "the situation in an Ndembu village closely parallels that found in Greek drama where one witnesses the helplessness of the human individual before the Fates: but in this case the Fates are the necessities of the social process." *Mutatis mutandis* the same basic situation prevailed in Iceland, and this is pithily revealed in *Njal's Saga* in its accounts of how men reacted to the rules forcing them to take part in the feud. Icelandic social structure never resolved the opposition between forces making for centralization and forces making for decentralization, between extreme individualism and family loyalty, between kinship and citizenship and, perhaps, also, between a bare subsistence economy and the aspiration to an aristocratic style of life. There may well have been increasing pressure on effective resources at that subsistence level which exacerbated disputes between adjacent *goðar* and their followers over scarce resources, such as timber and meadows, and activated other structural and cultural contradictions. A host of cultural considerations I have not been able to mention are relevant here; Njal, the man of peace, was a Christian but Icelandic standards of conduct remained vindictively pagan; it is constantly hinted that he was somewhat effeminate—his enemies called him mockingly "the Beardless Carle"—for if pursuing vengeance is defined as manly, seeking reconciliation with one's foes must be unmanly, and so on. But ultimately, for the author of the saga, Njal seems to symbolize the Commonwealth itself. This is perhaps best reflected in the celebrated scene when the burning begins. I must quote (from Dasent's translation):

> Flosi (from outside) said to Bergthora, Njal's wife, "Come thou out, housewife, for I will for no sake burn thee indoors."
>
> "I was given away to Njal young," said Bergthora, "and I have promised him this, that we would both share the same fate."
>
> After that they both went back into the house.
>
> "What counsel shall we now take?" said Bergthora.
>
> "We will go to our bed," says Njal, "and lay us down; I have long been eager for rest."
>
> Then she said to the boy Thord, Kari's son, "Thee will I take out, and thou shalt not burn in here."
>
> "Thou hast promised me this, grandmother," says the boy, "that we should never part so long as I wished to be with thee; but methinks it is much better to die with thee and Njal than to live after you."
>
> An ox hide was thrown over the three of them, and they spoke no more.
>
> Skarphedinn saw how his father laid him down, and how he laid himself out, and then he said, "Our father goes early to bed, and that is what was to be looked for, for he is an old man."

For me, these laconic, ironic, heroic words epitomize the fate of the Icelandic Commonwealth, and its attempt to find peace and order. It could not live but it made a good end, so good that its failure to survive became immortal literature.

5

The Icelandic Family Saga as a Genre of Meaning-Assignment

Concrete examples are more eloquent than abstract theorizing, even when that theorizing is based on much empirical observation and analysis of extended case studies. I would like to discuss with you a renowned literary genre which takes as its subject matter allegedly historical sequences of social events of the type I have called social dramas. I refer to the Icelandic family sagas, most of which are known to have been composed about two hundred and fifty to three hundred years after the events they purport to describe. Few anthropologists have written about Iceland in the saga period (covering events taking place between about A.D. 930 and A.D. 1030), yet these narratives are replete with materials on sociocultural processes, relations, and structures. Rosalie Wax is a fine exception. Her book, *Magic, Fate, and History: The Changing Ethos of the Vikings* (1969), which examines the question of whether the Icelandic writers' renowned "freedom from superstition" was indeed "a manifestation of a precocious, proto-scientific enlightenment," or not rather "a terminal expression of an extraordinary disenchantment" (p. 162), is full of penetrating insights, although I think she misses the proto-Romanticism behind the apparently "austere, proto-existential, warrior philosophy, within which a man's brave and honorable deeds were the most valuable and lasting of all things" (p. 162). If we look closely at the course and outcome of a great human social process, and especially if we have grasped the main principles—and antiprinciples—of the culture and *Weltanschauung* in which it is being conducted, she also misses the sheer reflexive delight in the meaningfulness of factuality. I have to admit that I also tried my hand at understanding an aspect of saga literature in an article which appeared in one of the many *festschriften* dedicated to the late Professor Evans-Pritchard, *The Translation of Culture* (1971), edited by T. O. Beidelman. This was called, rather grandiosely, "An Anthropological Approach to the Icelandic Saga" (see Chapter 4 in this book). I argued that Icelandic social structure "never resolved the contradiction between forces making for centralization and forces making for decentralization, between extreme individualism and family loyalty, between kinship and citizenship, and, perhaps, also, between a bare subsistence economy and the aspiration (among many leading Icelanders) to an aristocratic style of life" (p. 92 above).

Further on in this chapter, I shall pick out one of the major Icelandic family sagas or "prose epics," the *Eyrbyggya Saga*, to underline some new theoretical points. Meanwhile, some introduction is needed to Icelandic history, ecology, and to Old Icelandic literary genres. It must be understood, in the first place, that the Icelandic family sagas are not historical chronicles but highly structured and elaborated literary pieces. As just mentioned, they were mostly composed in the thirteenth century while the events they purport to narrate took place in the tenth and early eleventh centuries. Most scholars now agree that they are by no means oral traditions written down in the early days of Icelandic literacy (the so-called "Freeprose Theory"), but were original literary creations drawing on several centuries of written materials. This "Bookprose Theory" does not deny that oral histories and poems may have been used as sources, not only by the earliest writers of saga but also throughout the entire era of saga composition. The best-known sagas represent "bricolages" of oral and literate forms, motifs, formulae, framing devices and tropes. Each of them is a brilliant literary achievement in its own right. In her study, *The Laxdaela Saga: Its Structural Patterns* (1964), Margaret Arent Madelung is particularly critical of the notion that the saga stems directly from oral tradition. Her conclusion, arrived at by a close structuralist analysis of this great saga, is worth quoting in full:

> Rhetorical techniques such as the use of repetitions, increments, antitheses, negative alternatives, litotes [understatement for effect, in which something is expressed by a negation of the contrary—*e.g.,* Grettir the Strong's remark to Thorbjorn shortly before he slew him in *Grettis Saga* (p. 102), "I prophesy, Slowcoach, that you will not die of the smoke of the hearth, and yet perhaps you will not die of old age either. . . . my prophecies are not generally long-lived"—there is usually a sauce of irony in litotes!], chiasmal relationships [inversion of the second of two parallel phrases or clauses—in *The Laxdaela Saga,*

> Thorstein has much livestock but little land, while Halldor has little livestock but much land (p. 114) or where dreams of good omen are followed by dreams of bad omen, smooth sea crossings contrasted with difficult sea-crossings, or men with similar names have opposite characters], stylistic conventions such as the use of anticipatory devices, contrastives (after gladness, sorrow, *etc.*), incorporation of authoritative names, folk etymologies, poems, dreams; narrative techniques such as interspersing narration with dialogue, mingling of direct and indirect discourse, use of flash-backs [all these] are hardly new with the author of *Laxdaela*, and can be shown to be the result of long schooling with classical texts, however much they may have coincided with the devices of native poetry (p. 154).

What we are in effect dealing with is a type of social drama, characteristic of Icelandic culture, involving feuds between coalitions of households, examined within the frame of a set of rhetorical conventions that have developed within a literate tradition though borrowing certain stereotyped elements from a preexisting oral tradition. Most scholars agree that the kinds of situations prevalent in the Sturlung Period, when the sagas were mostly written, were similar in nature, though perhaps greater in intensity, to those in the earlier stages of Icelandic society. But the time lag between past deeds and later narration of those deeds is highly significant, for they raise most of the problems we have been discussing: reflexivity, the assignment of meaning, the influence of *Weltanschauungen*, variation in the processual form of social dramas in different cultures, and so forth. It enables me, furthermore, to revive a pet theory of mine in the area of comparative study of national epics, which I first broached at the University of Chicago in 1969 during a seminar I convened with James Redfield, when both of us were on the faculty of the Committee on Social Thought. We brought together a group consisting of: A. K. Ramanujan and J. Van Buitenen to discuss early Indian epic (they focused on the *Mahabharata*); David Grene and James Redfield himself for ancient Greek epic (Grene took the *Odyssey*, Redfield the *Iliad* for detailed study); Donald Levine, who gave a paper on the *Kebra Nagast*, the major epic of Amharic Ethiopia; Donald Shojai, an Iranian scholar who spoke about the *Shahnameh*, the great Persian epic by Ferdowsi; and I who contributed some thoughts on the Icelandic *Njal's Saga*, and a general paper on the comparative problems emerging from the series. Margaret Arent took part, and it is clear that her book on the *Laxdaela Saga* benefited from our discussions. She writes in her Preface that "some ten years after the inception of the whole idea" of her "study of a single saga" (p. ix), "I stumbled upon something totally unexpected . . . the saga metamorphoses into a *roman à clef*" (p. x). By this she means that the events and personages of the *Laxdaela Saga* referred to events and people contemporary with its author and not to those of early Iceland. I include a section from the general paper, "Comparative Epic and Saga," (unpublished manuscript, Cornell University Icelandic Collection) which I gave at the beginning of the Chicago seminar in 1969. The section called "The Epic Relation" betokens my earliest interest in the problem of cultural reflexivity. It will also serve as an introduction to my analysis in social dramatistic terms of the *Eyrbyggya Saga*, chosen because it relates to the vicissitudes of groups of people over time and not, as many sagas do, primarily to individuals or pairs, such as *Njal's Saga* does to Njal, *Laxdaela Saga* to Kjartan and Gudrun, *Grettir's Saga* to Grettir.

The Epic Relation

By "epic relation" I designate the relationship among three periods of time, each associated with a particular organization of society and culture. The first may be called the *heroic time* of the narrated events, with its implicit background of "heroic" society; the second is *narrative time* when the epic was first composed or believed to have been composed; the third is the *documentary time* which covers the period for which we have manuscripts of the epic in their various recensions (revisions). I have been forced to formulate this notion of the epic relation because I disagree, for once, with the great Scottish scholar, W. P. Ker, when he says that epic poetry is a *direct reflection* of an order of society where "the center of life is a great man's house, and where the most brilliant society is that which is gathered at his feast, where competitive boasting, storytelling, and minstrelsy are the principal intellectual amusements . . . where fighting is more important than anything else, *etc.*" (*Epic and Romance,* 1967 [1908]:12). Clearly, songs were sung in such settings, but the epics we know about seem to have achieved their definitive form at least several centuries after the events they purport to relate. Other genres, too, may evince a similar triadic relation between nodes of time, but the epic differs in the magnitude of the historical events related, the importance of *written* sources for the epic-maker, and, very often, the number of redactions, or recensions in parchment, vellum, or paper, made of the reputed first text.

Consider the epics in this series: (1) The *Shahnameh* tells the story of the Iranian Empire, from the creation of the world down to the Mohammedan conquest. This conquest took place in A.D. 636. But Ferdowsi completed his royal record, after thirty-five years of intermittent composing, in A.D. 1010. Thus there was a gap of almost four hundred years between the end of heroic time and the end of narrative time. I have no material presently available to me on the dating of the earliest manuscripts of the *Shahnameh*, but Reuben Levy suggests in the prologue to his translation that it may have been due to a redactor that the various episodes traditionally composed in no set sequence by Ferdowsi were finally put together in chronological order (R. Levy 1967:xvi). (2) According to Charles Drekmeier in *Kingship and Community in Early India* (1962:132), the conflict at the core of the *Mahabharata* "probably took place in the tenth or ninth centuries B.C., although popular tradition has located it as early as 3102 B.C. All India supposedly participated in the battle, which stormed for eighteen days on the plain of Kuruksetra, in the vicinity of modern Delhi." According to W. H. McNeill in *The Rise of the West* (1963:190n), "the *Mahabharata* existed in some form or other as early as 400 B.C.; but its present recension, which includes a tremendous bulk of priestly piety, presumably deposited around an original core of more secular poetry, dates from between 200 and 400 A.D." McNeill adds: "It is rather as though Homer had been reworked by the Christian Fathers into an allegory and handbook of Christian doctrine, leaving only traces of the original spirit of the poem." Other scholars I have read offer variant views, but the main point I wish to stress is that here again we have the epic relation, between heroic, narrative, and documentary time, the implications of which we will shortly consider. (3) George Steiner, in his Introduction to *Homer: A Collection of Critical Essays* (1962:4), tells us that the archaeological evidence suggests that Troy VIIA was sacked *in circa* 1180 B.C., at a time when "on both sides of the Aegean, the Mycenaean world, with its great palaces and complex dynastic and commercial relations, met with violent disaster. The citadels of Pylos and Iolkos were burnt around 1200, and golden Mycenae itself was destroyed within the century." Yet, "in the form in which we know them, the *Iliad* and the *Odyssey* were set down between *circa* 750 and 700 B.C." Although Steiner following Whitman states that the first manuscript might date from the second half of the eighth century and was initially set down in the Old Attic alphabet, the Ionic script in which the *Iliad* and *Odyssey* were handed down came into official use only in the fifth century B.C. (p. 6). Once more we have the epic relation. (4) About the Ethiopian *Kebra Nagast*, Edward Ullendorf has this to say in *The Ethiopians* (1960:143–44): "The greatest work not only of the time of Amda Sion (1314–44), but the foremost creation of Ethiopic literature generally, is the 'Glory of the Kings' which has been woven into Ethiopian life in the most intimate manner. It has as its *piece de resistance* the legend of the Queen of Sheba (based on the narrative in 1 Kings X. 1–13 and liberally amplified and embellished [and here we might remember what Ker said about the relationship between history and epic]), how she visited King Solomon, accepted his religion, bore him a son (Menelik I), and how the son visited his father and abducted the Ark of the Covenant, which was taken to Aksum, the new Zion [Don Levine in *Wax and Gold* (1965) points out that Ethiopians regard this ark-stealing as a sign that the

Promise has passed from Israel to Ethiopia]. Apart from numerous quotations and paraphrases from the Old and New Testaments, we find generous borrowings from apocryphal literature, the Book of Enoch, the *Book of the Pearl*, from the christological and patristic writings in Coptic, Syriac, Arabic and Greek, from the *Testamentum Adami*, from Rabbinical literature as well as the Koran....In fact, the main story must have had a very long period of gestation in Ethiopia and elsewhere and have possessed all the elements of a gigantic conflation of cycles of legend and tales. When it was committed to writing, early in the fourteenth century, its purpose was no doubt to lend support to the claims and aspirations of the recently established Solomonic dynasty. Its author, the *nebura ed* Yeshaq of Aksum, was thus mainly redactor and interpreter of material which had long been known, but had not until then found a coordinating hand, an expository mind, and a great national need."

What is interesting about this account is that a very large portion of the *Kebra Nagast* appears to be based solely on literary sources rather than upon oral tradition. I have no information about the dating of the earliest vellum or goatskin manuscripts of this epic, but I imagine they cannot long postdate their author Yeshaq of Aksum. Here the dominant epic relation would be between heroic and narrative time. I raise the matter of written versus oral sources because several of the literatures have been subjected to this controversy, as we shall see in a moment. What is also striking about the epics we have already considered is that in the Persian, Indian and Ethiopian cases major religious changes have occurred between heroic and narrative times: Ferdowsi wrote in Muslim times about Zoroastrian kings, Yeshaq in Christian times about ancient Israel, while many of the incidents of the *Mahabharata* "go far back into the remote Vedic period" (Drekmeier 1962:132), but have been then drastically modified by Brahmanical priests, writing in the second and first centuries B.C., "who expanded the meaning of the ballads," according to Drekmeier, "linked them together with prose narration, and interpolated treatises on ethical and theological problems." I cannot say whether a similar situation existed in the Greek epic, whether Homer, for example, lived under a religion radically different from that of heroic times—probably most authorities would agree that ancient Greek religion was far less ordered than Homer's pantheon of Olympians, being derived as McNeill writes: "partly from Indo-European sky and nature deities and partly from the autochthonous protectresses worshipped by pre-Greek populations" (*The Rise of the West* 1963:226). But the *Iliad* and the *Odyssey*, like much of the *Shahnameh*, have a pronouncedly secular tone, by comparison with religious literature of the same period.

In the case of the Icelandic literature we have large quantities of reliable evidence to show us fairly precisely the nature of the epic relation.

To begin with, we know that the poetic and prose epics and other genres were collected or composed by Christians, though they referred to pagan times or to the transition between paganism and Christianity. The great sagas of kings and of Icelandic heroes were written in the thirteenth and early fourteenth centuries, but they were usually about events that occurred between the latter part of the ninth century and about the middle of the eleventh. Most of the sagas are preserved in several manuscripts, both vellum and paper, dating from about 1350 to 1400, often in fragmentary vellums, to paper manuscripts from the seventeenth and eighteenth centuries copied from lost vellums. Scholars have been arguing for several centuries as to whether the different redactions of the same saga represent oral variants or manuscript variants: did the scribes copy down an oral tradition, did they copy the first manuscript and subsequent redactions of it, and did they interpolate in Saga A passages from sagas B, C and D?

If epics achieve their definitive form several centuries after the deeds they record, it is legitimate to ask: what has happened during those centuries and is the picture of the past presented by the epic-maker or compiler an accurate one? Modern Icelandic scholars are in more or less agreement that the family sagas "originated under the influence of the Kings' sagas, just as the Kings' sagas originated under the influence of hagiography and of other learned writing" (Turville-Petre 1953:231), not a sequence of development that one would have expected arguing from common sense! From saints to kings to folk heroes! From clerks to sagamen! Yet there is a mass of evidence for this development. I suspect that a number of popular stereotypes concerning the inevitability of the course from oral to written, collective to individual, folk to learned epics and lays may prove to be equally baseless in the other literatures with which we will deal.

The other problem, that of the relationship between the poet or redactor and "the heroic time," is one of fascinating complexity. Much of the tension and mystery of epic derives from the ambivalence of the poet to the past. For example, the Icelandic Saga of the outlaw Grettir the Strong is at once a set of Christian moral judgments upon a proud man of blood who came inevitably to a bad end—as contrasted pointedly with the pious end of his younger brother Thorsteinn who died a holy hermit—and a sustained panegyric on a great warrior who embodied the Icelandic heroic ideal. Much of the dramatic tension of this great tale comes from the simultaneous appraisal of Grettir's deeds in two contradictory evaluative frames. The result is somehow to make of Grettir a human being in the round, rather than an immaculate tragic hero in the romantic style or a saint in the hagiographic. The epic relation has similar consequences for the *Shahnameh*, as Reuben Levy writes (1967:xxii): "The overriding tragic fact of [Ferdowsi's] life is that the glory of which he sings is no more. But this is not to say that the *Shahnameh* is a defiant nostalgic lament. The intellectual horizon of Ferdowsi is that of a national and devout Muslim. Mohammed and Zoroaster are venerated as if they were of the same root, but Ferdowsi's pride in Iran is his constant muse," just as the sagamen's pride in Iceland was theirs, despite its former paganism. In both the Iranian and Icelandic instances, of course, the epic-makers were intensely conscious of other societies and political systems than their own, the Icelanders of Norway, Denmark and Ireland, the Persians of the Arabs, Indians, Afghans, and Turks. The India of the *Mahabharata*-makers and redactors was as yet unthreatened by outside invasion, and it would seem that its major tension was due to the rivalry between Kshatriya and Brahmanical world views. But there also appears to be in it a tension between tribal and caste ideas, too, which is reflected in what Drekmeier calls "the dual character of the lord Krishna" who is at once a *kshatriya* noble whose role as "*avatar*, protector of the dharma" would necessarily involve him in *kshatriya* functions, and a "tribal god," a "trickster, a master of deception, a wily fox" (1962:135). In all these cases, a complex relationship seems to exist between the imagined past, stimulated by the deposit of oral traditions available to the poet, either at firsthand, or second- and thirdhand in manuscript redactions, and the often painful present, a relationship in which sometimes the past and sometimes the present are by implication alternately negatively and positively evaluated vis-à-vis one another. Again since "the past" is never homogeneous but is itself stratified and the present is a hodgepodge of disparate tendencies and relationships, the poet is presented with a diversity of elements which he can combine in a diversity of ways.

What often seems to happen is that the struggles of the poet's own time are projected onto the teeming data, fanciful and factual, of the past. Thus Reuben Levy writes (1967:xxi) that "the bitterness of the mythical Iranian-Turanian epic struggle that permeates the Shah-nama and gives it its dramatic tension is largely the pressing phenomenon of the poet's own time. Thus he has experienced a reenactment of the final tragedy of his poem. The necessity of dedicating the Shah-nama to the very Turkic destroyer of the Iranian Samanids must have been a bitter and demeaning fact." In Iceland, too, such late works as *Njal's Saga* seem to reflect the turbulent Sturlung Period in which they were conceived, in the wide geographical range of their factional struggles and the number of homicides recorded, rather than the social situation of the late tenth century, when conflict must have been more localized.

When Levy goes on to mention that the tensions and contradictions in the poet's experience that are reflected in the tragic paradoxes of the epic are "not at all conscious or external" (1962:xxiii) he makes a point that I believe would hold good for other epic literatures as well. These inner conflicts, in assonance with the conflicting schemes of values accumulated by oral and written traditions, provide an emotional richness and complexity that give to the characters and settings of epic their peculiarly living quality. It may well be also that the derivation of epic's values, ethical imperatives and manners from several dissonant epochs may be the very cause of its well-known, universal-human quality. The poet is forced by his materials away from the familiar paths of systematically connected customs and norms to make original assessments of character and individual worth. He is at a sufficient distance from the standards of the heroic age to be objective about them and even daringly to judge those standards themselves by their good or bad effects on the fully human beings the multidimensional quality of his material has allowed to emerge. These are some of the motives that induce me to stress the "epic relation" rather than to regard epic as the direct expression or reflection of the heroic society in which it is supposed to be set. It is the anachronistic nature of epic that gives its characters their sculptural solidity; this "strength and weight" of character is not merely an invariable attribute of a heroic age. Like a fine wine, epic needs time to mature; it is not the news of the day.

Freeprose versus Bookprose

Theodore Andersson (1964) argues that what we think of saga origins is important because on it rests our assessment of their value for a study of the times of which they tell. For example, if we believe, as a number of patriotic Danish, Norwegian, and Swedish scholars have done and still do, that the sagas are vessels of authentic historical tradition going back to the ninth, tenth, and eleventh centuries, then we must count them as among our most valuable sources of information for that period on Northern Europe. On the other hand, if we hold them to be free compositions by authors with other interests than the transmission of strict historical facts, then much of their value for historians is reduced. At the extremes of the argument, the sagas, so Andersson shows us, may be thought of as either recorded history or late historical fiction. The most useful part of his book is the chapter on "Freeprose versus Bookprose," terms coined by Andreas Heusler (1941). The freeprose theory postulates a highly developed oral art of saga-telling before the sagas were written down. This shaped saga style as well as saga substance. "The relationship of the saga writer to his material was that of editor rather than a creator. He enjoyed the same freedom as any previous teller in addition to certain literary prerogatives denied to the oral sagaman, but [and this is crucial for the theory] he was always bound by his *oral source* or sources" (Andersson 1964:65). The proponents of this position include such celebrated scholars as Rudolph

Meissner, Andreas Heusler, Gustav Neckel, Per Wieselgran, and Knut Liestol, none of them, significantly, being Icelanders.

The bookprose theory regards the sagas as deliberate works of art, largely based on oral tradition, but making at times considerable use of written sources, allowing much freedom to the individual artist, and showing demonstrable variation of style, narrative, characterization and organizing ability. The saga writer is on this showing much more an author than an editor. The bookprose theory is associated with Iceland and stems essentially from the work of B. M. Olsen (1911). The formidable scholars Sigurdur Nordal (1953) and E. O. Sveinsson (1953) are his main followers; both are Icelanders. It is easy to see why Icelanders should support the bookprose theory, for a "bookprose" *Njal's Saga* or *Laxdaela Saga* will impress us more than ever before as a work of literature. Here the shaping power behind the saga is the genius in individual great men—the freeprose theory finds it in the collective representation of the "folk." Icelanders have always been inveterate individualists and would prefer to have great writers than a great folk spirit. Nordal, for example, reminds us that the literary quality of the sagas forbids us to regard them as popular art (S. Nordal, pp. 233–34, cited in Andersson, 1964:71). Where the freeprosaists argue that stylistic homogeneity in the sagas proclaims them vessels of folk tradition, Nordal retorts that this is like saying that all babies are alike, or the urbanite's view that all white sheep are alike! Close study of the sagas reveals that no two can with certainty be attributed to the same author. As for the problem of anonymous authorship—which the freeprosaists held to represent the transmission of an impersonal tradition—Nordal holds that "all *invented* sagas are transmitted anonymously, like all Eddic poems. Do *Voluspá* (the Eddic poem) and *Njála* (the prose saga), which are both anonymous, bear the stamp of their authors less than, for example, *Vellekla* and *Sverri's Saga* (the authors of which are known—Einar Skalaglamm for the first, Karl Jonsson for the second)?" Nordal, following B. M. Olsen, identified Snorri Sturluson as the author of *Egil's Saga*, while Bardi Gudmundsson, the late Keeper of the National Archives of Iceland, in his *Höfundur Njálu* (1958), has tried to locate the milieu, if possible the family or monastery, in which a saga was written, even if he has found it almost always impossible to identify the author by name. All this effort seems to be adding up to the emancipation of the author from a set oral tradition and suggesting that he was "open to those cultural and biographical influences which play such a large part in the study of modern authors" (Andersson 1964:74). Again, just as we suggested in considering the epic relation, scholars are now seeking out traces of contemporary life and events in the sagas. Andersson lists a number of identifications between saga incidents and happenings of the authors' own time, for example, Bley's suggestion that Snorri Sturluson's relationship to King Hakon of Norway was "the nerve of Egill's conflict with Erik Blood-Axe in *Egil's Saga*" (Andersson 1964:74). The bookprosaists also argue that the saga was not "hermetically sealed off from other genres," as the freeprosaists implied (Andersson 1964:75). "The influence of the romantic literature which spread from the Continent (of Europe) to Scandinavia in the thirteenth century was studied in *Gunnlaugs Saga* by B. M. Olsen (1911) and in *Laxdaela Saga* by E. O. Sveinsson. The historical writings which predated the family sagas came to be viewed to some extent as stylistic models . . . fluent style [is] no longer regarded as the true patent of oral tradition but as a sign of artistic ripeness gradually attained by several generations of saga writers" (Andersson 1964:75). These passages support and amplify what we have already said about the need to consider epic literature in its full context of different genres and in terms of written as well as oral developments.

These considerations lead me to regard the Bookprose theory as the more satisfactory of the two. For the bookprosaists do not rule out oral tradition as lying at the foundation of the sagas. But they do not see this tradition as being crystallized and transmitted *en bloc*, so to speak, in the sagas as we have them now. The unwritten tradition is rather a matter of bits and pieces—scraps not blocks—what is called in Icelandic *tháèttir* (singular: *tháttr*, literally "a single strand of a rope" and later, a "short story"), and it is the skill of the author who combines these scraps with material from earlier written sources, histories and sagas, into a unified whole that really counts.

I have gone into this debate in some detail because it bears on certain views about the nature of Homeric epic that have become extremely influential—those of Albert Lord. He is concerned with the oral transmission of poetic epics, not prose sagas, and it may be that poetry lends itself better than prose to this method, but it seems to me that his position is closely similar to that of the proponents of freeprose. (Unfortunately we cannot really use "freeverse" or "freepoetry" in English as the parallel term.) For example, he writes, in his chapter on "Homer," in *The Singer of Tales* (1960:141): "What is called oral tradition is as intricate and meaningful an art form as is its derivative, 'literary tradition.' In the extended sense of the word, oral tradition is as 'literary' as literary tradition. It is not simply a less polished, more haphazard, or cruder second cousin twice removed, to literature. By the time the written techniques come onto the stage, the art forms have been long set and are already highly developed and ancient." Lord then states boldly: "There is now no doubt that the composer of the Homeric poems was an oral poet. The proof is to be found in the poems themselves; and it is proper, logical, and necessary that this should be so." He then cites a series of techniques, such as are used today by Yugoslav oral poets, that permeate the Homeric poems—formulas, thematic structures, the line of verse as a metrical unit in itself, and so forth—as evidence that Homer worked inside an oral tradition of epic song. Finally, he claims that the *Iliad* and the *Odyssey* are "oral dictated texts," the result of collaboration between "a good singer and a competent scribe." Homer is alleged to be an "oral poet" who "must have sung them [the *Iliad* and the *Odyssey*] many times before and many times after those momentous occasions that gave us" the variants that we have now in written form. Lord also "feels sure that the impetus to write (them) down did not come from Homer himself but from some outside source."

Lord argues with the authentic voice of a freeprosaist, such as the Norwegian Knut Liestøl, who, according to Andersson, held that "the recurrence of stock phrases, the anacoluthon, the leveling of style and structure, the objectivity and the epic tendencies of expansion on the one hand and schematization on the other could only be interpreted as the product of oral processes comparable to the analogous processes studied firsthand in the (present day) Norwegian søgør"—the oral tradition of the remote valleys (Andersson 1964:68). Like Lord, too, Liestøl supports the claim that the saga style is really a preliterary achievement by observing that it appears in perfected form at the very outset. Such German scholars of Icelandic literature as Meissner and Heusler, like Lord, assert the idea of dictation, but Nordal sharply retorts that the faithful reproduction of the storyteller's version is a technique originated by modern folklorists! (Andersson 1964:71). His final coherent theory "sees the lines of a saga as the work of an author who imposed his artistic will on heterogeneous materials" (p. 79), including fragments from oral tradition, and who was in no way precluded from giving an air of spontaneity and verisimilitude to his work by using in his verse the techniques of an oral poet. Thus, as Baetke has argued, the references to saga telling in the sagas themselves lose their value because they are themselves contained in fictional sagas (p. 90). In any case the "oral" quality is no more than we would expect since it represents the writer's natural mode of expression. Walther Baetke (cited in Andersson 64:80–81) sums up: "The element of oral tradition must therefore be discarded in studying the sagas. They were the product of the Sturlung Age during which they were written. The feuds and vendettas are a reflection of the contemporary tumult, which contrasted so sharply to earlier conditions that the era after the settlement of Iceland in about 870 A.D. came to be viewed as a golden age and was cast in a heroic light. This nostalgic view of the past (though it was interpenetrated by ethical critiques of pagan behavior and other clerical interpolations) was nurtured by the imminent absorption under the Norwegian crown. The threat from abroad brought a reaction against the prevalent preoccupation with Norwegian history (as in the Kings' Sagas) and led to a literary concentration on Icelandic affairs. The literary counterpart to this historical activity was the creation of the family sagas. Viewed as a creation of the thirteenth century their development under the influence of the classical and medieval literature introduced by the church is set in better perspective. The saga cannot then be regarded as the last offshoot of Germanic heroic poetry, rather it filled a gap left by the departed heroic age."

The Eyrbyggya Saga

There is no reason to believe that the Icelandic social drama and the genealogies which form integral parts of them are mere fictions. Rather are they oral traditions of feuds and disputes reworked by original thinkers and artists within a rhetorical tradition which owes more perhaps to literary than to oral precedent. Interestingly, there is sometimes a poor fit between the "natural" processual segmentation of the social drama and the rhetorical structure of the "saga form," between what Bernard Bedseman (p. 21) called "*organic*" and "*formal*" segmentation. The reason for this is that the saga nearly always comments on the characters and deliberately sets the stage for its key events. In his analysis of the Icelandic family sagas Theodore M. Andersson in *The Icelandic Saga: An Analytical Reading* (1967:29) points out that a saga always begins with a preface about the main characters—this is often a simple presentation of the protagonists; where these characters are antagonists their future conflict is foreshadowed in their preliminary characterization. Or the preface can be a detailed account of the hero's family background with full genealogical details. Sometimes the preface is a virtually independent story which serves to give color and momentum to the main plot. In *Njal's Saga*, for example, it is the tale of Gunnar, his character, deeds, and betrayal, which occupies most of the first part, though Njal and his sons are introduced and we can see what manner of men they are, measured against the noble behavior of Gunnar.

According to Andersson, "the body of a saga is concerned with a conflict either between two individuals, between an individual and a group, or between two groups" (1967:29). To my mind, it always comes down to a conflict between two groups. This part of the saga is very much akin structurally to my formulation of the social drama, for, as Andersson writes, "the conflict is touched off by an insult or injury, sometimes inflamed by the malice of a troublemaker, and gradually intensified by a sequence of invective and assault" (1967:29). As you can see, he is talking about the stages of breach and crisis. Next he mentions in other terms what I call the deployment of redressive machinery. "This sequence mounts to a climax. In sixteen cases it culminates in the death of one of the protagonists (more often the hero than the villain), in three cases in the death of someone else, and in two cases in the bloodless discomfiture of the hero . . . The death or discomfiture of a protagonist is usually avenged. The revenge may either be effected by legal procedures, or (in the majority of cases) by blood vengeance, or by a combination of both. In a few sagas the revenge is followed by counterrevenge . . . The revenge section marks the termination of the action, but in about half of the sagas the termination of conflict is confirmed by an express reconciliation between the hostile parties. The reconciliation is either in the form of a personal agreement or of legal arbitration, to which the parties are bound" (p. 29). Although the hero's death is by no means a distinguishing feature of Icelandic saga—it is found in Persian, Anglo-Saxon, Spanish, and Japanese epic, for example—it well expresses the Diltheyan *Weltanschauung* "idealism of freedom," which stresses unconquerable will in defiance of fate. In the saga, the religious aspect is not prominent but the aesthetic is strongly emphasized. However, there is also a strong note of "naturalism," in Dilthey's sense, sounding throughout the sagas, an objectivity that is often pitiless, revealing the flaws in even the most heroic characters, and trying to picture persons in the round.

As an anthropologist, I am interested dominantly in how modes of crisis control developed as the settlement of Iceland proceeded. The sagas give quite self-conscious ("reflexive") exemplification of this growth and consolidation of redressive machinery. Pálsson and Edwards, in the introduction to their translation of the *Eyrbyggya Saga* (1973:11 – 12), saw the saga as an interpretation of Icelandic history, beginning with the pre-Christian anarchy of the Viking Age, moving rapidly to the settlement of Iceland (A.D. 874) and the beginnings of an organized society. Then followed a "period of internal strain and violence, as the laws are hammered out on the lives of proud and inflexible individuals"—reminding one of the expanding western frontier in America. Finally, Christianity comes and the more or less ordered civilization of medieval Iceland becomes established. Here I would again invoke "the epic relation," for the *Eyrbyggya Saga* was probably written "shortly after the middle of the thirteenth century at a time when many sagas had already been composed" (Pálsson and Edwards 1973:23). Other sagas are referred to in it, including the famous *Laxdaela Saga* which concerns events in much the same area of Iceland as *Eyrbyggya* and involving several of its main protagonists, notably Snorri the Priest, who was an ancestor of Snorri Sturluson, the greatest historian and man of letters of medieval Iceland. Some have argued that Snorri Sturluson wrote the *Laxdaela Saga*; he may well had a hand in writing the *Eyrbyggya Saga*. *Erybyggya's* author also drew on the *Landnámabók* (*The Book of Settlements*), probably written in the first half of the twelfth century, perhaps by Iceland's first historian, Ari Thorgilsson, the priest who is known to have composed his *Íslendingabók* between 1122 and 1133. All Ari's works are replete with precise genealogical information, richly supplemented in subsequent redactions by other authors including Sturla Thordarson (1214 – 1284), Snorri's nephew. The point is that *Eyrbyggya* was composed during the turbulent age of the Sturlungs—and other great rivalrous families—where "ordered civilization" gave way to a Hobbesian struggle for power between individual chieftains and their followings, so weakening Iceland that the Commonwealth submitted to King Haakon of Norway in 1262. The great chieftain and historian Snorri Sturluson had already been assassinated in 1241 at the instigation of the ambitious chieftain Gizur Thorvaldsson who had hoped to make himself supreme ruler of Iceland. Gizur had been made a jarl by King Haakon but turned against him for a while, only to declare renewed loyalty to him when it became clear that the Icelanders were now prepared to trade their once-valued independence for law, security, and trade-pledges. Treachery, turncoatism, cowardice, and sadistic cruelty in combat situations had replaced the simpler pagan ethic—unless indeed that ethic was itself the nostalgic creation of writers of the Sturlung Age. Thus the epic relation, involving both the projection of present conflicts onto the data of the past and idealization of the past's moral culture, holds good with regard to *Eyrbyggya*.

At the time of the main events in *Eyrbyggya*, the population of Iceland has been estimated to have been about 20,000. Although the island is nearly 40,000 square miles—about the size of Virginia—only a small percentage was habitable, let alone cultivable, mostly land lying "between fell and foreshore" as the adage had it. Not much more than 5,673 square miles, or about the area of Connecticut, can be used for farming purposes today, in the past perhaps even less. Yet it is likely that the early settlers came primarily for freehold land unencumbered by protofeudal constraints such as were beginning to bind men in Western Norway from which most of the pioneers came. Probably, too, pressure of population on resources and land-shortage were becoming acute in Norway. The "myth" in most of the sagas was that the settlers left Norway because they opposed King Harald Fairhair's policy of uniting the petty Norwegian chieftains under his own centralized rule. This, however, would not account for the twelve percent, or so, of settlers who, according to the *Landnámabók*, came from the Norwegian colonies in the British Isles—Ireland, the Isle of Man, the Hebrides, the Orkneys and Shetlands mainly. They must have come principally for pastures unoccupied by a hostile native population. However, these settlers must have brought a noticeable strain of Celtic culture with them, for they had Gaelic-speaking thralls and often wives and concubines and many were themselves children of

Celtic mothers. Some scholars have noted features shared by Icelandic skaldic poetry and Irish syllabic poetic forms (Turville-Petre 1953:37), and others have argued that the high art of Celtic storytelling has influenced saga-telling technique.

There is, I think, though, something more than myth in the view that many prominent men left Norway to settle finally in Iceland. The areas which the leading settlers laid claim to in the new country were not small plots of ground; they were as extensive as modern Scandinavian parishes and jurisdictional districts. Within these territories they apportioned the land among their kinsmen and followers. In response to the need for some kind of overall organization and for a forum for the discussion of common affairs the Icelanders set up a general assembly called the *Althingi*, with its meeting place at Thingvellir near the land's largest lake, *Thingvallavatn*, about fifty miles east of Reykjavik, the capital. The general assembly convened yearly in June. The legislative power was exercised by the *lögrétta*, which consisted of thirty-six, later forty-eight, *goðar*. *Goðar* (singular *goði*) were eminent men or chieftains who had built or were in charge of pagan temples (notably to Thor, Frey, or Odin) in their areas. Among them were descendants of the more notable among the first settlers. The *lögrétta* was presided over by the Law Speaker (*lögsögumaðr*). He was elected for three years and was required to know the law from memory, even to recite it in its entirety before the general assembly during his three-year term of office—another example of the remarkable memories of men in preliterate cultures. A court consisting of thirty-six members was also established. This was later divided into four independent courts, called district or quarter courts, one for each quarter of the country. To be valid, the verdicts of these courts had to be unanimous. Thus many cases could not be settled until a Fifth or High Court (*fimtardómr*) of forty-eight members was established shortly after A.D. 1000. Of these members only thirty-six were to participate at any one time in judging a case. If the District Courts failed to achieve unanimity, an appeal could be carried to the High Court, where a simple majority could provide a decision.

Much of the trouble in Icelandic society was due to the fact that the Icelanders created a legislative and judicial authority on an island-wide basis, but were unable to give it teeth by developing comparable executive and administrative authority. The very drive for independence that led to the first settlement continued to impel the leading *goðar* and other chieftains who could accept a forum for discussion but not an authority which could overrule their will. We will see many cases of litigation and descriptions of acts of vengeance in *Eyrbyggya*. It is clear that if a litigant succeeded in having a condemnatory sentence passed against his opponent in the Quarter Court or even High Court, it was his own responsibility to execute it; there was no police force, nor national penal system. The result was that matters were settled, as the proverb had it, by "point and edge," that is, by power and strength. Indeed, the court judgments themselves were sometimes dictated by the number of retainers and influential allies one could get to ride with one to the General Assembly. Scholars have commented wonderingly that "the role which power and violence played in litigation presents a sharp and strange contrast to the formalism and subtlety which were developed in legal procedure" (Hallberg, P., pp. 8–9). In my article I showed how the absence of centralized political and executive power led to the self-destruction of the Icelandic Commonwealth, rendering it vulnerable to internal disintegration as well as external pressures from Norway.

The rule was that every ninth farmer or *bóndi* (all land was freehold) had to go with his *hofgöði*, shortened to *goði*, "priest-chieftain" (or "temple-chief") to the General Assembly if the latter so desired. If they stayed home they had to pay the expenses of those traveling to the *Althing*. My wife and I had been working on pilgrimage and its sometimes ambiguous connections with *communitas*. The annual trip to the General Assembly could be conceived as a sort of pilgrimage, an exhibition of Icelandic antistructure as well as a source of structurations (which, however, were often aborted). At the *Althing* the leading men of the country met, and the *Thingvellir* site became the heart of Iceland's cultural life. As Peter Hallberg writes (p. 9): ". . . an intensive activity unfolded, which was not restricted to official business. In their free time the young men competed in ball games, wrestling, and swimming. Beer parties were given for friends and acquaintances. Poets and storytellers contributed to the entertainment. From all indications the assembly also played an important role in the dissemination of news, perhaps in a certain degree to the art of relating the news. There are various references to Icelanders who, having just returned home from abroad, related the 'saga' of their travels to the Assembly." We found similar features at pilgrimage centers not only at major Christian shrines but also in those of other religions. The key role of the *goðar*, or temple-owners, in Iceland gives this annual assembly more than a little of a religious character, since the *goðar* were the kernel of the *Althing*. This title is derived from *god* which, as in Anglo-Saxon and English means "god," perhaps ultimately connected with Sanskrit *hū*, "to invoke the gods." The *goðar* not only had charge of temples, but also had secular authority in their domains, called *godord*, which also stands for their office. They had authority in what was in effect the only administrative unit in Iceland. The *goði* was the chieftain of the district, and those subject to him were called his thingmen. But their relationship to him was quite free. True, they promised to accompany and support him, and he promised to protect them and take up their law suits. But if they fell out or their relationship cooled, *goði* and thingmen could dissolve their tie by mutual consent. A farmer of one *godord* could seek the protection of the *goði* of another; the phrase is "to declare oneself into the thing" of the latter. Correlatively, the *goði* was free to accept or refuse him. This meant that the *godord* was not strictly a territorial unit; rather it was a contractual union of thingmen under the provisional politico-religious authority of a *goði*. The *goði's* authority, power, and influence could wax or wane according to his initiative and popularity. The one with the biggest following usually had the biggest say, both locally and also when it came to settling cases at the National Assembly, the *Althing*. The *godord* was hereditary in theory, mostly in the patriline, but the sagas mention many cases in which *godords* were sold, temporarily transferred, or even divided and held in partnership. Truly Iceland was a collocation of individualists—at least the leading men and women were such; thralls and poor farmers were, however, quite dependent on their *goðar* and masters. Every year, before the *Althing* in June, the *goðis* held the "spring assemblies" at home on their *godords*. Three authorities comprised one assembly or thing. It is generally thought the Ulfljot and Grim Goatbeard who set up the first *Althing* in A.D. 930 modeled its constitution on similar moots in Norway.

The Eyrbyggya Saga as a Sequence of Social Dramas

Most sagas narrate events that took place between A.D. 930 and A.D. 1030; though framed as literature, scholars mostly agree that many of the events recounted in them are not fictitious, while others have been independently verified to be historically reliable. In any event, whether factually correct or not, the sagas manifest for us the processual form of social conflict and the key symbols which made such struggles meaningful for contemporary Icelanders. It is significant, too, that most sagas were written in the thirteenth century during the Sturlung Age. I mentioned the Epic Relation as a dynamic interplay of past and present relationships, events, values, and symbols—here the Sturlung Age and the Saga Age. Fortunately, we can read about the Sturlung Age in a unique, detailed, contemporary work, *Sturlunga Saga*. This describes the history of Iceland during the twelfth and thirteenth centuries. Most of it was written by Sturla Thordarson (1214 – 1284), a nephew of Snorri Sturluson, author of the *Heimskringla* and probably of several of the best-known family sagas. Sturla, like Snorri, was himself involved in violent factional struggles between great families. The *Sturlunga Saga* describes much the same kinds of conflicts as the tales of the Saga Age, which supports the view that these were not simply made up. The difference was that by the Sturlung Age, a polity consisting of many *goðar* with approximately equal power had been replaced by the subjugation of large territories by a few influential individuals and families, such as the Sturlungs themselves. Continuous conflict raged among these chieftains, reaching a climax in the early thirteenth century, and eventually led to the submission of Iceland to the rule of the Norwegian king. From this final perspective the sagamakers must have taken a retrospective, reflexive look back on the period of the Commonwealth's formation to try to figure out what went wrong. Clearly, the men and women of the sagas are presented as larger than life, far nobler, even far baser, than their contemporaries. This will emerge as we study one corner of Iceland—an important one, for the Sturlung Family were located at and near Hvamm (*Hvammr* means grassy hollow or little vale), an important settlement in the region we will be examining.

The *Eyrbyggya Saga* essentially concerns ten major dramas of conflict and resolution involving six groups of settlers on the southern and western shores of Hvammsfjord and the promontory of Snaefellnes to the south of Breidafjord, all in the northwest of Iceland, a territory that later produced the historians Ari the Scribe and Snorri Sturluson. *Eyrbyggya* does not treat a single drama or a few dramas in minute detail as do certain other sagas, but it presents a chain of conflicts involving persons living in the same region over a period of four genealogical generations. Among the Ndembu, we tried to collect historical data on social dramas involving matrilineally connected persons forming the core of Mukanza Village and others linked to the main village matrilineage as their slaves. We obtained these histories in 1953 to 1954, but the farthest we could go back in time in reasonable detail was 1925 to 1928—events from those years formed the staple of Social Drama VI in *Schism and Continuity* (Turner 1957:178–82). Thus good social dramatic data could not be obtained from an earlier period than about thirty years before. The oral traditions in Iceland which were eventually incorporated in Ari's histories and the sagamen's tales evidently had greater historical depth, perhaps because, as scholars have argued from Gudbrand Vigfusson (1879) onwards, the long northern winters in Iceland were conducive to storytelling, later storyreading, leading to the tenacious preservation of family and local traditions. In any case, we have long been on the lookout for connected narratives spanning several generations in the life of a given sociocultural community, for in the successive dramas so recorded, we can examine not only the diachronic profile of political development but also how meaning is assigned and sustained and prestigious paradigms and key symbols are preserved, undermined, or revived, for crisis, problem, and disaster provoke reflexivity and throw into relief the range of interpretations arising to explain them, and they find meaning and order in them. The *Eyrbyggya* is, at least, one sagaman's attempt to portray and partially understand the human problem of living together in peace.

There was not much sustained peace in the Saga Age if the tales are to be believed—and were not simply projections of the Sturlung Age onto the screen of the past. Of course, the armed struggles described mainly involved aristocrats; thralls and servants were deemed unworthy of killing, unless their deaths were to discomfit important rivals where they would have been seen as chattels rather than human individuals. In one sense, the old Mafia motto, "we only kill each other," would apply to the old Icelandic landed gentry, the *goðar* and wealthy homesteaders.

Eyrbyggya is at once a regional history dealing with the families on Snaefellsnes and Helgafell, and the story of Snorri Go*ði*. Insofar as it is Snorri's story (he crops up in other sagas, such as the *Laxdaela Saga, Njal's Saga,* and *Grettir's Saga*, but in *Eyrbyggya* he has a central role), this saga resembles others focused on individuals (*Gisla Saga, Kormak's Saga,* etc.). But Snorri is always seen in the midst of social intrigue, conspiracy, and conflict. Furthermore, as Theodore Andersson points out (p. 161), he is no standard saga hero, a tragic chieftain who succumbs in the end, or ends up dominating his neighbors, but "a shrewd, politic chieftain who is not afraid to assert his authority but who knows the limits of his power . . . . His career is not a progression of triumphs building up to a position of unchallenged supremacy or a web of circumstances leading to a noisy fall, but an alternation of nicely weighed successes and inconclusive setbacks . . . [His] attitude both in success and defeat is characterized by caution and moderation. He exposes himself neither to a loss of reputation through excessive yielding nor to retribution through excessive aggressiveness." His counterpart, perhaps, in Greek Epic is the "wily Odysseus." The point I wish to make here, however, is that Snorri Goði is a man of affairs, intimately involved in social process, shrewd rather than good, but not bad either, at once a catalyst and mediator of social conflict. In a society still in process of generating legal rules and procedures, strong men often had recourse to self-help and the ideal of *dreng-skapr*, "manly honor, high-mindedness, valor," made it a matter of *skömm*, "shame, dishonor, or disgrace," to sit idly by (*at sitja hjá*) when insulted or injured and fail to use one's weapons. Men like Snorri Goði gained power and legitimacy by manipulating this code and these means to their own advantage, and also finding it to their own advantage to create more effective public rules and sanctions against arbitrary violence. Perhaps this is why such a cool, amoral man urged the Icelanders so vehemently to accept Christianity. He saw it as a damper on *dreng-skapr*. In *Eyrbyggya*, Snorri represents the cautious tides of conscious historical change modifying the "honor-shame" system of beliefs that gave the feud what meaning it possessed.

The plot of *Eyrbyggya* is fairly simple. Like some other sagas it begins with a sketch of Harald Fairhair's attempt to dominate proud local chieflings in Norway. Then it homes in on two of these rebels, Thorolf Mostur-Beard and Bjorn the Eastman. It is important for the development of the saga that Thorolf was devoted to the god Thor and dedicated a mountain on Thor's Ness (between Vigra Fjord and Hofsvag) to the storm god. Thor, though, was also the guardian of law and justice in the community; oaths were sworn on holy rings kept in his temples, and the General Assembly of Iceland always opened on a Thursday (Thor's Day). Thorolf called the mountain Helga Fell, "sacred mountain." Thorolf was one of the original *goðar*, and he held his Thing (district assembly) on the point of the Thor's Ness headland where the high-seat pillars of his former temple to Thor in Norway had come ashore. Ari the Historian's *Íslendingabók* and the *Book of Settlements (Landnámabók)*, probably written by him too, show it as the common practice of the pioneer settlers to throw the high-seat pillars of their house or temple into the sea before landing, follow them in, then take possession of a large parcel of land behind where they came ashore. Bjorn Ketilsson had been befriended once in Norway by Thorolf at Mostur (whence Thorolf got his name Mostur-Beard— "he was a tall, strong man . . . very handsome with a long beard"). Bjorn had been outlawed by King Harald and Thorolf helped him escape to the Hebrides by giving him "a magnificent longship with a good fighting crew." Bjorn, a doughty pagan, could not stand the Christian faith of his kin who had settled in the Hebrides and after two years betook him to his old benefactor Thorolf, bringing with him Thorolf's son Hallstein who had been entrusted to him for fostering by his father. With Thorolf's approval Bjorn took possession of land between the Staf River and Hraun Fjord, and built his farm at Borgarholt in Bjorn's Haven. The saga declares (Pálsson and Edwards 1973:42) that "Hallstein Thorolfsson thought it a slur on his manhood (*dreng-skapr*) that he should be granted land by his own father, so he crossed over to the other side of Breida Fjord, staked his own claim there, and settled at Hallstein's Ness."

We can see already from this brief narrative how extraordinarily individualistic these settlers were. They did indeed respect family ties, but it was important for them to *choose* to respect them. No wonder Lewis Henry Morgan in his classical study of kinship terminology, *Systems of Consanguinity and Affinity of the Human Family* (1871), should have considered the Icelandic system of kin nomenclature the purest example of a "descriptive system," as opposed to the "classificatory systems" familiar to most anthropologists in preliterate societies. A kinship term that includes several kinship types is said to "classify" these kinship types together (as where father, father's brother, father's father's brothers, *etc.*, are classified together as "fathers"). A highly descriptive system like the Icelandic does not classify mother's brother and father's brother together as "uncle" as even English does, but, for example, distinguishes *föður-bróðir* from *móður-bróðir*, "father's brother" from "mother's brother" and *föður-móðor* from *móður-móðir*, "father's mother" from "mother's mother," instead of classifying them together as "grandmother" as we would in English. Highly descriptive systems tend to be accompanied by kinship statuses that are highly differentiated and involve different role expectations for nearly every one of Ego's kinsmen, while highly classificatory systems are likely to be accompanied by statuses with more general role obligations that are the same for large classes of Ego's kinsfolk. For example, in Iceland if one man slew another it was considered honorable either to seek blood-compensation or blood-vengeance from the killer *himself*; in many parts of Africa, however, retribution could be sought from any member—man, woman, or child—of the slayer's lineage or clan, all indeed, who "shared substance" with him. In the former case, the moral unit was a person; in the latter case, a group.

To return to *Eyrbyggya:* Icelandic women generally enjoyed high status and were also extremely individualistic. This is exemplified by the next prominent settler, Aud the Deep-Minded (who appears in several sagas and was one of the most remarkable personages in ancient Iceland), who is also known as Unn the Deep-Minded (*e.g.*, in the *Laxdaela Saga*). She was the sister of Bjorn the Eastman: both were children of a great chieftain in Norway and later great viking "who conquered and took over the Hebrides" (p. 36). Aud had been married to Olaf the White described in *Eyrbyggya* as the "greatest warrior-king at that time in the British Isles." When her son was killed fighting the Scots at Caithness, Aud fitted out a ship "loaded with rich cargo," according to *Laxdaela*, "and brought away with her all of her kinsfolk who were left alive. And there is scarcely an example known to men, of another woman having got away, single-handed, out of such great straits with so much wealth and so large a company" (Veblen 1925:6). After many adventures, Aud was received in grand style by her brother Bjorn the Eastman in the Breida Fjord country, finally building a large farmstead near the Hvammsfjord, at Hvamm. She also "took wide lands" round about, which she distributed among her kin and other followers, by her generosity showing her 'high-mindedness'." But her descendants do not really enter *Eyrbyggya*; interestingly enough, she was an ancestress both of Ari and Snorri Sturluson, the main known writers who have given us knowledge of ancient Iceland.

Four other pioneer settlers should be mentioned: Geirrod, whose sister Geirrid was also granted land west of Urthvalar Fjord, and whose farmstead was Ondurda Eyr, from which the saga takes its name; Asbrand of Kamb on the eastern shore of Hvamm Fjord; and Finngeir, who came with Geirrod, and who settled at Alftafjord. With Thorolf and Bjorn, they were founders of patri-groups, three to four generations deep, whose interactions, amicable or hostile, compose the main structural dynamic of the saga.

One of my difficulties in describing and analyzing episodes in *Eyrbyggya* as social dramas has been to locate physically many of the places mentioned in the text. I have quite a good map of modern Iceland, but its scale, even so, does not allow me to pinpoint individual farmsteads in small districts. Moreover, the names of places have changed in the thousand years that have passed from saga time to modern time. Surprisingly though, several have *not* changed and this has been a help in mapping the scenes of the saga. The translation I have of *Eyrbyggya* has no map, but several Everyman Edition texts of other sagas cover some of the region in which *Eyrbyggya's* events took place. But these very gaps have perhaps some heuristic value, for they enable me to mention the types of data an anthropologist should look for in trying to characterize the structure and properties of a field of social action. If one were to regard *Eyrbyggya*, for example, as an account construed from the narratives of several gifted and reliable native informants, one would list the principal actors and try to discover information about them which would partly account for their behavior vis-à-vis one another. One subset of information would be how they were related, if at all, by kinship and affinity, whether they were linked or separated by class, rank, wealth, political interest, religious role. One advantage of Icelandic data is that "thanks to the lively interest in history and genealogy of the early Icelanders we are able to follow the beginnings and growth of the nation . . . which is probably the only one in the Old World knowing its origin, since the settlement of the country took place within historical times, and no aborigines were to be found there when the Norwegian settlers arrived in the ninth century" (Hermannsson 1930:1). Thus we can trace the interrelations of groups of settlers, their loves, hates, feuds, coalitions, reconciliations, over several genealogical generations, noting how the way one drama was concluded may provide the conditions for the generation of another as time goes on. We can also trace the development of character as individuals mature. We can detect also a rhythm in individual lives and in groups' affairs. There is intense localization. As Gudbrand Vigfusson (1879:xxi) noted:

> Each cluster of dales opening on a separate bay, nay, each dale itself possessed an individuality and life of its own, within the circle of which a man's days were mainly passed; and the more so as nearly every firth had been originally the 'claim' of a single settler, who had divided it out by gift or sale among his kinsmen or dependents, later comers being obliged to buy of the earlier settlers where and how they could. Thus a series of almost 'family' groups was formed, each living its own life amid its own interests, cares, and politics.

There are also what Vigfusson called "two great outlets" (p. xxi). One was the *Althing*, the other the *Sea*. I would say that both of these represented "liminoid"* alternatives to life in the local community. The Althing

* "Liminoid" resembles "liminal," which refers to the middle phase of a rite of passage. Liminoid activities are marginal, fragmentary, outside the central economic and political processes.

gave the Icelander the sense of community, a "normative communitas" transcending narrow localized ties and of the growth of a generalized system of law as against the family feud. At the Althing and indeed at Quarter and District Things there were also feasts, fairs, and games (as at Tara in ancient Ireland and the Isthmus of Corinth in ancient Greece). The sagas are replete with descriptions of the bustling life of the Althing fortnight, which also contained the High Summer Festival, dedicated to the fertile power of the sun. We read of games of hurling and of football, of matchmaking, of feasting, and above all, of the recital of stories by those who could tell best the legends and traditions of their several districts—perhaps the setting for the preliterate oral beginnings of the family saga. We hear also of spring and autumn sacrifices (especially to Thor), which seem to have coincided with and were held at the district things. Vigfusson gives us some idea of the communitas that prevailed at yuletide, the winter feast when kin, friends, and neighbors, would get together at one of the larger farmsteads in the dale (p. xxii):

> The homely life of those days, while it kept every man in his own place, yet tolerated no formal separation of ranks, and the meanest thrall shared with the highest chief in the hospitality and relaxation of the season.

The other liminoid outlet was the Sea. The sagas have an almost obligatory chapter or two about the overseas wanderings of young well-born Icelanders, either to the motherlands of Scandinavia, or further afield, to the Mediterranean lands, even to Constantinople to fight in the Byzantine Emperor's Varangian Guard. Trade and war were the occupations of these young Vikings. Some went overseas because they were outlawed for feuding as was *Eirik the Red*, discoverer of Greenland. (He had killed Thorgest's sons and it was partly due to Snorri Goði's diplomacy that Eirik was not attacked by Thorgest's followers at the Althing.) The Sea was the great romance in a life that was mainly fishing in spring, haymaking, and, in spots, grain harvest in summer, in autumn killing beasts and salting meat for the winter; in winter itself, after woodcutting and stump-grubbing had procured fuel, weaving, spinning, boat building and the making and mending of farm implements. It seems that there were no specialized performative genres, such as music, dancing, or drama, but it is likely that the declaiming of verses and the telling of stories were full of dramatic, musical, and dialogical elements. They were performances indeed!

6

Conflict in Social Anthropological and Psychoanalytical Theory

Umbanda in Rio de Janeiro

In this paper I want to discuss conflict between and within people, *whether* and, if so, *how* they are connected, and if social anthropology and psychoanalysis can jointly contribute to a general theory of human conflict. I shall take as case material a study by Yvonne Velho of conflicts she observed in a cult center (*terreiro*) of the Umbanda religion in Rio de Janeiro. In three months the center was founded, experienced crisis, and came to an end, a process minutely observed by Velho. In addition, she collected life histories of four protagonists. These are not nearly as detailed as clinical analytic data, but nevertheless provide reliable clues to the motives, conscious and unconscious, impelling the actors in the social drama. Velho made a considerable impact on Brazilian social thought in her book entitled *Guerra de Orixá: Um Estudo de Ritual e Conflito; War of Orixá: A Study of Ritual and Conflict* (1975). *Orixá* means, for practical purposes, the supernatural entities, gods, or spirits who are "received" by mediums in Umbandist sessions or, to use another cultic idiom, are "incorporated" with them. A "war of *orixá*" refers, in this idiom, to a struggle between two mediums in which the gods and/or spirits who habitually "ride" those mediums as their "horses" come into conflict and try to capture and imprison their opposite numbers in the world of "invisibles." Such supernatural conflicts provide the idiom in which actual conflicts for important roles and offices in the cult are conducted. We will thus be considering conflict on three levels: (1) the network of actually existing social relations which comprises the "social structure" of a cult center; (2) the religious beliefs and practices of its members; and (3) the mental and emotional processes of these members; in other words, on the social, cultural, and psychological levels.

Two senses of "conflict" may be distinguished, both derived from *Webster's New World Dictionary:* (1) sharp disagreement or opposition, as of interests, ideas, and so on; clash; and (2) emotional disturbance resulting from a clash of opposing impulses or from an inability to reconcile impulses with realistic or moral considerations. The first falls easily into the province of the anthropologist. His notebooks, since Malinowski's *Crime and Custom in Primitive Society*, are filled with accounts of periodic irruptions of strife out of permanent struggles between types of persons, groups, or categories on different sides of a dominant cleavage or subsidiary cleavage in the total social system studied (tribe, province, village, family, and so on) or in one of its parts. Max Gluckman sees struggles arising out of what he sees as *conflict*—of interest or loyalty or allegiance or value in the system. Conflicts, in his view, can be resolved in the pattern of the prevailing system; what he calls *contradictions* cannot, but lead steadily to radical changes of pattern (Gluckman 1958:46f.). The second type of conflict can best be analyzed by psychologists. Here a distinction should be made between normal and neurotic "emotional disturbance." The first involves a conscious choice of loyalties or interests such as can be readily detected in the descriptive data of anthropologists. The second relates to unconscious conflict. In *The Ego and the Id*, Freud warned against deriving neuroses from a conflict, *tout simple*, between the conscious and the unconscious, regarding it rather as proceeding from the antithesis between the coherent ego and the repressed wish which is split off from it. In *The Question of Lay Analysis*, he elaborated on this by suggesting that the essence of a neurosis consists in the fact that the ego is unable to fulfill the function of mediating between the id and reality. In this paper I will suggest that the cultural symbols of Umbanda in some measure substitute for the feebleness of the ego in thus mediating. However, some cost to the cohesion of the ritual community is incurred, since actors who might otherwise have remained socially unviable through neurosis have been able to manipulate such cultural symbols to further their interests in social conflicts. Geza Roheim (1968:74) wrote that the difference between a neurosis and a sublimation is evidently the social aspect of the phenomenon. "A neurosis isolates; a sublimation unites." I would prefer, in this paper, to think of a neurosis as sealing off an individual from social contention in his/her enclosed domain of psychological conflict. But the "psychic defense system," which Roheim and, after him, Melford Spiro would identify with "culture," represented in this paper by the ritual and mythic symbols of Umbanda, in rendering the Umbandist "normal," enables him to enter into social conflict with gusto. Our data will provide us with some basis for considering the relationship between so-called "madness" and so-called "normality" or "culture," for Umbandists have their own definition of madness, which I think you may find interesting.

Velho found it useful to use my concept of "social drama" (see Chapter 9, pp. 215–221; Chapter 10, pp. 230–232; and Epilogue, pp. 291–292) in attempting to account for the disturbances and crises which she observed in the social life of the cult-center. I had developed this formula for handling situations of recurrent conflict during my fieldwork among the Ndembu people of northwestern Zambia. My observations were made in small villages whose cores were clusters of matrilineal kinsfolk. But I have since found the same processual form in societies of much greater complexity and scale. A social drama begins with a breach of regular norm-governed social relations, signalized by a public transgression of a salient rule normally binding on members of the group being studied. This may be an overt flouting of a law or custom to make inevitable a testing political process, or it may result from an outburst of previously suppressed feelings. This first phase, which I call "breach," is followed by a crisis in which its effects spread to the limits of the parties involved, threatening to mobilize the largest opposed groups of which they are members. This second phase I call "crisis." Various adjustive and redressive mechanisms are then deployed to seal off or heal the breach—a phase I call "redress." These lead either to reestablishment of relations or social recognition of irreparable breach between the contesting parties. Redressive and adjustive actions may range from personal and informal arbitration or mediation, to formal and legal machinery, and, to resolve certain kinds of crisis, to the performance of public ritual. Much of my data consisted of direct reporting, but I was already halfway towards psychological modes of explanation when I was forced at times—reluctantly, then, due to my Durkheimian background—to rely on the accounts of my informants. Soon I realized that it was their very bias that was of central importance. For the aim of the social drama is not to present a seemingly objective recital of a series of events; it is concerned, rather, with the different interpretations put upon those events, and the ways in which these give subtle expression to divergent interests or switches in the balance of power. I now consider that such interpretations are themselves influenced by unconscious factors—wishes, anxieties, ego-defense mechanisms—which are inaccessible to the research methods and techniques of social anthropology. The study of social dynamics, as opposed to that of social and/or cognitive structure, necessarily involves psychological approaches. A social drama engenders a sociopsychical "field" for whose "events" there are clearly several dimensions of interpretation, ranging from the biochemical, physiological, and neurological, to the psychological and sociological. Each type of interpretation answers some problems, but not all. Like Max Gluckman and Ely Devons, in their Introduction to *Closed Systems and Open Minds: The Limits of Naivety in Social Anthropology* (1964), I have always held that one must be scrupulously clear in which dimension one is operating. For actions may have different significance in the different dimensions. For example, a smile may be a token of social amity in a sociological analysis and overtly responded to as such, but for the depth psychologist may be a sign of repressed aggression which will have behavioral consequences for the actor later on. Nevertheless, and especially when one is dealing with ritual symbols and beliefs as the content of social forms, the anthropologist cannot escape the fact that the interactions he observes as they develop are constantly being shaped by intrapsychic factors and cannot be explained away as mere conformity with external cultural norms. As Melford Spiro has written: "Social behavior . . . is more likely to be the end product of a chain of interacting psychological events, including impulse (id), cultural and personal values (superego), conflict between them, and defense against conflict, which only then eventuates in behavior" (in ed. George Spindler 1978:356). Most of the time, behavior—the end product of this chain—does conform to norms, but in social dramas, the controls which ensure this are often broken and one encounters the behavioral manifestation of those "discontents" Freud saw as so important for sociocultural dynamics.

Velho experienced some difficulties in attempting to apply the social drama model to her study of Umbandistas in conflict. My model was derived from the study of African villages, in a small-scale society where the kinship system provided a structural frame for analyzing the regularities of the social process. Such a society has well-defined group boundaries with a correspondingly marked profile in the development of social events. Velho's cult center was embedded in a complex urban milieu. Its members were drawn from many walks of life; some were defined in Brazilian terms as "black," some as "white"; differences of class and education manifested themselves during the drama; in short their life experiences were greatly diverse. Again, unlike African villagers, they did not live together but in various urban localities. Even in their ritual practices they differed; coming from different cult centers, they had idiosyncratic views on how the rites should be performed, for Umbanda has no authoritative liturgical manual. Moreover, the cult center was the creation of voluntary action. In African villages, kin ties result from birth and involve culturally specific rights and obligation: status-roles are ascribed rather than achieved. A village headman is ritually invested with certain powers, privileges and capacities, and with legitimacy; in the cult center leadership tends to be charismatic and to emerge from successful mediumistic performance. A village is the scene of its members' total life, of their economic, domestic, religious, political and leisure activities. A cult center is only active when its members have finished work at their geographically scattered occupations. Their interaction is, as it were, single-stranded, simplex, not multiplex as in the case of villagers who perform most of their activities with the same set of people, a group of kin and affines. As Gluckman has written: "In the very conditions of a large city, looked at in contrast to tribal society, the various roles of most individuals are segregated from one another since they are played on different stages" (1962:35). One would, therefore, on this argument not expect to find conflict on the scale in which it existed in Velho's cult center, since, Gluckman continues, "in modern society not only are roles segregated but also conflicts between roles are segregated" (Gluckman 1962:38). Further, Gluckman argues that ritual is so frequent and fundamental in tribal society "because men and women . . . play so many of their purposive roles with the same set of fellows. Each action is [thus] charged with *high moral import*. A man's actions as worker are not segregated from his actions as father by being placed in a different building with a specialized set of fellows. His achievement as a farmer directly affects his position as father, as brother, as son, as husband, as priest, or as worshipper. That is, the moral judgment on a man who neglects his work as a cultivator applies to his relation with his wife, his brothers, his chief, his subsistence group as a whole. Conversely, if a man quarrels with his wife or his brother this may affect their ability to cooperate in farming. Every activity is charged with complex moral evaluations, and default strikes not at isolated roles but at the integral relations which contain many roles. I think that it is this compound of moral evaluation and the spreading effect of breach of role, which accounts for the way rituals are attached to so many changes of activity in tribal society" (Gluckman 1968:28).

Gluckman seems to be saying that rituals in tribal society are functional equivalents of spatial separation in modern society, for it is ritual, not space, which segregates roles from one another when relations are "multiplex." Ritual here seems to be a mechanism of the sociocultural mainstream, in no way a leisure activity set apart for voluntaristic participation. Now I am going to present Velho's data which documents a high level of conflict taking place on what Gluckman would call a "segregated stage"—that is, the cult center—in a complex urbanized society (note the theatrical metaphor). Why should ritualized conflict be shoved off on to this stage or "arena?" Let me state here at the outset, so that you can see what I am up to immediately and are put in a position to raise valid objections about my handling of Velho's data, that I have concluded on the basis of other studies that sociocultural activities can be roughly divided in all cultures between those which correspond with the *indicative* mood of verbs and others which have many of the properties of the *subjunctive* or *optative* mood. This distinction becomes more clear-cut as societies develop in scale and complexity and specialization, but already it exists in tribal societies, between pragmatic and ritual activities. The difference is between what is culturally defined as "what *is*" and "what *might be*," between what common sense presents as "cause and effect," "reality," and what may represent a range of plausible or fanciful alternatives to the tried and tested. These may range from scientific hypotheses, the domain of "as-if," which will be exposed to vigorous empirical reality-testing, to fantastical or utopian alternatives, where wishes predominate over practical experience. This distinction makes possible the view that in complex societies the arts, including literature and theater, science, in its creative aspect necessitating hypothesis, and ritual, both religious and secular, which often "plays" metaphorically with the factors of sociocultural experience, become the legitimate dialectical partners of "factuality," the domain of pragmatical handling of historical "reality" in any given culture. This provocative dichotomy between fact and play, indicativity and subjunctivity, at the cultural level makes possible, if not inevitable, a sort of plural reflexivity in societies, whereby a community of human beings sharing a tradition of ideas and customs may bend existentially back upon itself and survey its extant condition not solely in cognitive terms but also by means of tropes, metaphors, metonyms, and symbolic configurations, which may give it some existential sense of where it realistically, ethically, or prophetically stands with reference to its own past, its aspirations, and its relations to other sociocultural groups. The opposition, indicative/subjunctive, is not precisely homologous with the distinction, conscious/unconscious, in depth psychology, but inasmuch as the subjunctive is declaratively open to the influences of willing, desiring, and feeling, defenses against unconscious drives and ideas are to that extent reduced in scope and efficacy, allowing unconscious phenomena, openly or in congenial disguise, to emerge into public visibility. [This insight into the link between the subjunctive and emotions tallies remarkably with the link between the right cerebral hemisphere and the limbic system talked about in Chapter 11 of this book.] What may be cause for idiosyncratic, private repression, may not be cause for public, generalized repression; that which convulses an individual with painful affect, may have a healing function when mythologized as a datum of a subjunctive genre of cultural performance. A pleasure shared may be a pleasure doubled, but an "unpleasure" shared may be an "unpleasure" halved, or even extinguished by the elicitation of sympathy, the experience of what I have called communitas, which is relatedness among individuals without judgmentality.

My case, as against Gluckman's, is that a ritual system in a modern urban setting, such as Umbanda, is a reflexive institution, what Clifford Geertz has called "a metasocial commentary," albeit one acted out rather than intellectualized, whereby the "atomized" citizens (in Brazil these are often labor migrants from rural areas to the cities) act out in symbolic or metaphoric guise the conflicts and tensions produced by their uprooting and resituating in a world of commerce and industry framed by a political system based on military and police force. Umbanda is the subjunctive counterstroke which makes viable for many the social limitations of Brazilian industrialized indicativity.

Before we probe the empirical data, one final theoretical point. This is the concept of the "star group." In complex societies, where the style of voluntarism prevails, individuals are confronted with a multiplicity of social associations which they are free to join in their leisure time. The social impulse, constrained during the working day by contractual obligation, substituting for the ascriptive obligations of tribal life, is unpent in nonworking time. Indeed, in bureaucratic organizations of any complexity, room is left for joining subgroups within a firm, an academic institution, or a business or labor complex, during the working day. One's "star group" is a subjective category. It is made possible by a recognition of the social category of "the individual" as a voluntaristic entity and by the generation of many voluntary groups in a complex economico-political society. Almost everyone, except confirmed solipsists or the timid or fatigued, has a target-group to which he believes he could congenially belong. This group is one whose goals, values, and personnel come closest to his ideal model of how human beings should purposively behave. Many possibilities of affiliation are open to modern, urbanized man and woman. The group with whom one most wants to spend one's time, in which one finds one's deepest satisfactions, overt or disguised, is one's "star group." It may be the local philatelic society; indeed, I have known colleagues for whom it is a university senate subcommittee. It may be a church fraternity, a Union local, an athletic club, or an informal group of friends who regularly spend their vacations together. The point is that an individual *chooses* to belong to the group, regardless of its objective ranking or standing. In a complex society there are numerous institutionalized and informal groups, many of them arrayed in a hierarchy of status and influenced by criteria of social stratification. Among their members will be a minority for whom the group is their "star group." These tend to be the "activists," the leaders, the builders-up and sustainers of its esprit de corps, its defenders and negotiaters vis-à-vis the world outside. Such star groupers are in action in Velho's narrative. We shall also note that it is precisely this category of members who are most in contention: over policy, for office, as prime defenders of the group's honor, and so on. Indeed, we shall find among them many of the attitudes and orientations characteristic of members of an elementary family: sibling-rivalry, intergenerational conflict, ambivalent feelings, and the like. Since the Umbanda group is in the subjunctive mood, we should be able to detect in its symbolism and behavior the operation of what in the indicative domain would remain hidden, for instance, overt expressions of such unconscious defense mechanisms as *projection* where the outward tendency of an impulse or drive, instead of being recognized as such, gives rise to a feeling that it exists in other people; *introjection* and *identification*, where the ego behaves as if it had unconsciously absorbed or, respectively, adsorbed the characteristics of other people (processes obviously encouraged by the Umbandist idiom of "incorporation" of medium and deity or spirit); unconscious *displacement* (meaning to move from its usual or normal place, here the emotion is transferred to another, more acceptable object) where both the aim and the objects of impulses are affected; *condensation*, which affects the form of unconscious ideas and permits the expression of two or more impulses in one ideational presentation; and so on through the entire repertoire of Freudian unconscious mechanisms. Perhaps all of the above are dependent upon sublimation, since the beliefs and imageries of Umbanda are cultural expressions which mediate between individual unconscious impulses and intentions and the social processes of the group making for its cohesion and continuity. My argument is that for the Umbandist stargroupers, the cult center is, in the atomistic urban environment, a surrogate family. Nevertheless, since it is not a real family, the degree of repression of libidinal and aggressive drives must be less, allowing for more overt conflict, conflict which is mediated and reduced, if not extinguished, in its turn by symbolic sublimations which desexualize libidinal impulses and redirect aggressive drives to objects which do not threaten group solidarity. Nevertheless, as we shall see, group solidarity very often does break down in these urban cult centers, despite these cultural defense mechanisms. For we are dealing with an expanding industrial social system which bursts inherited cultural frames. The conflicts we shall observe are instructive. They dramatize the contradiction between established meaning and unprecedented social structural change.

The Birth, Life, and Death of the Tenda Espiritu Caboclo Serra Negra

Let us move from theoretical abstractions to concrete data, Velho's case-material. As you may know, the so-called Afro-American religions, as well as Kardecist spiritism, of French origin, are ebulliently on the increase in modern Brazil, where they were the object of rebuke from Pope John Paul II. Literally thousands of *terreiros* or cult centers (derived from the Latin and Portuguese term *terra*, meaning a piece or plot of land, with implications of the lost rural Africa) have sprung up in such cities as Rio de Janeiro, Saõ Paulo, Campinas, Belo Horizonte, and so on. Each *terreiro*, which is often no more than a hut in a yard, or a room, has a membership of twenty to thirty mediums, with a fringe of clients and consultants. There are several loose federations of terreiros on the urban, state, and even national levels, but the essential unit is the localized cult center. Although Umbanda has Afro-Brazilian antecedents in such cults as Candomblé, Batuqué, Kabula, Macumba, and others, it aspires to being a universalistic religion and has incorporated not only aspects of Catholic ritual but also beliefs and practices drawn from Spiritism, Amerindian religion, and also from Asian-based religions like Theosophy. Its membership includes many Whites, and Asians, as well as Blacks and mulattos.

Umbandists meet at least once a week to perform ritual in what is called a "session." In it the mediums "receive" supernatural beings, known as "*orixás*," "guides," "entities," or "saints" (these terms are interchangeable). Mediums are also known as "horses" to be ridden by the *orixá*, now called "horsemen or knights" (cabalheros). In the course of a typical session, seven categories or "lines" of orixás are invoked, "incorporate" with mediums, and are "despatched" to make way for the next "line."

The African influence is truly wide and deep. As in many liminal situations generated by poor or structurally "low" people, fictitious hierarchies abound in Umbanda. The main hierarchy is structured by African, mainly Yoruba, deities. The major orixá is called Oxalá or Zambi; Nzambi is the name of the otiose high god among the Ndembu and many other Central Bantu-speaking peoples. Oxalá has no "horse"—as the human *medium* (feminine, *media*) of an orixá is called. He only rules over the other orixás who are classified into seven "lines" (*linhas*), each line being divided into seven "phalanxes." These lines are broad categories which define how each orixá should "work" (*trabalhar*), that is, what his or her behavioral characteristics are when he or she "rides a horse," in other words, possesses a medium—the type of dance peculiar to that orixá, his or her bodily manifestations (dress, gestures, intonation, vocabulary, and so on), what colors are appropriate to him or her, what day of the week is dedicated to him or her, and so forth. The seven lines of Umbanda are as follows: (1) *the line of Iemanjá*, a female orixá who represents the sea and rivers; this line is also called "the line of the water-people." She is spoken of as the Mermaid of the Sea (*a Sereia do Mar*), and her image may be one of the advocations of the Virgin Mary; (2) *the line of Xangô*, a male Orixá, whose cult throve originally among blacks of Yoruba origin in the regions of Pernambucó, Alagoas, and Sergipe, representing thunder, tempests, and lightning, and the fire latent in stone (Oxalá is "the fire of heaven")—Xangô is portrayed by an image of the crusty Catholic Saint Jerome; (3) *the line of Oxossé* or of *Caboclos-Oxossé* is often spoken of as a "guide" and represents indigenous or rural symbolic types, otherwise referred to as Caboclos, a term of Amerindian origin. The Brazilian writer Dilson Bento (1979) speaks of this line in Eliadean terms as the "hierophany of ecology." It is the primordial *land*, as yet unravished by history. Oxossé is a conserver, related to vegetation and the healing properties of herbs. His own "phalanx" is known as Jurema; (4) *the line of Ogum*, a male orixá representing war and portrayed by an image of the now demoted Catholic Saint George. His physical manifestation is that of a strong man with a sword in his hand. He dances as if he were riding on horseback; (5) *the line of the Old Blacks* (Pretos Velhos). Individually these have names preceded by "Grand-Dad" or "Grandma" (*vovôs e vovás*) or "uncle" or "aunt" (*tios e tias*). A person possessed by an Old Black walks with a stooping gait, sometimes supported by a cane, and speaks in a rambling fashion. These ex-slaves have been aged medicine men or healers or aged warriors. Their ceramic images represent them as elderly Blacks with white hair and country-style white clothes. Invariably they smoke pipes. In Central African curative cults ancestral spirits act as agents of affliction; but when propitiated, they become a source of blessing. In Africa ancestral spirits are associated with particular families, lineages, and clans. But under New World conditions, these specific linkages were liquidated when slaves were separated from their kinsfolk and fellow tribesmen, and what was left of the lineage ancestors was a "symbolic type," to use Don Handelman's terms, representing "ancestorhood." The Old Blacks are generalized ancestors in Umbanda, and, indeed, in Kardecism, they can possess Whites as well as Blacks; (6) *the line of the Child (Crianca)*. The Child is an orixá which stands for archetypal Childhood. Members of this line are also called "children of Ibeji," African twin deities associated with the Catholic saints Cosman and Damian, whose ceramic images represent them. As individual "entities" they take names in the diminutive, such as Pedrinho ("little Peter"), Joãozinho ("little John"), and so forth; (7) *the line of Exú*. Exú or Leba is an entity who represents both good and evil. The name is clearly derived from that of the Yoruba and Fon Trickster God Eshu-Legba or Eshu-Elegba. I had discussed Eshu in an article I wrote on myth and symbol for the *International Encyclopedia of the Social Sciences* some years ago. Little did I think then that I would meet Exú face to face one night and be told that I had him "on my shoulder!" And, later still, that I was a "Son of Exú," a dubious distinction as we will see! In Brazil Catholic priests sometimes identify Exú with the Devil, while dismissing Umbanda itself as "devil-worship." His ceramic image certainly represents him as a man with goats' feet, pointed ears, sometimes clutching a trident, often clad in a red and black cape, and wearing a silk top-hat—a diabolic dandy in short! But he is also portrayed as a man with a bare chest. One just cannot pin Exú down! I speak of Exú, but Exús are usually thought of in the plural. Their "name is legion." When they enter the terreiro, they talk and gesticulate obscenely, utter piercing cries and strident peals of laughter. Because the symbolic type Exú is ambiguous, being at once good and evil, his manifestations and refractions may unexpectedly become dangerous and powerful. The relationship of men and women to the Exús is always a risky one, for these tricksters can dupe their "children" (as the mediums of orixás are called), telling them one thing but doing another. The Exús (as in West Africa) are the lords of the crossroads and of the graveyard, where offerings are made to them. One of the types of refractions of Exú is Exú of the Two Heads. His image was prominent among the images on the altar of the terreiro we visited. He wears a red cape and carries a trident. One of his heads is that of Jesus, the other of Satan. As a Catholic saint he is sometimes represented as Saint Peter, in the double sense of gate-keeper and denier of his Lord. Exús are customarily divided into two types: "Exús of Light," described as "superior" and "turned away from 'matter'." "Exús without light" are "less pure," and "closer to matter." They have to be controlled or they will "produce confusion in the works" (as Umbandist rituals are called). They are ruled by the Exús of Light. They can be used to work harm against people. As such they are the main "entities" in *Quimbanda*, the reverse side of Umbanda. Its rituals are those of "black magic." As you will have noted, this division among Exús is an attempt to resolve the ambiguity of this figure. In West Africa, Eshu-Legba is an explicitly phallic deity: in Brazil his phallicism is partly repressed.

Each of the seven "lines" has its chief and his or her subordinate entities. Each "line" is subdivided into seven "phalanxes," each with its own chief and subordinates, the whole group being under the hegemony of the line chief. For example, in the Line of Iemanjá, the water goddess, one phalanx is commanded by Iansã, a female orixá who dances balancing a cup or wineglass in her hand. She wears a gilded crown ringed with pearls. Her Catholic form is the image of Santa Barbara. Another phalanx in Iemanjá's "line" is Mamãe Oxum's. Mamãe Oxum is a female orixá, represented as a weeping woman, often as the Catholic Mater Dolorosa.

Each "line" is associated with a locality (sea, forest, crossroads, and so on), a color, a day of the week, and stipulated kind of food. There is also the category of *orixá cruzado*, "intersected orixá," which defines an orixá who belongs to two lines at the same time. For example, a Caboclo may be "crossed" with Exú; he may be half Caboclo and half Exú. This gives great flexibility to the system.

Umbandistas also speak of "nations of Candomblé" among the invisible entities. These include Queto, Jeje, Nagô (or Yoruba), Angola, Omoloco, Cambinda, and Quiné. Such names—there are supposed to be seven in all—refer to real or imaginary regions of Africa from which the slaves came in the colonial period.

I have discussed these categories mainly to prepare you for the social drama we will discuss. There is a hierarchy of human roles as well—or rather two hierarchies in each terreiro. These are known as the *hierarchia Espiritual* and *hierarchia Material* respectively. The spiritual hierarchy consists of either a *pai-* ("father") or *mãe-* ("mother") *de-santo* (literally "of saint or orixá"); a "little mother" (*Mãe Pequena*), the second-in-command; a *samba*, the helper of the little mother; the *filhos* or *filhas de santo*, the sons or daughters "of saint," who are also called *médiuns* or *médias*. A *medium* is a person who "works in the saint," who enters into trance and controls the idiom of possession. For there is nothing wild about Umbanda trance, except perhaps its first moments when the entranced one jerks and jackknifes galvanically, though never actually falling on the ground. Those who do fall on the ground are onlookers, and this behavior singles them out as candidates for mediumship. They become mediums by undergoing the initiatory ritual known as *fazer cabeça*, literally "to make (perhaps "inspire") head." Mediums are admired for the degree to which they control their trances. Evan M. Zuesse has pointed out (1979:198) that in Haitian voodoo similar in many respects to Afro-Brazilian cults, it is important that the medium should be trained to a *standard behavior* (Zuesse's emphasis) in trance: "bodily action and a genuine alter ego are defined and elaborated in the course of the induction, to replace the lost coherence of the ego-world." Since the "entities" who possess them have many human traits, it is fitting that the mediums in trance act more or less like normal human beings, although prominently displaying the distinctive behavioral features of the orixá or guide riding them. Some mediums "see" orixás (*médiuns videntes*), others "hear" their commands (*médiuns ouvintes*).

The maternal hierarchy organizes the internal affairs of the terreiro and deals with its finances. At the head is the president, but there may also be a secretary, a treasurer, and a councillor of the associates, those who contribute monthly dues for the general maintenance of the terreiro. Yvonne Velho's book contains case histories of the conflict between officers of the spiritual and material hierarchy in a single terreiro, the former rupturing ties with the mundane life outside, the latter injecting its criteria of prestige into the terreiro's organization of authority.

I mention all these classifications and organizational formats in order to give you some idea of how a terreiro is *framed* both culturally and organizationally. I published a paper in 1977 whose title, "Frame, Flow, and Reflection" indicates some of the main factors that I think important in analyzing most kinds of performance, whether these belong to the worlds of ritual or of entertainment. By "frame" I refer to that often invisible boundary—though here visibly bounded by the terreiro's limits—around activity which defines participants, their roles, the "sense" or "meaning" ascribed to those things included within the boundary, and the elements within the environment of the activity, in this case the Umbandista session, which are declared to be "outside" (*fora*) and irrelevant to it. I am indebted to such scholars as Bruce Kapferer, Don Handelman, Gregory Bateson, and Erving Goffman for this usage. The framing process continues throughout the whole time of the activity; indeed, what Goffman calls "frame slippage" is an ever-present danger. The occasional, unsolicited intrusions of Exú probably manifest this danger. But in Umbanda, as we shall see, there is a culturally programmed ritual process, an invariant sequence of episodes which keeps the frame intact until the end of the session. The order in which the entities of the lines appear varies in different regions of Brazil, but in each terreiro, the series is fixed. "Flow" is a term for which I am indebted to my former colleagues at the University of Chicago, John MacAloon and Mihali Csikszentmihalyi (see Csikszentmihalyi 1975). Flow, for them, is an interior state which can be described as the merging of action and awareness, the holistic sensation present when we act with total involvement, a state in which action follows action according to an internal logic, with no apparent need for conscious intervention on our part. Flow may be experienced, say these scholars, in play and sport, in artistic performance, and in religious ritual. Flow is made possible by a centering of attention on a limited stimulus field, by means of framing, bracketing, and usually a set of rules. In flow, there is a loss of ego; the "self" that normally acts as a broker between ego and alter becomes irrelevant. One might argue that the grammar and lexicon constituted by the rules and symbols of Umbanda can generate "frames," within which "flow" might emerge. But flow dispenses with duality and contrariety; it is nondualistic, nondialectical. And Umbanda sessions, like many ritual performances, are impregnated with problems, and problems always involve contradictions to be resolved. Mediums, especially the mãe-de-santo, are regarded as seers who can give spiritual, guided advice about problems and contradictions in people's lives. The members of a terreiro are also members of an urban society, subject to the stresses and alienating influences of a rapidly industrializing nation. Part of the reason they come regularly to the terreiro with its dominating mother and father figures as leaders is to get some authoritative advice about how to live their lives, at all levels, marriage, family, neighborhood, work, surrounded by urban crime and often assaulted by police. The terreiro session is a liminal, space-time "pod" in which they can distance themselves from immersion in the status-role structures of the present by identification with the gods, ancestors, and traditions of African roots organized in terms of "lines" that bring the gods of sea, rivers, waterfalls, forests, mountains, and other natural habitats into healing contact with the impurities of modern urban culture. This figure/ground relationship between a "pure Africanity" and "pure nature" on the one hand, and an impure post-slavery world in cities dominated by powerful Whites on the other, surely induces reflection and reflexivity. Reflexivity must be an arrest of the flow process, a throwing of it back against itself; framing procedures make this possible. The rejected ego is suddenly remanifested. In reflexivity one is at once one's subject and direct object, not only in a cognitive way, but also existentially. Or one might say, ransacking the terminology of depth-psychology, that the deepest reflexivity is to confront one's conscious with one's unconscious self. Flow perhaps elicits or "seduces out" the unconscious levels of the self. But these are then scrutinized by the conscious self, maybe not in scientific terms, in the case of Umbanda, for example, but certainly in terms of values preserved and elaborated in the innumerable performances of Umbanda that go on every night in the vast territory of Brazil, terreiro by terreiro. A ritual performance is a flow/reflexivity dialectic. One can only "know" this in performance itself. For knowledge, as Dilthey divined, is based on "structures of experience" that are at once cognitive, affective, and volitional—*all* of which contribute to the "form" of the actual performance itself. The protocols, scenarios, and scripts may be given sharp coherent "shape" by cognitive schemata. These guidelines would correspond, for example, to the taxonomies of Umbanda—there are many more—I have spent some time in elaborating. But into the final "form" must go the unique, once-only emotional experiences of the particular performance which are not only articulated by the formal grammar of Umbanda but which also succeed in "blurring" and "melting" its ideal outlines. In other words, the experience of the conjoined performers is a *primary* component in the specific performance. Similarly, it is not only the generic teleology or goal-structure of Umbandist religion that is important, but the specific goals, the multiple entelechies of the mediums and spectators actually present, their problems, dilemmas, sufferings, and successes, that must be taken into account if we are to characterize a performance, rather than spell out a cognitive paradigm. Ritual, as I said earlier, is multidimensional; any given performance is shaped by the experiences poured into it as much as by its conventional structures. Experiences make the structures "glow"; the structures focus and channel the experiences.

Velho differs from other scholars of Afro-Brazilian religion in focusing on conflicts within the cult center community and not on the ideology, cosmology, or therapeutic aspects. She presents in her book a diary of events from the terreiro's inauguration to its demise three months later. The dramatis personae of the social drama consisted of the mãe-de-santo, known as Apareçida; the president, Mario; the little mother, Marina; the pai-de-santo, Pedro, who replaced Apareçida after she had been removed to a psychiatric hospital; Sonia, a new little mother appointed by Pedro; about a dozen mediums regularly possessed in the *giras* (literally "whirls") or sessions; sundry clients of the mediums; and the previous mães-de-santo of Apareçida and Pedro. The short life of the group was virtually taken up with competition for leadership roles and struggles between officeholders for prestige and recognition. The Tenda Espiritu Caboclo Serra Negra (Tent of the Spirit Caboclo Black Mountain) became an arena for parapolitical conflict. Velho considers this situation not untypical: hundreds of terreiros rise and fall every year. They are thus in marked contrast to the cult centers of the older-established Afro-Brazilian cults—such as Candomblé in Bahia State which have lasted more than a century. The idiom of conflict depended on a native category, known as *demanda*, which means, literally, a demand or a contest, but which Velho's informants described as *uma guerra de orixá*, a "war between deities," or "a dispute of santo," or "a holy war." As they put it: "A medium who has a dispute, a question or case against another medium, mobilizes his/her orixá by means of 'works' (that is, rituals) so that they should harm his/her rival." The target medium then counters by mobilizing his own orixá, the entities or guides who regularly incorporate with him/her. Each tries to damage or neutralize the witchcraft works made by hostile orixás.

"*Demanda* is a very dangerous thing, it can go as far as death," said one of Velho's informants. It may take place between a mãe- or pai-de-santo and their "children," or between terreiros as whole groups. A pai- or mãe-de-santo has deeper esoteric knowledge than a "child," knows the "law" (*lei*), that is, the beliefs and practices of Umbanda, and may have acquired powers by presiding over the initiation of a medium (as they say, "the mother/father knows all about them" in the ritual known as "*fazer cabeça*," literally "making the head," which involves the medium's "giving" his/her head—the seat of will or intention—to the mother/father, as well as rendering him/her more accessible to the orixá). The process of demanda begins with an accusation or confession by a parent or child "de-santo." One or other party "makes works," that is to say, makes offerings to one of his orixá or guides (usually an exú) to get him/her to afflict the rival, who responds by involving his guides to defend him. A battle ensues among the "invisibles," spreading to all the "lines," with the aim of capturing one of the opposing lines, or an important member thereof. Once an orixá is captured, he/she can no longer protect his/her "horse." The medium faces the prospect of madness (*loucura*) or death. The moment that the medium loses contact with one or more of his guides, writes Velho (p. 50), he "loses his identity as a human being, as a person." One medium, who believed that her principal guide, an Old Black, had been captured, told Velho one day that she was relieved, because she had once more "received" her Old Black who told her to fear no more for he would protect her from the demanda." She added, "At last, I met my me (*encontrei o meu eu*)." *O meu eu*, it will be noted, is masculine, though the speaker is feminine. In Umbanda the identity seems to be composed of the guides that are "incorporated" with the medium, or rather of the relationship between the medium and his/her orixás. There is danger of madness, if even one of the principal guides is imprisoned. Each guide is conceived of as personally distinct even though belonging to a line. The "self" is thus regarded, as in most of Africa, as a multiplicity of components (more, indeed, than the Western trinity of ego, superego, and id, or foursome, if we add the ego-ideal!) all of which together represent a sane entity. If one part is subtracted, insanity may occur. At least this is so in the subjunctive domain of Umbanda.

The terreiro we are studying began partly in the context of a demanda between its first mãe-de-santo and *her* own mãe-de-santo in another terreiro. Apareçida had achieved a fine reputation as a consultant, when incorporated by her Old Black Woman in that cult group during optional private sessions held in Mario's house. Mario and his friends thought that she ought to be set up as the head of a terreiro of her own, certified under Brazilian law, though Mario proposed that he would pay the rent and be first president, head of the "material hierarchy." This led Apareçida into conflict with her mãe-de-santo, who did not wish her to leave her terreiro on Bishop Street. Some said she began a demanda against Apareçida at this point. In any event a new terreiro was established. On its altar in the altar room (*sala do gonga*, which is entered by the mediums in a state of incorporation) were ceramic figures owned by Apareçida and by her personal clients, and the Exú image and shrine (those of "Exú Manguera") set up beside the gateway into the yard were also hers.

The new terreiro, therefore, was the result of an irremediable schism accompanied by what amounted to witchcraft accusations. Perhaps that was why Mother Apareçida began her terreiro with an unorthodox ritual which was to prove her swift undoing. Her eye was on the past, not on the new terreiro. Velho did not observe the sequence of events herself, but informants' accounts, however, unverifiable empirically, have the merit of vividly rendering the values of the subculture being studied. I should mention that until this episode Apareçida had been highly respected by the members, not least because her Old Black Woman, known as "Avô" (Grandmother) Maria Conga, had helped all the group's mediums in the course of consultations about their problems, both mundane and esoteric. After a conventional inauguration ceremony, Apareçida decided, a week later, to set up "a work in the cemetery" or "an obligation," that is to say, a ritual in which offerings of food and drink appropriate to each orixá are made. The chief of the "people of the cemetery" is Obáluae—associated with the Catholic St. Lazarus—and he is classed among the Exús. He is head of the phalanx of Exús associated with death and disease, and, indeed, his Yoruba prototype Abaluaye was the god of smallpox. In choosing this kind of ritual Apareçida may have had in mind that she was being attacked by her former mãe-de-santo, to whom she had been little mother, for graveyard Exús are entities more often invoked in Quimbanda than in Umbanda. The offering may have been a placation. When the members of her terreiro arrived they found that another terreiro group was trying to *arriar obrigação*, to "lay down an obligation," in precisely the same place. Both groups of mediums were incorporated, "ridden" by their guides, and Marina, the first little mother, began to struggle with a medium from the other group. He, in trance, accused her of "being a traitor" to Apareçida, of being in demanda against her own mãe-de-santo. At that, all the mediums of Apareçida's group fled from the cemetery. Back at the terreiro, Apareçida seized Marina by the arms and thrust her bodily from the house. She then attacked most of the others, leaving in the terreiro only Mario, the president, and two or three mediums.

This was only the beginning. In the next few days Apareçida accused Marina of "working" against her, threatened to kill her, broke into Marina's house and smashed her furniture, entered the house of her "godmother" (the ritual sponsor for her Umbanda initiation), beat her up, and fiercely resisted the efforts of her mediums to restrain her. Eventually Mario, the president, on a doctor's advice, took her to Pinel Hospital in Río, whence she was transferred to the psychiatric hospital of Engenho do Dentro. The terreiro remained shut for some time.

The mediums provided their own mystical explanations for Apareçida's mad or crazy (*maluca*) behavior. She had made works against Marina and had put "seven Exús in her head." At sessions Marina could only "receive" these, and, in her turn, so she informed Velho, she nearly went mad (*doida*). She saw enormous insects (*bichos*) before her and could never get to sleep. Her own guides had been captured. The seven Quimbanda-type Exús (she had names for each of them) entered by the "breach" (*brecha*) in her head—which may describe a cut mark made during the making the head (initiation) ritual on the fontanelle. Sonia, who was to replace Marina as little mother, told Velho that Apareçida had placed her head below the altar, an act which would have removed her guides and made her mad. Mario, the president, reported that he had awakened once and found himself in Exú's house, located to the left of the entrance gate to the terreiro yard, and that he had broken all the images placed there. His clothes were all torn. At first the group explained all these untoward events as due to the demanda from the terreiro in Bishop Street. But after the mãe-de-santo began to say "strange things" and beat people, they agreed that her conduct was caused by her "madness" (*loucura*), her "sickness" (*doença*). They speculated that this, in turn, was due to exhaustion from performing the "works" involved in the opening of the terreiro. But her ritual sponsor then told them that Apareçida had previously been twice interned in psychiatric hospitals. Indeed, she had once had another terreiro, which had been closed down for the same reason. The doctor then told them that her madness was caused by traumas experienced in infancy. But the group asked the question by now familiar to anthropologists: "But why did she become mad just at that precise moment and at that particular place?" The answer they gave was within the Umbandist belief system. She had committed errors in the opening of the terreiro. She should not have "worked with Exú" in the inauguration ritual—it is best to wait seven months before doing this. If one works with Exús before the prescribed date, they are likely to be Exús without Light—called *Quiumbas*—"who don't want to bring charity (*caridade*—the great Umbandist virtue; in sessions, when a new guide appears, he or she goes round the whole group embracing each medium and client twice with great affection) but go on to cause confusion (*bagunça*)." It was these Exús who made mãe-de-santo mad and "caused the war between brother and brother and the pai-de-santo and his children." Note the use of familial terms here. Added to this, she did not have the guidance of her own mãe-de-santo, and she failed to "baptise the *atabaque* drums"—whose sonic driving in sessions induces possession and trance. She did not have the requisite guidance and approval (hence legitimation) from her mãe-de-santo because she was having "a war of orixás" with her.

Velho did not mention the psychiatrist's diagnosis of Apareçida's condition but it might be guessed that her guilt at leaving the Bishop Street terreiro and possibly being in demanda with its mãe-de-santo was a precipitating factor. When the medium from the other terreiro, in trance and hence speaking with some authority, pointed out Marina as a traitress—and one who occupied the same role, little mother, which she herself had occupied in the other cult center—she may have been pushed over the verge of paranoia. The fact that in both terreiros the tension was between members of the same sex may have some significance here. Velho elsewhere stresses that Apareçida and Marina had been very close friends. One thinks of some remarks on the link between paranoia and homosexuality by Freud in his article, "Some Neurotic Mechanisms in Jealousy, Paranoia, and Homosexuality," (1922:226–27): "The persecuted paranoiac sees in . . . others the reflection of his own hostile impulses against them. Since we know that with the paranoiac it is precisely the most loved person of his own sex that becomes his persecutor, the question arises where this reversal of affect takes its origin; the answer is not far to seek—the ever present ambivalence of feeling provides its source . . . and serves the same purpose for the persecuted paranoiac . . . of a defence against homosexuality."

I must abridge Velho's account of conflict in the terreiro, though I regret the consequent loss of much rich data. It was agreed that Apareçida should be deposed from her role as mãe-de-santo though she could participate in the sessions as an ordinary medium when she returned from the hospital. On the advice of several mediums a new pai-de-santo named Pedro was brought in, a bricklayer by trade in ordinary life, who had a good reputation for starting terreiros. He was said to be very knowledgeable in "things of santo." For a time he united the group behind him in "making works" against Apareçida, who, it was rumored, had secured the aid of a powerful Candomblé practitioner to "work ill" against the terreiro. She had made a spectacular reappearance about three weeks after her hospitalization. I translate Velho's account of it, not only because it contains interesting material on Umbanda ritual and theories about possession but also because it marks the beginning of a cleavage between Mario the president and Pedro the pai-de-santo. Velho writes:

> The mediums were assembled on Wednesday, July 26th, 1972, in the altar room. They were about to begin the ritual of "development" (*desenvolvimento*) which begins with a "lesson" instructing the mediums in "the things of the law," that is, the beliefs, rituals, and techniques of Umbanda. Suddenly Apareçida entered the terreiro screaming and howling as she did when incorporated. She was already in the small house of Exú and the ghosts and was receiving Exú. Mario rushed out to her and restrained her by the arms while she raved that she would "break everything up." He dragged her towards the altar room. Mario assured me that Apareçida was not (really) "with saint," in a state of possession that day, but Pedro insisted that she was indeed incorporated. Whatever may have been the case, Apareçida drew the symbol of an orixá (a design of lines, stars, triangles, arrows, and so forth, thought to have magical power drawn from the supernatural entity) with sacred white chalk (*pemba*) on the floor of the altar room near the altar, and pulled Mario into it. She wanted Mario to "fall in the saint" (*caisse no santo*) in the symbolic drawing, akin to the Western "pentagram of sorcery", that is, fall into a trance. But Mario "firmed up" (*firmou*), in other words he resisted falling into trance. [This technique may be employed to prevent an orixá "from descending into one's head" and gives the medium a measure of control over his or her orixás.]
>
> If Mario had succumbed, Apareçida would have succeeded in dominating him and thus demonstrated her power to be mãe-de-santo in the terreiro. While this was going on Pedro was piercing himself on an arm and foot with a needle and making other "works." The pai-de-santo was incorporated with his Old Black, and the Old Black was locked in mystical combat with Apareçida's Exú (*demandando*). As Pedro said, "One of them was making a work and the other was unmaking it."
>
> Finally, Apareçida "beat the head" before the altar. In this ceremony

> the medium lies down before the altar which is crowded with the images of the orixá, and beats his or her head three times on the ground, to the right, the left, and straight ahead, then three times with the forehead on the altar table, then three times before the pai-de-santo. This ceremony is done at the beginning and end of each session. Apareçida completed it, then said that she "had nothing against" anyone. When she turned towards the stairs, Mario caught her by the hands and said, "Don't be angry with me; you can come back, but only to help." Mario took her "beating of the head" to be a sign that she had accepted her defeat and was making a respectful farewell to the terreiro and its orixás.
>
> Mario and Pedro gave substantially the same account of the event, but Mario emphasized his own role in not having "fallen in santo," while belittling that of Pedro, who, he said, had driven the needle into his crippled arm (as a child he had been the victim of infantile paralysis), an arm which would have been insensible. Nevertheless Pedro had apparently consolidated his position in the terreiro, particularly for having succeeded in getting Apareçida out of the house without breaking anything [Velho 1975:59–60].

There followed a period during which Mario became increasingly disenchanted with Pedro's leadership. The two men were very different. Mario was reckoned to be "white" by Brazilian criteria; Pedro was "black." Both were young, Mario being thirty-one and Pedro twenty-seven. But Mario considered himself an educated man, and was, indeed, a part-time social science student at the Federal University of Rio de Janeiro. He was in one of Yvonne Velho's classes, and it was in class discussion that she had learned of his participation in Umbanda. At that time he was also working as a typist, and gave private classes in history, literature, and English to eight pupils. Pedro had an incomplete primary education, had been a college servant, then worked in the canteen, before learning his trade as a bricklayer and plasterer. Mario was an immigrant from the rural interior of the State of Alagoas. His father was probably a dirt farmer, though he always claimed to have come from a family of "*fazendeiros*," or great landowners. He lived in the working class northern zone of Rio. Pedro, on the other hand, lived in the residential southern zone. While Mario was relatively new to Umbanda, Pedro had been "thirteen years in *Macumba*" (a generic term for possession cults; it may also stand for a musical instrument used in them). He had originally been a drummer (*ogã* or *macumbeiro*), and had after five years become chief-drummer (*ogã-iao*). His mãe-de-santo was his cousin, Leda by name, and eventually she allowed him to "open his own *gonga*," a terreiro "where they don't beat drums." To open a terreiro one must have at least thirteen mediums. He managed to recruit this number, and with the help of two mediums seconded from Mother Leda's terreiro "developed" the mediums, teaching them how to control possession and how to receive appropriately each type of orixá. In brief, Pedro picked up his ritual skills in practice in "works." During the dispute with Mario, Pedro introduced Mother Leda to the group, to confirm his assertion that he had been "baptized into Macumba" (that is, properly initiated). She supported his claim to know "how to work in all the lines of orixá" that is, he could direct any type of ceremony and was familiar with the behavior-patterns of each orixá. Pedro further asserted that he had "a good crown" (*corôa bonita*), that is, that he "received many strong orixás," chiefs of phalanxes, not minor entities. He was also, he said, a clairvoyant medium, a clairaudient, who heard the words of Orixás, and "a radiant," one who received orixás. Pedro also insisted that though he was an uneducated man, when he was incorporated with an orixá he could understand Yoruba, the language of the high gods. Mario, against this, asserted that he himself "had studied," he was a university man, a "person of culture." He attempted to manipulate Yvonne Velho, whom he had introduced at the inauguration ritual, as "my professor," hoping thereby to enhance his standing with the group. But his formal education reacted against him, for the majority of the mediums, themselves mostly uneducated, murmured that "book learning" was no substitute for "knowledge of the things of santo." Mario, moreover, had never passed through the rites of making the head (initiation). Velho found Pedro a more consistently reliable informant than Mario, less given to fantasy about his own importance. "He told me his life-history three times in substantially the same form. He was never given to exaggeration, and told me facts and dates almost mechanically. He hardly ever gave me autobiographical information in casual conversation, but tried, rather, to give me information about ritual practices, always in a professional tone. He laughed a lot at my questions, and always said that the 'fundamentals' of Umbanda were very difficult, and that I would need a lot of time, perhaps a lifetime, to grasp them" (Velho 1975:110). A typical professional answer—true experience is verbally almost incommunicable! Professionals create hermetic circles of shared experience. Mario, on the other hand, was the sort of person that in the States might be called an "achiever," despite, or perhaps because of, certain disabilities. More than a smattering of education tilted him in the direction of the bureaucratization of the terreiro. Here his role as president, that is, acknowledged head of the "material hierarchy," and incidentally the actual lessee of the property on which the terreiro functioned, encouraged him to propose the "rule" (one thinks here of Catholic monastic orders forced by Rome to generate rules to curb their charismatic beginnings) for routinizing the terreiro mediums' behavior. This took place on the heels of the excesses that Mario thought followed Pedro's insistence on the group's making works to counteract Apareçida's deadly demanda. Velho's diary for August 20, 1972, documents the broaching by Mario of the "rule."

> Mario arrived at the terreiro early, well before the session began, and immediately confronted Pedro. They both sat on tree stumps in the altar room. [Such stumps are symbolic reminiscences of the "natural" character of the supposedly ancient tradition—actually the first Umbanda rites were performed in Niteroi, across the Bay from Rio, in the early twenties—but Candomblé or something like it, such as Katimbu and Kabula, probably developed among the slaves of the Portuguese settlers at the very beginning of colonization, in the early sixteenth century.] Mario spoke in loud tones, Pedro replied in a low, calm voice. Mario held a piece of paper—a symbol of literacy—in his hand. He said; "This is the Rule—it contains regulations for mediums. They must not smoke, arrive late, and the session must end at ten P.M." [Pedro had kept the group up all night performing works to frustrate the demanda; hence mediums who had daytime jobs were getting worn out—the subjunctive mood was becoming indicativized, the symbolic "works" of Umbanda were becoming really laborious.] Mario continued: "You, Pedro, must impose that rule on them here." Pedro replied: "I don't have to say that. What I say goes anyway. I have started three terras, and I know what I have to do. You are well aware that we are in a state of demanda and must 'work'." Mario yelled back; "I don't want to know about your terras. Our business is right here. Either you lay down that rule or you get out. You will get out because I will get another pai- or mãe-de-santo, for things are impossible as they are."
>
> The two got up, and the pai-de-santo started the session with the usual drawing of an orixá's symbol below the altar in white chalk. Mario approached me about some faculty business at the University. I could not grasp what he said for I was trying to figure out what was happening around me. I replied rather laconically, but when I glanced at the altar, I saw a blaze of fire. A medium ran to put it out, pulling off the burning altar cloth. Due to the heat, an Umbandist necklace or rosary, known as "guide," broke in pieces scattering the small beads all over the room. The mediums fled. When the fire was extinguished they looked at the broken rosary with fear. Sonia, the new little mother, said to me, "See how strange it is! Whatever could have happened?" The pai-de-santo, Pedro, unperturbed by the fire, finished drawing his Umbanda sign, stood up, and said: "All this is because someone came to the terreiro with a hot head." [The consensus among mediums was that the fire was a sign of war between Mario and Pedro, in other words, that a state of demanda existed between them.]
>
> After this episode a typical Sunday session began. But an important change took place. Mario received his Pomba-Gira ("Whirling Dove"), the wild, gypsy feminine form of Exú, and stayed with her until the end of the session. He explained to me afterwards that Pedro asked for her to "protect the gira" (the session). From that time onward Mario's Pomba-Gira played a leading role in the sessions [Velho 1975:67–68].

The mediums now began to take sides. Most of the office-holders in the spiritual hierarchy supported Pedro, while a small group, known as

"Manuel's Little Gang," including three mediums, as well as mere dues-paying associates, supported Mario, arguing that the terreiro ought to "have order." They were also concerned that the money Pedro and other mediums had obtained from consultations with nonmediumistic clients should be accounted for and divided fairly among the group. But, to their surprise, Mario supported Sonia, the little mother, who should have dealt with this, the result being that Manuel's Little Gang quit the terreiro, declaring that Mario was "dishonest" and wanted to "take control of everything himself." I understand that Manuel had always been Mario's rival, and had a large durable following which had accompanied him from the terreiro in Bishop Street. In those days Mario had been close to Apareçida and Manuel's gang had hoped to benefit from her counsel in the new cult center. But, in a way, Mario had ditched her in an attempt to fulfil his own ambitions for leadership.

Mario had now, in an odd fashion, isolated himself from the group. As he told Yvonne Velho: "They are ignorant people totally dominated by Pedro and scared of the demanda. But I have no fear, for my guides are strong and I am a cultured person. I am on a high cultural level and have nothing to learn from Pedro. The group is obsessed with learning from him. They have no confidence in their own resources. They are only secure when they are 'in santo'. Unpossessed they know nothing. But I can even change the structure of Umbanda ritual for the better—not because I have more culture, but also due to the intuitive power of my guides, who are from the Oriental line" (Velho 1975:140). He is here referring to the influence of theosophy and other Asian-based religions which, as in California and other parts of the United States, are acquiring considerable religious prestige with the failure of traditional Judeo-Christian symbols and norms among, particularly, the young—and the average age of Umbanda adherents is in the middle twenties. For Mario, the main thing about the "Oriental line" was that it was opposed to the traditional lines linked to Africa in Umbanda. The line of "Exús without Light" would be contrasted by those intellectuals or semi-intellectuals like Mario who have recently taken up the manifold literature on Eastern religions now being translated into Portuguese, with Hindu/Buddhist thought, and would be designated as "African witchcraft" (for example, the seven "dark" lines of Quimbanda).

All kinds of strange events followed, which I will not vex you with, so aberrant they are to our scientific tradition. Even psychoanalysts become uncomfortable confronted by fantasies that have become culturally standardized rather than emerge in secrecy from individuals under controlled conditions. I will not mention the various fire ordeals Pedro and Mario imposed on one another, nor the constant possession of Mario by his female gypsy guide. Suffice it to say that Mario's financial power over the property which provided the terreiro's material basis prevailed, but he was virtually abandoned by all the mediums three months after the terreiro he sponsored began, though remaining the titular head of the house and yard. The note I really want to conclude on is what seems to have been happening in Mario's "mind" or "psyche," insofar as Velho's life history gives us access to this obscure dimension.

Both Mario and Pedro seem to have had unusual relationships with their mothers—a fact not to be ignored in view of the close "star group" relationship between a mãe-de-santo and her "child" in Umbanda. But while Pedro duplicated his mother's physical paralysis, Mario's connection with the mother he abandoned to go to Rio from the farm seems more complicated.

Although she does not mention his place in the sibling order, Velho tells us that Mario was one of nine children—while Pedro apparently had only a few siblings. Mario went to live with a mother's brother when he first moved to Rio. Women meant a lot in his life. For a time he stayed with various female cousins. He taught himself typing, shorthand, English, French, and passed all his tests in matriculation except mathematics. Math first introduced him to Umbanda, oddly enough, for a female friend made him consult a pai-de-santo in Umbanda in Laranjeiras, a suburb of Rio. This man told him that "he had the great protection of Ogum," and it so happened that the college where he was to do his math test was just opposite a church dedicated to St. George—who is the Catholic modality of Ogum, god of war and blacksmithing. According to his account a black boy emerged from the church, just after he had lit a candle to Ogum/St. George, and handed him a sheet of answers to the questions he later encountered in his math exam—which naturally he passed! This was not enough to dispel Mario's skepticism about Umbanda, so he told Velho, but having said this he went straight on to speak of his mother. He said that it was now clear to him that she was clairvoyant. As mediums possessed by Caboclos or Old Blacks do, she smoked two cheroots every night, and saw "everything that was going to happen." She loved Mario best of her children, even though he stuttered and did not like to ride or hoe like his brothers. He was only ten when she died. It was not long before he dreamed about her. She sat on the edge of his bed and gave him what he thought was advice, but he was so scared he could never remember it. Later, when he was in Rio, an Umbandist medium told him that his late mother was in a state known as *encostada*, in the technical vocabulary of Umbanda and similar spiritist cults. This, in its literal sense, means "dependent, leaning against, propped up." It meant, so it was explained to him, that her spirit had become "passionate" (*apaixonada*) or had "fallen in love" with him, and had become "dependent" on matter (*encostado na matéria*). Dependence (*encosto*) occurs when a dead person's spirit needs something, especially prayers to obtain light (*luz*). The gnostic component in Umbanda is clear here, as it is in the distinction between Exús with and without "light." The living person on whom it "fastens itself" is both "confused" or "troubled" (*atrapalhada*) and helped (by spiritual advice) when in this state. But Mario remained skeptical about such interpretations, though he was shaken when, during an Umbanda session he was persuaded against his inclination to attend, a woman near him "received the spirit of his mother, cried, and said she felt the taste of blood in her mouth," for his mother had died of an internal hemorrhage. Nevertheless, he still held it all to be "buffoonery" (*palhaçada*). "What would I, a student of sociology, be doing to believe in that stuff?" he told Velho.

Mario, at that time, was afflicted both by being cross-eyed and having a stutter. He had been hospitalized in August 1971 for an operation on his right eye, but while in bed, received "pinpricks" (*alfinetadas*), a "spiritual warning" (*aviso*) that he should leave. He did so, then consulted Apareçida, who would later become the mãe-de-santo we have been discussing. She, or rather her Old Black Woman, confirmed that he had a dependency from his mother and drew it out (*tirou o encosto*). Since the spirit was "seeking light," she advised him to light a candle for her and make some prayers. From then on, his stuttering diminished and he was in distinctly better general health. Apareçida urged him to "work" in Umbanda and "wear the white clothes" (a mark of the Umbanda medium). Her Old Black Woman also improved his eyesight, he told Yvonne Velho. Though unconvinced that his improvement was due to supernatural influences, he began to sense strange things. For example, when he went to a session as he had taken to doing, he could not hear a song or drum rhythm dedicated to an orixá (*um ponto*), without feeling totally "disconnected" (*desligado*), as if he were "in another world." He was "extinguished," "switched off" (*apagado*). Later, he accepted Apareçida's invitation to "make an obligation" in the woods to the Caboclo, or Red Indian spirits. When he began to watch a waterfall, he began to feel a sensation of emptiness, as if he were entirely lost. Apareçida was being ridden by her Caboclo, Serra Negra, after whom the terreiro would be named, and "he" called Mario and placed "his" hands on Mario's. Mario told Velho: "At that moment I saw no more . . . it was the first time this had happened to me. I did not just 'receive', I sprang up (*pulava*). I felt vibrations. It was like an electric shock. The more the Caboclo seized hold of me, the more I jumped. I did not control myself, I fell and became beside myself" (Velho 1975:100). After that he became a regular attender at the sessions of the Bishop Street terreiro, put on the white clothes, and within two months was "receiving normally"—note that to receive is classified as "normal" behavior in Umbanda—further evidence that the cultural symbols and processes of Umbanda substitute in persons of neurotic disposition for the weakness of the ego in mediating between the id and reality. Under the alienating circumstances for the poor and displaced of urbanization in a land hitherto rural and post-feudal it is perhaps not so surprising that people would find such means of ego-reinforcement. This is true even of the Brazilian white upper classes who have also been joining Umbanda groups in considerable numbers, for they too are experiencing the stresses of rapid industrialization. Umbanda is not a single-class or single ethnicity phenomenon: it crosses all social structural taxonomic lines, although its basic membership is drawn from lower-middle class urbanites. Both Sonia and Marina, for example, were beauticians, and, indeed, Esther Pressel, from Columbia University, who studied Umbanda in São Paulo, found that her shortest route to an Umbandist session was to visit a hairdresser's shop and inquire both from the beauticians and the customers where the next one would be held. Women usually outnumber men by about three to one among the mediums, though pais-de-santo are about equal numbers with mães-de-santo. There is some stigma attached to male Umbandists, in a land that worships machismo, but Yvonne Velho reports that pais-de-santo are more frequently heterosexual, with families, than homosexual. Of course, all mediums, often in the course of a single session, are incorporated with "entities" of both sexes, and display in their behavior the attributes of male and female orixás. More of this presently, in the case of Mario.

As the rivalry grew between Mario and Pedro, president and pai-de-santo, significant changes occurred both in Mario's conduct and in the way he "received" his guides. Undoubtedly, Yvonne Velho's presence in the terreiro had an influence on these changes, and on Mario's self-image. As she writes:

> At first, Mario's attitude was humble enough. He said that since he had only a year "in santo," he didn't "understand it well; the babalao (pai-de-santo) is the one who can explain matters well." He confided several times that he had many doubts about Umbanda, and sought for psychological explanations of the facts. My presence there as his professor inhibited him (*o inibia*). Sometimes he would be amused at his anomalous position as sociology student and medium at the same time. But, on the other hand, my presence undoubtedly helped to increase his power in the terreiro. Just as Leda had confirmed Pedro's legitimacy as pai-de-santo, so did my presence as his professor confirm Mario's status as a university student. The group appreciated this, but, nevertheless, Mario's 'having studied' had negative implications, for it could make him proud and desire to know more than the pai-de-santo. There was a conflict between the latter's esoteric gnosis and Mario's academic knowledge. A crisis came when I interviewed Mario on tape, and committed the ethnographic gaffe of failing to inform Pedro—who was chagrined by what he thought was an undermining of his ritual authority. Mario now began to condemn the group as being "ignorant know-nothings." He belittled Pedro's

> expertise, saying that "when you've been a drummer in terreiros for twelve years, you can't help picking up some knowledge of the magic (*sic*) of the terreiro." He, on the contrary, had "more culture," his guides were from "the Oriental line, from a more advanced branch of culture." He was certain that he could become the chief of a terreiro and could "modify the structure of an Umbanda ritual for the better."

It must be clear by this time that Mario was a highly competitive person, despite, or as Alfred Adler would have argued, on account of his disabilities, his stammering, his poor vision. One of nine siblings, his mother's favorite son, and obviously the most intelligent member of his rural family, he had set out to become a person of importance in the big city. Older women, his mother and a series of mother surrogates, including Apareçida and perhaps Yvonne herself, played important roles in determining the directions taken by his career. There is obviously much ambivalence in his attitude towards them. He had a problem in ridding himself of his mother's spirit "who had become dependent" on him and passionate for him. She represented perhaps, inter alia, the hold his rural background still exerted on him. Next, he turned to Apareçida for help, and was not content until he had rented a house for her in which to play her role as a kind of mother, a mãe-de-santo. In his own role of president, complementary and equal to her, perhaps he could even see himself as his surrogate mother's spouse, thus fulfilling in legitimate, cultural disguise his Oedipal wish. Apareçida's madness, however, quashed that relationship. Powerful female figures, however, seemed central to his own aspirations. As we shall see, if he could not enter into a relationship with one, he had the route open to him in Umbanda belief and ritual of identifying with a female guide. This turn seems connected with his tacit decision to abandon his "urban, civilized, university student's" pose towards Umbanda, and try to beat the pai-de-santo at his own game—esoteric cultic gnosis and techniques of possession. Let me return to Velho's narrative.

> In the early days of the new terreiro, Mario received mostly male guides, for example: two Caboclos, namely the Cowboy (*Boiadeiro*) João Menino ("Little John") and His Honor Seven Stars of the East; an Old Black, Pai Benedito of Angola; a Child Spirit, Pedrinho da Mata ("Little Peter of the Wood"); a Pomba-Gira Gypsy (*cigana*), called Salomé; Ogum Seven Stars; and an Exú, His Honor Seven Crossroads (Seu Sete Encruzilhada). His "front guides" (*guias de frente*), that is, his most important orixás, were Xango and Mamäe Oxum [a female phalanx commander in the line of Iemanjá; Mamäe Oxum is represented on Umbandist altars as a weeping woman, and as a Christian santa, as the Mater Dolorosa].
>
> Mario explained to me that in Umbanda there are seven cosmic forces or lines, and that there always exists a duality, masculine and

feminine. Consequently, a medium (male or female) always receives a "feminine entity" and a "masculine entity." He said that he liked to receive the Cowboy best, and at first this was the one he received most. He explained: "While I am an individual of great sensibility, indeed almost of a feminine sensibility . . . I find that I have within me a truly masculine force. This is exteriorized through the Cowboy guide, with whom I feel most at home . . . The first guide to give me advice was the Cowboy, by means of a dream . . ."

He said that at this stage he had no desire to receive the Pomba-Gira. "She is extremely feminine," he said, "and I did not feel like receiving her well. But I was steadily coming to the conclusion that it would be necessary for me to receive her more often. Not only because of what she could do for others but also because of what she could do for me personally." He did not want to receive her because "automatically, if she is feminine, I become effeminate, and that's just the problem. Most people never come to see me as a man. They think of me as effeminate, even after she has gone . . . and indeed she causes a series of disturbances. Just because she is very feminine, she likes long hair. Similarly she loves jewelry. She wants clothes. Last time she came, she ordered me to take off the shirt I had from the Preto-Velho and she wound a cloth around my breasts (*meus peitos*)." I asked if this did not conflict with the Cowboy, since he was masculine? He replied: "Each force has its own mode of being (*maneira de ser*) . . . when I receive the Cowboy I am masculine, when I receive her, I take on her appearance. If I did not receive a cosmic force, how could I from one moment to another change my identity? . . ."

Mario rationalized his frequent incorporation with Salomé by pointing out that she was the one who organized the lesser guides. She must have been a nuisance for Pedro, since she would not stop riding her "horse," Mario, throughout an entire session, and tried to dictate the course of events in a flamboyant way.

As the conflict between Mario and Pedro grew, the Pomba-Gira stripped Mario of his white medium's shirt, replacing it by a red cloth. He was obliged to buy a wine glass from which she sipped champagne. Next, he bought earrings, bracelets, and a headcloth of colored silk, in which were caught up, gypsy-style, innumerable golden medals. At first, his dancing was stiff and limited in movement, but he began to choreograph it more elaborately. [Yvonne Velho pictures him for us whirling around in his "giras," with long hair, wrapped in silk cloth, with jingling bracelets and earrings.] When possessed, he spoke in a cultured voice and very slowly, using an educated vocabulary, in contrast with the other Pomba-Giras, who "sputtered and used crude language."

One day, when Mario was incorporated with his Pomba-Gira, she asked me: "What difference do you see between this material (*materia*) here, the horse in the terreiro and in the (university) faculty?" I replied that they were two different things. She looked me in the eye and said: "You don't understand in the least. This material here (the

> horse) is the same, only it has a little of me in it, a portion of my personality." I then asked why she only "descended" in the terreiro. She replied: "This is my terra [a play on words, indicating both "earth," with implications of "nature" as against "artificiality," and the cult center itself]. Here I can come and no one is going to be scared by my material. Elsewhere people just don't understand. Here is my terra, my true ground, there I never felt at home. I work like this, as you see me doing, because I feel at home" [Velho 1975:102 – 4].

Much of what I wrote in the first part of this paper applies here. Clearly, Mario, in his Pomba-Gira *persona*, is stating that a large part of his real life is in what I called "the subjunctive mood" of culture, and that much freedom from constraint exists in the social modes tolerated there. Here, too, culture and personality are in agreement, for Brazilian culture has often been characterized as rich in genres of cultural performance, involving reversal or inversion of the social and political structures. Furthermore, it is a point of honor in Carnaval, for example, that one should express in public one's fantasies—indeed, the Portuguese term for a Carnaval costume is *fantasia*. In Carnaval there is a good deal of transvestitism: men even have silicon implants in their breasts for greater verisimilitude. But these reversals are restricted to institutions defined as festivity, play (including the complex symbolism associated with soccer matches), or the madness (*loucura*) of Mardi Gras. In the life of everyday, machismo prevails, postfeudal and bureaucratic hierarchies organize the family, business, industry, the military, and so on. Rules of etiquette and politeness appear to involve distancing, the reverse of the frankly intimate behavior found in the subjunctive mood genres. This is because there are elaborate rules for switching from indicative to subjunctive behavior and vice versa. Recently much discomfort has been caused in São Paulo and Campinas when "gays" formed their own samba schools and blocos during Carnaval and introduced their sexual reality into that figurative and symbolic domain, thereby revealing it as a cultural defense-mechanism against indicatively illicit impulses.

At the level of Mario's psychosomatic "idioverse"—to use Theodore Schwartz's term for "the distributive aspect of culture," or the total set of implicit constructs of each individual in a cultural system, we can, I believe, see in the Pomba-Gira a symbolic archetype which props Mario's weak ego-development in crisis and solves—at least for a time—his problems in relation to femininity and authority. One can say that his mother's "dependence" on him in the Umbanda idiom really represents his dependence upon his mother, a dependence on mother figures which progressively is reduced as it is transferred from mother to ritual mother (Apareçida) to teacher mother (Yvonne), until he himself, as Pomba-Gira, is transformed into a kind of anti-mother. The Pomba-Gira is the "bad woman of the world" as against the virtuous nurturant protectress of the domestic family. Mario perhaps could only obtain his independence from his various "dependencies," not by becoming fully a man but by becoming, in the subjunctive mood where fantasies are objectivated, a different, even opposite kind of woman to the series of "mothers." It is also possible that his connivance in the "killing," that is, expulsion of his ritual "mother" (Apareçida) expedited his feminine identification, for identification often follows the loss of a loved object.

But in achieving this partial resolution of his personal problems Mario seems to have become a loser in the social drama, for, in the end, he drove away not only the pai-de-santo, Pedro, but also all the other mediums from the terreiro, whose lessee, of course, he remained. In the terreiro he had thought to have found his star-group, his subjunctive star-group, but instead he succeeded in alienating its other members, perhaps because, more than the others, he had brought into the public domain in the symbolic guise of demanda many of the unconscious conflicts of childhood in the Brazilian lower-class family that would have otherwise lain dormant in the world of "indicative-mood" groups to which the Umbandists belonged.

I have not given you a blow-by-blow account of the demanda which developed between Mario and Pedro, including such exotica as fire-ordeals and self-stabbings, since I have already overburdened you with detail. Suffice it to say that in successive sessions, the hostility between those two became evident to all. In the religious hierarchy, Pedro, though his junior, was Mario's "father" (pai). The group that began in demanda ended in demanda, and in all its stages, it set ritual "parents" against ritual "children." In the end, Pedro and most of the others left ostensibly over a financial issue—Sonia the little mother had been a hundred cruzeiros short after adding up fees paid by clients to mediums for consultations. She had offered to repay this sum from her own pocket to the joint funds. Pedro wanted all the consultation fees to be divided up among the mediums and not put in the terreiro's joint account. Squabbling arose. Mario ordered the expulsion of all mediums who took Pedro's side. He explained this in mystical terms; he said that his main orixá, Ogum (St. George) had defeated the demanda against him, as St. George had slain the dragon. But soon the terreiro had to be closed down, for only the president remained with one woman helper, a non-medium named Zilda, Mario's colleague on the university faculty. Yvonne herself, by her own account, clearly took the side of those whom Mario expelled. "When I said goodbye to the other mediums, they observed that I was in the grip of emotion, though Pedro's sister hesitated to say so aloud" (Velho 1975:80). Anthropologists rarely describe their own feelings so honestly, preferring to pose often as cognitive machines for which third person language is appropriate.

How, then, may an anthropologist, working in collaboration with a psychoanalyst, handle this kind of data which clearly is Janus-faced—looking directly at both disciplines? I have made some amateurish suggestions along the lines of psychoanalytic interpretation of portions of the behavior observed by Velho. I know that these are inadequate. I know that I am capable, however, of handling the social and cultural contexts of the dramas described. Obviously, some division of labor would be desirable. Sociocultural systems are, after all, at the level of observation, quite different from, though interdependent with, psychical or mental systems. They involve different kinds of sustentative processes and have different developmental mechanisms. Indeed I lament the lack of adequate social structural contextualization of Velho's terreiro in the contemporary Brazilian society, with its multitudinous problems of class stratification, ethnicity, labor migration, urbanization, political control, and so on. And I wonder about the typicality of her group of mediums. Is the life of the average terreiro really as short as three months? I would also have desired more information about the extant social structure of the group, its basic organizing norms and perdurable relationships, and, in addition, its division into transient alliances and factions (information on these is provided but not systematized), for both persisting structural forms and recurrent types of conflict and self-serving interests tend to be stereotyped in the ritual symbolism. Nevertheless, I still regard her book as very nearly a tour de force. Psychoanalysts could make a decisive contribution to the study of sociocultural fields such as these by entering into a working field partnership with anthropologists. For example, our understanding of such dramatis personae as Apareçida, Mario, Pedro, Sonia, Marina, Leda, and the like, would have been immeasurably enhanced if it had been possible to bring them regularly into clinical interview situations, during and after the events described—even though the events themselves would then have taken a radically different turn. One wonders, of course, if the events would have followed the course described had Yvonne Velho not been present most of the time!

Finally, it has sometimes been argued by anthropologically oriented psychiatrists such as T. Adeoye Lambo and Ari Kiev that patients should be referred to traditional practitioners to complete their therapy, in cultures where such ritual modes of therapy are still a going concern. But Velho's data show that when Pedro was insisting that his mediums should perform works lasting through the night several nights a week to resist and dispel the demanda laid on the group by Apareçida, they all had problems in their daily work and some experienced accidents because they were exhausted. In industrializing societies, it is clear that the Western notion of "the individual in general" as the source of rational choice has replaced the corporate group as the responsible, even ethical unit, and that it is not really feasible to turn the clock back to cultural forms that are appropriate to preindustrial and nonurbanized societies. The ego has to achieve its own strength assisted by the findings of a rationally oriented culture; it can no longer rely on forms, even as beautifully and potently numinous as those of the subjunctive subculture of Umbanda, to keep neurosis at bay or sublimate it into socially viable behavior.

7

Process, System, and Symbol

A New Anthropological Synthesis

Just beyond our present horizon, I like to think, lie the Delectable Islands. But I think that anthropologists will reach them only if they reverse the process of fission into subdisciplines, each with its awesome jargon, which has characterized the history of anthropology in the past decade or so, and move toward a renewed fusion which will lead to discussion of an animated sort among, say, the biological, ecological, structural, semiotic, semiological, "etic," "emic," ethno-this and ethno-that, kinds of anthropologists. Our expulsion from various colonial research Edens may be an opportunity rather than a loss. We can now take stock—and also assess our relationship, in this breathing space, to other entrenched sciences and humanities.

Anthropology should not flinch from looking at creative art and literature in complex societies, but always as these reflect upon the "tides of history" which form their processual contexts. Texts not only animate and are animated by contexts but are processually inseverable from them. The

Reprinted with permission of *Daedalus*, Journal of the American Academy of Arts and Sciences, *Discoveries and Interpretations: Studies in Contemporary Scholarship*, vol. 1, Summer 1977, Boston, Massachusetts.

arts are germane to the ebbs and flows of human understanding as these awaken or fade at given moments on the scale of global history; the sciences show anthropology the constraints of the human condition. In terms approvable by William Blake, we oscillate between "single" and "fourfold" vision, but neither is inappropriate to us, exhausts us, or cannot be seriously studied.

My personal view is that anthropology is shifting from a stress on concepts such as structure, equilibrium, function, system to process, indeterminacy, reflexivity—from a "being" to a "becoming" vocabulary—but with a tender perpetuative regard for the marvelous findings of those who, teachers of the present generation, committed themselves to the discoveries of "systems" of social relations and cultural "items" and "complexes." The validly new never negates the seriously researched immediate past in any science; it incorporates it in "a wider orbit of recovered law."

As Tom Kuhn and others have shown, the sociopolitical situation in any disciplined field of knowledge, whether classified as a science or not, exhibits the conflicts of processuality (as our Italian colleagues, literally translating, put it). Actual persons represent theoretical stances. Older persons command stronger positions in the microcosmographia academica—persons trained and working valuably in earlier periods than the present. Younger persons are doing the experiments, the fieldwork. Paradigms supported by the "good old boys" are challenged by new facts, new hypotheses grounded in them. Anthropology is presently experiencing this stress rather sharply.

The discipline of anthropology undoubtedly shares this crises with other academic disciplines. To my possibly naive European eye, stress on the individual as the grant-seeking unit, on "chaps rather than maps," has virtues certainly, but it also makes for theoretical fragmentation. And behind it is often a covert, unhealthy collectivism. For certain of the major departments of anthropology in the United States show a kinship to the city states of antiquity. Each department specializes in a certain kind of anthropology (ethnoscience, symbolic anthropology, ecological anthropology, applied anthropology, etc.), and it would be a bold student who successfully obtained support for what his tutors considered an "adversary position" in terms of his grant proposal or thesis research.

This combination of a myth of individualism and a reality of departmental theoretical orientation often tends to create for imaginative students the classical Batesonian double-bind situation. Their best thoughts may be tabooed and their integrity undermined by "city state" shibboleths in the way of concepts and styles to which they must render at least lip service to obtain support from nationally and locally prestigious departmental faculty. Students often seem to suffer from the guilt of "self-betrayal"—which pursues them even into their fieldwork in far places. I am sure this is not an optimal condition for fieldwork. For they have to process their fieldwork into Ph.D. dissertations acceptable by their sponsoring departments.

One remedy would be to seek means to overcome the overspecialization of departments and the atomism of funding. My paper indicates that a new breakthrough in anthropology depends upon a serious sustained effort by the proponents of severely segregated subdisciplines (who bestow on their students the emblems of this segregation as "professional competence") to relate the best findings of their separated years. The major funding agencies, the NSF, NIMH, SSRC, Ford Foundation, and so forth, should be approached to provide the basis for a series of "summit" meetings among the leaders of the various modes of "anthropologizing." None of the major think-tanks (Palo Alto, Princeton, etc.) has promoted this immense work of collective reflexivity. Not that conferences alone can do this, but they are signals that the reconstitution of anthropology at a higher level under the aegis of processualism is under way. Otherwise the centrifugal drift, indeed, the suicidal *sparagmos*, will go on and on.

The device of encouraging representation on the faculties of certain departments of all the major subfields of current anthropology tends to be a palliative rather than a remedy if it is not cognizantly and authoritatively reinforced by the shared understanding of the discipline that such specialization must be accompanied by authentic integration under a major paradigm whose lineaments have been indicated by the acknowledged creative leaders of the total discipline.

Although it may not be possible to point to a definitive breakthrough, exemplified by a single book or article, in the past decade or so in world anthropology, one can make a fair case for a general disciplinary drift toward a theoretical synthesis to which processual studies have largely contributed. However, process theory is no longer linked, as in its earlier heyday, with L. Gumplowicz's notion (1963:203) that "man's material need is the prime motive of his conduct"; it now recognizes the critical importance of meaning and symboling. Furthermore, its theoretical focus is now "an individual and specific population studied in a multidisciplinary frame of reference and with a stress on specific human behavior rather than generalized norms or averages" (Bennett et al. 1975:179). Processes of conflict and competition of the social Darwinian type, or of cooperation (accommodation, assimilation) modeled on Kropotkin's zoological "mutual aid," are no longer regarded as being at the dynamic core of social development. Material need is not rejected but is rather viewed as part of "the simultaneous interaction among biology, ecology, and culture" which some anthropologists call *biological ecology* (Bennett et al. 1975:164).

In this junctural analysis of various systems—not *a* systems analysis but, rather, an *inter*systemic analysis—culture has to be seen as processual, because it emerges in interaction and imposes meaning on the biotic and ecological systems (also dynamic) with which it interacts. I should not say "it," for this is to reify what is, regarded processually, an endless series of negotiations among actors about the assignment of meaning to the acts in which they jointly participate. Meaning is assigned verbally through speech and nonverbally through ritual and ceremonial action and is often stored in symbols which become indexical counters in subsequent situational contexts. But the assignment and reassignment of meaning must be investigated as processes in the domain of resilience possessed by each population recognizing itself to be culturally perduring. For human populations are periodically subjected to shocks and crises, in addition to the strains and tensions of adjustment to quotidian challenges from the biotic and social environments. These involve problems of maintenance of determinate institutional structures as well as of creative adaptation to sudden or persisting environmental changes, making for indeterminacy.

Processual analysis has undoubtedly gained from the phenomenological critique of positivist anthropology. Whereas positivist anthropology held that social phenomena are qualitatively the same as natural phenomena, that the techniques of analysis developed in the natural sciences are applicable with little modification to anthropological investigation, and that anthropology should strive to develop empirically based theoretical propositions which would support predictive statements about social phenomena, the phenomenologists, notably Schutz, insisted that the social world is in many important respects a cultural construct, an organized universe of meaning in the form of what Harold Garfinkel calls a series of "typifications" of the objects within it. Garfinkel follows Schutz and Husserl in their view that "by naming an experienced object, they are relating by its typicality to preexperienced things of similar typical structures, and we accept its open horizon referring to future experiences of the same type" (A. Schutz 1962:285). Garfinkel argues that when a member of a collectivity accounts for his unique actions he is at the same time typifying them in terms of a framework of meaning which he shares with all other members. This framework is what the phenomenological social scientists call *common sense*. Garfinkel argues that even the practical, mundane activities of members of sociocultural groups are "reflexive" at the common sense level, because the social existence of a member's experiences can be established only through their typification, through the effort of relating their uniqueness to the world of meaning generated and transmitted by the group. For these scholars Durkheim's famous attempt to treat social phenomena as "things" is misdirected. What Durkheim fails to do is to analyze the processes, involving shared symbols, gestures, and language, by which social interaction generates an emergent social reality distinct from and external to that of the individuals who produce it. Processual analysis, like phenomenological anthropology, dereifies collective representations into the purposive and cross-purposive actions of persons in sequences of negotiations to maintain or retain, modify, or subvert social meanings, even, in some cases, to change the character and structure of common sense. By focusing attention on processes of meaning assignment it may be possible to locate the principles and rules which generate what D. E. Brown has called "presumptively perpetual social units" (1974:40). Brown refers specifically to corporations, which he regards as more readily classifiable than many noncorporate statuses, but like many structural-functionalists, he regards as unproblematical the processes by which corporations and other "surface structures" come into existence, are maintained against disintegrative processes, and are constantly reevaluated by actors. Social meanings cannot be taken for granted. It is not enough to make taxonomies or inventories of jural norms and cultural values, based on formal statements by informants. We have to develop strategies for ascertaining how the actors deal with discrepant norms: what are their standards of appropriateness, how they assess the respective weighings of stated and unstated rules, in short, how they assign meaning to their transactions and interactions.

Processual analysis has recently been considerably advanced by Sally Falk Moore's "Epilogue" to *Symbol and Politics in Communal Ideology* (1976). Moore proposes that "the underlying quality of social life should be considered to be one of theoretically absolute indeterminacy." Such indeterminacy is only partially reduced by culture and organized social life, "the patterned aspects of which are temporary, incomplete, and contain elements of inconsistency, ambiguity, discontinuity, contradiction, paradox, and conflict" (p. 232). She goes, in fact, further than Schutz, Garfinkel, and other phenomenological sociologists, who seem to find some system, vocabulary, and syntax in common sense. Here they share with the structural-functionalists some notion of the priority of determinacy. Moore, however, argues that even where rules and customs exist, "indeterminacy may be produced by the manipulation of the internal contradictions, inconsistencies, and ambiguities within the universe of relatively determinate elements" (p. 233). For Moore, determining and fixing are processes, not permanent states. The seemingly fixed is really the continuously renewed. This model assumes that social reality is "fluid and indeterminate," although regularizing processes continually transform it into organized or systematic forms. These, however, never completely lose their indeterminacy, and can slip back into an ambiguous or dismembered condition unless vigilantly attended. Moore calls the processes in which persons "arrange their immediate situations (and/or express their feelings and conceptions) by exploiting the indeterminacies of the situations or by generating such indeterminacy or by reinterpreting or redefining the rules or relationships, 'processes of situational adjustment' " (pp. 234–5). A major advance made by Moore in process theory is her proposal that processes of regularization and processes of situational adjustment "may each have the effect of stabilizing *or* changing an existing social situation or order." Both should be taken into account whenever the complex relationships between social life and the continuously renewed web of meanings which is culture are being analyzed. Both types of process contain within themselves the possibility of becoming their schematic opposites, for strategies used in situational adjustment, if often repeated, may become part of processes of regularization. Per contra, if new rules are made for every situation, such rules cannot be said to "regularize" and become elements of situational adjustment. The process of creating "legal fictions" may perhaps be regarded as mediating between processes of regularization and situational adjustment (Owen Barfield 1962:60 – 64).

A caveat should be interpolated here. It has sometimes been forgotten by those caught up in the first enthusiasm for processualism that process is intimately bound up with structure and that an adequate analysis of social life necessitates a rigorous consideration of the relation between them. Historical hindsight often reveals a diachronic profile, a temporal structure in events, but this structure cannot be understood in isolation from the series of synchronic profiles which compose the structure of a social field at every significant point of arrest of the time flow. Processual studies, as Moore has shown us, do not replace a research focus on regularity and consistency. They may, however, give us clues to the nature of forces of systemic maintenance even as they shed light on the countervailing forces of change. When I speak of *structure* here I am well aware of the phenomenological critique of structural-functionalism that it reifies social order and structure. Thus, I am in agreement with David Walsh's comment that "the requirement for a sociological analysis of the problematic character of social order is a suspension of the belief in the facticity of that order so as to concentrate on the routine practices and procedures of interpretation by which members accomplish it in interactional settings" (P. Filmer et al. 1972:21). But Walsh's view that what is important is not formal rules but the procedures by which members demonstrate that activities are in accordance with the rule and therefore intelligible seems to me to put too much stress on what Moore would call processes of regularization and not enough on the processes of situational adjustment, which in certain cases may bring about a shift from regularity to indeterminacy. There is much merit in the phenomenological sociologists' argument that in accounting for their actions in a rational way, group members are *making* those actions rational and thus making social life a coherent and comprehensible reality in a way that underlines the constructed nature of all reality—a view particularly developed in the work of Garfinkel, following Schutz (with Husserl shadowing both!). But scientists of "Man," anthropologists in the strict sense, must find "interesting" not only what Garfinkel ironically terms the "uninteresting" "commonplace" events and activities in social life, involving constant negotiations about typifying conduct in endless constructions of common sense, but also what is genuinely interesting, extraordinary, rare—"spare, original, strange." Perhaps anthropologists are in a better position than sociologists in this respect, for their fieldwork is conducted—or has been until recently—mostly among populations having sometimes widely different cultures from their own. The common sense of those whom they study from the outset seems extraordinary though ordinary enough to their subjects. Sociologists, on the other hand, share understandings with their subjects because they share their culture and have to work hard at transforming the taken-for-granted into a fascinating object of study. Anthropologists, sensitized from the outside to the alienness of many of the symbols and meanings shared by those they investigate, often go on to discover what is extraordinary by any reckoning. The profession of anthropology has in its archives so many variant organizations of commonplace everyday activities, every one of which no doubt seemingly exotic or bizarre as apprehended from the standpoint of the others, that it is led to probe beneath this surface layer of reflexivity for processes and mechanisms of a generally human type. French structuralism, whose leading anthropological exponent is Claude Lévi-Strauss, attempted this task. Bob Scholte has succinctly summarized Lévi-Strauss's argument: "conscious, empirical, and ethnographic phenomena are assumed to be the concrete and comparable realizations of unconscious, structural, and ethnological systems. These, in turn, are said to be the results of neurological, cybernetic, and physico-chemical universals. Not only does structuralism as a discipline stand or fall on the basis of this premise, but it also provides the paradigmatic closure for the enterprise as a whole: an encompassing movement from the empirical description of ethnographic models on to their final reduction to unconscious, comparable, and universal structures" (Bob Scholte 1973:680).

Two comments may be made here. First, Lévi-Strauss's dates are drawn from completed texts such as myths and culinary recipes. Second, the neurological and physicochemical bases of human behavior are clearly not exhausted by genetically fixed enduring neuronal pathways but have a high potential for innovative behavior. Even if there are inherited genetic structures of cognition, categories or engrams, it is not impossible that at levels of mentality at least as deep there is a capacity for plastic, adaptive, and manipulative behavior in response to changing circumstance. In other words, processual potential may be preconstituted in the physicochemical infrastructure. In any event both structural and processual foundations in biology remain as yet unverified. I wish only to make the point that we are not here dealing with a behavioral surface crawling with processes contrasted with deep unconscious structures. Indeed, it might be possible to reverse the order of depth and regard the structures inferable in collections of myths and kindred phenomena as convenient means of ordering collective experiences arising from the contestation of deep processes of regularization and situational adjustment. Phenomenologists might even argue that structural arrangements (binary logic, split representation, mediation, and the rest) provide boundary conditions for framing that which actors take for granted, "typified conceptions that make up the actor's stock of knowledge, ecological settings, common linguistic usage, and biophysical conditions" (A. Cicourel, see Filmer et al. 1972:21). From this perspective the structural oppositions and transformations detected by Lévi-Strauss in the "concrete logic" of mythical narratives may not so much provide clues to fundamental cognitive constraints as represent a convenient and simplistic coding of items of common sense knowledge. We must look elsewhere for intimations of human depth. It is here that we must turn once more to the investigation of processes, but now to processes heavily invested with cultural symbols, particularly those of ritual, drama, and other powerful performative genres.

Van Gennep was the first scholar who perceived that the processual form of ritual epitomized the general experience in traditional society that social life was a sequence of movements in space-time, involving a series of changes of pragmatic activity and a succession of transitions in state and status for individuals and culturally recognized groups and categories. Certainly he was ahead of his time; other investigative procedures had to be developed before his discovery could become the foundation of salient hypotheses. He might be compared with Hero of Alexandria, who described the first known steam engine in 120 B.C. Unlike James Watts's model nineteen hundred years later it performed no useful work, merely causing a globe to whirl, but not a world of invention to turn! Van Gennep, a folklorist, had what he considered an almost mystical inspiration as he attempted to elicit the processual structure of two types of rite: those which mark, and, in indigenous thought, bring about the passage of an individual or social category from one cultural state or social status to another in the course of his, her, or their life cycle; and those which mark culturally recognized points in the passage of time (first fruits, harvest, mid-summer, new year, new moon, solstice, or equinox). He found that *rites de passage*, viewed cross-culturally, had three principal stages: rites of separation, margin (or *limen* = threshold), and reaggregation. The duration and complexity of these stages varied according to type of rite, though initiatory rites tended to have a protracted liminal stage. Max Gluckman has taken van Gennep to task for stressing the mechanisms of ritual rather than the role which "whole ceremonies and specific rites play in the ordering and reordering of social relations" (Gluckman 1962:4). However, descriptive social anthropology had not in van Gennep's time provided the holistic characterization of social systems which would have made this possible, whereas the coolness displayed by Durkheim and his school to van Gennep's work must have discouraged van Gennep from attempting to relate his processual discovery to the early structural-functionalist formulations of the *Année sociologique* group. American scholars were among the first to note the theoretical significance of van Gennep's discovery. As early as 1942 E. D. Chappell and C. S. Coon (1942) had attempted to discuss his analysis of rites of passage in a framework of equilibrium-maintenance theory, and had added a fourth category, "rites of intensification," which had as their main goal the strengthening of group unity. J. W. Whiting and I. L. Child (1953), Frank W. Young (1965), and Solon T. Kimball (1960), are among those scholars who have in recent years seen the relevance of van Gennep's formulation for their work in varied fields. Kimball has noted how van Gennep went beyond his analysis of the triadic processual structure of rites of passage "to an interpretation of their significance for the explanation of the continuing nature of life." Van Gennep, continues Kimball, believed that rites of passage with their symbolic representation of death and rebirth illustrate "the principles of regenerative renewal required by any society" (Kimball 1968:113). The present author, stimulated during his fieldwork by Henri Junod's use of van Gennep's interpretative apparatus for understanding Thonga ritual (Junod 1962 [1912–13]), came to see that the liminal stage was of crucial importance with regard to this process of regenerative renewal. Indeed, van Gennep sometimes called the three stages "preliminal, liminal, and postliminal," indicating that importance. But he never followed up the implications of his discovery of the liminal beyond mentioning that when individuals or groups are in a liminal state of suspension, separated from their previous condition, and not yet incorporated into their new one, they present a threat to themselves and to the entire group, requiring their segregation from quotidian life in a milieu hedged around by ritual interdictions. In 1963, while awaiting a visa to live in America, suspended between cultural worlds, I wrote a paper, later to be published in the *Proceedings of the American Ethnological Society for 1964*, whose title expresses what for me is the distinctive feature of liminality: "Betwixt and Between: The Liminal Period in *Rites de Passage*" (1964). "Liminars," who may be initiands or novices in passage from one sociocultural state and status to another, or even whole populations undergoing transition from one quadrant of the solar year to another in a great public ceremony, are "neither here nor there"; they are betwixt and between the positions assigned and arrayed by law, custom, convention, and ceremonial. Van Gennep pointed to the many symbols of birth, death, and rebirth found in the liminal stage in many societies and religions. But for me the essence of liminality is to be found in its release from normal constraints, making possible the deconstruction of the "uninteresting" constructions of common sense, the "meaningfulness of ordinary life," discussed by phenomenological sociologists, into cultural units which may then be reconstructed in novel ways, some of them bizarre to the point of monstrosity (from the actors' own "emic" perspective). Liminality is the domain of the "interesting," or of "uncommon sense." This is not to say that it is totally unconstrained, for insofar as it represents a definite stage in the passage of an initiand from status A to status B in a ritual belonging to a traditional system or sequence of rituals, liminality must bear some traces of its antecedent and subsequent stages. To use Robert Merton's terms, some symbols must accord with the "manifest" purposes of the ritual (to transform a boy into a man, a girl into a woman, a dead person into an ancestral spirit, etc.). But others have the "latent" capacity to elicit creative and innovative responses from the liminars and their instructors. The study of masks and costumes in African and Melanesian initiation rituals, whether of puberty or into secret societies, demonstrates the imaginative potential unlocked by liminality, for maskers (representing deities, arch-ancestors, territorial guardian spirits, or other supernaturals) typically appear in liminal sites sequestered from mundane life. Among the Ndembu of Zambia, for example, the *makishi*, masked figures, said to be ancient ancestors, of awesome shape and power, are believed by boy novices secluded in the bush camps during the *Mukanda* rites to spring from the blood-soaked site in the deep bush where they had recently been circumcised. The woodcarvers who create the masks, though they portray a limited range of types (the Foolish Young Woman, the Crazy One, the Wise Old Chief, the Fertility Binder, etc.), display a wide range of personal aesthetic initiative in generating variant forms.

In other words, there is an aspect of play in liminality. Huizinga's *Homo Ludens* (1955 [1938]) has sensitized anthropological thought to the play element in the construction and negotiation of meaning in culture, by his scrutiny of all kinds of playing from children's games to the dialectic of philosophy and the judicial process. After him, play is a serious business! Not all play, of course, is reserved, in any society, for liminal occasions in the strict van Gennepian sense of ritual stages. In tribal societies, children and adults play games in nonritual, leisure contexts. But the serious games which involve the play of ideas and the manufacture of religiously important symbolic forms and designs (icons, figurines, masks, sand-paintings, murals in sacred caves, statues, effigies, pottery emblems, and the like) are often, in traditional societies, reserved for authentically liminal times and places. In "Betwixt and Between" I invoked William

James's "law of dissociation" to clarify the problem of liminal monsters—so often presented through different media to initiands. James argued that when *a* and *b* occurred together as parts of the same total object, without being discriminated, the occurrence of one of these, *a*, in a new combination, *ax*, favors the discrimination of *a, b,* and *x* from one another. As William James himself put it in his *Principles of Psychology:* "What is associated now with one thing and now with another, tends to become dissociated from either, and to grow into an object of abstract contemplation by the mind. One might call this the law of dissociation by varying concomitants" (1918 [1890]:506). Liminal monsters and dragons are compounded from various *discriminata*, each of them originally an element in the common sense construction of social reality. In a sense, they have the pedagogical function of stimulating the liminars' powers of analysis and revealing to them the building blocks from which their hitherto taken-for-granted world has been constructed. But in another way they reveal the freedom, the indeterminacy underlying all culturally constructed worlds, the free play of mankind's cognitive and imaginative capacities. Synthesis, as well as analysis, is encouraged by monster construction! In many cultures, liminality is often the scene for immolative action which demonstrates, usually subverbally, this innovative freedom. Symbolic structures, elaborately contrived, are exhibited to liminars at most sacred episodes in the marginal rites, and are then, despite the time and labor taken to construct them, destroyed. Shakespeare's "cloud-capped palaces," as his master of liminality, Prospero, declared, "leave not a rack behind." The fabrications of liminality, being free from the pragmatics of the common sense world, are "baseless fabrics of this vision"—like *The Tempest* itself. Yet the products of ritual and dramatic ritual are surely not ineffectual—at least they survive in ways not altogether to be expected. How, then, should they be assessed in the terms of sociocultural science?

Let me advert to the ecological anthropological concept of resilience mentioned above (A. P. Vayda and B. J. McCay 1975:4). This holds that ecological systems (including those ordered by culture) survive "in so far as they have evolved tactics to keep the domain of stability, or resilience, broad enough to absorb the consequences of change." Here we are not only once more in the presence of the constant negotiation of meanings of the phenomenological anthropologists, and the mutually modifying processes of regularization and situational adjustment elicited by Sally Moore, but we begin to see the evolutionary, and, indeed, mere survival, value of the cultural carving out by negotiation, over the ages of sapient development, of ritualized spaces and times, given over as most sacred, privileged, and inviolable moments, to the manufacture of models for behavior and conduct, even if the cost is oftentimes the production of weird and extravagant forms. Evolutionary theory, since Darwin, has always stressed the importance of variability, as it permits a given species to adapt to changing conditions; and selection, at the zoological level, is often for variability rather than for homogeneity, which demands a single limited environment. Anthropologists such as Malinowski and Lévi-Strauss have always found the distinction between nature and culture a useful one, and I share their conviction. I see liminality, in tribal societies, even when they have inhabited a single ecological environment for a long time by any measure, as the provision of a cultural means of generating variability, as well as of ensuring the continuity of proved values and norms. This is done sometimes by mirror inversion of mundane life, so that liminars become the simple antitheses of their antecedent secular "selves" (the bundle of roles occupied preritually). Thus, in many puberty rites boys are invested symbolically with feminine attributes, and girls with masculine traits, on the way from juniority to seniority in social classification, or political inferiors may be liminally endowed with the marks of political authority (see Turner 1969 for examples). With increasing frequency, however, inversion gives way, as societies increase in scale and complexity, to the liminal generation of many alternative models.

The primacy of play does not go uncontested, especially in societies that have been long in one place and have had time to consolidate their common sense structures into plausible semblances of "natural systems." Here, in the dangerous realm of challenge to all established jural-political, kinship, and other structures, it is necessary, above all, to maintain, even through the liminal stage, a strong thread of "common sense-ically" constructed order. This is often represented by *sacra*, carefully concealed and seldom revealed symbols and configurations of symbols, which are exposed only on rare liminal occasions. They represent the axiomatic rules and definitions of the culture—usually one that has been well consolidated by continuous occupancy of a single territory over a goodly period of time. In such relatively homogeneous cultural groups where understandings are widely and deeply shared, the liminal periods of ritual have episodes in which the axioms and principles which govern mundane life have solemn representation in myths and symbols which do not contravene or criticize the mundane order (as ludic constructions often do) but present it as based in the primordial cosmogonic process. Here ritual is less play than work, and the culture that has such liminality tends to be nonreflexive as well as nonadaptive. Where religious systems and their rituals are backed by superior political force and power they tend to lose their ludic innovativeness and variability, for the success of a single form tends to reduce the need to "carry" a store of alternative forms. That this may be shortsighted is seldom recognized, for climatic, geological, or historical processes may bring disasters and traumas for which the single-model ritual system, represented by a set of paradigmatic myths and their ritual translation into action, may provide inadequate models for mental and physical response. What, paradoxically, may be more functional is a culture which carries with it over time a store of seemingly nonfunctional, even ridiculous liminal schemata for behavior, in evolutionary terms, a repertoire of variant deep cultural models, one of which may prove to be adaptive in drastically changed ecological and biotic conditions. It may even be said that when structure, in the French cognitive sense, penetrates the partially ludic space-time of liminality, imposing on it a "grammar and lexicon" of rules found to be successful in mundane, extraritual contexts, the society thus beset has so much the less adaptive resilience.

Another feature of liminality is that it may be said to contain at least one, and probably more than one, "metalanguage." The term is Gregory Bateson's (1972), a thinker who, if it can so be claimed for anyone, has given the social sciences a new way of talking about the phenomena and processes we study. Bateson talks about "a play frame which is involved in the evaluation of the messages which it contains" (1972:188). He argues that in human systems of communication, and also in many nonhuman, zoological systems, certain signals are emitted in relations among actors, which frame the subsequent proceedings for a variable period of time, in which communication is not direct but which is about the forms of communication used in the day-to-day processes of ensuring survival—in mankind's case, the productive relations and the forms of social control guaranteeing their orderliness and relative freedom from conflict. Metacommunication is self-conscious, but plurally and cumulatively self-conscious. It is the way a population or group evaluates its own routine behaviors. Because it is collective and cumulative it perhaps lacks the trenchancy of individual commentary, but compensates by its positing of generic thought against generic experience. Because it represents the reflexivity of many it has perforce to clothe itself in multivocal ("susceptible of many meanings") symbols, and against the univocal signs in which the logical thought of gifted individual philosophers is expressed. We have the plural self-consciousness of men experiencing and thinking together as against the singular self-consciousness of a master craftsman of cognitive reflexivity. Plurality brings feeling and willing (*orexis*) into the act. One might even argue that the founders of major religions (whose adherents still can be counted in hundreds of millions, "objectively"—hence "scientifically"—speaking) occupied a medial position between tribal (and plural) reflexivity and industrial (and singular) reflexivity (as represented by the Western European thinkers), in that they spoke for collectivities and their common sense values, and, at the same time, provided their critique; whereas the Western philosophical tradition, losing much of the plural, social component, spoke for the individual, cognitively liberated though orectically alienated, as against the "damned compact majorities" of Ibsen's Dr. Stockman in *An Enemy of the People*.

If liminality in tribal, traditional ritual is a mode of plural, reflexive, often ludic metacommunication (though containing the countervailing processes and symbols of system maintenance), we have to ask the question—whether it can be satisfactorily answered or not is another set of questions for investigation—what are the functional equivalents of liminality in complex societies, high on the dimensions of scale and complexity, with ever increasing division of labor and specialization of crafts and professions, and where the concept of the individual as against the mass is positively evaluated?

Before we can answer this question we might consider the distinction between indicative and subjunctive moods of verbs—those classes of words expressing action, existence, or occurrence (for we are concerned with the processual aspects of nature and culture). The indicative mood commonly designates the expression of an act, state, or occurrence as "actual"; it asks questions of "fact"—in terms of the definitions of tested facts acceptable in the common sense world of a given human population. Where the subjunctive mood is found, it tends to express desire, hypothesis, supposition, possibility: it may or might be so. In its expressive range it embraces both cognitive possibilities ("hypotheses" = unproved theories or propositions tentatively accepted to explain certain facts or relations) and emotional ones (though here the optative mood might be a better appellation, because it expresses wish or desire). Enacted fantasies, such as ritual and carnival disguises, probably belong here. At any rate one might classify ordinary, quotidian life as indicative, even much of ceremonial or ritual. But one would have to reckon liminal processes subjunctive or optative, for they represent *alternatives* to the positive systems of economic, legal, and political action operating in everyday life. But if the indicative is "bread," mankind "does not live by bread alone." It seems that the dialectic between *is* and *may be*, culturally elaborated into the distinction between pre- and post-liminal, on the one hand, and liminal, on the other, forms a continuous human social process, involving biological, ecological, and sociocultural factors, and made reflexive by the search for meaning raised above common sense to a higher power.

The great social thinkers have indicated a drift, trend, or direction in cultural history, which, whether it may be called progressive or regressive, at any rate indicates a series of linear developments. Henry Maine hypothesized a modal shift "from status to contract," Durkheim a move from "mechanical" to "organic" solidarity; Marx and Engels postulated a stage of "primitive communism" subverted by the development of productive forces which generated class oppositions around the issue of property.

Private property, in its turn, generated the notion of individuality and elevated it to philosophical respectability, even as it assured the impoverishment and alienation of the masses of mankind—who had no property other than their "labor-power" to put to use in earning a living. They predicted, in Hegelian fashion, an abolition of private property and class ownership of the means of production by a regenerated communism among the propertyless masses, organized ironically—and dialectically—by the very means of production from which the ruling classes derived their profits, which, directed by an elite cognizant of the laws of historical development, that is, the Communist Party, would overthrow the instruments of class hegemony, army and police forces, and restore at a higher material level the primordial communism which was mankind's best pre-class state.

Major social thinkers have posited a developmental sequence in types of sociocultural systems in which emphasis shifts from the collectivity as the effective moral unit to the individual. This is paralleled by a growing stress on achieved as against ascriptive status, and by an ever more precise division of labor in the domains of economics and social control. The obligatory component in social relationship yields to the optional or voluntaristic, status gives way to contract. Corporate groups constructed on the model of kin ties are replaced as effective social centers of action by associations of those having like interests. Rational and bureaucratic organization lords it over groups bonded by ties to locality. The city prevails over the rural hinterland. Industrialization has decisively split work from leisure by its "clocking in and out" devices and has reserved play for the leisure sphere wherein work is complemented or rewarded (J. Dumazedier 1962). Ritual which, particularly in its liminal stage, contained both work and play (many tribal societies speak of ritual activity as work, for ceremonies are part of the ongoing process of the whole group) now becomes a leisure activity. Moreover, its liturgical structures accentuate the solemn and attenuate the festal aspects, as codes for moral behavior become increasingly internalized as "conscience." When it loses its capacity to play with ideas, symbols, and meanings, when it loses its cultural evolutionary resilience, ritual ceases to be an effective metalanguage or an agency of collective reflexivity.

Some anthropologists, and scholars in adjacent fields, influenced by developments in adjacent disciplines, such as history and literary criticism, are beginning to turn their attention to both the folk and high culture of complex societies and civilizations (C. Geertz, M. Douglas, R. Firth, J. Peacock, B. Myerhoff, and R. Grimes spring readily to mind). In these they find that the obligatory rituals and ritualized bonds characteristic of complex, rurally based civilizations have been supplanted by city-based associational and professional linkages. The dismemberment of ritual has, however, proved the opportunity of theater in the high culture and carnival at the folk level. A multiplicity of desacralized performative genres have assumed, prismatically, the task of plural cultural reflexivity. The *sparagmos* (dismemberment) of major liturgical systems, or, in some cases, their relegation to the periphery of the social process, has resulted in the genesis and elaboration of esthetic media, each of which takes as its point of departure a component subgenre of traditional ritual. Thus the dramatic scenario—frequently the enactment of a sacred narrative—now becomes a performative mode sui generis breeding a multiplicity of plots most of which are far from sacred! Song, dance, graphic and pictural representation, these and more, broken loose from their ritual integument, become the seeds of concert music, ballet, literature, and painting. If ritual might be compared to a mirror for mankind, its conversion into a multiplicity of performative arts gives us a hall of magic mirrors, each reflecting the reflections of the others, and each representing not a simple inversion of mundane reality, but its systematic magnification and distortion, the ensemble composing a reflexive metacommentary on society and history as they concern the natural and constructed needs of humankind under given conditions of time and place.

The fragmentation of a collective liturgical work, such as ritual, paves the way for the labeling of specific esthetic works as the production of individuals. But, in fact, all performative genres demand an audience even as they abandon a congregation. Most of them, too, incarnate their plots or scores in the synchronized actions of players. It is only formally that these esthetic progeny of ritual may be described as individual creations. Even such forms as the novel involve a publishing process and a reading process, both of which have collective and initiatory features. A great opportunity is opening up for scholars in both social sciences and humanities who are interested in the reflexive or dialectical relationship between common sense processes in the "getting and spending" (biocultural-ecological) dimensions of sociocultural life and the popular and high performative genres which continually scrutinize, criticize, subvert, uphold, and attempt to modify the behavior of the personnel, their values, activities and relationships, centrally concerned with the maintenance and management of those processes; or which make statements, in forms at least as bizarre as those of tribal liminality, about the quality of life in the societies they monitor under the guise of "entertainment"—a term which literally means "holding between," that is, "liminalizing." Instead of studying socioeconomic processes in isolation from these "magic mirrors," or dramatic types as texts in vacuo, it is possible to envision a creative collaboration among literary critics, anthropologists, sociologists, historians, art historians, philosophers, historians of religion, and other kinds of scholars, on the shared field of the relationship, say, between Noh,

Kabuki, Kyogen, Bunraku, and other Japanese theatrical genres, and the social and cultural history of Japan at the time of genesis and in the successive periods of development and decline of these genres—always with the stress on the reciprocal relationship between social process and dramatic medium under varying conditions of time and place. A formidable undertaking? But a great one. The same might be said of dynamic studies of Elizabethan and Stuart drama, Greek high and low comedy, the commedia dell'arte, the theater of the absurd, and the theater of cruelty, not merely in sociocultural context but in live reflexive relationship to the fluctuant problems of their times—in terms of competent, dynamic sociological and anthropological analysis, both synchronic and diachronic.

In a recent appraisal of modern social anthropology Sir Raymond Firth has commented on its inward-turning disposition in the sense that modern anthropology is concerned not solely with the behavior of the populations investigated but mainly with their models for perceiving and interpreting their materials and generating their behavior, with their modes of thought, not modes of action (1975:8). The position that I am presenting, on the contrary, stresses attention to the relationship between modes of thought and of action. Furthermore, if models are to be considered, I would draw on recent work on the role of metaphor in assigning meaning to social behavior, conduct, and action, and argue that, at least implicitly, many sociocultural systems, insofar as they may be considered to be systems, are oriented, through the cumulative effect of their performative genres, to what I have called *root paradigms*. These are not merely cognitive clusters of rules from which many kinds of social actions can be generated, but represent consciously recognized (though only on occasions of raised consciousness) cultural models of an allusive, metaphorical kind, cognitively delimited, emotionally loaded, and ethically impelled, so as to give form to action in publicly critical circumstances. Such root paradigms are often based on generally accepted narratives of climaxes in the careers of religious or political leaders, having thus an existential rather than merely morally edifying character, and often emphasize the primacy of social over individual goals when choices appear between these in extreme situations, to the point of endorsing personal sacrifice for others. Key decisions in the lives of religious founders, such as Gautama, Moses, Jesus, and Mohammed, and of political leaders such as Lenin and Gandhi, are portrayed as exemplary through a wide range of performative genres, and form an almost engrammatic component of socialization. Biocultural anthropologists might regard this stress on sacrifice of self for society as possessing survival value at the transcultural species level. When we shift our perspective to that of the performative genres, we may see these paradigmatic acts in terms of such "loaded" values as supreme love, compassion, and heroism. It may be that our future task as scientists of the human condition is to establish a set of concepts occupying a liminal ground between objective estimation of values promoting species survival and subjective response to stirring exemplifications of self-sacrifice for group survival.

If one is to be as bold as the editor of *Daedalus* would have us in assessing whether or not breakthroughs have happened in anthropology, one would have to record that the potentiality for a major breakthrough exists today. It may be that such a breakthrough is possible only in the United States, for British, French, and other European and third world anthropology, partly through the limited number of their practitioners, tend to be more homogeneous and committed to the pursuit of agreed-upon goals—structuralism and neo-Marxism in France, sophisticated structural-functionalism and conflict theory in Britain, and the political evaluation of all established metropolitan theories in the Third World. It is only in the United States that a "thousand flowers" have truly blossomed in a rigorous theoretical way, because of the huge size and cognitive individualism of the subcontinent, where each major department may be likened to an autonomous Hellenic city state—where each, through the diaspora of its graduates, has a nimbus of satellites, both individuals and groups. The outcome has been that a number of perspectives on the human condition, each technically and theoretically of excellent quality, have sprung up in virtual independence of one another. One thinks at once of cultural anthropology, social anthropology, symbolic anthropology, ecological anthropology, biocultural anthropology, phenomenological anthropology, structuralist anthropology, biocultural ecology, legal and political anthropologies, plus the many hybridizations between anthropology and other scholarly approaches: anthropological linguistics and ethnography of speaking; the uses of systems theory in archeological research; Marxist approaches in anthropology; applications of the sociology of knowledge to anthropological data; and others.

My suggestion is that, instead of working in blinkers, anthropologists and scholars in adjacent disciplines interested in cross-cultural problems should make an earnest (and "ludic") attempt at mutual empathy—earnest in the sense that the disciplines mentioned above, and significant others, might be treated at least as a unified field whose unity might have something to do with the systems theory view that there are systems and systemic relations so fundamental that they occur in many different living and even inorganic phenomena. This would not be to reduce the distinctive features of the disciplines entering into the field to some bland interactional average, but would respect the natural independence of each within their dynamic interdependence. It would also represent a struggle against disciplinary chauvinism. For example, vulgar Marxists and others who have placed their faith in the primacy of economic forces and relations, could not imperialistically claim that ways of thinking about and appreciating man's relationship to the cosmos and his fellows were, by definition, a transmitted load of "false consciousness"—false at least until the defeat of all adversaries of the proletariat. Rather, they should hold the evaluation of the nature and magnitude of productive forces and the conflicting classes resulting from them as at least as problematic as "ideology." Why so much, so fast, and so wastefully employed? The perspectival view from the infrastructure may be at least as false as any superstructural cosmology. What is required is a firm, scholarly, yet imaginative grasp of the total phenomena produced by Man alive and Woman alive. It is strange that both the Hegelian and Marxist logics should conceptualize dialectic so uncompromisingly from the positive and structuralist position of thesis. It is not so much a question of the content of a process of self-transformation being made up of opposing factors or forces as of any cognitive or jurally normative structuration of human processes and relationships encountering, as the indicative confronts the subjunctive mood in verbs, a virtually unlimited range of alternative ways of doing things or relating people. Limits may be set, of course, by biotic or ecological and often by historical conditions. But for the dialectical negation we should perhaps substitute liminality, a plurality of alternatives rather than the reversal or inversion of the antecedent condition. Moreover, the motor of historical dialectic is not so much a matter of quantitive increments cumulating to a qualitative change as deliberate formulations of human thought and imagination—often made in liminal situations, such as exile, prison, or even in an "ivory tower"—first presenting, and then perhaps backed up by organized action, a new vision. Liminality is a major source of change rather than the embodiment of a logical antithesis. Science is not mocked—but then neither is art. If what has been durably regarded as the "interesting" by the informed opinion of thousands of years of human attention cannot be incorporated into the serious study of mankind, then that study is surely in the hands of the "philistines"—the "bourgeois and the bolshevik" of D. H. Lawrence—who were so intent on securing by force general assent to their opposed views on the nature of material property (one said "private" should be the basic label, the other "public") that the richness and subtlety of human "immaterial" culture (especially, one might add, its liminal constructions) escaped this Tweedledum-and-Tweedledee pair of dedicated materialists.

What is needed in anthropology is work under the aegis of a *wider orbit of recovered law* in which specialists in its hitherto separate subdisciplines, biological, ecological, social, and cultural anthropology, utilize systems theory to integrate their finds and research procedures in a single field, stress the primacy of processual approaches, incorporate what phenomenologists have to say about the negotiation of meaning, and remain aware of the powerful role of sociocultural liminality in providing conditions for reflection, criticism, rapid socialization, the postulation of variant models of and for conduct and social organization, and the reformulation of cosmologies religious and scientific.

Signs of renewed interest in processual and systems theory abound in the recent literature. If one glances through the articles in *Annual Review of Anthropology* for 1975 one finds Jane F. Collier writing: "Legal processes are social processes. Law . . . is an aspect of ongoing social life," and so forth, and her article is peppered with items of "process" vocabulary and with references to the legal handling of conflict as framed by extended-case analysis (1975:121). E. A. Hoebel in the United States (1954), following his classical use of the case method (Llewellyn and Hoebel 1941), and Max Gluckman in Britain (1955a) may be said to have been among the pioneers of processual analysis through their studies of law as social process, as Collier recognizes. Fred T. Plog in "Systems Theory in Archeological Research" shows how processual thought is influencing the new archeology where it is intrinsically linked to general systems theory: "The interest in general systems theory in archeology has been expressed primarily by 'processual archeologists' and has been a component of the 'systemic approach' that these archeologists have advocated" (1975:207).

A. P. Vayda and B. J. McCay, in their essay "New Directions in Ecology and Ecological Anthropology" (1975:298–99) in effect support Sally Moore's view that processes of regularization, processes of adjustment, and the factor of indeterminacy must be taken into account in studying sociocultural populations, when they attempt to rescue the notion of *homeostasis* from its previous association with concepts of static equilibria and unchanging systems. They cite Slobodkin as emphasizing that "some properties of homeostatic systems must at times change so as to maintain other properties that are important for staying in the existential game—. . . e.g. resilience and what might be described as flexible enough to change in response to whatever hazards and perturbations come along" (p. 299). Systems theory, in fact, can be modified to handle the irruption of sudden unprecedented changes, making it processually viable and disencumbering it from those structural-functional assumptions which metaphorized sociocultural systems either as organisms or machines.

The present author has for some time tried to analyze ritual processually in a number of settings, ranging from African traditional societies to medieval and modern pilgrimages in several universalistic religions. Ritual studies led him into the analysis of ritual symbols and, later, of social symbols in general. This type of investigation, which is sometimes called *processual symbolic analysis*, is concerned with the interpretation of the meaning of symbols considered as dynamic systems of signifiers, signifieds, and changing modes of signification in temporal sociocultural processes (Turner 1975b). Here the focus is meaningful performance as well as underlying competence. Ritual is a transformative performance revealing major classifications, categories, and contradictions of cultural processes. It is not, in essence, as is commonly supposed in Western culture, a prop for social conservatism whose symbols merely condense cherished cultural values, though it may, under certain conditions, take on this role. Rather does it hold the generative source of culture and structure, particularly in its liminal stage. Hence, ritual is by definition associated with social transitions, whereas ceremony is linked with social states and statuses. Ritual symbols, in processual analysis, are regarded as the smallest units of ritual behavior, whether object, activity, relationship, word, gesture, or spatial arrangement in a ritual situation (Turner 1967:19). They are factors in social action, associated with collective ends and means, whether explicitly formulated or not (Turner 1968:269).

Because the analytical frame is processual and embeds meaning in contexts of situation, definitions assigned to terms do not always coincide with those made by linguists and cognitive structuralists. Thus symbol is distinguished from sign both by the multiplicity (multivocality, polysemy) of its signifieds, and by the nature of its signification. In symbols there is always some kind of likeness (metaphoric/metonymic) posited by the framing culture between signifier (symbol-vehicle) and signified(s); in signs there need be no likeness. Signs are almost always organized in "closed" systems, whereas symbols, particularly dominant symbols (which preside over or anchor entire ritual processes), are semantically "open." The meaning is not absolutely fixed, nor is it necessarily the same for everyone who agrees that a particular signifier ("outward form") has symbolic meaning. New signifieds can be added by collective fiat to old signifiers. Moreover, individuals may add personal meaning to a symbol's public meaning, either by utilizing one of its standardized modes of association to bring new concepts within its semantic orbit (metaphorical reconstruction) or by including it within a complex of initially private fantasies. Such private constructions may become part of public hermeneutics or standardized interpretations provided that the semantic manipulator has sufficient power, authority, prestige, or legitimacy (e.g., he may be a shaman, prophet, chief, or priest) to make his interpretation stick. Political symbols have been analyzed in similar terms by A. Cohen (1974), R. Firth (1973), A. Legesse (1973), and V. Turner (1974), among others.

The anthropological study of symbolic forms and processes and the functions of symbolism has generally thrived in the past decade. Where it has been influenced by linguistics or structuralism the stress has been on the eliciting of abstract systems of symbols and meanings from cultural "products" (myths, kinship nomenclatures, iconographic forms, ethnotaxonomies, texts on customs drawn from native informants by questionnaires, etc.). Processualism, on the other hand, demands a kind of fieldwork in which the investigator becomes involved with central sociocultural processes. He recognizes his own role in social interaction with his informants and tries to account for the biases this may impart to his subsequent analyses. Symbolic analysis here rests on data generated in the heat of action in ritual, legal, formal, informal, interpersonal, domestic, ludic, solemn, and so forth, processes to which the anthropologist has become party and privy. Such data are quite different from those obtained by a stance of detachment. This stance is best for the taking of measurements (gardens, hut sizes) or the counting of heads (village census-taking), but worst for coming to an understanding (itself a process) of how actors perceive, generate, and negotiate meaning, using words and symbols. The present author has suggested that there are natural units of sociocultural process, which tend to have, like raw *rites de passage*, a temporal structure, with successive phases cumulating to at least a temporary resolution. The duration, internal structuring, and style of processual units are influenced by biotic, ecological, and cultural variables which must be empirically investigated in each population under survey. Extended case histories may contain a sequence of several processual units of different types, ranging from those which maximize cooperation to those which maximize conflict. Different kinds and intensities of social control functions are brought into play. What is required is a workable cross-cultural typology of processual units. For it is in the analysis of the "social drama" (1957:91 – 93) and the "social enterprise" (Firth 1964) that we recognize the merit of Sally Moore's comment: "An anthropology exclusively focused on clear regularities of form, symbol, and content, and their presumed congruence (whether 'structural,' 'cultural,' or 'processual' in orientation) is leaving out fundamental dimensions. The negotiable part of many real situations lies not only in the imperfect fit between the symbolic or formal level and the level of content, but also in the multiplicity of alternatives and meaning within each, which may accommodate a range of manipulation, interpretation, and choice. Individuals or groups may exaggerate the degree of order or the quality of indeterminacy in their situations for myriad reasons" (Moore 1975:233). How they do this, and why, can be ascertained only if the investigator has also become an actor in the field of living relationships. There are risks in not staying aloof, of course, but the acquisition of knowledge has always been beset by dangers, here physical as well as intellectual!

In conclusion, it may be permissible to indulge in a few personal opinions and speculations. Clearly, the great breakthrough or paradigm shift has not yet occurred, if by *paradigm* we mean, with Thomas Kuhn, "an accepted example of actual scientific practice—which includes law, theory, application and instrumentation together which provides the models from which spring coherent traditions of scientific research" (Kuhn 1962:10, 41). But there are signs of convergence among hitherto isolated subdisciples, as mentioned above. If these can be united in a single work, either by a single mind, or by a team of interdependent specialists, then the reflexivity among biological, ecological, social, and cultural anthropologists, systemically relating their concepts (and modifying them mutually in the process) in relation to a body of both phenomenologically and empirically generated data, may produce a paradigm comparable in its own way to those from which have sprung coherent traditions of natural science research. But to achieve this goal anthropologists will have to sink certain unimportant structural differences, and processually achieve a relationship of *communitas* with one another, a relational quality of full unmediated communication, even communion, between definite and determinate identities. Such *communitas* would essentially be a liminal phenomenon, consisting of a blend of humility and comradeship—such as one sees among liminars in the ritual process in simple societies "on the edge of the world."

PART TWO

Performance and Experience

8

The Anthropology of Performance

For years, I have dreamed of a liberated anthropology. By "liberated" I mean free from certain prejudices that have become distinctive features of the literary genre known as "anthropological works," whether these are field monographs, comparative studies, or textbooks. Such features have included: a systematic dehumanizing of the human subjects of study, regarding them as the bearers of an impersonal "culture," or wax to be imprinted with "cultural patterns," or as determined by social, cultural, or social psychological "forces," "variables," or "pressures" of various kinds, the primacy of which is still contested by different schools or coteries of anthropologists. Briefly, this genre apes natural scientific treatises in style and intention—treatises which reflect the thinking of that period of five centuries which in the West is known as the "modern era." The modern is now becoming part of the past. Arnold Toynbee coined the term "postmodern," Ihab Hassan has given it wide prominence, and a recent book, *Performance in Postmodern Culture* (1977) edited by the late Michel Benamou, attempts to give it greater specificity. I do not like these labels, but it is clear to me that there has been what Richard Palmer, (in an article in the Benamou volume, "Towards a Postmodern Hermeneutics of Performance"), called a "postmodern turn" taken in recent thinking which is having a liberating effect on anthropology, as on many other disciplines. Premodern, modern, postmodern—these are crude and inelegant terms for the naming of cultural eras of disparate duration. But they may give us a preliminary purchase on the data on performance which will form the staple of this essay.

Premodern represents a distillation or encapsulation of many worldviews and cosmologies before and, later, outside the specific emergence in Western consciousness, about five centuries ago, of the modern perspective. Indeed, the Swiss cultural historian Jean Gebser holds that it was, quite literally, the rise of perspective which, as Palmer writes, is "the key to modernity." He summarizes Gebser's argument as follows:

> Perspective spatializes the world; it orients the eye in relation to space in a new way . . . it represents a 'rationalization of sight' (William M. Ivins). . . . Perspective leads to the founding of mathematical geometry, which is the prerequisite for modern engineering and modern machinery . . . for steadily increasing naturalism in European pictoral representation (but also for its purely schematic and logical extensions) . . . both are due to the growth and spread of methods which have provided symbols, repeatable in invariant form, for representation of visual awareness, and a grammar of perspective which made it possible to establish logical relations not only within the system of symbols but between that system and the forms and locations of the objects that it symbolizes . . . the combination of the abstractedness of numbers as symbols that measure, with perspective, a way of relating those numbers as symbols to the visual world, leads to a sense of space as measured, as extending outward from a given point; ultimately the world is measurable—epitomized in Galileo's maxim, 'to measure everything measurable and to make what is not measurable capable of being measured' [this attitude is still common among anthropologists; thus George Spindler remarks in the book he edited, *The Making of Psychological Anthropology* (1978:197–98), we were taught: "if it happens you can count it"]. The spatialization of vision has metaphysical and epistemological implications . . . the overemphasis on space and extension divides the world into observing subject and alien material objects . . . words are seen as mere signs for the material objects in the world . . . time itself is perceived in spatialized terms . . . it is regarded as measurable, as a linear succession of present moments . . . the perspectival model makes man the measure and measurer of all things . . . technologized rationality harmonizes with the protestant ethic—God places his blessing on the individualistic, competitive person (implicitly male) who exercises restraint and represses desires in the interest of more 'rational' goals: power and control . . . History, perceived as a straight line that never circles back on itself, becomes the story of man's gradual self-improvement through the exercise of reason [Spindler 1978:22–25].

What Spindler drew attention to was the "modern" climate of thought in which my anthropological training took place. It was a climate in which academic disciplines had clearly defined boundaries which one transgressed at one's peril: boundary ambiguity was, in Mary Douglas' words, a form of pollution; much interdisciplinary work was regarded as an abomination. Within anthropology there was a tendency to represent social reality as stable and immutable, a harmonious configuration governed by mutually compatible and logically interrelated principles. There was a general preoccupation with consistency and congruence. And even though most anthropologists were aware that there generally are differences between ideal norms and real behavior, most of their models of society and culture tended to be based upon ideology rather than upon social reality, or to take into account the dialectical relationship between these. All this follows from the perception of reality in spatialized terms. So, too, did the study of statistical correlations between social and cultural variables such as we find in G. P. Murdock's *Social Structure* (1949). In all this work, as Sally Moore has pointed out in her book *Law as Process* (1978:36): "Whether ideology is seen as an expression of social cohesion, or as a symbolic expression of structure, whether it is seen as a design for a new structure or as a rationalization for control of power and property, the analysis is made in terms of *fit*" (italics mine).

During my fieldwork I became disillusioned with the fashionable stress on fit and congruence, shared by both functionalism and different types of structuralism. I came to see a social system or "field" rather as a set of loosely integrated processes, with some patterned aspects, some persistences of form, but controlled by discrepant principles of action expressed in rules of custom that are often situationally incompatible with one another. This view derived from the method of description and analysis which I came to call "social drama analysis." In fact this was thrust upon me by my experience as a field worker in the central African society of the Ndembu of Northwest Zambia. In various writings I have given examples of social dramas and their analysis. More to the point for this essay, since we will be dealing with the anthropology of performance, I would like to bring to your attention a man of the theater's discussion of my schema. He is Richard Schechner, professor of drama at New York University's School of the Arts, and director of The Performance Group, an avant-garde theater company. As he sees it (in the chapter "Towards a Poetics of Performance," *Essays on Performance Theory, 1970 – 1976*, pages 120 – 123): "Victor Turner analyses 'social dramas' using theatrical terminology to describe disharmonic or crisis situations. These situations—arguments, combats, rites of passage—are inherently dramatic because participants not only do things, they try *to show others what they are doing or have done*; actions take on a 'performed-for-an-audience' aspect. Erving Goffman takes a more directly scenographic approach in using the theatrical paradigm. He believes that all social interaction is staged—people prepare backstage, confront others while wearing masks and playing roles, use the main stage area for the performance of routines, and so on. For both Turner and Goffman, the basic human plot is the same: someone begins to move to a new place in the social order; this move is accomplished through ritual, or blocked; in either case a crisis arises because any change in status involves a readjustment of the entire scheme; this readjustment is effected ceremonially—that is, by means of theater." In my book, *Drama, Fields, and Metaphors* (pp. 37–41), I define social drama as units of aharmonic or disharmonic social process, arising in conflict situations (See also Chapter 9, pp. 215–221; Chapter 10, pp. 230–33; and Epilogue, pp. 291–92). Typically, they have four main phases of public action. These are: 1) *breach* of regular norm-governed social relations; 2) *crisis*, during which there is a tendency for the breach to widen. Each public crisis has what I now call liminal characteristics, since it is a threshold (*limen*) between more or less stable phases of the social process, but it is not usually a sacred limen, hedged around by taboos and thrust away from the centers of public life. On the contrary, it takes up its menacing stance in the forum itself, and, as it were, dares the representatives of order to grapple with it; 3) *redressive action* ranging from personal advice and informal mediation or arbitration to formal juridical and legal machinery, and, to resolve certain kinds of crisis or legitimate other modes of resolution, to the performance of public ritual. Redress, too, has its liminal features, its being "betwixt and between," and, as such, furnishes a distanced replication and critique of the events leading up to and composing the "crisis." This replication may be in the rational idiom of the judicial process, or in the metaphorical and symbolic idiom of a ritual process; 4) the final phase consists either of the *reintegration* of the disturbed social group, or of the social recognition and legitimation of *irreparable schism* between the contesting parties.

First let me comment on the difference between my use of the term "ritual" and the definitions of Schechner and Goffman. By and large they seem to mean by ritual a standardized unit act, which may be secular as well as sacred, while I mean the performance of a complex sequence of symbolic acts. Ritual for me, as Ronald Grimes puts it, is a "transformative performance revealing major classifications, categories, and contradictions of cultural processes." For Schechner, what I call "breach," the inaugurating event in a social drama, is always effected by a ritual or ritualized act or "move." There is some truth in this. For example, in the very first social drama I present in my book on Ndembu social process, *Schism and Continuity*, a series of social dramas focused on one individual ambitious of the power and influence that goes with the office of village headman, this protagonist, Sandombu, "dramatizes" to others in his effective sociocultural field that he is weary of waiting for the old headman, his mother's brother Kahali, to die, by ostentatiously refraining from giving him portions of meat appropriate to Kahali's status, age, and relationship after he had killed an antelope. This refusal to follow custom might be regarded as a ritualized act as well as a transgression of a custom with ritual implications, for the dividing of a slain animal implies the sharing of sacred substance held to constitute matrilineal kinship. The symbolism of blood has a strong correlation with matrilineal kinship, especially with the procreative aspect of motherhood, and there are many rituals connected both with matriliny and the hunting cults which contain symbols for blood. But I would prefer the terms "symbolic transgression"—which may also coincide with an actual transgression of custom, even of a legal prescription—to "ritual" in the frame of phase 1 (*Breach*) of a social drama.

What is more interesting to me than the definition of ritual is the connection established by Schechner between social drama and theater, and the use made of "the theatrical paradigm" by Goffman and myself. For Goffman, "all the world's a stage," the world of social interaction anyway, and is full of ritual acts. For me the dramaturgical phase begins when *crises* arise in the daily flow of social interaction. Thus, if daily living is a kind of theater, social drama is a kind of meta-theater, that is, a dramaturgical language about the language of ordinary role-playing and status-maintenance which constitutes communication in the quotidian social process. In other words, when actors in a social drama, in Schechner's words, "try to show others what they are doing or have done," they are acting consciously, exercising what Charles Hockett has found to be a feature peculiar to human speech, reflectiveness or reflexiveness, the ability to communicate about the communication system itself (Hockett 1960). This reflexivity is found not only in the eruptive phase of *crisis*, when persons exert their wills and unleash their emotions to achieve goals which until that time have remained hidden or may even have been unconscious—here reflexivity follows manifestation—but also in the cognitively dominant phase of redress, when the actions of the previous two phases become the subject matter for scrutiny within the frame provided by institutional forms and procedures—here reflexivity is present from the outset, whether the redressive machinery be characterized as legal, law-like, or ritual.

You must have noticed how Goffman, Schechner, and I constantly stress process and processual qualities: performance, movement, staging, plot, redressive action, crisis, schism, and reintegration. To my mind, this stress is the "postmodern turn" in anthropology, a turn foreshadowed in anthropological modernity perhaps, but never its central thrust. This turn involves the processualization of space, its temporalization, as against the spatialization for process or time, which we found to be of the essence of the modern.

Although there is a major difference between linguistic and anthropological definitions of performance, something of the change from modern to postmodern ways of thinking about sociocultural problems can be aptly illustrated by considering Edmund Leach's recent attempt to apply the linguist's vocabulary to matters anthropological in his article, "The Influence of Cultural Context on Non-Verbal Communication in Man" (Hinde 1977:321–22). Leach writes that "the anthropologist's concern is to delineate a framework of cultural *competence* in terms of which the individual's symbolic actions can be seen to make sense. We can only interpret individual *performance* in the light of what we have already inferred about competence, but in order to make our original inferences about competence we have to abstract a standardized pattern which is not necessarily immediately apparent in the data which are directly accessible to observation." It was Chomsky who introduced this competence-performance dichotomy, competence being mastery of a system of rules or regularities underlying that kind of language behavior which, for example, we call "speaking English." It was Dell Hymes who pointed out the hidden Neo-Platonism or Gnosticism in Chomsky's approach, which seems to regard performance as generally "a fallen state," a lapse from the ideal purity of systematic grammatical competence. This is clearly exemplified in J. Lyons' article "Human Language" in the same volume as Leach's essay just quoted. He is writing (p. 58) of three stages of "idealization" in "our identification of the raw data" of language-behavior. "First of all," he says, "we discount all 'slips of the tongue,' mispronunciations, hesitation pauses, stammering, stuttering, *etc.*; in short, everything that can be described as a 'performance phenomenon'." He then goes on to "discount" (p. 59) a certain amount of the "systematic variation between utterances that can be attributed to personal and sociocultural factors."

The "postmodern turn" would reverse this "cleansing" process of thought which moves from "performance errors and hesitation phenomena" through "personal and sociocultural factors" to the segregation of "sentences" from "utterances" by dubbing the latter "context dependent" (hence "impure") with respect both to their meaning and their grammatical structure. Performance, whether as speech behavior, the presentation of self in everyday life, stage drama, or social drama, would now move to the center of observation and hermeneutical attention. Postmodern theory would see in the very flaws, hesitations, personal factors, incomplete, elliptical, context-dependent, situational components of performance, clues to the very nature of human process itself, and would also perceive genuine novelty, creativeness, as able to emerge from the freedom of the performance situation, from what Durkheim (in his best moment) called social "effervescence," exemplified for him in the generation of new symbols and meanings by the public actions, the "performances," of the French Revolution. What was once considered "contaminated," "promiscuous," "impure" is becoming the focus of postmodern analytical attention.

With regard to the structure-process dichotomy mentioned earlier, which is similar, if not identical, to other oppositions made by anthropologists: ideal norms—real behavior; mechanical models—statistical models; structure—organization; ideology—action, and so forth, Sally Moore has many pertinent things to say in *Law as Process*.

She is aware that, as Murphy has argued, "It is the very incongruence of our conscious models, and guides for conduct to the phenomena of social life that makes that life possible" (Murphy 1971:240), but also insists that "order and repetition are not all illusion, nor all 'mere' ideology, nor all fictive scholarly models, but are observable [and I would add often measurable] on a behavioral level, as well as in fixed ideas" (p. 38). She proposes that social processes should be examined in terms of the interrelationship of three components: "the processes of *regularization*, the processes of *situational adjustment*, and the factor of *indeterminacy*" (p. 39). This is really a revolutionary move on Sally Moore's part for she is challenging the Idealist formulations of her prestigious contemporaries. Like Heraclitus she is insisting that the elements (in her case, the sociocultural elements) are in continual flux and transformation, and so also are people. Like Heraclitus, too, she is aware that there is also a strain towards order and harmony, a *logos*, within the variability, an intent, as James Olney puts it (1972:5) to transform "human variability from mere chaos and disconnection into significant process." This is, in effect, what the redressive phase in a social drama (the processual microcosm) attempts to do, and for what, in complex cultures, the liminoid performative genres (see Turner 1982:20 – 60) are designed.

Moore's experience as a practicing lawyer underlies her view that (p. 39) "social life presents an almost endless variety of finely distinguishable situations and quite an array of grossly different ones. It contains arenas of continuous competition. It proceeds in a context of an ever-shifting set of persons, changing moments in time, altering situations and partially improvised interactions. Established rules, customs, and symbolic frameworks exist, but they operate in the presence of areas of indeterminacy, or ambiguity, of uncertainty and manipulability. Order never fully takes over, nor could it. The cultural, contractual, and technical imperatives always leave gaps, require adjustments and interpretations to be applicable to particular situations, and are themselves full of ambiguities, inconsistencies, and often contradictions." But Moore does not see everything social as amorphous or as unbounded innovation or limitless reinterpretation. She sees that common symbols, customary behaviors, role expectations, rules, categories, ideas and ideologies, and rituals and formalities shared by actors do exist and frame mutual communication and action. But she is claiming that the fixing and framing of social reality is itself a process or a set of processes. Whereas anthropologists like Firth and Barth have contrasted structure and process (Barth sees process as a means of understanding social change), Moore sees structure as the ever-to-be-repeated achievement of processes of regularization. As she writes (Moore 1978:40–41):

> The whole matter contains a paradox. Every explicit attempt to fix social relationships or social symbols is by implication a recognition that they are mutable. Yet at the same time such an attempt directly struggles against mutability, attempts to fix the moving thing, to make it hold. Part of the process of trying to fix social reality involves representing it as stable or immutable or at least controllable to this end, at least for a time. Rituals, rigid procedures, regular formalities, symbolic repetitions of all kinds, as well as explicit laws, principles, rules, symbols, and categories are cultural representations of fixed social reality, or continuity. They represent stability and continuity acted out and re-enacted; visible continuity. By dint of repetition they deny the passage of time, the nature of change, and the implicit extent of potential indeterminacy in social relations. [Whether these processes of regularization are sustained by tradition or legitimated by revolutionary edict and force, they act to provide daily regenerated frames, social constructions of reality, within which] the attempt is made to fix social life, to keep it from slipping into the sea of indeterminacy.

But as Moore points out, however tight the rules, in their application there is always "a certain range of maneuver, of openness, of choice, of interpretation, of alteration, of tampering, of reversing, of transforming" (1978:41). In brief, "within the cultural and social order there is a pervasive quality of partial indeterminacy" (Moore 1978:49). Processes of situational adjustment involve both the exploitation of indeterminacies in sociocultural situations and the actual generation of such indeterminacies. Or they may be concerned with the reinterpretation or redefinition of rules and relationships. By regarding a field of sociocultural relations, which may include networks and arenas as well as relatively persisting corporate groups and institutions, as a plurality of processes, some of regularization (or *reglementation* as Moore [1978] prefers to call them: see pages 2–3, 18, 21, 29), others of situational adjustment, Moore proposes a model of social reality as basically fluid and indeterminate, though transformable for a time into something more fixed through regularizing processes. "This is a framework," she holds, "usable in the analysis of particular situations and their detailed denouement, and equally usable in the analysis of larger-scale phenomena such as institutional systems" (Moore

1978:52). She warns that "whether the processes are unchanging or changing is not the dichotomy proposed. Processes of regularization and processes of situational adjustment may *each* [italics mine] have the effect of stabilizing or changing an existing social situation and order. What is being proposed is that the complex relationship between social life and its cultural representation may be easier to handle analytically if the interlocking of processes of regularization, processes of situational adjustment, and the factor of indeterminacy are taken into account" (Moore 1978:52–53).

My own work for many years had inclined me in a similar theoretical direction. This direction is towards postmodern ways of thinking. Clearly the factor of indeterminacy has assumed greater importance in today's world. Historical events have played their part: wars, revolutions, the holocaust, the fall and fragmentation of colonial empires. But scientific developments in many fields have helped to undermine the modern views of time, space, matter, language, person, and truth. Processes of regularization are still potent in politics and economics; capitalistic and socialistic bureaucracies and legislatures still attempt to fix social reality. In the sciences and humanities work is still done within the constraints of prestigious "paradigms" (in Thomas Kuhn's sense). In the political macrocosm sharp divisions continue to exist fostered by the regulatory processes of nationalism and ideology. Nevertheless, there is detectible an extensive breakdown of boundaries between various conventionally defined sciences and arts, and between these and modes of social reality. In sociocultural studies the spatiality of modern thought, dependent on what Richard Palmer calls "one-point perspective," shows signs of giving way to multiperspectival consciousness, a field with several variables. The notion of society as an endless crisscrossing of processes of various kinds and intensities is congruent with this view. Time is coming to be seen as an essential dimension of being as well as multiperspectival, no longer merely as a linear continuum conceived in spatial terms.

With the postmodern dislodgement of spatialized thinking and ideal models of cognitive and social structures from their position of exegetical preeminence, there is occurring a major move towards the study of processes, not as exemplifying compliance with or deviation from normative models both etic and emic, but as performances. Performances are never amorphous or openended, they have diachronic structure, a beginning, a sequence of overlapping but isolable phases, and an end. But their structure is not that of an abstract system; it is generated out of the dialectical oppositions of processes and of levels of process. In the modern consciousness, cognition, idea, rationality, were paramount. In the postmodern turn, cognition is not dethroned but rather takes its place on an equal footing with volition and affect. The revival of what has been termed "psychological anthropology," exemplified in *The Making of Psychological Anthropology* edited by George Spindler, is, in my view, not unconnected with this view of process and performance, of which the units are total human beings in full psychological concreteness, not abstract, generalized sociocultural entities, but each, in Theodore Schwartz's term, an "idioverse" with his/her "individual cognitive, evaluative, and affective mappings of the structure of events and classes of events" (Spindler 1978:410) in his/her sociocultural field. If Schwartz's formulation seems to be derived from the products of processes of reglementation, and hence to be somewhat abstract, the notion of idioverse is a valuable one, for it postulates that "a culture has its distributive existence as the set of personalities of the members of a population," thus allowing for negotiation and dispute over what should be authoritative or legitimate in that culture, in other words, for social dramatic action (Spindler 1978:423–24). As Schwartz writes: "The model of culture as a set of personalities does not preclude conflict; rather the inclusion of the differences as well as the similarities among personalities in the culture makes social coordination a central research problem implied by this model. Differences may lead to conflict or complementarity. The perceptions of commonality or difference are themselves construals which, at times, may mask their opposite" (Spindler 1978:432). This view of Schwartz's of a culture as consisting of "all the personalities of the individuals constituting a society or subsociety, however bounded," is entirely consistent with Sally Moore's processual position, since it allows scope for the coexistence of processes of regularization (overall "social coordination") and situational adjustment ("conflict," "masking of commonality or difference," and *situational* modes of social coordination). Schwartz is also aware of "indeterminacy."

> A given personality (the individual's version and portion of his culture) is not necessarily representative in a statistical sense, nor is the approximation to some central tendency the aspect of culture stressed by a distributive model. Rather, this model emphasizes the whole array of personalities, the constructs they bring to and derive from events, and their structuring of events in construct-oriented behavior. Centrality (or typicality) would not necessarily be predictive or (it may even be negatively correlated with) the contribution of a given personality to the structuring of events. *It is essential, then, to emphasize that although individual personalities and their cognitive-evaluative-affective constructs of experience are the constitutents of culture, they may be discrepant and conflicted among (and within) themselves or with central tendencies or configurations in the overall population of personalities comprising a culture or subculture* [italics mine]. Similarly the constructs of the individual will vary in the adequacy with which individuals anticipate and conduct the course of events (Spindler 1978:432).

If performance seems then to be a legitimate object of study for postmodern anthropology, it seems appropriate that we should examine the literature on types of performance. We need not confine ourselves to the ethnographic literature. If man is a sapient animal, a toolmaking animal, a self-making animal, a symbol-using animal, he is, no less, a performing animal, *Homo performans*, not in the sense, perhaps, that a circus animal may be a performing animal, but in the sense that man is a self-performing animal—his performances are, in a way, *reflexive*; in performing he reveals himself to himself. This can be in two ways: the actor may come to know himself better through acting or enactment; or one set of human beings may come to know themselves better through observing and/or participating in performances generated and presented by another set of human beings. In the first instance, reflexivity is singular though enactment may be in a social context; in the second case, reflexivity is plural and is based on the assumption that though, for most purposes, we humans may divide ourselves between We and They, or Ego and Alter, We and They share substance, and Ego and Alter mirror each other pretty well—Alter alters Ego not too much but tells Ego what both are!

When we scan the rich data put forth by the social sciences and the humanities on performances, we can class them into "social" performances (including social dramas) and "cultural" performances (including aesthetic or stage dramas). As I said earlier, the basic stuff of social life is performance, "the presentation of self in everyday life" (as Goffman entitled one of his books). Self is presented through the performance of roles, through performance that breaks roles, and through declaring to a given public that one has undergone a transformation of state and status, been saved or damned, elevated or released. Human beings belong to a species well endowed with means of communication, both verbal and nonverbal, and, in addition, given to dramatic modes of communication, to performances of different kinds. There are various *types* of social performance and *genres* of cultural performance, and each has its own style, goals, entelechy, rhetoric, developmental pattern, and characteristic roles. These types and genres differ in different cultures, and in terms of the scale and complexity of the sociocultural fields in which they are generated and sustained. But let us take a look for a while at some theories of communication, particularly nonverbal communication, because the genres we shall study in this essay, ritual, carnival, theater, spectacle, film, and so forth, contain a high proportion of nonverbal symbols. Nonverbal communication is a topic which forces us to give heed to what ethologists, primate sociologists, and other scientists of animal behavior have to say. I have myself always argued for the importance of biological components in symbolism, since I see the planet Terra as essentially a single developing system, based, in its vital aspect, on cellular structures which display a remarkable uniformity in different genera and species of living things. I am sure that a biologist from outer space would find the various Terran life-forms to be made of similar stuff, a planetary kinship group, from biological amoeba to high-cultural products like the works of Homer, Dante and Shakespeare, Leonardo and Beethoven. Mankind differs from most other "kinds" in the degree of its self-consciousness, its evolving reflexivity, made possible by language and the dialectic then made mandatory between linguistic and biological modes of responding to environments of varying kinds.

In an article entitled "Formal Analysis of Communicative Processes" (Hinde 1977:3–35), D. M. MacKay uses the "information-system approach" in order to understand what is going on in non-verbal communication. His detailed argument results in a simple model:

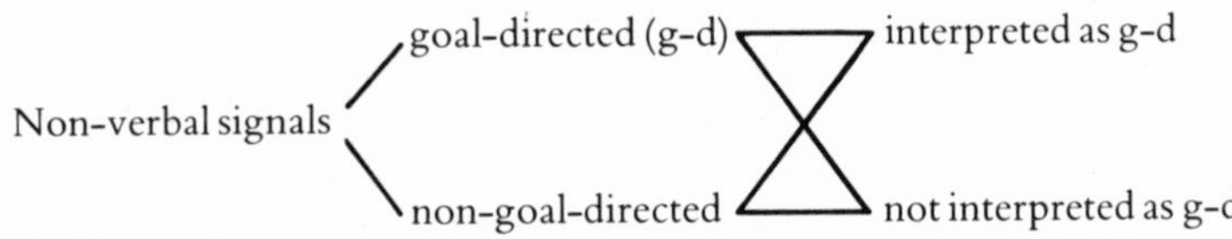

MacKay argues that "communication" in the strict sense only occurs when the originator of a nonverbal signal A's action is goal-directed to a recipient B. One must use a more neutral expression, he argues, when there is no goal-directedness or "intention" (from *intendere arcum in*, Latin for "to draw a bow at," implying A's selection of B as a "target"). For example, we may simply say that B perceives whatever he does about A, or that information flows from A to B. He gives several examples of how to distinguish communication proper from mere perception or information flow. "Suppose," he says, "that in the Boy Scout tent, A, poor fellow, turns out to have sweaty feet, B's internal state of readiness is likely to be very different according to whether he perceives A as an unsuspecting sufferer or as one who knows his olfactory armament and has the *aim* of stimulating B with it" (Hinde 1977:20). Only the second case would constitute *communication*. MacKay distinguishes between *in such a way as* and *in order to*. For example, "a new-born baby cries *in such a way as* and *in order to*. Later on, it may learn to cry *in order to* get attention" (Hinde 1977:24). MacKay claims that his model raises a whole series of scientific questions for further research. In this case, the question is posed as to what are the stages by which the baby's crying "in such a way as" develops into crying "in order to" get attention. "What kinds of behavioral situation might be diagnostic of the presence and nature of evaluative feedback upon the action concerned? . . . and so on" (Hinde 1977:24).

Robert Hinde has criticized MacKay's model, though mainly from the viewpoint of an evolutionary biologist. These scientists have (Hinde 1977:88) tended "to focus on the distinction between behavior which appears to have become adapted in evolution for a signal function, and that which does not . . . [But] behavior adapted for a signalling function may or may not be 'goal-directed' to that end. Indeed, some such behavior may be goal-directed in a sense, but towards broadcasting signals rather than towards affecting the behavior of a particular individual. Furthermore, behavior which is goal-directed towards affecting the behavior of others may be idiosyncratic and not adapted through processes of natural selection to that end." Nevertheless, MacKay is saying some useful things about *human* communication which may be applied to performance theory.

If we take into account the Freudian model according to which human personality consists of several differentiated, but interrelated structures (*e.g.* id, superego, ego), involving unconscious, preconscious, and conscious levels of awareness, we may conjecture that nonverbal signals may be goal-directed by unconscious *id* wishes and desires of the sender and interpreted either consciously or unconsciously by the receiver in terms of some internal goal criterion of his/hers. Similarly signals may be emitted from the *superego*, or normative-prescriptive system of the sender to a receiver who may interpret them at the cognitive-perceptual or *ego* level—or at the unconscious level by *id* or *superego* structures. There may also be conflict within the personality of the receiver over the interpretation of the nonverbal signal on both levels and in and between the structures. A woman's smile might be interpreted, for example, by a male receiver as at once politeness, invitation, and temptation, with the consequent problem as to which was really intended, and if so what signal to emit in response. How nonsensical, even arch, the "communication engineering" type jargon sounds!

Social and cultural performance is infinitely more complex and subtle than the nonverbal communication of animals. Its messages are through both verbal and nonverbal media, and its verbal media are varied and capable of communicating rich and subtle ideas and images. This may be a good opportunity to discuss some of the approaches which I have found useful as conceptual underpinning for the analysis of types and genres of performance.

In the first place, the Western anthropological tradition has moved well away from the study of what D. H. Lawrence called "man alive," or, better today, "man and woman alive." It shared the Western passion from Plato on, (even some aspects of Heraclitus, his backing of the Logos, for example) for explanation via models, frames, paradigms, competence, plans, blueprints, preliminary representations, hypothetical or stylized representations. In practice, this way of thinking rests on the real political power of effecting what one proposes, making one's *archetypes work by the effective application of force*. The Western philosophical tradition—Plato, Aristotle, Descartes, Hegel, Kant, to name but a few, and all the anthropological structuralisms—is hooked on this belief in predetermined orderings. In my view there is such a thing as "natural" or "social" law; communitas rests on Buber's I-Thou and "essential We." Extreme individualism only understands a part of man. Extreme collectivism only understands man as a part. Communitas is the implicit law of wholeness arising out of relations between totalities. But communitas is intrinsically dynamic, never quite being realized. It is not being realized precisely because individuals and collectivities try to impose their cognitive schemata on one another. The process of striving towards and resistance against the fulfillment of the natural law of communitas necessitates that the unit of history and of anthropology (which takes into account the sociocultural schemata) and also the unit of their analysis is drama, not culture or archive. And certainly not structural relationship. Structure is always ancillary to, dependent on, secreted from process. And performances, particularly dramatic performances, are the manifestations par excellence of human social process.

In saying these things I reveal myself an adherent of that epistemological tradition which stresses what Wilhelm Dilthey calls "lived experience." For Dilthey experience is a many-faceted yet coherent system dependent on the interaction and interpenetration of cognition, affect, and volition. It is made up of not only our observations and reactions, but also the cumulative wisdom (not knowledge, which is cognitive in essence) of humankind, expressed not only in custom and tradition but also in great works of art. There is a living and growing body of experience, a tradition of communitas, so to speak, which embodies the response of our whole collective mind to our entire collective experience. We acquire this wisdom not by abstract solitary thought, but by participation immediately or vicariously through the performance genres in sociocultural dramas.

I will now call attention to the distinction between such static models for thought and action as cosmologies, theologies, philosophical systems, ethical systems, and ideologies, and what Dilthey calls a Weltanschauung. The former are static, the latter is dynamic. And since Dilthey insists that experience is equally woven from the three strands of thought, feeling, and will, a Weltanschauung has, like a prism; a triple structure. Thus it consists first of a *Weltbild*, that is, a body of knowledge and belief about what is cognitively taken to be the "real world"; secondly, on this is raised a set of value judgments expressing the relation of the adherents to their world and the meaning (*Bedeutung*) which they find in it. (Dilthey sees value as dominantly formed by affect.) Thirdly, this set, in turn, supports a more or less coherent system of ends, ideals, and principles of conduct, which are the point of contact between the Weltanschauung and praxis, the sociocultural interaction, making it a force in the development of the individual, and, through him, of society at large. This last component represents the action of the will, the connative aspect of systematized experience. The point is that for Dilthey the Weltanschauung is not a permanent, fixed structure of eternal ideas but itself represents at any given moment a dispensible stage in mankind's unending struggle to find a convincing solution to what Dilthey calls "the riddle of life." He seems to mean by this the mysteries and paradoxes that surround the great crises of birth, mating, and death, the seasonal round, and its perils of drought, flood, famine, and disease, the endless battle of man's rational activity against the forces and necessities of nonhuman nature, the neverending task of satisfying with limited means his unlimited appetites, the paradoxes of social control in which a person's or group's loyalty to one legitimate cause, or moral principle, automatically renders them disloyal to others equally valid—in summary, the whole mystery of humanity in the world. Weltanschauungen, then, are built up as much on tropes as on reasons, as much on metaphors and synechdoches as on concepts. What is unknown is guessed at on the analogy of the known, what is unintelligible is explained on the analogy of the intelligible. But Weltanschauungen are continually subject to revision, their personifications and metaphors are much more mutable than cognitive constructs. Their forms differ as the collective experiences underlying them differ, in ways conditioned by climate, topography, history, technological invention, and by the genius of rare individuals. I am sufficient of a cultural Darwinist to suppose that there is a kind of competition among Weltanschauungen, whereby the fittest survive and are selected to receive detailed development at the hands of successive generations. Particular periods of history and particular clusters of societies and nations become dominated and characterized by a particular Weltanschauung.

But Weltanschauungen, like all else that motivates humankind, must be performed. Dilthey saw this clearly and argued that every type of Weltanschauung expresses itself in at least three modes. These are what he calls "religious, esthetic, and philosophical forms." An anthropologist might find this distinction to be itself the mark of a specific cultural type, "Western Civilization," for these three categories have arisen in that cultural tradition. Nevertheless, let us bear with him awhile, for his discriminations proceed from one of the most creative minds in social science.

The ground of *religion*, according to Dilthey, rests on two opposite types of reflection; mankind is a reflexive species, as I have so often insisted. The first is those regular but mostly uncontrollable processes of nature, both meteorological and biological, with which we all have to come to terms. The second is represented by those mysterious accidents by which our lives are sometimes so powerfully affected, even when our circumstances seem to be most fortunate. Religion posits that both regular processes and unexpected accidents are due to the agency of invisible, transhuman powers or beings, and in each Weltanschauung the idea of such powers is gradually elaborated by mythological fantasy and theological speculation. Since, so Dilthey argues, a Weltanschauung must give meaning to the practical life, the question arises how we are to order and systematize our relations with these unseen powers. In Sally Moore's terms means must be found to reduce the indeterminacy of their action and to regularize their relations with us. Therefore, says Dilthey, primitive societies generate over time a system of symbolic ideas and practices, a ritual system, which eventually gives rise to and comes under the control of a group or class of priestly regulators. Dilthey further supposes that as societies increase in scale and complexity something like the notion of an "inner life" develops and individuals of genius, shamans, prophets, and mystics emerge who begin to develop a reflexive system of doctrine which reinterprets traditional ritual and mythology in terms of inner experience. Today anthropologists would demur. They believe that shamans, and other types of inspirational religious specialists, are more prominent in hunting and gathering societies, considered simpler, than in societies with well developed agricultural systems, in which calendrical cults, supervised by priests, and with cognitively well-developed cosmologies are dominant. However, Dilthey is correct in supposing that prophets, shamans raised to a higher power tend to emerge when relatively stabilized agricultural societies are seriously threatened by political and cultural change. Mystics, on the other hand, may emerge in response to the growing banality of ritualistic action in well-bonded societies characterized by the absence of variety, let alone change, over many generations. Viewed from the religious standpoint, a Weltanschauung sees the meaning of visible social life to be determined by its relation to an unseen world from which the known experienced world has proceeded. For social peace and development, it is held to be necessary that individuals and groups, through cultic observances and solitary prayer and meditation should find meaning and value to be derived from messages credibly transmitted from the unseen world through various media: prophecy, visions, apparitions, miracles, heroic acts of faith such as martyrdoms, divination, augury, and other extraordinary processes and phenomena. Ethical standards are believed to be promulgated by invisible powers; they are put beyond the range of human wisdom and creativity.

Dilthey considers that the esthetic or artistic viewpoint, which can be detected in many Weltanschauungen, is not only different from the religious, but also antithetical to it. The artist tries "to understand life in terms of itself," rather than in terms of the supernatural. The thoughts and passions and purposes of human beings, and the relationships into which they enter with one another and with the natural world provide for the artist a sufficient basis from which to derive the meaning of life. He is alert to all the senses, not merely sight, and it is in intense and complex sensory codes that he attempts to give performative reality to that meaning. He is often a fierce opponent of theory, particularly cognitive theory. He scorns to contribute to philosophy. Yet, for an anthropologist, given to inference, a Weltanschauung is fairly easily inferrable from esthetic production. Esthetics, in complex cultures, are pervaded by reflexivity. The style and content of novels, plays, and poems reveal what Geertz has called meta-social commentary. In literature of all types writers directly or through their characters proliferate in reflexive generalizations, which nevertheless stop short of cognitively elaborated theories. The strain towards system, paradoxically, seems to be strongest in preliterate or barely literate agricultural cultures, and in the heads of sophisticated literate urbanized individuals of Western high cultures. Artists tease their readers or viewers with works which the latter treat as a type or "re-presentation" of reality, which they compare with the rest of their experience and are compelled to reflect upon their meaning. The esthetic form of Weltanschauung, one might say, cleaves closest to the experiential ground of all valid knowledge.

According to Dilthey, the philosopher differs from both the man of religion and the artist. His great aim is to elicit from experience a system of concepts and universal truths bound together by a chain of mutual logical implication. Although most philosophers have been, as anthropologists would assert, "culture bound," their goal is to know, if possible, all that is to be known, and to find for that knowledge a logically exact and valid foundation. To this end, particularly since Kant, they engage in an endless criticism, whose goal is to reduce every experience to its constituent factors and to trace every proposition to its ultimate ground, never resting till they have related all facts to an ultimate reality, all knowledge to a highest truth, and all value to a supreme good. Their ideas are derived from every possible source, including religion and art, as well as empirical science, but the intelligible whole in which these data are evaluated has a distinctive character. The world is represented as a rational system whose structure and properties can be made the object of a demonstrable science. For Dilthey, this science is "metaphysics." Religion, esthetics, and philosophy are what he regards as the three media of expression of every Weltanschauung. As an anthropologist, I propose to translate these epistemolgical media into cultural media, that is, such institutions as ritual, carnival, theater, literature, film, spectacle, and television.

But Dilthey, with his German passion for classification, and his scientist's drive to comparative study, proceeds to classify Weltanschauungen into three types. Personally, I regard this taxonomic frenzy of Dilthey's as a culture-bound denial of his own true position, as we shall see. For what he sees as separate types are often processes which have different characteristics at different times. Nevertheless, his types are useful heuristic devices, helping us to find our way into a new sociocultural "field." For Dilthey, Weltanschuungen may be classified into three broad types: 1) *naturalism;* 2) *the idealism of freedom*; and 3) *objective idealism*. Naturalism sees the criterion of the good life either in *pleasure* or *power*, both regarded by Dilthey as representing the *animal* side of human nature. In religion this represents an assertion of the claims of the world and the flesh and proclaims a revolt against other-worldliness, even, in some instances, against religion itself as the epitome of other-worldliness. In art, naturalism takes the form of "realism," the picturing of people and things as it is thought they really are without idealizing. Its use in literature must, however, be distinguished from philosophical Realism, which is, of course, the doctrine that universals or abstract terms are objectively actual (here the opposed term would be Nominalism which asserts that universals and abstract terms are mere necessities of thought or conveniences of language and therefore exist as names only and have no general realities corresponding to them). For Dilthey, though, realism in art tends to manifest the dark forces of passion, thereby exposing higher ideals and principles as illusory or even hypocritical. At the philosophical level, Dilthey regards naturalism as a view of the world as a mechanical system composed of elements all of which are clear and distinct, that is, mathematically determinable. The natural world, known and experienced scientifically, is all that exists; there is no supernatural or spiritual creation, control, or significance. This view, says Dilthey, may be held as a doctrine of the nature of reality—in which case it is better termed materialism—which explains thought, will, and feeling only in terms of matter, that is, whatever occupies space and is perceptible to the senses in some way, either directly or by means of instruments. It may also be held, more cautiously as a methodological principle, as in the case of Positivism, established by Auguste Comte, and still, *au fond*, influential in the thinking of the social sciences. Here philosophical thought is held to be based solely on observable, scientific facts and their relations to one another; speculation about or search for ultimate origins is firmly rejected. Naturalism, in Dilthey's sense, is associated with sensationalism in philosophy, the belief that all knowledge is acquired through the senses, the ability of the brain and nerves to receive and react to stimuli. In *ethics* Naturalism is either *hedonistic*—that is, it conceives that pleasure, variously regarded in terms of the happiness of the individual or of society, is the principal good and proper aim of action—or preaches *liberation* through enlightenment and the destruction of illusion—false perceptions, conceptions, or interpretations, particularly unscientific notions and prescientific prejudices persisting through tradition. In his *Introduction to Weltanschauungslehre*, Dilthey mentions Democritus, Protagoras, Epicurus, Lucretius, Aristippus, Hulme, Feuerbach, Buechner, Moleschott, and Comte as representatives of this philosophy (Kluback 1914–36:75–118).

The second type of Weltanschauung, the idealism of freedom, is based, Dilthey tells us, on our inner experience of free will and was "the creative conception of the mind of the philosophers of Athens." This interprets the world in terms of *personality*; its exponents "are pervaded to the tips of their fingers by the consciousness of totally disagreeing with naturalism" (Kluback 1914–36:61, 62). Their basic premise is that there exists in man a moral will which we can know to be free from physical causation; this will is bound, not physically but morally, and therefore freely, to other wills in a society of moral persons. For many of these idealists of freedom the relations between these persons is held to depend upon an absolute, free, personal agent, in other words, Deity, God. In religion, this Weltanschauung appears as theism, in particular, Christian theism where the fundamental premise of naturalism, that *ex nihilo nihil fit*, "nothing is made from nothing," that is, *something*, for example, is eternal, is contradicted by the doctrine of creation *ex nihilo*. In art, and this is what has pertinence for our later study of modern drama from an anthropological perspective, the idealism of freedom emerges as the conception of the world as a "theater of heroic action," for example, in the works of Corneille and Schiller. Corneille liked to set up historically true but surprising situations that forced a number of characters into action and in which the individual, through his heroic and magnanimous decisions, his heinous crimes, or his renunciations, proves his powers of transcendency. Corneille favored what is called "the ethics of glory," by which the hero convinces himself and seeks to convince others of his self-possession and superiority of spirit. Freedom of the will appears in the elucidation of the hero's inner conflicts as well as great feats whereby he tries to reconcile his will and his passions in order to achieve his goal. Some heroes rationalize their motives while acting in bad faith—a source of irony. For Schiller the artist's role is to show the moral growth of the individual pitted against the necessities of reality. The idealism of freedom or personality, in Dilthey's view, developed in philosophy from the conception of reason as a formative power in Anaxagoras, Plato, and Aristotle, to the medieval conception of a world governed by the personal providence of God, and thence in Kant and Fichte to the idea of a supersensible world of values, which are real only in and for the infinite will which posits them. Dilthey finds among its modern representatives Bergson, the Neo-Kantians, and the pragmatists.

The third type of Weltanschuung, objective idealism, is based, says Dilthey, on a contemplative and affective attitude to experience. We read our own feelings and mental activities into the external world, regarding it as a living whole which continually realizes and enjoys itself in the harmony of its parts; we find the divine life of the Whole immanent in every part, and rejoice to find ourselves in sympathy with this life. This Weltanschauung, he goes on, emerges in the Pantheism of Indian and Chinese religion; in art its most notable exponent is Goethe. The epistemology of this third type of philosophy lays emphasis on "intellectual intuition"—the intuitive grasp of the wholeness of things. Dilthey finds examples of it in Stoicism, in Averroes, Bruno, Spinoza, Leibnitz, Shaftesbury, Schelling, Hegel, and Schleiermacher.

Dilthey argues in *Die Drei Grundformen der Systeme in der ersten Halfes 19 Jahrhunderts* (1959 [1921]) that the history of recent philosophy can be described and elucidated in terms of a conflict between the three types. Since Weltanschauungen are more than merely cognitive structures, but are ways of looking at the world and life, in which cognitive, affective, and volitional elements are bound together and alike are primary, they are seldom found in their pure form, often hybridize, and must be seized as lived experience.

But I do not want to become involved in Dilthey's philosophical speculations in this essay, only to give you a notion of how his general approach to cultural dynamics provides some reinforcement for my views on the anthropology of performance. As I insisted earlier, the truly "spontaneous" unit of human social performance is not role-playing sequence in an institutionalized or "corporate group" context; it is the *social drama* which results precisely from the suspension of normative role-playing, and in its passionate activity abolishes the usual distinction between flow and reflection, since in the social drama it becomes a matter of urgency to become reflexive about the cause and motive of action damaging to the social fabric. It is in the social drama that Weltanschauungen become visible, if only fragmentarily, as factors giving meaning to deeds that may seem at first sight meaningless. The performative genres are, as it were, secreted from the social drama and in turn surround it and feed their performed meanings back into it.

The social drama is an eruption from the level surface of ongoing social life, with its interactions, transactions, reciprocities, its customs making for regular, orderly sequences of behavior. It is propelled by passions, compelled by volitions, and it overmasters at times any rational considerations. Yet reason plays a major role in the settlement of disputes which take the sociodramatic form, particularly during the redressive phase—though here again nonrational factors may come into play if rituals are performed (performance here being in terms of regularizing process) to redress the disputes.

In other words, there is a structural relationship between cognitive, affective, and conative components of what Dilthey called lived experience. This is clearly shown in the characteristic sequential structure of the social drama. Although all these psychological processes coexist during every phase of a social drama, each phase is dominated by one or the other. In detailed analysis it would be possible to demonstrate how the verbal and nonverbal symbolic codes and styles employed by the actors correspond to some extent with the primacy of a particular psychological tendency. For example, in the first phase—Breach—affect is primary, though an element of cognitive calculation is usually present, and the transgressor's will to assert power or identity usually incites the will to resist his action among representatives of the normative standard which he has infringed. The stage of Crisis involves all three propensities equally, as sides are taken and power resources calculated. Quite often, however, when a social field is divided into two camps or factions, one will manifest in its words and deeds the more romantic qualities of willing and feeling. One thinks immediately of the American Civil War, the American and French Revolutions, the Jacobite rebellions of 1715 and 1745, and the Mexican Insurgentia of 1810. All these are on the scale of macropolitics, but my studies of micropolitical situations directly among the Ndembu, and indirectly from anthropological literature, indicate that a similar dichotomy exists on the small scale order. As mentioned, a cognitive emphasis tinges social attempts to remedy disorder, though first will must be applied to terminate the often dangerous contextation in Crisis. Cognition reigns primarily in judicial and legal redressive action. Where such action fails, however, to command sufficient assent, will and emotion reassert themselves. This reassertion may proceed in opposite directions. On the one hand, there may be reversion to Crisis, all the more embittered by the failure of restitutive action. On the other hand, there may be an attempt to transcend an order based on rational principles by appealing to that order which rests on a tradition of coexistence among the predecessors of the current community, whether these are conceived as biological ancestors or bearers of the same communal values. This kind of ordering is better regarded as the crystallization of joint experience, handed down in striking or potent cultural forms and symbols, and bears rather the character of orexis (feeling and willing) than rational planning. Thus when legal redress fails, groups may turn to activities which can be described as "ritualized," whether these "rituals" are expressly connected with religious beliefs or not. Anti-religious states and societies have their redressive ceremonies, sometimes involving public confession by those held responsible for breaching the norms or transgressing the values of societal tradition. Legal action itself, of course, is heavily ritualized. But in these more fully ritualized procedures what is being introduced into situations of crisis is the nonrational, metaphorically "organic" order of society itself, felt rather than conceived as the axiomatic source of human bonding. It is the "social will." The potency of ritual symbols is well recognized by the antagonists in the phase of Crisis. In *Dramas, Fields, and Metaphors*, I show how, in the Mexican *Insurgencia*, Hidalgo seized the banner of Our Lady of Guadalupe to rally the peasants, while Viceroy Venegas of Spain endowed Our Lady of Remedios with a field marshall's baton to strengthen the loyalty of the people of Mexico City.

In the final stage, the Restoration of Peace, which entails either a reestablishment of viable relations between the contending parties or a public recognition of irreparable schism, cognitive criteria tend to come uppermost again, if only in the sense of a rational acceptance of the reality of change. Every social drama alters, in however miniscule a fashion, the structure (by which term I do not mean a permanent ordering of social relations but merely a temporary mutual accommodation of interests) of the relevant social field. For example, oppositions may have become alliances, and vice versa. High status may have become low status and the reverse. New power may have been channeled into new authority and old authority have lost its legitimacy. Closeness may have become distance and vice versa. Formerly integral parts may have segmented; formerly independent parts may have fused. Some parts might no longer have belonged to the field after a drama's termination, and others may have entered it. Some institutionalized relationships may have become informal, some social regularities become irregularities or intermittencies. New norms and rules may have been generated or devised during the attempts to redress conflict; old norms may have fallen into disrepute. Bases of political support may have altered. The distribution of the factors of legitimacy may have changed, as did the techniques (influence, persuasion, power, etc.) for gaining compliance with decisions. These considerations, and many more, have to be rationally evaluated by the actors in a social drama, in order that they may take up the threads of ordinary, regular, custom- and norm-bound social life once more.

From the standpoint of relatively well-regulated, more or less accurately operational, methodical, orderly social life, social dramas have a "liminal" or "threshold" character. The latter term is derived from a Germanic base which means "thrash" or "thresh," a place where grain is beaten out from its husk, where what has been hidden is thus manifested. That is why in my first study of social dramas in Ndembu society, *Schism and Continuity*, I described the social drama as "a limited area of transparency on the otherwise opaque surface of regular, uneventful social life.

In the social drama latent conflicts become manifest, and kinship ties, whose significance is not obvious in genealogies, emerge into key importance . . . Through the social drama we are enabled to observe the crucial principles of the social structure in their operation, and their relative dominance at successive points in time" (Turner 1957:93). Manifestation, to revert to the "thrashing" metaphor, is the "grain" and "husk" of social life, of the values and antivalues, of the relationships of amity and enmity, which are revealed in the often passionate action of the social drama, and the "grain" of manifestation thus becomes part of a community's reflexive store, its knowledge of itself, stored in the bins of legal precedent, common knowledge, and even ritual symbolism—if the drama is redressed by ritual means.

Let me make the simple point again that I regard the "social drama" as the empirical unit of social process from which has been derived, and is constantly being derived, the various genres of cultural performance. One phase of the social drama in particular deserves attention as a generative source of cultural performances. This is the Redressive Phase, which, as we have seen, inevitably involves a scanning of and reflection upon the previous events leading up to the crisis that has now to be dealt with. I have mentioned legal and judicial processes as having an important place here and that these are often highly formalized and ritualized. As Sally Moore and Barbara Myerhoff put it in *Secular Ritual* (1977:3): "Collective ritual can be seen as an especially dramatic attempt to bring some particular part of life firmly and definitely into orderly control. It belongs to the structuring side of the cultural/historical process." Since law is concerned with orderly control, legal and religious ritual have much in common. One difference is that in law cognitive processes assume priority, while in religion orectic processes prevail, though both have similar procedures involving repetition; conscious "acting"; stylization (as Moore and Myerhoff put it: "actions or symbols used are extraordinary themselves, or ordinary ones are used in an unusual way, a way that calls attention to them and sets them apart from other mundane uses" [1977:7]); order (collective ritual is by definition "an organized event, both of persons and cultural elements, having a beginning and an end, thus bound to have some order. It may contain within it moments of, or elements of chaos and spontaneity, but these are in prescribed times and places," [Moore and Myerhoff 1977:7]); evocative presentational style of "staging" ("collective rituals are intended to produce at least an attentive state of mind, and often an even greater commitment of some kind," [*Secular Ritual* 1977:7]), and have social "message" and "meaning."

These formal characteristics of collective ceremony or "ritual" are clearly transferrable to other genres, and are shared with, for example, theater and games. Law and religious ritual, seen as a pair, however, can be distinguished from other kinds of performative genres, Myerhoff argues, in "the area of meaning and effect." She sees collective ceremony (law-ritual) as a container, a vehicle that holds something. It gives form to that which it contains—for ritual is in part a form, and a form which gives meaning (by "framing") to its contents. The work of ritual (and ritual does "work," as many tribal and post-tribal etymologies indicate) is partly attributable to its morphological characteristics. Its medium is part of its message. It can "contain" almost anything, for any aspect of social life, any aspect of behavior or ideology, may lend itself to ritualization, as the late Professor S. F. Nadel argued in *Nupe Religion* in 1954 (p. 99). And as Myerhoff points out, once an event or person or thing has been put into the ritual form and mode recognized by a given culture it has "a tradition-like effect" whether "performed for the first or thousandth time" (Moore and Myerhoff 1977:8). She describes "such a once-and-only event, a graduation ceremony in an urban social center for the aged. The graduation combines many elements from the several cultural backgrounds of the members to make a unique composite ("bricolage") . . . Though performed only once it is supposed to carry the same unreflective conviction as any traditional repetitive ritual, to symbolize for the participants all that they share in common, and to insist to them that it all fits together by putting it together as one performance" (Moore and Myerhoff 1977:8 – 9). Here I would take mild issue with Myerhoff's term "unreflective." I would see such a ritual, which the context of her book shows to have been itself a phase in a communal social drama, as involving *reflection* on the past myths and history of the group's culture (Judaism and Yiddishkeit). The "tradition-like" ceremony was, in terms of her own analysis, "an effort to have that past make sense in the situation of their peculiar collective present" (Moore and Myerhoff 1977:9).

Both religious ritual and legal ceremony are genres of social action. They confront problems and contradictions of the social process, difficulties arising in the course of social life in communities, corporate groups, or other types of social fields. They are concerned with breaches of regular norm-governed relationships, involving action of the sort we would call in our culture crime, sin, deviance, offense, misdemeanor, injury, tort, damage, and so forth. In addition to the redress of immediate issues, the reconciliation of the parties involved, and, in extreme cases, the condign punishment, elimination, or ostracism of inverterate offenders, legal and religious rituals and ceremonies are what Moore calls "a declaration against indeterminacy" (Moore and Myerhoff 1977:16). Through "form and formality they celebrate man-made meaning, the culturally determinate, the regulated, the named, and the explained. . . . Ritual is a declaration of form *against* indeterminacy, *therefore* indeterminacy is always present in the background of any analysis of ritual. Indeed there is no doubt that any analysis of social life must take account of the dynamic relation between the formed and "the indeterminate" (Moore and

Myerhoff 1977:16 – 17). Of course, what is socioculturally indeterminate may be biologically, even sociobiologically determinate; or an indeterminate phase of social process may result from contradiction between principles or rules, each of which would produce systematic social action if it were conceded an unimpeded validity. Thus being a "good son" may mean being a "bad citizen," if family loyalty obstructs civil justice. When we examine some Icelandic family sagas we will see how confused states of affairs, crises of conscience, arise from sociostructural contradictions.

My contention is that the major genres of cultural performance (from ritual to theater and film) and narration (from myth to the novel) not only originate in the social drama but also continue to draw meaning and force from the social drama. I use "force" here in the Diltheyan sense. For him, *Kraft*, "force" meant something different in the humanistic studies from what it means in natural science. In the human studies, force means the influence which any experience has in determining what other experiences shall succeed it. Thus a memory has force insofar as it affects our present experience and actions. All the factors which together lead up to a practical decision are forces, and the decision itself is a force insofar as it leads to action. This category, so conceived, is an expression of something we know in our own lives. In natural science, Dilthey argues, it is different. There the concept of force is not drawn from experience of the physical world, but projected into it from our inner life; and it is bound up with the idea of laws of nature and physical necessity, to which the human studies offer no parallel. In other words, in the natural sciences "force" is used metaphorically; in physics the definition of force as "the form of energy that puts an object at rest into motion or alters the motion of a moving object" derives ultimately from human inner experience of acting vigorously and effectively, of controlling, persuading, or influencing others.

Thus the "force" of a social drama consists in its being an experience or sequence of experiences which significantly influences the form and function of cultural performative genres. Such genres partly "imitate" (by *mimesis*), the processual form of the social drama, and they partly, through reflection, assign "meaning" to it. What do *I* "mean" by "meaning" here? I am aware of the formidable ambiguities of this term, and of the controversies surrounding it. To "mean" is, in its simple lexical definition, to have in mind, to have an opinion, to intend, and it derives ultimately from the Indo-European base *maino-*, from which are derived, O. E. *maenan*, and German *meinen*, all of which signify "to have an opinion." Broadly speaking, a "meaning" is "what is intended to be, or in fact is, signified, indicated, referred to, or understood." But in the context of the humanistic studies, I would prefer to look at the term, again influenced by Dilthey, somewhat as follows: If a given human collectivity scans its recent or more distant history—usually through the mediation of representative figures, such as chroniclers, bards, historians, or in the liminal lens of performative or narrative genres—it seeks to find in it a structural unity to whose total character every past, culturally stressed, collective experience has contributed something. If the relevant agents of reflexivity go further and seek to understand* and interpret (*deuten*) the structural unity of their past social life, to explore in detail the character and structure of the whole and the contradictions made by its various parts, we must develop new categories to understand the nature of their quest. One is *meaning*, which Dilthey employs in two ways. The first defines the *meaning* of a part as "the contribution it makes to the whole." The "whole" here would seem to be a complex of ideas and values akin to Clifford Geertz's notions of "world view" (itself akin to Dilthey's *Weltbild*) and *ethos* (or moral system). The resultant character of the whole is also said to possess "meaning" (*Bedeutung*) or *sense* (*Sinn*).

Dilthey throws in for good measure the categories of *value* (*Wert*) and *end* (*Zweck*) or *good* (*Gut*), and relates them along with *meaning* to the three structural "attitudes of consciousness" cognition, affect, and volition, mentioned earlier. Thus, the category of *meaning* arises in *memory*, in *cognition* of the *past* (*i.e.* meaning is cognitive, self-reflexive, oriented to past experience, and concerned with negotiating about "fit" between present and past, as the phenomenological sociologists like Garfinkel and Cicourel might say today). The category of *value* arises, according to Dilthey, dominantly from feeling or affect, that is, value inheres in the *affective* enjoyment of the *present*. The category of *end* (goal or *good*) arises from *volition*, the power or faculty of using the will, which refers to the *future*. These three categories, says Dilthey, are irreducible, like the three structural attitudes, and cannot be subordinated to one another.

Nevertheless, for Dilthey, value, end, and meaning are not of equal value insofar as they may be regarded as principles of understanding and interpretation. He defines value, for example, as belonging essentially to an experience in a conscious present. Such conscious presence, regarded purely as present moments, totally involves the experience. This is true to the extent that the present moments have no inner connection with one another, at least of a systematic, cognitive kind. They stand behind one another in temporal sequence, and, while they may be compared as "values" (having the same epistemological status), they do not form, since they are quintessentially momentary, *qua* values, transient, anything like a coherent whole; if they are interconnected, the ligatures that bind them are

*Dilthey uses the term *Verstehen*, around which numerous methodological and theoretical controversies have raged since the late nineteenth century, especially when it has been contrasted with the German term, *Wissen*, "knowing, acquaintance," which is conceived as denoting a form of conceptual activity peculiar to the physical sciences but which sociological positivists believe is also applicable to the data of the social sciences.

of another category. As Dilthey sees it, "From the standpoint of value, life appears as an infinite assortment of positive and negative existence-values. It is like a chaos of harmonies and discords. Each of these is a tone-structure which fills a present; but they have no musical relation to one another." Dilthey's view of value phenomena differs, markedly, of course, from that of many contemporary scientists. Robin Williams sums up their position quite well: "It seems all values contain some cognitive elements . . ., that they have a selective or directional quality, and that they involve some affective component . . . When most explicit and fully conceptualized, values become criteria for judgment, preference, and choice. When implicit and unreflective, values nevertheless perform *as if* they constituted grounds for decisions in behavior" (Williams 1968:283). Williams does not analyze so finely as Dilthey; he gives *value* cognitive and conative attributes which Dilthey reserves for other categories. The advantage of Dilthey's position, it seems to me, resides in the articulating (as well as reflexive and retrospective) character he assigns to *meaning*. The category of *end* or *good*, for example, shares the limitation of *value*, and, indeed, for Wilhelm Dilthey, depends upon it. It can show life as a series of choices between ends, but finds no unity in this sequence of choices. Ultimately, it is only the category of *meaning* that enables us to *conceive an intrinsic affinity between the successive events in life*, and all that the categories of value and end can tell us is caught up into this synthesis. Moreover, Dilthey tells us, since meaning is specifically based on the *cognitive attitude of memory*, and "history is memory," meaning is naturally "the category most proper to historical thought" (Dilthey 1927:201 – 2, 236). I would add, to socio-processual thought also.

Now I see the social drama, in its full formal development, its full phase structure, as a process of converting particular values and ends, distributed over a range of actors, into a system (which may be temporary or provisional) of shared or consensual meaning. The redressive phase, in which feedback is provided by the scanning mechanisms of law and religious ritual, is a time in which an interpretation is put upon the events leading up to and constituting the phase of crisis. Here the meaning of the social life informs the apprehension of itself; the object to be apprehended enters into and determines the apprehending subject. Sociological and anthropological functionalism, whose aim is to state the conditions of social equilibrium among the components of a social system at a given time, cannot deal with *meaning*, which always involves retrospection and reflexivity, a past, a history. Dilthey holds that the category of meaning is all-pervading in history. The storyteller, at the simplest narrational level, for example, "gains his effect by bringing out the *significant moments* in a process. The historian characterizes men at significant, turning points in life (*Lebenswendungen*—what I would call "crises") as full of meaning; in a definite effect of a work or a human being upon the general destiny he recognizes the *meaning* of such a work or such a human being" (Dilthey 1927:234). Meaning is the only category which grasps the full relation of the part to the whole in life. In the category of *value*, or again in that of good or *end*, some aspect of this part-whole relation is of course made visible; but these categories are, as Dilthey insists, abstract and one-sided, and, he holds, we cannot think of them without finally encountering some brute fact, some empirical coexistence of experiences, which these categories do not help us to resolve into a living whole. It is at this point that we should invoke the comprehensive category of meaning, a category by definition inclusive, laying hold of the factors making for integration in a given situation or phenomenon, and the whole, the total sociocultural phenomenon, becomes intelligible, of which value and end were but aspects. Meaning is apprehended by looking back over a process in time. We assess the meaning of every part of the process by its contribution to the total result.

Meaning is connected with the consummation of a process—it is bound up with termination, in a sense, with death. The meaning of any given factor in a process cannot be assessed until the whole process is past. Thus, the meaning of a man's life, and of each moment in it, becomes manifest to others only when his life is ended. The meaning of historical processes, for example, civilizational processes such as the decline and fall of the Roman empire, is not and will not be known until their termination, perhaps not until the end of history itself, if such an end there will be. In other words, meaning is retrospective and discovered by the selective action of reflexive attention. This does not, of course, prevent us from making judgments, both quick and studied, about the meaning of contemporary events, but every such judgment is necessarily provisional, and relative to the moment in which it is made. It rests partly on the positive and negative values we bring to bear on events from our structural or psychological perspective, and for the ends we have in mind at the time.

The encounter of past and present in redressive process always leaves open the question whether precedent (Moore's "processes of regularization") or the unprecedented will provide the terminal "meaning" of any problem situation. At every moment, and especially in the redressal of crises, the meaning of the past is assessed by reference to the present, and of the present by reference to the past; the resultant "meaningful" decision modifies the group's orientation to or even plans for the future, and these in turn react upon its evaluation of the past. Thus the apprehension of the meaning of life is always relative, and involved in perpetual change. Of course, cultural devices, such as religious dogmas, political constitutions, supernatural sanctions and taboos against breaking crucial norms, attempt to fix or crystallize meaning, but, as we said earlier, these are subject to manipulation and amendment.

9

Experience and Performance

Towards a New Processual Anthropology

In my professional life as an anthropologist, the terms "function" and "structure" have had almost talismanic value. Both are borrowings from other disciplines: function from biology and mathematics, structure from architecture, engineering, and linguistics. I am not going to linger on plains of contention littered with so many broken spears. Too much time is wasted on negative polemics. I would like to revive our abiding anthropological concern with "experience." We have not borrowed this term from other human studies; it is peculiarly our own. It has long been the jest of anthropologists that field "experience" equals our "rite de passage." But this remark is no metaphor; it describes a true psychological passage from one way of seeing and understanding to another, a passage not vouchsafed to those who hold hard to the values, meanings, goals, and beliefs they have grown up to think of as reality. Few others are professionally committed to entering the lifestream of conspecifics with different, often deeply different, cultural traditions for a considerable stretch of time, during which they are enjoined to render themselves vulnerable to the total impact not just of the other culture but of the intricate human existences of those they are "hired" to "study." "Good" fieldworkers are those who are prepared to have good "trips," that is, suspend as far as possible their own social conditioning in order to have sensory and mental knowledge of what is really happening around and to them. If they open themselves in this way—and learning not only the language but also the nonverbal codes of communication as key to the opening process—they may well be transformed by fieldwork experience. Not all experience is transformative; did not T. S. Eliot write: "to have the experience but miss the meaning?" Experience must be linked with performance for there to be transformation. Meaning is generated in transformative process as its main fruit. But what do *I* mean by these terms?

I suspect that most of those who have read my writings regard me as essentially an ethnographer, a describer of particulars, who is, nevertheless, given to making occasional generalizations—one of my favorite critics would say *over*generalizations—from the sets of data I have studied (Ndembu ritual and political processes, Gisu circumcision rites, pilgrimages in Mexico and Ireland, and so on). Some of these generalizations seem to have been found useful—even outside anthropology—but the criticism remains well-founded that I have not set out systematically the epistemological foundations of my inferences. The plain truth is that I am prejudiced against system-building, though seduced by it: the elegance of a *summa* entrances; with all logical loopholes closed, each part crafted to sustain the whole, the whole a hierarchy of consistently interrelated logical elements, who could resist the temptation to make of all he knows or might conceivably know such a crystalline ediface? But I am not prejudiced against attempts to find the systematic in nature and culture. Every society has its sets of interrelated ideas, principles, procedures, norms, and the like. But the life, the animating force, the source of vitality that we experience as biotic and social beings continually destroys and creates all types of systems, rendering even the most apparently marmoreal and enduring of them, even the oldest rocks, provisional, evanescent, and open-ended. A common human delusion is that the very-slowly-changing is the timeless—even, cognitively, the axiomatic. Fear of change is the mother of the structuralist gods. Change, for them, is an illusion, a matter of altering a given set of objects in a group, a matter of permutation not mutation. Death, the termination of life for structuralists, is in a sense the legislator of life. For life is essentially transitional; it aspires to alter, to modify, to transform: biological evolution is its changing series of footprints in the rocks (merely sands) of time. It only seems to be repetitive because organisms are brief, and conscious organisms, ourselves, deny our brevity by adoring general, universal, and "eternal" laws. But it is the lust for life that drives us to propose such laws in the first place: as Nietzche wrote, "*Alle Lust will Ewigkeit.*"

I am, therefore, in favor of building life and the experience of life into any disciplined account of human affairs, whether in particular societies or concerning what is known about our species generally. Be sure that I am no iconoclast in this, for I love the iconic systems and systematic icons that the incessant doing and thinking of my own kind have imprinted and landscaped on minds. Each is a clue, a sign, of a species-specific interiority we can fathom in no other way than through its most widespread and its rarest manifestations, its tools and customs, its poems and imagings, its praxis and philosophy. It requires a Moses, a Buddha, a Jesus, a Homer, a Dante, and a Shakespeare, to reveal to us what has been inside us all along. We are a species whose members must help one another to understand what it is that our species is *for*, what it *means*. Each individual experiences life too briefly to communicate to his coevals and successors the conscious derivatives of that experience—though some have more fully than others the gift of penetrative communication. But we learn from each other not merely how to survive, poorly or sumptuously, but how to find meaning in our singular lives and in our intersubjective life with those whose life-spans overlap our own. We learn that it is not merely a full belly or a warm skin in winter or a blissful copulation that makes for a full life but also the abandonment ("sacrifice") of personal goals for the sake of significant others (sometimes known as "love") which makes for satisfaction, even when we know that our own unique life has to be snuffed out for the sake of a family, a clan, a tribe, a nation, a religion, or some similar image of ongoing humanitas. For our species, "meaning" is entwined with inter-subjectivity, how we know, feel, and desire one another. Our means of communication (languages, cultural codes) are saturated, whether we know this or not, with the experiences of our progenitors and forerunners. But these codes can never be re-experienced unless they are periodically, or at least occasionally, *performed*. We have to try to re-experience in performance, whether as ritual, festival, theater, or other active modalities of religion, law, politics, or art, as best we can, the socially bequeathed sparks of lives now biologically extinguished. Rules, rubrics, commandments, codes, regulations lie heavy on us, unless we can render them resilient once more in the heat of social action, transformed into guidelines rather than dogmas. (In Lincoln's sense: "the dogmas of the quiet past are inadequate to the stormy present".)

Dilthey's "Structures of Experience"

Bob Scholte, in a fine study of Claude Lévi-Strauss' structural analysis (1973: 692), pointed out that the main difference between structuralism and phenomenology or dialectics is clear: "for structuralism, intellect precedes praxis—not vice versa." He cites Jean Pouillon's summary of the paradigmatic differences: "For Lévi-Strauss, [anthropology] is a question of discovering 'mental circuits,' universal laws about the functioning of the spirit which, in the final analysis, would depend upon certain cerebral mechanisms; in short, it is a question of finding the matter behind man and not a freedom in him. One is therefore dealing with two radically opposed concepts of the relation of consciousness to reality. For Sartre, consciousness of oneself and of things discovers itself in praxis and, for this reason, it is an understanding of reality: dialectics is constitutive. For Lévi-Strauss, consciousness, whether pure intellect or practical consciousness, has no such privilege; it thinks it understands the real, but its truth is merely functional: reason is always constituted. In the first case the relationship to the real is before me and the real is contemporaneous with me; in the second this relationship is behind me and the real is less the object I think than the condition of the fact that I think it. In the first case the relationship is established by praxis; in the second it is revealed by structure" (Scholte 1973:692–93).

Several comments are in order here. In the past decade many discoveries about cerebral functioning have been made through neurobiological research (see pp. 249–89; also d'Aquili et al. 1979 and Konner 1982). Also, an undeniable affinity exists between structuralism as defined above and what Paul Ricoeur (1963:9) has called "a Kantian unconscious," that is, "a categorical, combinatory unconscious." Ricoeur qualifies this by pointing out that, unlike Kant's notion of mind, the structural unconscious is "a categorical system without reference to a thinking subject; that is why structuralism, *qua* philosophy, develops a kind of intellectualism [which is] thoroughly anti-reflexive, anti-idealist, and anti-phenomenological. This unconscious spirit may also be said [to be] homologous to nature; perhaps it even is nature" (Scholte 1973:647). Since this "self-objectifying, systematic-relational, and synthetic *a priori* intellect" (Scholte 1973:647) is held to be a neurological and unconscious entity, it remains an unproven assumption until very much more detailed experimental work has been done which is aimed at disclosing relationships, for example, between the functional bisymmetry and asymmetry of brain organization and perception, cognitive and linguistic processes, emotion, and personality. My final comment on Pouillon's summation of Gallo-structuralism—that it tries to discover universal laws about the functioning of the spirit (l'esprit humaine), which are themselves dependent on the nature of the central nervous system, thus constituting the whole project as a sort of transcendental materialism standing Kant's transcendental idealism on its head, as it were—would be that such an aim is truly to restrict anthropological research to texts, artifacts, and mentefacts, products of human activity, rather than man and woman alive, the producers of such forms. It is thus concerned with tiderows rather than tides, the limits reached by human energies at the moment of their exhaustion, not those energies in full production. These sets of products are then probed in the hope of finding in them implicit systems of rules. The trouble is that this sort of analysis presupposes a corpse, and the "limit or outward bound of Energy" (William Blake) somehow becomes the lawgiver; death prevails over life; entropy always increases and available energy diminishes in a closed system, the "universe" of human culture. Whether or not this vision of the futility of all endeavor will ultimately prove correct, it fails to account for the dynamic complexities of cultural experience discovered by field anthropologists and forming the staple of their enterprise.

Lévi-Strauss has always been firmly opposed to experience, which he seems to confound with that vulgar empiricism which is based on practical experience without reference to scientific principles. In *Tristes Tropiques*, for example, he damns phenomenology for assuming "a continuity between experience and reality . . . To reach reality we must first repudiate experience, even though we may later reintegrate it into an objective synthesis in which sentimentality plays no part." One might ask here why experience should necessarily involve "sentimentality." Blake, for example, thought of experience as contrasted with "innocence." One sometimes wonders whether Lévi-Strauss is the sentimentalist here, when he praises primitive cultures for their "harmony" and "coolness," while civilized societies are repressive, exploitive, and "hot." He looks back, with Rousseauesque romanticism to an age of "innocence," which presumably would be favorably contrasted with our "entropic" loss of innocence. It would seem that his "quarrel is with Time at last, and History its wayward child," both of whom are "cheerfully dismantling millions and millions of structures and reducing their elements to a state in which they can no longer be integrated" (Lévi-Strauss 1955:397). Since most "tribal" or "preindustrial" societies remain for us in the "structurable" forms of ethnographic reports or texts dictated to Western ethnographers by the most intelligent of "native informants," and not in the form of reports of social dramas, extended case histories, life-histories of individuals, biographies, autobiographies, or chronicles of culturally stressed past events, it is possible for structuralists to posit a golden age, or rather crystalline age of structural forms, reposing on universal principles of rationality, and hence, as Geertz writes, "in the great tradition of French moralism, of *virtue*." The many-levelled messiness of human social life may not be a "fallen" state. However, after all, it may be life, *leben, elan vital*, behavior that responds more faithfully to the true character of the central nervous system (full as it may be of still unused evolutionary potential) than the cerebral model of the structuralists responds to the laws they find "beneath" or "behind" linguistic and cultural symbol-, sign-, and signal-systems.

Lévi-Strauss has dismissed the distinction between *Geisteswissenschaften*, usually translated as "human studies"—oddly enough, the German word was originally a translation of John Stuart Mill's "moral sciences"—and *Naturwissenschaften*, natural sciences, as "mythical" and "irrational" (1967:16). As we have seen, he prefers to found his own method on a "naturalistic basis." But those approaches that stress dynamics, process, and meaning-for-man have an awkward habit of not remaining dismissed by French "thought-structuralists." The neglect to which Durkheim's *Année Sociologique* school subjected van Gennep has not been continued by the world community of scholars in the "human studies." Rather his "death" at the hands of the structuralist "sacrificateurs" has proven merely a phase in his liminal regeneration and ultimate "reaggregation" to the world of creative scholarship. A similar happy fate should befall the *de facto* originator of the distinction between the human and natural science studies. I refer, of course, to Wilhelm Dilthey, described by R. G. Collingwood, who appreciated but failed to completely understand him (as an anthropologist *will* be able to do) as "the lonely and neglected genius" (1977:171). "Life" (*Leben*) and "experience" (*erleben*, literally, "living through"), are key concepts in Dilthey's attempt to provide an epistemological and methodological basis for a humanistic science of the individual and the intersubjective sociocultural domain. Dilthey remained opposed to any approach that abstracts from the given continuities of life, as when he referred to Husserl, with whom in many ways he agreed, as a "true Plato, who first conceptually fixes the things that become and flow, and then adds the concept of flow" (quoted by Georg Misch 1957:cxii). When I first encountered Dilthey's work some five or so years ago it became plain to me that here was a philosopher who had vitalizing messages for an anthropology withering on the structuralist vine. Commentators in English on Dilthey's work have been few as yet. Most of them—Herbert Hodges, H. P. Rickman, Rudolph Makkreel, and Richard H. Brown, for example—have been philosophers. Translations have been rare: Hodges' excellent book, *The Philosophy of Wilhelm Dilthey* (1952), is peppered with translated extracts and paraphrases from Dilthey's *Collected Works* (*Gesammelte Schriften* [hereafter *GS* followed by volume and page number]), which now amount to seventeen volumes. William Kluback translated *GS* (VIII:220–26), which he entitled "The Dream" for his book, *Dilthey's Philosophy of History* (1956:103–9). Stephen A. Emery and William T. Emery translated *GS* (V:339–416) for their book *The Essence of Philosophy* (1969). An unknown translator contributed a range of selections from *GS* (VII) to the book edited and introduced by H. P. Rickman entitled *Pattern and Meaning in History: Thoughts on History and Society* (1962). Fredric Jameson translated *GS* (V:317–31) as "The Rise of Hermeneutics" (1972:229–44). William Kluback and Martin Weinbaum included a translation of *GS* (VIII:75–118) in their book *Dilthey's Philosophy of Existence* (1957). J. J. Kuehl translated *GS* (VII:205–20) as "The Understanding of Other Persons and Their Life-Expressions" in *Theories of History: Readings in Classical and Contemporary Sources*, edited by Patrick Gardiner (1959). Makkreel includes many translations from the *Collected Works* in his complex, stimulating argument for the centrality of Dilthey's aesthetic writings and their philosophical implications for his theory of history. I have the *Collected Works* at hand for translations, but my own knowledge of German is insufficient to explore in detail the historical and literary case studies which approach most clearly to anthropological modes of analysis. The *Gesammelte Schriften* cry out to be translated in full: their impact on social thought would be resounding. In 1976, H. P. Rickman edited, translated, and introduced the widest selection of Dilthey's work yet, but clearly the whole oeuvre must be made available in English.

Nevertheless, enough Dilthey has leaked into English, and he has been well enough interpreted, to enable me to make a plausible case with its aid for an "anthropology of experience" in the Diltheyan sense, modified somewhat by recent anthropological research in cultural performance and symbolic action. In Dilthey's theory of knowledge there is no *a priori*. Hodges explains his position very well:

> All thought-structures arise out of experience, and derive their meaning from their relation to experience. There is no "timeless world" of meanings, or essences, or rational principles; there is no clear-cut distinction, such as is drawn by the German Neo-Kantians, or the Italian Neo-idealists, or Collingwood, between the rational level of experience and the irrational, the "spirit" and the "psyche"; there is no "metaphysical subject" or "transcendental self" such as is found in orthodox Kantian and post-Kantian theories of knowledge. There is only the human being, the mind-body unit (*psychophysische Einheit*), living his life in interaction with his physical and social environment; and out of this interaction all experience and all thought arise (Hodges 1952:XVIII–XIX).

Like an anthropologist in the field Dilthey begins, so to speak, *in media res*. He makes the obvious point that we feel and think immediately, we "live through" (*erleben*) our own thoughts and feelings, experience them directly. But experience is not, as the structuralists assert, invertebrate, assigned its "reality," so to speak, by conformity to a coherent set of intellectual principles. Dilthey writes of "structures of experience." These are not cognitive structures, though they contain thinking. They also involve emotions and volitions, in other words they are structures of action. It is important to realize that for Dilthey an *Erlebnis*, an experience, is not an immediate, self-enclosed unity since it carries within it direct relations with the past. One *Erlebnis* is distinguishable from another in that it has a specific function in relation to the life of an individual or a group as a whole—every experience is a part of a whole. As we shall see, experience is contrasted with "life" (*leben*) in being inherently structural, not a flow of ephemeral moments (Makkreel 1979:388). As Makkreel writes: "[*Erlebnis*] is truly temporal and yet it contains a dynamic structural unity which allows the momentary value of the *present* to become a meaningful *presence*" (1979:389). He cites Dithey to the effect:

> The qualitatively determinate reality which constitutes *Erlebnis* is structural. To be sure, it flows in time and is experienced as sequencial; [but the concrete] temporal relations in it can be apprehended. That which is preserved as a force in the present, receives thereby a peculiar character of presence (*Präsenz*). Although it constitutes a flow, *Erlebnis* is a dynamic unity, and this not only objectively, but in our consciousness (*GS* VI:315).

Makkreel comments that *Erlebnis*, when interpreted as a "presence," is "able to structure life without fixing it." A tension is set up in any given experience between the determinate character of what is held to be the past—regarded as a source of the reality of the present (like the role of ancestral spirits in tribal religion)—and the indeterminacy of the future, which "keeps open the possibilities in relation to which the significance of *Erlebnis* will change and makes it subject to reinterpretation" (Makkreel 1979:390). What is characteristic of each *Erlebnis* is extended by Dilthey to the nature (*Wesen*) of man, which he declares to be *bestimmt-Unbestimmbares*, that is, "something determinate but nondeterminable, enduring but not fixed" (Makkreel 1979:391). As Dilthey himself puts it: "Implicit in this is that any change incorporating influences from without on the centralized context of life is at the same time determined by this life itself" (*GS* VII:244).

Thought, of course, has a role to play in the processual structuring of experience, and it is in connection with thought that the difference between Kantianism and Lévi-Straussian structuralism and Dilthey's approach becomes clear. Hodges is a reliable guide here. Kantianism, he says, begins by "deducing" the principles of thought as the *a priori* forms of all possible experience, and then declares objects to be "real" or "objective" insofar as they form a coherent system within these principles. Overtly or implicitly, Lévi-Strauss and his structuralist followers take the same position. Dilthey, as we have seen, makes "lived experience" the primary reality, and finds, Hodges writes (1952:65) "the reality even of the external world in the lived experiences of action and reaction which signalize our dynamic involvement with the not-self. *Thought enters in, of course, but only to clarify and integrate what is given in lived experience*" (italics mine). Dilthey himself claimed that his constant aim was to establish "a theory of knowledge on realist or critically objective lines"; and in so doing, "in contrast with the idealistic doctrine of reason, I did not go back to an *a priori* of the theoretical understanding or of practical reason, founded on a pure self, but to the structural relations in the mental (*psychischen*) system, which can be actually pointed to (*die aufzeigbar sind*)" (*GS* VII:13n.). Thought, for him, is "the interpreter of lived experience" (Hodges 1952:66).

During my first field "experience," which is recorded in my book, *Schism and Continuity in an African Society* (1957), I can see now that I was a Diltheyan all along. Perhaps this was partly because I had, prior to fieldwork, encountered dialectics through Marx, then through Hegel, as well as earlier from Kierkegaard, who also gave me some grounding in what I afterwards found was "existential philosophy." But it should not be forgotten that Dilthey by no means rejected many aspects of positivism and empiricism, both of which strongly influenced the British anthropological tradition known as "structuralism-functionalism." He insisted that what could be objectively described and quantified should be objectively described and quantified. But added to this requirement, especially in the study of historical and social data, was the need to explore the interior structures of experience, how an event or linked series of events was received by our consciousness. At present, I will not raise the Freudian critique of Dilthey, that he ignores the forces at work in the unconscious psyche. I will say in passing that, especially in his work on aesthetics, and in the study of what he calls "objectivated mind" (*objectiver Geist*) and "expressions" (*Ausdrucken*), literally "what has been squeezed or pressed out," that is of subjective and inter-subjective experience as a commemorable resultant of some key "lived through" experience, Dilthey recognized the salience of unconscious experience. Indeed, from his perspective, it is mainly through the interpretation, and later comparative study—leading to explanation—of such "cultural" expressions that we can develop a valid psychology. Introspection by individuals is not enough, since repression blocks off from even the most honest self-appraisal large areas of the psychical system. Such areas, however, become "visible," objectivated, in human mentifacts and artifacts, to the scrutiny of third parties, uninvolved as they are in the emotional causes of their authors' repressions. When social units—groups, communities, consociations—significantly modify tradition, generate a new tradition, "squeeze out" and authenticate a new symbol shaped by a new metaphor which enlarges the bounds of "meaning" (a term we shall consider in detail), unconscious principles are also at work, as well as preconscious ones. These, too, are available to that retrospective analysis (akin to Dilthey's *Nacherleben*, "re-experiencing, restoring the past") which was for him the "highest task of understanding." *Nacherleben* must not be confused, as some have confused it, with "empathy," a term used by American anthropologists meaning the ability to share in another's emotions or feelings. For Dilthey, re-experiencing involves interpretation, and interpretation involves placing an

Erlebnis in sociocultural and individual psychical context when seeking its meaning retrospectively. This is how Dilthey rendered Kierkegaard's maxim: "we live forward and understand backwards." Makkreel understands Dilthey to be saying that "whereas life and experience move on into the future, our attempts to understand them lead back into the historical past" (Makkreel 1979:328).

Dilthey's notions came then as heady stuff to an anthropologist whose close association with the "life" of an Ndembu village led him to formulate the major unit of social process he observed as an internally segmented "social drama." Social life appeared to him as an alternation of "dramatic" and "non-dramatic" sequences of events, the whole amounting to that strip of social "experience" directly accessible to the investigator—who was himself, directly and indirectly, an "actor" in the dramas, and a participant in the smoother passages of social time.

Clearly social dramas are a sub-category of *Erlebnisse*, defined by Dilthey as "that which in the stream of life forms a unity in the present because it has a unitary meaning . . . Going further, one may also call each encompassing unity of parts of life bound together through a common meaning for the course of life an 'experience'—even when the several parts are separated from each other by interrupting events" (R. Brown 1978:42). According to Brown, *Erlebnis* "suggests neither merely experience (for which the conventional German term is *Erfahrung*), but the involvement in, the lived experience of, some whole unit of meaning—as, for example, a work of art, a love affair, a revolution" (1978:41), and, I would add, a social drama.

Before I discuss social dramatistic analysis in the light of Dilthey's thought, I should further attempt to clarify Dilthey's formulation, "a structure of experience." Dilthey had the characteristic Western thinker's preoccupation with triads (for instance, ego, id, superego; binary opposition + mediation; thesis, antithesis, synthesis; production, distribution, consumption—truly Dumezil is not mocked!). One way of grasping what he means by *Erlebnis* is by the relations among three sets of terms, each a triad. These are: meaning (*Bedeutung*) or sense (*Sinn*), value (*Wert*), and end (*Zweck*) or good (*Gut*); past, present, and future; and cognition, affect, or feeling, and volition, described as "structural attitudes of consciousness." Put briefly, the category of *meaning* arises in *memory*, in *cognition* of the *past*, and is cognitive, self-reflexive, oriented to past experience, and concerned with what phenomenological sociologists might call "negotiation" with the "fit" between present and past. The category of *value* arises dominantly from *feeling*, that is, it inheres in the *affective* enjoyment of the *present*. The category of *end* (goal or good) arises from *volition*, the power or faculty of using the will, which refers to the *future*. These three categories, says Dilthey, are irreducible, as are the structural attitudes, and cannot be subordinated to one another. Makkreel, indeed, takes Rickman to task for making "meaning" their "common denominator" (1979:381). Ultimately, it is "only the category of *meaning* that enables us to conceive an intrinsic affinity between the successive events in life, and all that the categories of value and end can tell us is caught up into this synthesis" (Hodges 1952:273).

Erlebnisse may be individual or social (intersubjective). We shall consider the relationship postulated by Dilthey between personal experience, autobiography, biography, and history presently. Here I want to make tentative linkages between Dilthey's model and the processual structure of social drama. Like *Erlebnisse*, social dramas are open-ended, not hermetically sealed: they refer to antecedent dramas, and their denouements are never quite conclusive. Nevertheless, social dramas, since they impinge upon public attention, do have distinguishable beginnings—though in cultures marked by extreme politeness, it may be only their members who can detect them. Typically, a social drama has four phases, each of which has its own style, tempo, and duration, though these vary cross-culturally as well as within each society, between different kinds of groups and levels of organization.

Phase 1. The first phase is *Breach* of regular norm-governed social relations, signaled by the infraction of a law, a rule, a contract, a code of etiquette, in fact, any regulation for action authorized by the group or community. Such a breach may be premeditated and deliberate, like the Boston Tea Party or a military invasion. Or it may be a spontaneous or uncontrollable act, an unwitting word by a diplomat, a *crime passionel*, a border exchange of rifle-fire. Whether it is a performative utterance, a chance word, or an act of calculated violence, if the social circumstances are "ripe" for drama, the next phase begins.

Phase 2. Crisis follows breach as other persons and subgroups take sides for or against the rule-breaker. Factions become visible or are newly formed. Coalitions are made. Representatives of tradition or "law and order" try to seal off the breach before it spreads widely enough to threaten the group's structural or cultural survival. Faction leaders use various "stratagems and ploys" to recruit followers and stigmatize opponents. Attempts are made to settle old scores. For social dramas, as mentioned above, are not isolated events but follow others involving substantially the same sets of relations, with overlap of personnel. Crisis is usually one of those turning points or moments of danger and suspense when a true state of affairs is revealed, when illusions are dispelled and masks torn off or made impossible to don. It is a test of the strength of loyalty and duty. If crisis persists, persons have to take sides in terms of deeply entrenched moral imperatives and constraints, often against their own interests or predilections. For many it can be a key learning experience, but it can drive others to despair. Since the "reciprocal violence" (to use Rene Girard's terms), verbal and/or physical, released in crisis tends to be contagious, those who claim to lead the group seek to apply redressive and adjustive mechanisms to end the crisis, penalize, discipline, or otherwise punish proven peace-violators, reconcile contending parties, assign compensation to those suffering loss in crisis, and, above all, to restore confidence in the meanings, values, and goals defining the group as a perduring sociocultural entity. Sometimes leadership loses its legitimacy and either new personnel seek to replace the old or revolutionaries focus their action on restructuring the politicojural order.

Phase 3. But if the majority of its members indicate that the existing social order and its ideological or cosmological supports are still deeply meaningful for them, it is likely that they will accept the arresting of contestative action proposed or imposed by political, legal, or religious authorities, as well as the inauguration of redressive processes and procedures. These may be institutionalized, formal, and ceremonious, or informal, personal, and advisory. A great range of redressive procedures are available, from secular to sacred ritual, from socially sanctioned force, diffuse ridicule, to priestly curse and anathema. What is important about Phase 3 is its *reflexivity*. In it the disturbed social group turns back upon itself, and whether its self-scrutiny be through the judicial process in courts of law or divination into purportedly magical or supernatural causes of social upheaval, an attempt is made to assign *meaning* to what has happened, to articulate events in a way that makes *sense*. This is where Dilthey's views have been helpful to me, particularly his notion that the category of meaning "can do justice to a temporal continuum" (Makkreel 1979:382). You will recall that, for Dilthey, value is deeply implicated in the present, and unlike the American sociological sense of the term, is dominated by feeling, whereas goal, end, or purpose are oriented to the future and are essentially volitional.

One of Dilthey's best-known passages is his formulation of the nature of *value*. It is from the *Collected Works* (*GS* VII:201 – 2):

> From the perspective of value, life appears as an infinite assortment of positive and negative values of existence (*Daseinwerten*). It is like a chaos of harmonies and discords. Each of these is a tone-structure (pattern of chord) that fills a *present* moment; but these chords have no musical relationship to one another. The category of end or purpose which apprehends life from the perspective directed towards the *future*, depends upon that of value. From it, too, the totality of life (*Zusammenhang des Lebens* = "connectedness, hanging together-ness of passing one's life") cannot be constructed. For the relations of purposes (ends) to one another are restricted to those of possibility, choice, and subordination.

Life, in other words, can be viewed, from this standpoint, as a series of choices between ends, or, alternatively, as the subsuming of everything to a single end—in the first instance, no unity, no interdependence, can be found in the sequence of alternating choices; in the second, the complexity of life, including its ambiguity and the problem of competing, equally licit choices, is reduced: will and desire prevail, not *meaning*. Dilthey goes on to say that "only the category of meaning overcomes the mere juxtaposition and the mere subordination of the parts of life" (p. 202).

Makkreel comments that for Dilthey the "value category gives a too dispersed view of reality. Through evaluation we may enjoy the richness of experience (and appreciate its multiplicity) but lose any sense of unity. The variety of life can only be held together by a nexus of meaning" (1979:381 – 82). If one adopts Dilthey's standpoint, one can indeed see that in the context of social drama, Phase 2, *Crisis*, is indeed "a chaos of harmonies and discords . . . with no musical relation to one another." Each person, party, and faction strives to "maximize its gratifications," to advance its own interests, and to minimize and retard those of its opponents. Each certainly has its own purposes—primarily that of securing power and/or authority, but also of establishing legitimacy—and means are devised—tactics, strategies, plans—to attain their ends, but each is blind, so to speak, to the total domain of interdependent interests of which it is a part. Dilthey consistently defines meaning as a relationship which parts have to a whole. Thus he sees meaning as intrinsically "structured," since it implies a circumference, boundedness, internal partition, and the ultimate as well as immediate constraints indigenous to such a condition. Meaning, we have also seen, is connected with a reflexive relation between immediate, lived-in experience and past experience, which may take the form of perpetuated customs, laws, and other cultural institutions, that is, *Ausdrücken*, "expressions" of "objectivated mind." Or the "presence" of the past in the meaning-assigning, and even the meaning-generating (semiogenic?) contemporary situation may be represented not by "collective representations," but more fluidly by the memories of the living as they attempt to relate present deed to acceptable precedent. In law, the redressive machinery of the judicial process strikingly illustrates how "meaningfulness" is systematically imposed in a retrospective framing of events on the crisis that produced them, thereby rendering it intelligible to the parties involved and hence manageable. Its disruptive potential has been, so to speak, defused. J. W. Peltason defines the judicial process as

> a set of interrelated procedures and roles for deciding disputes by an authoritative person or persons whose decisions are regularly obeyed. The disputes are to be decided according to a previously agreed upon set of procedures and in conformity with prescribed rules. As an incident, or consequence, of their dispute-deciding function, those who decide make authoritative statements of how the rules are to be applied, and these statements have a prospective generalized impact on

> the behavior of many besides the immediate parties to the dispute. Hence the judicial process is both a means of resolving disputes between identifiable and specified persons and a process for making public policies (1968:283).

The judicial process, then, sifts the "chaos of positive and negative existence-values," that is, by the cross examination of witnesses, and through its judges brings to bear the various norms current in a society, its legal "past," on a variety of disputes, each of which, as Max Gluckman has often argued, is potentially unique. The judges' task is to give what they consider to be "justice"—we might call it "meaning" in the present context—in the case before them by selecting and combining rules drawn from a wide repertoire and applying them in terms of a culturally acceptable logic. Apparently disparate "parts" are carefully articulated to form a system of meaning applicable to the dispute. In giving decisions that "have a prospective generalized impact on the behavior of many besides the immediate parties to the dispute," the judges formulate a set of new ends for the group at large.

All societies have some kind of judicial process, but often it coexists with religious and magical procedures for resolving crises. Wherever invisible, transhuman beings and/or powers are regarded as the first and final causes of perceived phenomena and processes, such entities may be regarded as crucially involved in social dramas, both as causes of untoward events and as providers of remedies for them, if approached by the proper cultural means—including divination, ritual, prayer, sacrifice, spells, and other magical procedures.

In my own fieldwork among the Ndembu of Zambia, I found that judicial mechanisms tended to be invoked where conflict was overt and rational investigation into the motives and actions of the contending parties was obviously possible. Ritual mechanisms (here divination into the hidden motivations of witches or ancestor spirits, followed by the performance of rituals of affliction to exorcise familiars or placate ancestral wrath) tended to be employed when conflict was at a deeper level. Often deep conflict surfaced as death or severe illness, believed to be due to the secret, malevolent action of living witches. Illness was regarded as ancestral punishment for discord in the community. Illness, accident, bad luck at hunting, reproductive disorders, and death are all symptoms of hidden, moral disorder to which what we regard as the "natural order" is sensitively responsive. Part of the total ritual process, including divination by various means, such as the use of apparatus and symbolic objects and mediumistic trance, and the public confession of secret grudges before improvised shrines, involves retrospective and reflexive scrutiny of the actions of those close to the deceased or sick person. This amounts to establishing a sort of tally or inventory of the current level of covert divisiveness of the group. Remedial action, often in the form of conciliatory moves between hitherto "veiled antagonists," or attempts to remove grudges, may take place in the aftermath of ritual performance. In small-scale societies, with a limited economic base, there is practical sense in W. H. Auden's "we must love one another or die." A high degree of potential cooperativeness and readiness to share has survival value.

In most social systems, the basic structuring principles (caste, class, age- and sex-categories, rules of succession and inheritance and the like) are discrepant, even, at critical times, contradictory. It is when they cannot be judicially or rationally resolved that one most often finds religio-magical procedures and redressive mechanisms deployed, ways of assigning meaning to actions which seem all the more puzzling because they are initiated and conducted by men and women who are sure that they are acting not only intelligently but also morally and virtuously; and *yet*, the group is torn by strife! It seems that every human social group has its own "social unconsciousness," below the level of its rational control and knowledge of cause-and-effect. The development of cross-cultural, cross-temporal, and trans-societal comparative studies has had the aim of overcoming to some extent the emic and plural subjectivity of single group introspection. Marx, for example, hoped to elicit the "general laws of motion" underlying successive "formations of society" by his vision of radical contradiction between "the forces of production" and "the relations of production" at certain "nodal points" of historical development. He attained this vision after careful historical and comparative studies of major sociocultural systems. It is possible, however, that under the influence of nineteenth-century prejudices drawn from political economy and biology, he failed to notice that "the forces of production," controlled types and sources of energy and the technologies they energize, are themselves impregnated with "meaning," with the constant, creative struggle to relate past technical designs, layouts, blueprints, plans, projects, charts, and so on, to new, unprecedented social and personal *experience* evoked often by technological change itself. The new experience has cognitive, affective, and conative aspects and strives to be articulated in verbal and nonverbal codes (including the performative arts). Hence the characteristic "Western" dichotomy between economic "base" or "substructure" and "ideological superstructure" may in the end prove to be somewhat misleading in an exhaustive comparative perspective. For the tools may be charged with "ideas" and the ideas imaged in technical metaphors.

To return to our study of simpler groups: ritual mechanisms are often called upon when the causes of social crisis seem to be beyond the scope of legal arbitrament or commonsensical adjustment of any type. The invisible powers are held responsible, and since they cannot be brought to court, they must be exorcised, placated, or given sacrifices. This inevitably brings the cosmological system into the social drama, the attempt to assign meaning in terms of myths and scriptures concretized and dramatized in ritual processes. Current troubles are ritually related to root paradigms embedded in etiological myths concerning the origin of human frailty, divisiveness, aggressivity, and remedies assigned for these by God, the gods, ancestors, primordial lawgivers or other categories of authoritative and often numinous entities. In a sense, the petty local quarrels are elevated to the level of pristine, generative events and revitalize the powers of such events. The present troubles are, so to speak, dehistoricized, and given sempiternal meaning. Not every kind of redressive or curative ritual, of course, exemplifies or contains the whole cosmology, but each refers to that part of it which is considered to confer meaning on the events constituting the group's or individual's affliction. Certain gods or spirits specialize in certain troubles or ailments. Certain myths describe the habits of certain demons and how to deal with them. In many parts of Africa it is thought that if natural disasters, ranging from individual illness to plague, strike while a group or community is filled with suppressed interpersonal tensions, the breaches in physical order are symptomatic of social and moral disorder, and hence can only be dealt with by ritual means.

Phase 4. After the deployment of legal or ritual mechanisms of redress, there is either reversion to crisis (Phase 2) or acceptance of decisions made by those recognized as legitimate representatives of the group. Full acceptance entails the restoration of peace, of "normal relations." The group can now go about its usual business once more, getting and spending, begetting and producing. If some significant segment does not accept the settlement proposed, it may split off from the original group, and settle or "set up shop" elsewhere under a new set of rules or a fresh constitution. This may be on the scale of a few villagers moving a few miles from their former site or the exodus of an entire people from a national territory. I have called this phase *re-integration or recognition of irremediable schism.*

There can never be a complete replication of the social state before the social drama declared itself. Former allies may have become opponents. New allegiances will have been made. Factions may have shifted size and power. Leaders may have lost or gained legitimacy through their deeds in the drama. Lovers may have discovered they are no longer or have never been lovers. Former sources of authority or power may have been eroded; new resources may have been tapped, with new leaders to control them. The seeds of a new social drama may have been sown, even in the soil of the resolution of the present crisis. Nothing remains permanent in human affairs. What the functionalists called "equilibrium" is no more than a transient balance of power, or even a moment of general exhaustion, a rest between confrontations. Nevertheless, some sort of social "climax" has been attained, or better, achieved, since much time, effort, and ingenuity have gone into the resolution of crisis. In African societies, the fact of climax of outcome is sometimes celebrated by a ritual which enjoins collaboration on the principal adversaries in the antecedent drama. The round of experience that is a social drama is thus completed.

The Meaning of "Experience"

"Experience" is a word with a tenacious pedigree in Western etymology. I am well aware of the dangers of tracking a word back to an earlier period in the history of a language, or as it appeared in some allied or foreign language from which it may have long ago been borrowed. Many words, and more than words, affixes, phrases and other forms, have undergone strange changes in the wear and tear of time, even reversals, which people like Freud, attuned to the ambivalences of meaning, have attributed to the drives which consciously formulated key terms so strenuously repressed. So we find that our word "play," "to game or sport," derives from the Anglo-Saxon "to strike or clap," whence *plega*, "a fight, a battle." Gregory Bateson might have been glad of this reversal. Play is now a ritualized, not a lethal battle. But "experience," like "love," goes back, without many modifications in connotations, to an Indo-European root; "love" to the Indo-European base *lubh*—whence also "libido," "lief," "lust"; experience to *per*, or *par*, "to attempt, venture, risk."

Let me first quote Webster and interlard comments. Webster traces the noun from Middle English through Old French to the Latin term *Experientia*, to which the modern Anglo-American senses, "trial, proof, experiment" are allocated. Webster assigns five major modern meanings to experience. The first is the act of living through an event or events: personal involvement in or observation of events as they occur.

Both traditional facets of anthropology are here engaged: participation and observation—"science" for anthropologists involves both, but we are seldom fated honestly to encounter their mutual involvement. Experience is, therefore, from its inception ambiguous, being "in flow" with intersubjective events and yet being "detached from" or "out of flow" with them. Our ambiguity is, in a way, irresoluble. To be loyal, existentially, paramountly, and affectively, to the group we study (and "experience" most vividly, perhaps more than we have ever experienced our natal societies), is to depart from, even "betray," the comparative stance we have adopted as "cross-cultural social scientists." To be loyal to the Western European model of objective comparison, is often to deny what we, immersed sometimes for years in the "other" culture, have come to know of its indefeasible uniqueness. Experience as "living through" an event or events takes us back, before phenomenology or existentialism in their developed modern forms, to Wilhelm Dilthey, who, though unaware of even contemporary developments in the history of the concept of culture by Boas and his followers, nevertheless was concerned not only with "lived through" experience, but also with its perduring "objectifications," those handed-down inscribed forms we now call components of "culture."

The second sense of "experience," according to Webster, is "anything observed or lived through." This is Dilthey's meaning, already discussed earlier.

Webster's third sense of experience has two parts. One is "all that has happened to *one* in his life to date," and the other, "everything done or undergone by a *group*, people in general, etc."

Experience clearly involves biography, life-history, case-history, and local, tribal, national, and universal history. The anthropologist's fieldwork has to be sensitive to these modes of reflection upon individual and corporate experience. He must also be aware of the narrative structures of these genres in his own cultural tradition if he wishes to communicate the modes of other traditions to Western scholars and scientists.

Webster's fourth definition raises the problem of how to collect life-history and how to evaluate autobiography even more sharply: "*Effect* on a person of anything or everything that has happened to him; *individual reaction* to events, feelings, etc."

Several anthropologists have recently paid considerable attention to the collection of personal documents in the field; one thinks immediately of Barbara Myerhoff, Paul Rabinow, Renato Rosaldo, and Vincent Crapanzano, who in his book, *Tuhami: Portrait of a Moroccan* (1980:8–9), had these almost Diltheyan remarks to make:

> Like the autobiography and the biography, the life history and the case history are literary genres, and, as such, they shape a particular preselected range of data into a meaningful totality. They reflect not only the more superficial concerns of a particular historical epoch or a particular tradition but also, and more importantly, the more fundamental attitudes toward and evaluation of the person, of time, nature, the supernatural, and interpersonal relations . . . The case history, like the biography, presents a view of the subject from the perspective of an outsider; it bears the impress of a narrator who may even permit himself the luxury of "objectively" analysing and evaluating his subject. The life history, like the autobiography, presents the subject from his own perspective [here I would say, the subject's "subjunctive mood" of self-appraisal, the mood of desiring and feeling, and "as-if," which often prevails over his "indicative mood," his concern with factuality]. It differs from *autobiography* in that it is an immediate response to a demand posed by an Other and carries within it the

> expectations of that Other. It is, as it were, doubly edited: during the encounter itself and during the literary (re)-encounter. Not only do the specific questions posed by the Other reflect certain generic expectations within his own culture but the very question of life history itself may be an alien construct for the subject and cause in him alienating *prise de conscience* (awakening to consciousness).

Webster's fifth definition of "experience" applies directly to the anthropologist's own experience: "(a) activity that includes training, observation of practice, and personal participation; (b) the period of such activity; (c) knowledge, skill, or practice resulting from this."

An anthropologist's training, like rehearsal for the public performance of a play, should perhaps include some preparation for the *experience* of fieldwork. I have suggested elsewhere that part of the training of fieldworkers might include deriving playscripts from the best descriptive ethnographies, preferably of social dramas (of the sort, for example, presented by Malinowski in *Crime and Custom*), and encouraging the trainees to enact them, as far as possible using the symbols, speech idioms, technology, dress, insignia, and so forth, of the culture to be visited. The kinship, political, economic, and ritual roles occupied by indigenous actors in the social drama should be carefully designed in accordance with the best ethnographies available. The meaning of actions and events for members of the culture, its values and ends, should be underlined. Such a play—or "foreplay," if you like—such a pre-experience would be valuable, even if it turned out that actual fieldwork eventually called into question the "meaning" of the whole performance. At the very least, potential fieldworkers would begin to grope, in a more than cognitive way, towards an experiential or "inside view" of the other culture. They would also learn something about reflexivity, since they would be learning about themselves and their own value and modes of assigning meaning even as they attempted to grasp and portray those of the other group. What Dilthey calls a "real transposition" of minds—one way in which he defines the term *Verstehen*, "understanding, comprehension," "one's mind engaging another's mind," later taken up by Max Weber in a rather different sense—should not be seen as the *I-It* "objectivity" of the natural sciences, but as an intersubjective relationship between I and Thou.

But valid knowledge of others is not to be won merely through introspection (the "if-I-were-a-horse-what-would-*I*-do-when-confronted-with-a-fence" approach). Nor is it gained by some direct metaphysical communication, some mystical participation, with the mind, conscious or unconscious, of the Other. Dilthey anticipates modern anthropology in seeing that knowledge of others (and hence, as Lévi-Strauss has so rightly said for years about human cognitive structures, of ourselves) is best achieved through exegesis of the "objectifications," the "expressions," the *Ausdrücken* of that other mind, expressions that can be found in the sociohistorical world, the world of law, politics, art, religion, of language and gesture, and particularly for the fieldworker, of the shared community of experience in its living (and hence microhistorical) aspect. It would greatly assist the development of the anthropology of experience if fieldworkers kept in mind the possibility of scripting the sociocultural actions encompassing them into scenarios reproducible in the classroom or drama workshop.

Dilthey's possibility of intercultural reflexivity, though a sustained focus on penetrating another mentality by interpretation of its cultural expressions, rests on two assumptions. One is the abiding anthropological postulate of the psychological unity of humankind: psychological differences between populations are of degree not kind. The second is that mental components are linked in complex ways to cultural expressions so that we may learn more about our *own* minds from *them* than by introspection, for these expressions express unconscious contents often denied to personal introspection. Dilthey argues that understanding (*Verstehen*) proceeds from lived-through experiences. A lived experience is a basic unit of meaning having its inner pattern of connected elements. *Verstehen* is a process, a hermeneutic circling, whereby the essential reciprocal interaction of the parts and the whole of the lived experience, the *Erlebnis*, is finally grasped.

Perhaps this is no more than to say that knowledge is contextual, and that understanding is a process of clarifying and extending or expanding the contextual relationships of the meaning unit under study, made up as it is both of objectifications and immediate intersubjective experiences of the *I-Thou, Essential We* type. Here I will repeat what I said in discussing Crapanzano's *Tuhami*, that fieldworkers should focus their professional attention far more than they have hitherto done on performances, narrative, life histories, case histories, biographies, and, indeed, personal documents of all kinds. To play or re-play meaning-units of a dynamic culture, its social dramas and political *causes célèbres*, is a mode of *verstehen*, of intercultural understanding. It is, too, a form of "*experiment*," a term, like "experience," derived from the Latin *experiri*, "to try, test." Here we need not slavishly follow the model of eighteenth-century natural science. By experiment I mean something more like the modern "experimental theater." The differences between experimental anthropology and experimental theater are, however, important. The former does not leave any of the social factors which influence what happens implicit, taken for granted, unmeasured. Before such anthropological experimenting is undertaken, each form of social relationship and the structure of each group and subgroup involved has been carefully described and analyzed.

How far principles of organization are independent of, or dependent on, one another has been assessed. There is no shirking of statements of the obvious, the relevant demographic and ecological parameters of the meaning-unit under investigation, and the like, since, as Gluckman wrote in *Politics, Law and Ritual* (1965:302): "the problem of explaining what is obvious is often the most difficult in science." Thus, to be explicit and to labor at accurate definition means avoiding in one preliminary characterization of the field setting the evocative and metaphorical devices and tropes of the playwright and novelist. This awareness of typicality and repetitiveness is always the background of any attempt to script and enact social dramas.

Despite these necessary empirical and positivist methods intrinsic to the anthropology of experience, the anthropology of experience is also sensitive to evidences, as in works of art and religion, of expressions (*Ausdrücken*) of what have variously been called "peak-experiences," poetic visions, experiences of what the experiencers sometimes call "a higher reality," or mystical experiences. The life that is "lived through" in such experiences and even in those humbler kinds associated with what Csikszentmihalyi and MacAloon have called "flow" is perhaps uncapturable in any "expression." Truly to experience is "to know without saying," though paradoxically such knowledge presses insistently out to the light of cultural day. Silence mothers eloquence. One of the best expressions of this paradox, or creative double-bind, is a poem of Kabir's (translated by Robert Bly) to which Barbara Myerhoff recently drew our attention:

> There is nothing but water in the holy pools.
> I know, I have been swimming in them.
> All the gods sculpted of wood or ivory can't *say* a word.
> I know, I have been crying out to them.
> The Sacred books of the East are nothing *but* words.
> I looked at their covers one day sideways.
> What Kabir *talks* of is only what he has *lived* through.
> If you have not lived through something, it is not *true*.

The fact remains that some expressions are more "re-liveable through" than others. Objectifications of great artists, philosophers, or prophets seem to have a capacity to make the hearer or reader re-experience the creator's experience, are more limpid to life's inner movement. Consequently, any anthropology of experience must take such utterances seriously, not dismissing them to some structured, "elite culture." Vision often almost immediately converts into simple concreteness without mediating levels of declining abstraction. A poet's intuition may be more available to a peasant than to a philosopher. We may better find our way to "intelligibles" through "sensibles" than through concepts.

A continually repeated word of the natural language is worthy of this kind of attention, though with caveat that etymological shifts of meaning may deform or denature supposedly original stem-meanings. So, what have been the etymological vicissitudes of experience, highly suspect in purist cognitive circles?

Scholars trace the word right back to the hypothetical Indo-European base *per,* "to attempt, venture," whence the Greek, *peira*, πεῖρα, "experience," whence we also derive "empirical," and the Old English, *faer*, "danger," from which we derive our modern word "fear." More directly, "experience" derives, via Middle English and Old French, from the Latin *experientia*, denoting "trial, proof, experiment," and is itself generated from *experiens*, the present participle of *experiri*, "to try, test," from *ex-* "out"+base *per* as in *peritus*, "experienced," which is, of course, related to *periculum*, "danger" or "peril." Etymologists like Skeat relate the Greek *peirao*, πειράω, "I try" to *perao,* περάω, "I pass through." If culture is really to be regarded as the crystallized secretion of once living human experience, (which is still capable of liquefaction back into similar if not identical lived-through experience under favorable conditions, like the reputed miracle of Saint Januarius' dried blood), then we may perhaps see the term "experience" in its connotational penumbra at least, as preconsciously, if not unconsciously, linked with *rites de passage*, with danger, with "faring" or travel and "ferrying," its Anglo-Saxon form, and with "fear" and "experiment," which is, of course, "test, trial, the action of trying anything, or putting it to proof" (Oxford English Dictionary). Thus, experience is a journey, a test (of self, of suppositions about others), a ritual passage, an exposure to peril, and an exposure to fear. Does this not sum up to something akin to fieldwork, even to pilgrimage, which is, again etymologically, a journey "through fields" (*per agros*), a peregrination? Anthropological fieldwork surely deserves its very own kind of *experiential theory*, its own edifice of practical, yet poetical, knowledge.

10

Images of Anti-Temporality

An Essay in the Anthropology of Experience

The jagged, cacophonous title of this essay must jar on ears expectant of a disquisition on immortality. By "anti-temporality," I denote that which is opposite in kind to being temporal, that is, pertaining to, concerned with, or limited by time. By "time" I provisionally accept the first definition offered by the Oxford English Dictionary: "A limited stretch or space of continued existence, as the interval between two successive events or acts or the period through which an action, condition or state continues: a finite portion of 'time'." Here, however, I would detect a certain ambiguity in the phrase, "interval between two successive events or acts," for such intervals may, in many societies, be culturally detached from natural or logical sequentiality and formed into a domain governed by anti-temporality. Here the very definition of time implies its opposite. Indeed, I will argue that human cultural time, which is history, can only proceed meaningfully by generating, by cultural fiat, rituals and other genres of cultural performance, which deny quotidian systems of measuring or reckoning the passage of time any

Reprinted from the *Harvard Theological Review* 75 (2):243–65.

existential grounding. "Time" itself, as all dictionaries attest, is a multivalent term. For example, it can be regarded as unbounded, an indefinite, continuous duration, "the measure of changeable things" as Aristotle said, or as in Robert Blair's *Grave*, "Think we, or think we not, Time hurries on With a resistless, unremitting stream." Here time is evanescence itself, unsystematized, often "implacable," even "insupportable," as Baudelaire wrote of "life," which he sometimes saw as antithetical to the poet's vision. But time may also be seen as a period in the existence or history of the world; an age, epoch, or era. For example, Mircea Eliade's *illud tempus* refers to a mythical, cosmogonic time when the manifest cosmos took shape in a succession of events, waves, vibrations, or divine acts and deeds. This was the *first* time, the *primavera* of the world, when its conditions, instrumentalities, and powers were laid out, as it were, in their pristine vulnerability yet naked puissance. Eliade has argued, persuasively, that major rituals, viewed cross-culturally, aspire to annihilate measurable temporality, and evoke, in order to reinstate, that generative time of beginnings, to draw on its unfailing, unstinted, and ineradicable efficacies, to redress the failures of the present "time," to purify it of its stains, sins, and stigmata, and to restore the primaveral past as paradigmatic reality. Forgetting of, declension from, pollution of the constitutive cosmogonic time, is characteristic of the religious narratives central to many cultures.

Yet most cosmogonies intimately involve the chaos from which they are often deemed to have come. Chaos is the confused, unorganized state of primordial being, wanting in order, sequence, organization, or predictable operation, which is often thought to "precede" (if precedence is possible in pretemporality) cosmos, though as such mystics as Eckhart and Boehme have asserted in the Western tradition, in a way entirely unexplained, "a will to manifestation," and hence, I suppose, order, "arises in the abyss," in the timeless time before time. The cosmogonic motive has never been explained—why there should have been an embryonic (and this very term implies temporality) Logos in Chaos escapes the greatest intellects, including Aquinas—though Boehme sees the impulse by which "the Nothing became Something" as Love, which should be adored rather than understood, a matter of revelation rather than comprehension, the true first Mover, that moves Dante's "Sun and the other stars," the uncaused Cause.

I am an anthropologist, not a theologian or a mystic, and make no claim to understand such high matters. I have done fieldwork among African villagers and Mexican and Irish countrymen, with some brief glances at the rituals of Brazilian and Japanese townsmen. I have read quite widely in anthropological descriptive literature. From these direct and surrogate experiences I have developed some working hypotheses given probability by experimental and comparative evidence, if not conclusively established, after the manner of *natural* science, as a set of laws. Some of these bear on the subject of anti-temporality. In the first place, I conceive human life to be dominantly social life and to be fundamentally in flux, in motion. That is, human beings are not smoothly nude, enclosed subjectivities, but from conception are prepositional entities, projecting lines and plugs and covered with sockets, metaphorically speaking, which represent potential relationships: with, against, into, for, of, among, inside, outside, above, below one another. In brief, men and women come into existence connected with, opposed to, or disconnected from *one another*: "I-Thou is the first word uttered"; "no man is an island"; "we are all members of one another," both as members of natural species and Erik Erikson's cultural "pseudo-species." Thus, we tend to form groups, whether by ascription through kinship and neighborhood, or by choice, through friendship or common tasks or interests. But groups are neither simple nor enduring: they are composite, consisting of leaders and led, factions, segments, coalitions of sub-groups, dividing and uniting with reference to ever-changing issues and interests. Members leave them; recruits join them. The prepositions change over time: those we are "with" or "for" today may become those we are "against" or moving "away from" tomorrow. Time makes friends foes, foes friends, lovers indifferent, divorces spouses and espouses divorcees. Groups split, like cells in nature, and splice with the splinters from other groups. Our sociability is mutable though we yearn for permanence. We also seek to rest our restless minds in meaningfulness. Later we shall consider some of the implications of bonding and dissevering through language, which for human beings has superceded genetically implanted instinct as the ground of attraction and repulsion. For, through language, we impute meaning to flux and endeavor to order and border indeterminacy. This is never fully successful for, as Sally Falk Moore has written: "Order never fully takes over, nor could it. The cultural, contractual, and technical imperatives always leave gaps, require adjustments and interpretations to be applicable to particular situations, and are themselves full of ambiguities, inconsistencies, and often contradictions" (Moore and Myerhoff 1975:220).

As an anthropologist, I have to resist the temptation to foreclose the issue even by means of the most enlightened solutions handed to us in the traditions of the great salvation religions. I have to ground what I will say in my own field experience and that of my fellows who for varying periods of time have dwelt among members of cultures other than their own and have been professionally as well as personally committed to try to understand their lives and persons and the flow and ebb of their mutual relationships.

It has been a fact of my experience in many societies, including our own, that the life of perduring groups is punctuated, *de temps en temps*, by what I have called "social dramas." Time, that is to say, does not flow together altogether evenly, uneventfully. Would that it did, for I am not a combative, polemical person! If life on earth replicated Dante's *Paradiso* I would be content. I am not molded after Dostoevsky's "underworld man" with the "cynical and sneering face." Yet I cannot, corrupted by science, reject what is most evident. What is most clear is that all social groups, including monasteries, ashrams, and dojos, let alone university departments and university committees, give birth to social dramas, "tensional irruptions," as my friend, the Polish sociologist Stanislaw Andrzejewski, once called them.

Kurt Levin, the psychologist, divided social "time" into "harmonic" and "aharmonic" phases. The aharmonic phases, I have found, respond well to Aristotle's paradigm for tragedy. Empirically, though, I have found them fairly regularly to have four phases, the acts of the social drama (see Chapter 9, pp. 214–221). They often begin with a visible breach in one of the major expectable regularities of group living. This may be deliberate, or it may be spontaneous, such as a criminal or passionate outbreak, or perhaps a cry of outraged virtue against persistent injustice. Whatever the motive, the group has to take cognizance, for the breach or norm takes place in some visible, public arena, "cannot be hid," and challenges its main assumptions of unity and continuity. The second phase "crisis," represents a turning point in group living, a moment of choice, in which sides must be taken—even abstention from choice is a "position"—and conflict is apt to be contagious. Factions emerge, whether traditional or new-born round an unprecedented issue, coalitions are formed, scapegoats pointed to, degrees of opposition—from harsh words to physical violence—are mooted and/or resorted to; if things are left to themselves the crisis may manifest that ultimate *dichotomous* cleavage which thinkers from Zoroaster to Marx saw as the problem confronting all human attempts at group unity, empirical or metaphysical.

The third phase begins when those considered representative of the unity and continuity of the group—whether religious, political, economic or familial, or all combined—use their authority and legitimacy to isolate and constrain the spreading conflict within the bounds of law or religion or both. Here unity puts forth all its strength against the breach of norm promulgated by the peace-disturber and judges the case according to traditional legal standards, exonerating or penalizing the parties not only by those standards but also in accordance with the judges' assessment of contemporary reality which can always modify and elasticize standards. When law proves to be inadequate because the contending parties can convincingly appeal to cultural principles that are logically contradictory, though equally upheld, magical and even religious procedures (ranging from ordeal and divination to complex rituals propitiating ancestral spirits or deities) may be prescribed, in which members of the conflicting parties are enjoined to cooperate, having in preliminary rites purified their hearts or, as many societies say, livers of animosity towards one another. Religion, in the mode of faith, flies toward unity, despite material causes that deny it. But historical religions beget doctrinal terms which inflexibly determine modes of unity and exclude those who find themselves, for a variety of causes, unable to accept them. Here culture, as discriminatory, would seem to reject the unity of nature, if indeed, the inter-breeding capability of different human stocks would indicate natural affinity.

The third phase of social drama, that is, application of legal or religious means, in formal fashion, to the persons and issues of crisis, may succeed or fail in its endeavor to restore peace or at least equilibrium to social relationships in the group, however large or small, from family to international community. Success or failure is, of course, of equal analytical relevance. Success indicates that despite individual or subgroup critiques, the center can hold; failure demonstrates that the extant "structure" is rejected deeply by present experience of social reality. Both are diagnostic of "the human condition" in a given space-time continuum.

The fourth and last stage of this "strange eventful [yet all too familiar] history" is the *outcome*, whether this be some attempt to restore or reconstitute the group, the community that has been lacerated, even broken, by those who have denied its perduring meaningfulness,or an acceptance of its splitting, even its spatial severance. Obviously, when human beings gaze upon other human beings, unmasked by pressured events, nothing can afterwards be quite the same, with regard to relationships, as it was before the social drama began. Perhaps Blake wrote truly when he said, "In heaven the art of living is forgetting and forgiving," but usually on earth, living together is more "the art of the possible." People are now aware of what was hidden before, but they also know that they *must* continue to cooperate if the group is to continue, economically, politically, or in other ways, and that new terms must be created in which this cooperation can be carried on realistically. Every social drama entails a loss of innocence, compensated for by a gain in experiential knowledge. To be honest, let us look at our own lives. Do we not, even freed from the constraints of kinship, incumbent upon our tribal brothers, feel deeply, libidinally, or aggressively committed to *some* group, whose values and norms frame our own sense of self, our own feeling of identity? Even recluses, or hermits, are such through disappointments, or perhaps see themselves as members of an ideal society, absent from earth, and an invisible church. Let us call such a group, whether it be the local philatelic society, a set of close friends, even a university committee, our personal "star group." For many the star group may affectively replace the elementary family, the family in which one was raised. For that very reason its internal relationships, particularly those of authority and control, become highly ambivalent and emotionally charged beneath the surface of manners and civility, and are liable to manifest themselves periodically in social dramas. Voluntary associations may become tightly closed communities for their "star groupers." Rituals are devised to call a halt to crisis, redress wrongs, air grievances, find remedies that enable the group to continue.

I must admit that I find the third phase of social drama, redressive ritual and symbolic action, the most interesting one, for in it I find the seeds of practically all those ramifying genres of cultural performance that "wage contention with their time's decay," to cite Shelley. In pre-industrial societies, what we in the West have come to distinguish as the "natural" order, the "social" order, and the "moral" order, are often perceived as a single order, and when a social drama arises it may well involve events, such as the sickness or death of group members, which we would regard as irrelevant to the pragmatic issues at stake. Just as the apparition of Hamlet's father's ghost indicated that "something is rotten in the state of Denmark," so does the coincidence of what we call "natural disaster" with social conflict (for example, competition for high office, chieftainship or village headmanship) indicate in many pre-industrial communities the arousal of the punitive wrath of ancestral spirits against the dissension of their living descendants who are thus spurning the heritage of unity and order bequeathed to them, or the hidden presence of lethal witchcraft directed by the living against the living, often close kinsmen against close kinsmen—the "nearer in blood, the nearer bloody," as Shakespeare declaimed in *Macbeth*. I have often observed complex rituals performed during the third phase of social dramas during which, in incidents of divination, confession, exhortation, and prayer, it was clear that the community was thoroughly and seriously examining its corporate self. Hidden grudges and tensions were being brought to light, related by the elders and sages to models of ideal behavior, and, as the ritual process continued, reconciliation was being sought between the living and the ancestors, and among the living themselves. Ritual was at once a process of plural reflexivity, an inventory of the current state of social relationships, and an attempt to assign meaning to untoward events. At the social level it was an endeavor to purify relationships of envy, jealousy, hate, undue possessiveness, grudges.

Social structure is provocative of competition and conflict, even as it restrains its public expression. Social and political systems contain offices, high, medial, and low; chains of command; bureaucratic ladders. There are systems of promotion, rules, and criteria for status elevation and degradation, laws concerning the protection, disposal, transference, and inheritance of property, and succession to public office. There are social controls over sexuality and reproductive capacity, rules governing marriage and prohibitions on incest and adultery. In this many-leveled, ordered, and sanctioned field, individuals may find it hard not to envy their neighbor's good fortune, covet his ox, ass, lands, or wife, strive with him for office, compete with him on the promotion ladder, become greedy or miserly, or succumb to despair at their own lack of success. But when a member of, say, a Central or East African village group riddled with conflict was stricken down by illness—and the victim was usually not one of the main antagonists but an innocent member, perhaps a child, at any rate some kind of scapegoat—and his/her affliction was divined as ancestral wrath against the total community's divisiveness or as the malignancy of a witch in one or another of its contending factions, ritual was performed for which a cardinal rule was that the entire group had to cooperate, as officiants or congregation, in the healing process. This meant not only external purification, by lustrations and prayers, but also cleansing of the heart/liver by public confession of grudges against community members. By such means the ancestral shades might be placated and persuaded to remove the affliction. Ritual also involved remembering the ancestors, and, indeed, restoring the past, to some extent and selectively, a past which had once been or they had supposed to have been their present.

In many pre-industrial societies, cosmogonic myths, or fragments thereof, may be recited or enacted during such "rituals of affliction," as I have called this genre to distinguish them from rites of passage, seasonal celebratory rites, rites of intensification, and other modes of worship or veneration. In rituals of affliction, there is a strong element of reflexivity, for through confession, invocation, symbolic reenactment and other means, the group bends back upon itself, so to speak, not merely cognitively, but with the ardor of its whole being, in order not simply to remember but also to remember its basic relationships and moral imperatives, which have become dismembered by internal conflict. We do not have here a dispassionate moral stocktaking of the community's joint and several declensions from an objective set of ethical standards, though clearly such a stocktaking is a component in the ritual process. But it would be more correct to think of a ritual of affliction as a passionate attempt to heal the breaches caused by social structural conflict and competition and by egotistical or factional strivings for power, influence, wealth, and so forth by reviving feelings of an underlying bedrock *communitas*, a generic human relationship undivided by status-roles or structural oppositions, which is also vouched for by myths and histories stressing the unity and continuity of the widest group to which all belong by birth and tradition. Here a culturally structured social antistructure, an anti-temporal stretch of ritual time, opposes and ameliorates the divided, all too temporal world of institutionalized social structure, recognized as necessary, if polity and economy are to work, but sensed also as the forked root of all social sunderings.

Briefly summarizing the argument so far, then, we regard the social process within a given community, from pair or family to nation and even international fields of interdependence, commercial, professional, or political, as that which moves through undramatic and dramatic periods, harmonic and disharmonic phases. The social drama is an isolable processive form, proceeding from breach, through crisis, then attempted redress, to its climax or satiation in renewed equilibration of key relationships or the social recognition of irremediable schism. Of course, there is no certitude concerning the outcome; failure to redress can reanimate crisis. In situations of rapid, especially catastrophic social change, redressive devices may simply fail, since consensus about meanings, values, and goals—religious, political, or economic—may have broken down, and multiple ideologies, heresies, and outlooks may mobilize substantial groups against the banners of orthodoxy and tradition. Such situations may precipitate radical structural reforms, and even revolution, when basic modes of framing are reformulated, and hence new means of redress are authoritatively decreed.

But in the majority of pre-industrial tribal societies, this kind of breakdown of redress does not occur, though the intrusion and subsequent overlordship of advanced societies can precipitate those crises in tribal societies which generate millenarian movements, attempts to revitalize traditional beliefs and relationships, sometimes by syncretizing what are perceived as the powers of the conquerors' religion with the chthonian powers of the conquered land. But, my argument here supposes a relatively firmly framed tribal order, in which the third phase of social dramas regularly employs divination and rituals of affliction as means of redressing or resolving crisis by assigning accepted cosmological meaning to events of local or sectional significance. Such rituals often possess, though in briefer and truncated form, the structure of van Gennep's *rites de passage:* (1) rites of separation detaching the ritual subject from quotidian, secular reality, and often involving symbols of killing and death; (2) rites of margin or limen, often involving the subject's seclusion in a special hut, shelter, or cave, where former rules no longer apply and new ones remain in abeyance, a state at once liberating and terrifying for the subject, who is also an initiand into cultic membership; and (3) rites of re-aggregation, in which the subject is returned to the mundane realm, restored to health and integrity. Since the whole community, particularly those closest to the subject by kinship, affinity, friendship, or shared interests, not only participates in the ritual of affliction but also, in varying measure, must observe taboos on eating certain foods and on sexual activity, it may be said to share the subject's passage from illness to health, from solitary near-death to sharing again the communal life process. I am allowing myself in this talk the luxury of broad generalization since in various books and papers I have labored almost obsessively over what William Blake calls "the minute particulars," minutely observed ethnographic details of social and symbolic action.

Rituals of affliction spring fairly immediately from contemporary conflicts. They are, in a sense, obliquely remedial. But other types of ritual are prophylactic, generic all-purpose attempts to forestall conflicts arising from the deadly sins of men entrapped in and controlled by social structure. Van Gennep broadly distinguished three major types of ritual in pre-industrial society of which the third would include "rituals of affliction." He called his classification

> *rhythmic* in the sense that it begins by considering the human life, the principal object of our interest, from its beginning to its end; then the cycle of the year; and lastly the manifestation of various activities diverging in direction yet all radiating from Man as the center of energy. This rhythm, which is rectilinear in the first data series, then cyclic in the second, is alternating in the third. For here the action is directed from subject to object, then rebounds back from object to subject (van Gennep 1937, quoted in Belmont 1974:98).

Van Gennep is here, in fact, distinguishing between those rites of passage which mark the nodes of individual development in any human life from beginning to end, varying chronologically from culture to culture, but marking changes of state and status, from womb to tomb, and those rites, which often involve popular festival with dramatized status, gender, and age reversals, and Rabelaisian emphases on catabolism and fecundity, which mark nodes in the agricultural cycle or calendar such as sowing, first fruits, and main harvest of the staple crop, or in the solstices, or the intersection of solar, lunar, and/or Venusian cycles. The former rites, referring to human development, are centered on individuals, who are initiated by adepts or elders and taught the meanings of symbols materialized as rock-paintings, masks, medicine-bundles, riddling utterances, gestures, dance-movements, figurines, sand paintings, and many other modes of sacral communication—or at least as much as the elders desire novices to know in the innocency of their initiation. Some of these figurations are what Grathoff and Handelman call "symbolic types," akin to Jung's "archetypes" but derived from that portion of significant social experience transmitted and learned as culture rather than from the emergence into subjective awareness of genetically transmitted discrete numinous structures, unknowable in themselves, but clothed like caddis-fly larvae in forms derived from personal experience. As Aphrodite was born from sea-foam, such symbolic types are generated from liminality; they are its markers rather than its symbols, so to speak. They do not "stand for" liminality; they constitute it. Handelman, considering the array of liminal symbols cross-culturally—the masks, costumes, paintings, myths, and so forth—uses capital letters to represent symbolic types, distinguishing them thus from mundane instances of those types. Thus we have CHIEF, SHAMAN, TRICKSTER, MAIDEN, CLOWN, MOTHER, HERO, VILLAIN, SAINT, ANGEL, ENEMY, REDEEMER, HEALER, PROPHET, FOOL as against lower-case instances of these typifications. He argues that, should such symbolic types escape from their liminal habitat, they would generate around them a field of social relations and cultural expectations filled with numinosity; they would impose upon indicative reality their subjunctive potency. Suppose, says Handelman, a pope, a symbolic type of coronation, were to walk into one's lecture room. Would he not produce there a set of dispositions and attitudes of an idiosyncratic and autonomous sort, almost regardless of the religious or anti-religious affiliation of those present? Sophocles' tragedy *Oedipus at Colonnus*, indeed, derived its tension from the blinded, exiled king's resistance to becoming a symbolic type, a *genius loci*. His complex individual humanity resists this transmogrification.

But liminality is not wholly concerned with the transmission of sacra. It is also, even in tribal ritual, a time outside time in which it is often permitted to *play* with the factors of sociocultural experience, to disengage what is mundanely connected, what, outside liminality, people may even believe to be naturally and intrinsically connected, and to join the disarticulated parts in novel, even improbable ways. Even in solemn rites of passage and far more in calendrical festivals and carnivals it is considered licit to fool around with the factors of cultural construction, liberating the signifiers from the signified, filling the liminal scene with dragons, monsters, caricatures, fantasies made up of elements of everyday experience torn out of context and improbably combined with other disrupted elements. Alternatively, the ordinary, the expectable, is distorted. Human heads, limbs, genitalia are monstrously enlarged or unnaturally diminished, leaving the rest of the body of normal size. Such devices are used for mocking, critiquing, detaching the group from sober, normal, indicative orderings, and subverting the grammars of their arrangements.

Thus we have two kinds of anti-temporality: the perennially sacred, rooted perhaps in the primordial manifestation of the eternal, generative unmanifest, the Logos, that was "in the beginning," but was Son of the beginningless fathering will to manifestation; the perennially sacrilegious, human freedom to resist and even transgress the culturally axiomatic, the most sacred texts, the mightiest rulers and their commandments.

This antinomian egg, which contains both law and freedom, is ritual's tribal form, but, as society becomes more complex and increases in scale, with an ever more refined and specialized division of labor, it cracks open and discharges a secularizing progeny of performative genres, some collective in inspiration, others authored and crafted by known and named individuals.

Ritual, in tribal society, represents not an obsessional concern with repetitive acts, as Freud sometimes supposed, but a sensitive orchestration of many strands of symbolic action in all available sensory codes: speech, music, singing; the presentation of elaborately worked objects, such as masks, shrines, triptychs; wall paintings, body paintings; sculptured or carved forms; elaborate costumes; nakedness, which as Mircea Eliade has pointed out, embodies the magico-religious strength of women, while men enhance their magico-religious potentialities by disguising themselves, by masking; dance forms with complex grammars and vocabularies of bodily movements, gestures, finger movements, and facial expressions. As society increases in scale and complexity, and as mind increasingly becomes the substructure of the generation of forces and relations of productions, these strands of symbolic action are torn from their original connection in ritual and become independent modes of expression: folk and high cultural theater, musical composition; epic, ballad, and the novel; painting, sculpture, architecture; genres of dance, including ballet and morris-dancing; opera; sports and athletics, stemming from sacred ballgames and funeral games; games of chance devolving from divination; miming, clowning, circus performance in general; tumbling and juggling; postmodern experimental theater, and the various electronic genres, film, television, and rock concerts. Nevertheless, something of the anti-temporal character of ritual continues to adhere to the best of these genres and their best instances. Theater, for example, is almost ritual's firstborn, and the oldest forms of theater have much in common with ritual. Theater, though, breaks the unity of the congregation which is ritual's characteristic performative unit, converting total obligatory participation into the voluntary watching of actors by an audience. Such dualism and distancing create the possibility of critique. The whole group is not so directly involved in the inner and outward transformation of one or more of its members, through the invocation of supernatural powers, from one state of inward and social being to another. Rather, the gods and heroes themselves, as in Greek and Japanese tragedy and comedy, may be turned to ambiguity, and the possibility of subjunctive evaluation of what was tribally most sacred and beyond question may be a lively item on the cultural agenda.

As an anthropologist I am uneasy at so much generalization. Let me, therefore, give a detailed example of the presence of anti-temporality in Oriental theater. During a visit to Japan in 1981, I heard a fascinating lecture by Professor Gunji of the National Theater of Japan, on the roots of such genres as Nō, Bunraku (Puppet Theater), and Kabuki in Shinto ritual and cosmology, but it is not with these that I would begin. Two fascinating papers by Farley Richmond (1980; Richmond and Richmond 1980) make cogent use of van Gennep's and my analyses of rites of passage, and are concerned with Kutiyattam, one of the oldest forms of theater in India, traceable back to the tenth century A.D. Richmond does not, as I would have done, place a specific performance in its social, cultural, and political processual contexts in a well studied community. But he presents us with a symbological analysis of a transitional form between ritual and theater which has held its own for a thousand years. The plays—on mythical and epic themes—are written in Sanskrit and Prakrit, languages known and understood by a only a few priests and scholars who witness the performances. The local language Malayalam is incorporated into the show by the clown character (Vidusaka) who improvises and expounds on the text at great length.

> He speaks in a relatively realistic manner in contrast to the other characters who chant their verses and dialogue according to prescribed rules of execution. The actors use a highly complex system of gesture language to interpret the text; however, the meaning of this language too is known to a very few spectators. The eye and facial movements are also highly stylized, removing the form further from the understanding of the layman (Richmond 1980:2).

You will recognize in this opposition between actors and clown the opposition typical of ritual liminality in initiations between the perennially sacred and the perennially sacrilegious, between *illud tempus* and the scandalous news of the day. This is how Richmond describes the clown:

> Ancient texts . . . describe him as a hungry Brahmin, friend and companion of the chief character, having a hump back, protruding teeth, and a bald head with a long strand of hair. He carries a crooked stick and walks with a limp.
>
> In the course of time the Kutiyattam actors have taken this figure and expanded his role to that of a central character in the dramas in which he appears. They have done so at the expense of the text but to the sheer delight of the audience . . . According to tradition, he must recite in Sanskrit, repeat the words of his hero companion in Prakrit and enlarge upon their meaning in Malayalam. Armed with the tool of direct communication with the audience, the clown has been invested with unusual power. It is said he may criticize members of the audience, as well as society as a whole, with impunity . . . so powerful is his license that even kings have restrained themselves from taking offense at his remarks. One of the highpoints of a . . . performance is his satire on the aims of Hindu life. In four successive evenings he holds forth entirely alone upon the stage, often improvising for six hours at a stretch, wittily chastising society and prominent individuals with his barbed invectives. Because of his freedom to

> criticize all members of society, regardless of their social rank and caste, the audience experiences a unique sense of communitas. In this the clown serves as a leveller of society. It is no wonder then that the clown role may be played only by the eldest and most respected members of the actor community (who, incidentally, belong to a marginal caste called Cakyars . . . the mother being of one caste and father of another, whose line was traditionally carried on as a result of a plea to the king to allow them to adopt children who were illegitimate, born of a union of a Brahmin woman and a non-Brahmin man). A quick wit, excellent grasp of Sanskrit literature, Hindu philosophy, and religious practices, and perception of the weaknesses and foibles of mankind are necessary accomplishments before an actor dares assume the role . . . We have an in-between figure who mediates between the world of the play and the world of reality, given the utmost license to criticize, and given the power to pollute absolutely if its power is challenged (Richmond 1980:11 – 12, 13).

The clown pollutes, apparently, by removing his headdress; this brings the performance to an abrupt halt, polluting the entire temple in which it takes place. You may say that the clown's role hardly exemplifies the anti-temporality of the liminal domain, since it involves detailed commentary on the conduct and mores of contemporary personages. Nevertheless this commentary is really what Geertz would call a "meta-commentary" since it takes place within a frame which, as we shall see, is basically religious and composed of cosmological symbols. The clown is what we have earlier called a "symbolic type" and has something numinous about him. He sees history *sub specie aeternitatis*, an eternal vision not without rough humor, reminding us of Puck's gleeful aside to Oberon: "Lord, what fools these mortals be." The illusions of time are judged by eternal truth, the cosmic as comic.

The contrast between time and anti-time is quite clear when we look at the setting, the theatrical space, the costumes, and the actors in Kutiyattam. Performances are set in temple theaters (*kuttambalam*) situated in front and to the right of the main shrine within the precincts of Hindu temples. Such temple theaters, as the Richmonds make clear, are patently microcosms, sacred structures replicating the eternal cosmos.

> The *kuttambalam* is considered an *anga* or limb of the *vastapurusa* or 'personage' of the temple. Let us examine the word *vastapurusa*. The *vastapurusamandala* is a ritual diagram or plan which guides the form or existence of a sacred place—in this instance the Hindu temple and, by extension, the kuttambalam. The diagram (*mandala*) is not an architect's blue print. It is not a ground plan to be followed during construction. Rather, it is a *yantra*. Professor Stella Kramrisch, in her scholarly opus, *The Hindu Temple*, defines the word *yantra* as a "geometrical contrivance by which any aspect of the Supreme Principle may be bound to any spot for the purpose of worship." This sense of "binding" or "tying down" is a theme which is played upon with

> many variations in respect to space and time. The word *vastu* means site or residence. In the context of the word *vastapurusamandala* it means boundaries of existence, boundaries of space, the boundaries of an ordered universe, the boundaries, in this instance, of the temple or *kuttambalam*. As the universe is the outward manifestation of the Divine Essence, so is the temple, and by extension, the *kuttambalam*, the outward form of the Divine Cosmic Essence, *Purusa*. Who is this Purusa? The Purusa of the *Rig Veda* is the creator god. In the *Brahamanas* he is known as *Prajapati*. In a famous hymn to Purusasakta we are told how the world was fashioned by the gods by sacrificing this primordial giant. The sun sprang from his eyes, the moon from his mind; from his breath the wind sprang forth and Indra and Agni from his mouth. The four castes (*varnas*) too are equated to parts of his enormous being—the *brahmins* to the head, the *kshatriyas* to the arms, the *vaishyas* to the thighs and the *shudras* to the feet. The universe was thus created and both cosmic and social order came into being at this sacrifice. Purusa/Prajapati is the thirty-fourth god, he who contains all the others in his being. He is all there was, is, and will be. Thus he is both the sacrificer and the sacrificed, the victim and the god. Through sacrifice he brings into being the cosmos. Through death, there is life. The humblest and the most exalted of Vedic sacrifices recreate this great death and birth of the cosmos. When, out of chaos, violence, and sacrifice the universe comes into being, it takes on shape and becomes ordered, and out of the vast nothingness, space is circumscribed. So also the building of a temple theatre and the performance of the Kutiyattam. But these sacrifices, that original moment and act of creation is captured (Richmond and Richmond 1980:1 – 3).

You may have noticed how, in a complex metaphorical way, the cosmogony implicit in these arrangements of sacred and theatrical space (the two overlap) is homologous with the movement of the social drama from the phase of crisis to that of redress, when indeterminacy is reordered. Here the contemporary unruliness is directly connected to primordial chaos and redress to cosmos construction. An appropriate setting for a play which mediates between immemorial sacred tradition and contemporary social reality! I do not want to deploy here the full range of the Richmonds' argument that the Kutiyattam performance "is regarded as a visual sacrifice in honor of the deity and the stage charged with cosmic significance." They have gone into great detail: for example, relating the squareness of the stage to the Hindu notion that "totality is symbolized as 'four-squared'," and that the square,

> with its four directions of North, South, East and West, encompasses the cyclical movement of the rising sun in the East and its setting in the West. . . . Therefore the square stage is a microcosm of the universe. The gods and the planets have their abode here. On the ceiling of the stage their image is carved. They take their residence there,

> protecting the stage and the performance, ensuring that the "visual sacrifice" (*chakshusayagna*) will be completed without interruption. On this stage, the action of gods, demigods, demons, and heroes, personages of the three worlds, is played out. In the center of the ceiling resides Brahma, out of whose creative power and life force, the universe came into being (Richmond and Richmond 1980:3 – 5).

The actors wear costumes that are

> non-realistic in appearance. Oddly-shaped crowns, peculiar bustle-like skirts, red-striped jackets, makeup of greens, yellows, black and white, are some of the most striking visual impressions that meet the eye. As representatives of the cosmic world, a world peopled by gods and demons, of mythological kings and their retinues, a world in which men can fly, demons can change their shape at will, a world in which supernatural powers and insights are commonplace, a world we mortals cannot enter, it is no wonder that the characters dress in apparel that looks totally different from that which we wear. There is no attempt made to recreate a specific historical period either, for the characters are beyond the concept of time and space—they are cosmic figures, figures not of this profane world (Richmond and Richmond 1980:7).

Lest we should think this South Indian genre of cultural performance exotic, let us recall our own electronic attempts in film and television, in the so-called "science fiction" and "horror movie" genres, to body forth just such liminal "worlds" of gods, demons, shapeshifters, and curiously clad or cosmeticized people. I do not need to dwell on the etymological link between cosmetic and cosmos. The Kutiyattam actor transforms himself into a cosmic being by the application of skillfully arranged cosmetics. As is often the case in folk drama, the stage has no scenery, in contrast to Western dramatic realism where almost every item of property or scenery makes a specific statement about the characters and places them in a given time frame. Kutiyattam is not set in historic time, but the "timeless time" of the drama is created by the actors by means of manifold conventions. For example, images of time and space are conveyed by actors to the audience through a symbolic gesture-language. Thus, in a traditional performance, a passage of dialogue is repeated three times.

> First the actor chants the Sanskrit lines and executes the stylized gestures for each word, including nouns, pronouns, verbs, adjectives, prepositions and so forth. Then the gesture text is repeated with a marked reduction in tempo and an exaggeration of eye movements and facial expressions. All this is done to the accompaniment of the drums. The passage is chanted once again with gesture accompaniment. What would take only a few minutes to recite in western realistic theater often requires more than half an hour to perform in Kutiyattam. By freeing the spectacle of historical reference points, of

> realistic detail, of the drama of everyday life, the Kutiyattam takes on epic proportions assuming a scale appropriate to the cosmic world (Richmond and Richmond 1980:8).

I see that I have dallied overlong over this case study, which in many ways exemplifies other South, South-East, and East Asian types of theater. Clearly, Kutiyattam is the firstborn child of ritual, perhaps even a younger sibling. Nevertheless, though still oriented to the sacred, it is already (as Jane Harrison might have said) an "exhibition," "something shown," an emergent from true ritual liminality, which engrosses its participants existentially, catching them into the inner momentum of a society's life. Already there is an element of voyeurism, an increase in reflexivity, especially in connection with the hypertrophy of the vernacular clown, and the split between actors and audience. Cognitive detachment is growing: the spectators witness divine, demonic, heroic, and anti-heroic deeds and their denouements; they are no longer kinetically engaged in them. The ritual flow is broken; the possibility of questioning and even rejection is being mutely mooted.

As theater becomes increasingly separated from its ritual and cosmological moorings, it will become less transformative, less initiatory, more a presention of models which are expected to revivify fidelity to the religious meaning they convey. But what T. S. Eliot calls "the shadow" has already fallen between "the experience" and "the meaning." Certainly the clown scoffs, lampoons, and judges people's foibles, crimes, sins, and folly from the perspective of the ideal model. But his license to criticize moves the principle of criticism into the wings of the action. Unthinkable though that might presently seem, the model itself may be doubted. Truly, he comes dangerously near to doing this. According to the Richmonds,

> at one point he parodies the four aims of Hindu life (*purutharsas*) by misconstruing them to be license for overindulgence rather than self-control. He identifies them as enjoyment of sexual pleasure, gorging oneself on food, making oneself averse to sexual pleasure after having enjoyed it, and rendering service to the king and making money by doing so. On one day alone, he requires eight to nine hours to elaborate on the numerous types of hosts in Kerala, on the preparation for cooking various delicacies of different communities. He compares one dish to a beautiful woman and proceeds to devour it with relish (Richmond and Richmond 1980:9).

The clown is obviously a symbolic type, and hence timeless. He is partly the voice of the cosmology which frames his action, condemning the foibles of the time, casting down the mighty, and at the same time representing what Mikhail Bakhtin might have called "the people's second world," the racy and earthy folk meta-commentary on *Homo hier-*

archicus. He represents a sort of sacred secularity, whose ridiculing of solemn pretension by "stunning unpretension" (to borrow Emily Dickinson's phrase) has something imaginative and poetic about it, escaping didacticism and moral hauteur. As has been said about kyogen, the traditional farces of Japanese drama, inserted in performance between aristocratic No plays which they often parody, the Kutiyattam clown seems to state that laughter is lord over all, beginning with the bucolic but extending ultimately to embrace humankind.

It is perhaps time to recapitulate the argument: Social dramas or "dramas of living" (Kenneth Burke) are simultaneously expressions of conflict in corporate groups or groups that aspire to assign meaning to the untoward events by relating the problems of temporality to anti-temporal cosmological schemata, to legal standards and precedents, or to perennial commonsense often operating through ridicule. The third, redressive phase of the social drama, which continues to exist as a cross-cultural, trans-temporal, processual mode, since it is semiogenetic, "meaning assigning," and conflict-resolving, contains primordial modes of cultural performance, ritual, and judicial processes, which, over time, as societies become more complex, larger in scale, with specialized institutions, ramify into genres whose direct connection with the social drama becomes increasingly attenuated. In tribal, nonindustrial societies, social dramas and their redressive means are context-sensitive; in complex societies, ritual, theater, and performances are no longer context-sensitive; in the sense of local community context, however, they may be sensitive to the larger macrosocial contexts—political, familial, economic, and ideological. The germ of reflexivity always present in the social drama develops into theology and jurisprudence in the perduring primary genres, to some extent impoverishing their performative aspects. But with industrialization, urbanization, spreading literacy, labor migration, bureaucracy, the division of the leisure sphere from the work sphere, the growth of the market and money economy, the cleavage in each of us between the choosing "individual" and the structurally ascribed "persona," the professionalization of the arts, the former integrity of the orchestrated religious gestalt that once constituted ritual has burst open and many ramifying performative genres have been born from the death of that mighty *opus deorum hominumque*. Such genres of industrial leisure would include theater, ballet, opera, film, the novel, printed poetry, the art exhibition, museum displays, classical and rock music, carnivals, processions, folk drama, major sports events, and dozens more. *Sparagmos*, the dismemberment of Orpheus, has been accompanied by secularization. Traditional religions, their rituals denuded of much of their former symbolic wealth and meaning, hence their transformative capacity, persist in the leisure sphere but have not adapted well to modernity, save at the cost of relinquishing their healing and inspiriting numinosity. Modernity perhaps means, *inter alia*, the exaltation of what I have called culture's "indicative mood."

But in what some have seen as the "post-modern turn," there are signs of a return to subjunctivity and a rediscovery of cultural transformative modes particularly in some forms of theater. I have vividly in mind a performance of Euripides' *Bacchae* I saw in Japan which was directed by Tadashi Suzuki, which combined traditional ritual and dramatic kinetic and oral "languages" with the innovative use of alternate Japanese and English dialogue by a Japanese and American cast. Pentheus, the doubting and eventually dismembered king, was played in English. Cadmus also spoke his lines in English, as did a messenger. Dionysius was played in Japanese by Kayoko Shiraishi, a widely acclaimed actress of genius, who also played Agave, Pentheus' mother. The Bacchae themselves had no dialogue, and the chorus was half and half, English and Japanese. A reviewer, writing under the initials D. R., for the Tokyo *Japan News* (14 September 1981), wrote, quite justly, that

> the astonishing conversations in Japanese and English create a heightened sense of theater which is as rare as it is impressive. The two characters understand each other, but we understand only one of them. One is a mortal and the other is a deity. If we do not understand, say, Japanese, the deity is really god-like in his incomprehensibility. If we do not understand English, the all-too-human ruler is even more human in his agonized attempts to make *us* understand. It works either way, or both, and the result is perhaps the kind of ritual theater that Euripides had in mind. . . . total incomprehensibility makes for boredom, but half incomprehensibility keys us up, awakens our sense of wonder, makes us give all our attention—in short creates ritual theater. The director knows this very well: music, processions, dances, declamations and that very special sense of the inexorable which is perhaps what Greek drama was originally about.

Thinking the production over, I wondered whether perhaps the Catholic rejection of Latin and the Anglican muting of King James' biblical English may not be remedied by a post-modern turn towards combining the archaic with the modern languages or dialects in liturgy—not simply assigning the modern language to the resacralized clown (who is now seen as a legitimate model for religious action in various Christian denominations), as in Kutiyattam, but putting temporality (including significant moments of Church history) into living dialogue with anti-temporality, through the alternate use of significant liturgical languages. At any rate the dismemberment of traditional religious ritual may be a prelude to its creative re-membering, which is not merely the restoration of some past intact, but setting several formative "pasts" in living relationship, through symbolic action, to our fullest experience of the present.

Ritual must recover much of what it has lost to its multiple progeny, the many genres of cultural performance, which in the frames of play and entertainment have in fact often been entrusted with the reflexive, evaluative, redressive, and semiogenetic tasks once undertaken by religious ritual. In complex cultures with developing electronic media it might be possible to view the ensemble of performative and narrative genres, not as a single mirror held to nature, but as a hall of mirrors. Today we can draw our metaphors from science. In the December 1980 issue of the *Scientific American*, David Emil Thomas shows how the mirror image is not always a faithful reflection, but can be inverted, its handedness reversed, or distorted in other ways by such forms as plane, convex, concave, convex/cylindrical, concave/cylindrical, saddle, or matrix mirrors, while images can be reflected from one to another of these varied types. In similar fashion the multiple performative genres bounce the "real world" problems, issues, and crises of our social dramas—from political *causes célèbres* to marital and familial disputes—from one to another, giving diverse images, transformed, magnified, refracted in terms characteristic of each genre, then flashed on to another better able to scrutinize other aspects of those problems, and so forth.

A complex social process may require complex forms of performative self-scrutiny. In this hall of mirrors, which has its origin perhaps in the third stage of social drama, though varyingly elaborated in different cultures, the reflections are manifold, distorting, dwarfing, bloating, dimming the faces peering into them, provoking not merely thought, but also strong emotions, and perhaps the will to change. The flaw, the ugliness, may be in the mirror, the means through which we represent the world and ourselves in order to evaluate them, inducing people to find perhaps simpler and clearer cultural modes of reflecting experience.

But, in any case, it seems that there is a dynamic relation between social drama and the ensemble of expressive cultural genres, such that each, to quote Ronald Grimes, is the "dialectical dancing partner" of the other. What is unconscious and implicit in one may be conscious and explicit in the other, and perhaps humankind may only advance in understanding, and hence also even technically and organizationally, by fully recognizing this yin-yang type of dynamic interdependence. If one defines "immortality" as "that which is destined to persist through the ages," this "dialectical dance" between event and cultural mirrorings may be called "immortal." The difficulty here is that humankind has found a sure way to terminate itself by means of weaponry derived from its sour knowledge of nuclear fission and fusion, for matter is easier to probe to the root than spirit and can be put to baser uses. Thus, the "immortality of man" may be delusory, not only individuals but the species may be mortal, a word equivalent, as the dictionary tells us, to "human."

Eternity or eternal life is another matter—or is it? Here I must lamely admit that in considering the mechanisms of the human social and cultural dramas, I have omitted the meaning-content of the ritual process as it is utterly manifest in many religions. The complex temporality of all the social and cultural processes I have been discussing demands a moment of experienced eternal life as its cognitive and ontological counterstroke, the factor constructive of processual meaningfulness. And here I will conclude with a *salto mortale*, a leap of faith, which you may construe, according to your varied lights, as a coda, a non sequitur, or a capstone of my argument. In the tradition of positivist anthropology in which I was raised, the reading of Friedrich Von Hügel was considered worse than pornography. But now I will venture to conclude with a paragraph from his book *Eternal Life: A Study of Its Implications and Applications*. You may deduce from it my secret thoughts about what I have openly said:

> Eternal Life, in the fullest thinkable sense, involves three things—the plentitude of all goods and of all energizings that abide; the entire self-consciousness of the Being Which constitutes, and Which is expressed by, all these goods and energizings; and the pure activity, the non-successiveness, the simultaneity, of this Being in all It has, all it is. Eternal Life, in this sense, precludes not only space, not only clock-time—that artificial chain of mutually exclusive, ever equal moments, but even *duration* [here Von Hügel glances at Hénri Bergson, whom in so many ways he deeply admires], time as actually experienced by man, with its overlapping, interpenetrating successive stages. But Eternal Life precludes space and clock-time because of the very intensity of its life. The Simultaneity is here the fullest expression of the Supreme Richness, the unspeakable Concreteness, the overwhelming Aliveness of God [perhaps, in a nontheistic setting, like Zen Buddhism, one could speak of *satori* here, the sudden enlightening flash that *this, here, is* the Great Eternity, or as William Blake might have put it in our Western way, "Eternity is in love with the productions of Time," with a love denying any dualism]; and is at the opposite pole from all empty unity, all mere being—any or all abstractions whatsoever (von Hügel 1912:383).

In the general anti-temporality or contra-temporality or meta-temporality of social dramatic redress, the continuous sense of limitation and inadequacy, the frustratedness of historical experience, are often intuited as the very means in and through which historical humankind apprehends increasingly (but only if he opts to do so) the counterstroke of simultaneity, spontaneity, infinity, and pure action of that quintessence of anti-temporality which has been called absolute timelessness, Eternity.

PART THREE

The Brain

11

Body, Brain, and Culture

The present essay is for me one of the most difficult I have ever attempted. This is because I am having to submit to question some of the axioms anthropologists of my generation—and several subsequent generations—were taught to hallow. These axioms express the belief that all human behavior is the result of social conditioning. Clearly a very great deal of it is, but gradually it has been borne home to me that there are inherent resistances to conditioning. As Anthony Stevens has written in an interesting book which seeks to reconcile ethological and Jungian approaches: "Any attempt to adopt forms of social organization and ways of life other than those which are *characteristic of our species* must lead to personal and social disorientation" (italics added; Stevens 1982:24). In other words, our species has distinctive features, genetically inherited, which interact with social conditioning, and set up certain resistances to behavioral modification from without. Further, Robin Fox has argued: "If there is no human nature, any social system is as good as any other, since there is no baseline of human needs by which to judge them. If, indeed, everything is learned, then surely men can be taught to live in any kind of society. Man is at the mercy of all the tyrants

---

Reprinted with permission of the Joint Publication Board of *Zygon: Journal of Religion & Science*, vol. 18, no. 3 (September 1983).

who think they know what is best for him. And how can he plead that they are being inhuman if he doesn't know what being human is in the first place?" (Fox 1973:13). One of those distinctive human features may be a propensity to the ritualization of certain of our behaviors, from smiling and maternal responsiveness onwards.

Theories of Ritualization

In June 1965, I took part in a discussion on "ritualization of behavior in animals and man" organized by Sir Julian Huxley for the Royal Society and held—perhaps appropriately—in the lecture hall of the Zoological Society of London, near the Mappin Terraces, where the monkeys revel. The "hard core" of the conference consisted of zoologists and ethologists, Huxley, Konrad Lorenz, R. A. Hinde, W. H. Thorpe, Desmond Morris, N. M. Cullen, F. W. Braestrup, I. Eibl-Eibesfeldt, and others. Sir Edmund Leach, Meyer Fortes, and I spoke up for British anthropology in defining ritual, but by no means as unanimously as the ethologists did in defining ritualization. Other scholars represented other disciplines: psychiatrists included Erik Erikson, R. D. Laing, and G. Morris Carstairs. Sir Maurice Bowra and E. H. Gombrich spoke about the ritualization of human cultural activities, dance, drama, and art. Basil Bernstein, H. Elvin and R. S. Peters discussed ritual in education and David Attenborough shared his ethnographic films on the Kava ceremony in Tonga and land-diving in Pentecost, New Hebrides.

The nonethologists generally accepted Leach's position that "it cannot be too strongly emphasized that ritual, in the anthropologist's sense, is in no way whatsoever a genetic endowment of the species" (Leach 1966:403). I took up no public position at that time, since I was secretly, even guiltily impressed by the ethologists' definition of "ritualization" which seemed to strike chords in relation to human ritual, summed up by Huxley as follows: "Ritualization is the adaptive formalization or canalization of emotionally motivated behavior, under the teleonomic pressure of natural selection so as: (a) to promote better and more unambiguous signal function, both intra- and inter-specifically; (b) to serve as more efficient stimulators or releasers of more efficient patterns of action in other individuals; (c) to reduce intra-specific damage; and (d) to serve as sexual or social bonding mechanisms" (Huxley 1966:250). Actually, much of Huxley's definition is better applied analogically to those stylized human behaviors we might call "communicative," such as manners, decorum, ceremony, etiquette, polite display, the rules of chivalry (which inhibit the infliction on one another of damage by conspecifics) than to ritual proper.

In various publications I have suggested that ritual was "a *transformative* performance revealing major classifications, categories, and contradictions of cultural processes." In these respects it might conceivably fulfill Huxley's fourth function, that of "serving as sexual or social bonding mechanisms," by transforming social and personal life-crises (birth, initiation, marriage, death) into occasions where symbols and values representing the unity and continuity of the total group were celebrated and reanimated. The cultural rituals which seem most to embody something resembling Huxley's definition of "ritualization" are "seasonal, agricultural, fertility, funerary, and healing ones, because they make explicit the interdependence of people with their physical environments and bodies" (Grimes 1982:34). But as I have written elsewhere, ritual is not necessarily a bastion of social conservatism; its symbols do not merely condense cherished sociocultural values. Rather, through its liminal processes, it holds the generating source of culture and structure. Hence, by definition ritual is associated with social *transitions* while *ceremony* is linked with social states. Performances of ritual are distinctive phases in the social process, whereby groups and individuals adjust to internal changes and adapt to their external environment.

Meyer Fortes, influenced by Sigmund Freud, defined ritual at the London conference as "procedure for prehending the occult, that is, first, for grasping what is, for a particular culture, occult (i.e., beyond everyday human understanding, hidden, mysterious) in the events and incidents of people's lives, secondly, for binding what is so grasped by means of the ritual resources and beliefs available in that culture, and thirdly, for thus incorporating what is grasped and bound into the normal existence of individuals and groups" (Fortes 1966:411). This formulation might well identify psychoanalytical clinical procedure as ritual process. Fortes makes his Freudian affiliation quite clear when he goes on to write that "ritual is concerned with prehending the unconscious (in the psychoanalytical sense) forces of individual action and existence, and their social equivalents, the irreducible factors in social relations (e.g., the mother-child nexus, at one end of the scale, the authority of society at the other). By bringing them, *suitably disguised*, or symbolized in tangible material objects and actions, into the open of social life, ritual binds them and makes them manageable" (italics added; Fortes 1966:413).

Unlike Leach, Fortes sees ritual more as the handling of otherwise unmanageable power than the communication of important cultural knowledge. For Fortes irreducible ambiguities and antinomies are made visible and thus accessible to public and legitimate control—a position to which with important modifications I myself have subscribed—while for Leach the emphasis in ritual is cognitive and classificatory. As he writes, "it is characteristic of many ritual and mythical sequences in primitive society that the actors claim to be recapitulating the creation of the world and that this act of creation is mythologized as a list of names attached to persons, places, animals, and things. The world is created by the process of classification and the repetition of the classification of itself perpetuates the knowledge which it incorporates" (Leach 1966:405). Ritual's multicoded redundancies inscribe its "messages" on the minds of the participants. Clearly, the main difference between anthropologists of the Leachian persuasion and the ethologists in their concept of ritualization or ritual lay in the emphasis of the former on ritual as learned, culturally transmitted behavior, intrinsically linked with the development of language, and of the latter on ritual as genetically programmed behavior with important nonverbal components.

The Neurobiology of the Brain: Culturetype and Genotype

The years passed. I continued to treat ritual essentially as a cultural system. Meanwhile exciting new findings were coming from genetics, ethology, and neurology, particularly the neurobiology of the brain. I found myself asking a stream of questions more or less along the following lines. Can we enlarge our understanding of the ritual process by relating it to some of these findings? After all, can we escape from something like animal ritualization without escaping our own bodies and psyches, the rhythms and structures of which arise on their own? As Ronald Grimes has said, "They flow with or without our conscious assent; they are uttered-exclamations of nature and our bodies" (Grimes 1982:36). I also asked myself many of the questions raised by Ralph Wendell Burhoe in his part of the introduction to the September 1983:213 issue of *Zygon*—especially, following Edward O. Wilson, what is the nature of the alleged "chain," and how long is it, by which genes hold cultural patterns, including ritual patterns, to use the idiom of sociobiology, "on leash"? This, it seemed to me, is where the neurobiology of the human brain begins to be relevant.

We shall have occasion to look at the findings of Paul MacLean, the neuroanatomist, again later, but something should be said now about his work on what might be called "archaic" structures of the human brain. His early work dealt with what is called the limbic system, an evolutionarily ancient part of the brain concerned with the emotions, cradled in or near the fringes of the cortex. In a 1949 paper he suggested that the limbic system is "the major circuit that would have to be involved in psychosomatic diseases, such as gastrointestinal ulcers caused by social or psychological stress, a now widely accepted hypothesis since it has been demonstrated that this system controls the pituitary gland at the base of the brain and the autonomic nervous systems, which in turn control the viscera" (Konner 1982:147). He further proposed in 1952 that the frontal lobes of the cerebral hemispheres, shown to be "the seat of the highest human faculties, such as *foresight and concern for the consequences and meaning of events*, may have these functions and others *by virtue of intimate connections between the frontal lobes and the limbic system*" (italics added; Konner 1982:147). Here we see that the highest and newest portion of the cerebral cortex has by no means detached itself from an ancient, "primitive" region, but functions as it does precisely "by virtue of its relationship to the old emotional circuitry" (Konner 1982:147). Later, Walle Nauta, a celebrated neuroanatomist, has referred to the frontal lobes as "the neocortex of the limbic system" (Nauta 1971:167 – 87). As Melvin Konner concludes: "Just as other parts of the cortex have been identified as the highest report-and-control centers for vision, hearing, tactile sensation, and movement, so the frontal lobes have emerged as the highest report-and-control center for the emotions" (Konner 1982:147). Thus evolutionarily recent and archaic patterns of innervation interarticulate, and the former is pliant to conditioning while the latter is quite resistant.

Paul MacLean's work, and related studies by Jason Brown, raise the question neatly formed by Burhoe: What is the role of the brain as an organ for the appropriate mixing of genetic and cultural information in the production of mental, verbal, or organic behavior? Burhoe raises further important questions: To what extent is the lower brain, including the limbic system and its behavior (to continue the metaphor), "on a very short leash" under the control of the genotype? (Konner uses the term genetically "hard wired.") In other words is genetic inheritance a definitive influence here? The corollary would seem to run as follows: To what extent is the upper brain, especially the neocortex, which is the area responsible in mammals for coordination and for higher mental abilities, on a longer leash in terms of control by the genotype or genome, the fundamental constitution of the organism in terms of its hereditary factors? Does socioculturally transmitted information *take over* control in humankind and, if so, what are the limits, if any, to its control? Does the genotype take a permanent back seat, and is social conditioning now all in all? The picture thus built up for me was of a kind of *dual control* leading to what Burhoe calls a series of symbiotic coadaptations between what might be called culturetypes and genotypes. MacLean's hypothesis about the anatomical relations of the frontal lobes to the limbic system is certainly suggestive here. Subsequently, MacLean went further and gave us his model of the "triune brain." (As we shall see later, J. P. Henry and P. M. Stephens [1977] have argued that the dominant or left cerebral hemisphere represents a fourth and phylogenetically most recent system peculiar to our species.) According to his model, MacLean sees us as possessing three brains in one, rather than conceiving of the brain as a unity (see Fig. 1). Each has a different phylogenetic history, each has its own distinctive organization and make-up, although they are interlinked by millions of interconnections, and each has its own special intelligence, its own sense of time and space, and its own motor functions (MacLean 1976). MacLean postulates that the brain evolved in three stages, producing parts of the brain which are still actively with us though modified and intercommunicating.

The first to evolve is the *reptilian brain*. This is the *brain stem*, an upward growth of the spinal cord and the most primitive part of the brain, which we share with all vertebrate creatures and which has remained remarkably unchanged throughout the myriads of years of evolution. In lizards and birds this brain is the dominant and controlling circuitry. It contains nuclei which control processes vital to the sustenance of life (i.e., the cardiovascular and respiratory systems). Whereas we can continue to exist without large portions of our cerebral hemispheres, without our reptilian brain we would be dead! What MacLean did was to show that this "struc-

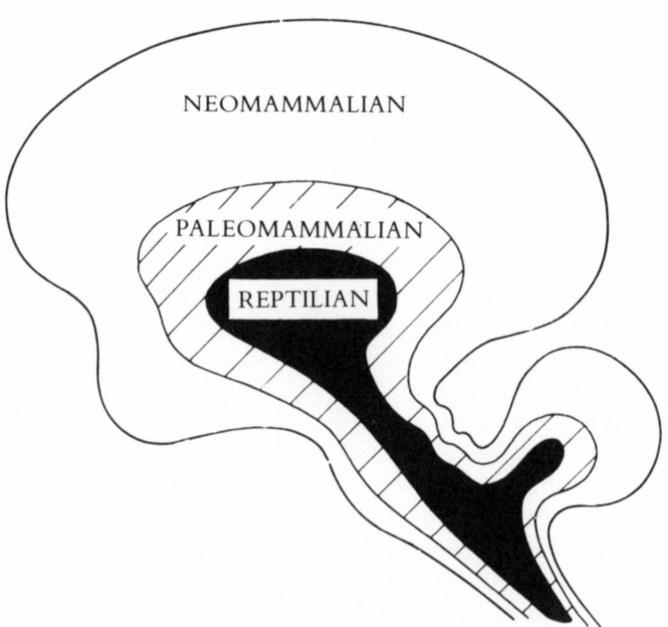

Fig. 1. MacLean's three brains (after MacLean 1973).

ture" or "level," as some term the reptilian brain, whether in reptiles, birds, or mammals, is not only concerned with control of movement, but also with the storage and control of what is called "instinctive behavior"—the fixed action patterns and innate releasing mechanisms so often written about by the ethologists, the genetically preprogrammed perceptual-motor sequences such as emotional displays, territorial defense behaviors, and nest-building. According to J. Brown, reptilian consciousness at the sensory-motor level is centered on the body itself and not differentiated from external space; yet it constitutes, I suppose, a preliminary form of consciousness. The reptilian brain also has nuclei which control the reticular activating system, which is responsible for alertness and the maintenance of consciousness. It is a regulator or integrator of behavior, a kind of traffic control center for the brain. Reptiles and birds, in which the *corpus striatum* seems to be the most highly developed part of the brain, have behavioral repertoires consisting of stereotyped behaviors and responses: a lizard turning sideways and displaying its dewlap as a threat, or a bird repeating again and again the same territorial song. I am not suggesting that mammals have no such behavior—clearly many have much—but rather that birds and reptiles have little else.

MacLean's "second brain" is the one he calls the *paleo-mammalian* or "old mammalian brain." This seems to have arisen with the evolution of the earliest mammals, the monotremata, marsupials, and simpler placentals such as rodents. It is made up of those subcortical structures known as the midbrain, the most important components of which are the limbic system, including the hypothalamus (which contains centers controlling homeostatic mechanisms associated with heat, thirst, satiety, sex, pain and pleasure, and emotions of rage and fear), and the pituitary gland (which controls and integrates the activities of all the endocrine glands in the body). The old mammalian brain differs from the reptilian brain generally in that it is, as the neuroanatomist James Papez defines it, "the *stream of feeling*," while the older "level" is the "*stream of movement*." The hypothalamic and pituitary systems are homeostatic mechanisms *par excellence*; they maintain normal, internal stability in an organism by coordinating the responses of the organ systems that compensate for environmental changes. Later, we shall refer to such equilibrium-maintaining systems as "trophotropic," literally "responding to the 'nourishing' (*trophē*) maintenance of organic systems," "keeping them going," as opposed to the "ergotropic" or aroused state of certain systems when they do "work" (*ergon*), "put themselves out," so to speak. These trophotropic systems, in Stevens's words,

> not only maintain a critical and supremely sensitive control of hormone levels [hormones, of course, being substances formed in some organ of the body, usually a gland, and carried by a body fluid to

> another organ or tissue, where it has a specific effect], but also balance hunger against satiation, sexual desire against gratification, thirst against fluid retention, sleep against wakefulness. By this evolutionary stage, the primitive mammalian, the major emotions, fear and anger, have emerged, together with their associated behavioral responses of flight or fight. Conscious awareness is more in evidence and behavior is less rigidly determined by instincts, though these are still very much apparent. The areas concerned with these emotions and behaviors lie in the limbic system, which includes the oldest and most primitive part of the newly evolving cerebral cortex—the so-called *palaeocortex*. . . . In all mammals, including man, the midbrain is a structure of the utmost complexity, controlling the psychophysical economy and many basic responses and attitudes to the environment. An animal deprived of its cerebral cortex can still find its way about, feed itself, slake its thirst, and avoid painful stimuli, but it has difficulty in attributing function or "meaning" to things: a natural predator will be noticed, for example, but not apparently perceived as a threat. Thus, accurate perception and the attribution of meaning evidently requires the presence of the cerebral hemispheres (Stevens 1982:264–65).

The *neo-mammalian* or "new mammalian" brain, the third in MacLean's model, corresponds to "the stream of thought" proposed by Papez and achieves its culmination in the complex mental functions of the human brain. Structurally, it is the *neocortex*—the outer layer of brain tissue or that part of the cerebrum which is rich in nerve-cell bodies and synapses. Some estimate there to be 10,000 million cells. Functionally, it is responsible for cognition and sophisticated perceptual processes as opposed to instinctive and affective behavior.

Further questions are triggered by MacLean's model of the triune brain. For example, how does it fit with Freud's model of the id, ego, and superego, with Carl Jung's model of the collective unconscious and archetypes, with neo-Darwinian theories of selection, and especially with cross-cultural anthropological studies and historical studies in comparative religion? One might further ask with Burhoe: to what extent is it true that human feelings, hopes, and fears of what is most sacred are a necessary ingredient in generating decisions and motivating their implementation? This question is connected with the problem of whether it is true that such information is necessarily filtered through the highly genetically programmed areas in the lower brain, the brain stem, and the limbic systems. Further questions now arise. For example, if ritualization, as discussed by Huxley, Lorenz, and other ethologists, has a biogenetic foundation, while meaning has a neocortical learned base, does this mean that creative processes, those which generate new cultural knowledge, might result from a coadaptation, perhaps in the ritual process itself, of genetic and cultural information? We also can ask whether the neocortex is the seat of programs largely structured by the culture through the transmission of linguistic and other symbol systems to modify the expression of genetic programs. How far, we might add, do these higher symbols, including those of religion and ritual, derive their meaning and force for action from their association with earlier established neural levels of animal ritualization? I will discuss this later in connection with my field data on Central African ritual symbols.

Hemispheric Lateralization

Before I examine some recent conjectures about the consequences for the study of religion of a possible coadaptation of cultures and gene pools, I should say something about the "lateralization" (the division into left and right) of the cerebral hemispheres and the division of control functions between the left and right hemispheres. The work of the surgeons P. Vogel, J. Bogen, and their associates at the California Institute of Technology in the early sixties, in surgically separating the left hemisphere from the right hemisphere to control epilepsy by cutting the connections between the two, particularly the inch-long, quarter-inch-thick bundle of fibers called the *corpus callosum*, led to the devising of a number of techniques by R. W. Sperry (who won a Nobel Prize in 1981), Michael Gazzaniga, and others, which gained unambiguous evidence about the roles assumed by each hemisphere in their patients (see Fig. 2). In 1979, an important book appeared, edited and partly authored by Eugene d'Aquili, Charles D. Laughlin, and John McManus and entitled *The Spectrum of Ritual: A Biogenetic Structural Analysis*. In an excellent overview of the literature on ritual trance from the neurophysiological perspective, Barbara Lex summarizes the findings of current research on hemispheric lateralization. She writes: "In most human beings, the left cerebral hemisphere functions in the production of speech, as well as in linear, analytic thought, and also assesses the duration of temporal units, processing information sequentially. In contrast, the specializations of the right hemisphere comprise spatial and tonal perception, recognition of patterns—including those constituting emotion and other states in the internal milieu—and holistic, synthetic thought, but its linguistic capability is limited and the temporal capacity is believed absent. Specific acts involved complementary shifts between the functions of the two hemispheres" (Lex 1979:125). Howard Gardner, following Gazzaniga, suggests that

> at birth we are all split-brained individuals. This may be literally true, since the corpus callosum which connects the hemispheres appears to be nonfunctional at birth. Thus, in early life, each hemisphere appears

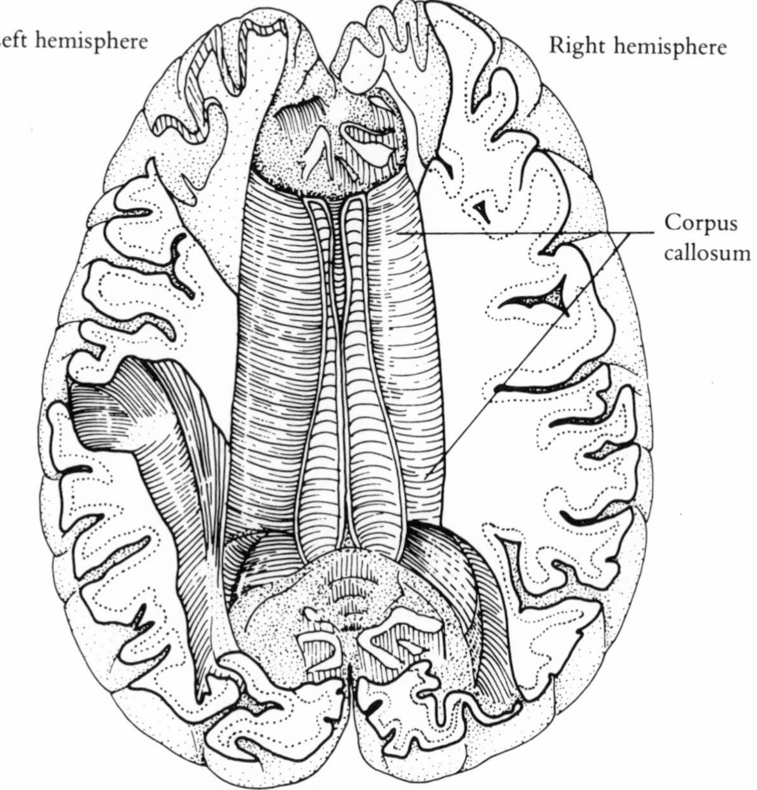

Fig. 2. The corpus callosum seen from above after partial removal and dissection of both cerebral hemispheres (from Stevens 1982).

> to participate in all of learning. It is only when, for some unknown reason, the left side of the brain takes the lead in manipulating objects, and the child begins to speak, that the first signs of asymmetry are discernible. At this time the corpus callosum is gradually beginning to function. For a number of years, learning of diverse sorts appears to occur in both hemispheres, but there is a gradual shift of dominant motor functions to the left hemisphere, while visual-spatial functions are presumably migrating to the right. . . . The division of labor grows increasingly marked, until, in the post-adolescent period, each hemisphere becomes incapable of executing the activities that the other hemisphere dominates, either because it no longer has access to its early learning, or because early traces have begun to atrophy through disuse (Gardner 1975:386).

D'Aquili and Laughlin hold that both hemispheres operate in solving problems "via a mechanism of mutual inhibition controlled at the brain stem level." The world "is approached by a rapid functional alternation of each hemisphere. One is, as it were, flashed on, then turned off; the second flashed on, then turned off. The rhythm of this process and the predominance of one side or the other may account for various cognitive styles [one thinks of Pascal's contrast between *'l'esprit de geometrie'* and *'l'esprit de finesse'*], from the extremely analytic and scientific to the extremely artistic and synthetic" (d'Aquili and Laughlin 1979:174). These authors and Lex then make an interesting attempt to link the dual functioning of the hemispheres with W. R. Hess's model of the dual functioning of what are termed the ergotropic and trophotropic systems within the central nervous system, as a way of exploring and explaining phenomena reported in the study of ritual behavior and meditative states (Hess 1925). Let me explain these terms. As its derivation from the Greek *ergon* (work) suggests, ergotropic is related to any energy-expending process within the nervous system. It consists not only of the sympathetic nervous system, which governs arousal states and fight or flight responses, but also such processes as increased heart rate, blood pressure, sweat secretion as well as increased secretion of catabolic hormones, epinephrine (a hormone secreted by the medulla of the adrenal gland, which stimulates the heart and increases muscular strength and endurance), and other stimulators. Generally speaking, the ergotropic system affects behavior in the direction of arousal, heightened activity, and emotional responsiveness, suggesting such colloquialisms as "warming up" and "getting high." The trophotropic system (*trophé*, in Greek, means nourishment—here the idea is of system-sustaining) includes not only the parasympathetic nervous system, which governs basic vegetative and homeostatic functions, but also any central nervous system process that maintains the baseline stability of the organism, for example, reduction in heart rate, blood pressure, sweat secretion, pupillary constriction, as well as increased secretion of insulin, estrogens, androgens, and so on. Briefly, the trophotropic system makes for inactivity, drowsiness, sleep "cooling down," and trancelike states (Gellhorn and Kiely 1972).

Developing the work of Hess, d'Aquili and Laughlin propose an extended model, "according to which the minor or nondominant hemisphere [usually the right hemisphere] is identified with the trophotropic or baseline energy state system, and the dominant or major hemisphere [usually the left] that governs analytical verbal and causal thinking is identified with the ergotropic or energy-expending system" (d'Aquili and Laughlin 1979:175). They present evidence which suggests that when either the ergotropic or trophotropic system is hyperstimulated, there results a "spillover" into the opposite system after "three stages of tuning," often by "driving behaviors" employed to facilitate ritual trance. They also use the term "rebound" from one system to the other; they find that when the left hemisphere is stimulated beyond a certain threshold, the right hemisphere is also stimulated. In particular, they postulate that the rhythmic activity of ritual, aided by sonic, visual, photic, and other kinds of "driving," may lead in time to simultaneous maximal stimulation of both systems, causing ritual participants to experience what the authors call "positive, ineffable affect." They also use Freud's term "oceanic experience," as well as "yogic ecstasy," also the Christian term *unio mystica*, an experience of the union of those cognitively discriminated opposites, typically generated by binary, digital left-hemispherical ratiocination. I suppose one might also use the Zen term *satori* (the integrating flash), and one could add the Quakers' "inner light," Thomas Merton's "transcendental consciousness," and the yogic *samadhi* (Mandell 1978:80).

D'Aquili and Laughlin believe that though the end point of simultaneous strong discharge of both the ergotropic and trophotropic systems is the same in meditation and ritual, the former begins by intensely stimulating the trophotropic system through techniques for reducing thought and desire in order to maintain "an almost total baseline homeostatis" (d'Aquili and Laughlin 1979:176). This results in "spillover" to the ergotropic side, and eventually to strong excitation of both systems. Ritual, on the other hand, involves initial ergotropic excitation. The authors have previously speculated that *causal* thinking arises from the reciprocal interconnections of the inferior parietal lobule and the anterior convexity of the frontal lobes, particularly on the dominant, usually left side, and is an inescapable human propensity. They call this brain nexus "the causal operator" and claim that it "grinds out the initial terminus or first cause of any strip of reality" (d'Aquili and Laughlin 1979:170). They argue that "gods, powers, spirits, personified forces, or any other causative ingredients are automatically generated by the causal operator" (d'Aquili and Laughlin 1979:170). Untoward events particularly cry out for a cause. Hence "human beings have *no choice* but to construct myths to explain their world," to orient themselves "in what often appears to be a capricious universe." Cause-seeking is "inherent in the obligatory functioning of the neural structures." We are, indeed, back, via neurobiology it would seem, to Aristotle's "first cause that is uncaused" or "Prime Mover unmoved"! We humans cannot do otherwise than postulate first causes to explain what we observe. They write, "since it is highly unlikely that humankind will ever know the first cause of every strip of reality observed, it is highly probable that humankind will always create gods, powers, demons, or other entities as first causes" (d'Aquili and Laughlin 1979:171).

Myths present problems to the verbal analytic consciousness. Claude Lévi-Strauss has made us familiar with some of these problems: life and death, good and evil, mutability and an unchangeable "ground of being," the one and the many, freedom and necessity, and a few other perennial "posers" (Lévi-Strauss 1963, 1963, and 1964). Myths attempt to explain away such logical contradictions, but puzzlement remains at the cognitive left-hemispherical level. D'Aquili and Laughlin argue that *ritual* is often performed situationally to resolve problems posed by myth to the analytic verbalizing consciousness. This is because like all other animals, man attempts to master the environmental situation by means of motor behavior, in this case ritual, a mode going back into his phylogenetic past and involving repetitive motor, visual, and auditory driving stimuli, kinetic rhythms, repeated prayers, mantras, and chanting, which strongly activate the ergotropic system (d'Aquili and Laughlin 1979:177). Ergotropic excitation is appropriate because the problem is presented in the "mythical" analytical mode, which involves binary thinking, mediations, and causal chains arranging both concepts and percepts in terms of antinomies or polar dyads. These are mainly left-hemispheric properties and connect up, in the authors' view, with the augmented sympathetic discharges mentioned earlier: increased heart rate, blood pressure, sweat secretion, pupilary dilation, increased secretion of catabolic hormones, and so on. If excitation continues long enough the trophotropic system is triggered too, with mixed discharges from both sides, resulting often in ritual trance. Lex writes that "driving techniques [also] facilitate right-hemisphere dominance, resulting in gestalt, timeless, nonverbal experiences, differentiated and unique when compared with left-hemisphere functioning or hemisphere alternation" (Lex 1979:125). One solution, if it can so be termed, of the Sphinxian riddles posed by myth, according to d'Aquili and Laughlin, is that "during certain ritual and meditation states, logical paradoxes or the awareness of polar opposites as presented in myth appear simultaneously, *both* as antinomies and as unified wholes" (italics added; d'Aquili and Laughlin 1979:177). There is an ecstatic state and a sense of union, brief in ritual, prolonged in meditation, where culturally transmitted techniques and intense personal discipline sustain the peak experience. One is aware of paradox, but rejoices in it, reminding one of Sören Kierkegaard's joyous celebration of the paradox of the cross as the heart of Christianity.

The problem therefore is resolved in d'Aquili and Laughlin's view not at the cognitive, left-hemispheric level but directly by an experience which is described by the authors as ineffable, that is, literally beyond verbal expression. Presumably the frequent embodiment or embedment of the myth in the ritual scenario, either verbally in prayer or song, or nonverbally in dramatic action or visual symbolism, continues to arouse within the ritual context the "cognitive ergotropic functions of the dominant hemisphere" (d'Aquili and Laughlin 1979:177). If the experiences of participants have been rewarding—and ritual devices and symbolic actions may well tune a wide range of variant somatic, mental, and emotional propensities in a wide range of individuals (amounting to the well-known redundancy of ritual with its many sensory codes and multivocal symbols)—faith in the cosmic and moral orders contained in the myth cycle will obviously be reinforced. A. J. Mandell argues in "Toward a Psychobiology of Transcendence" that "transcendent consciousness, suggested by William James to be the primary religious experience, is a neurochemically and neurophysiologically definable state, an imperturbable hypomania. . . . blissful, empathic, and creative" (Mandell 1978:1).

Play

It is clear that all this refers to the serious work of the brain, as distinct from "play." Full ergotropic, left-hemisphere behavior tends to be dramatic, agonistic behavior. I am not too happy about some authors' tendency to localize mental functions somewhat specifically in cortical regions rather than in interrelational networks, but there does seem to be, broadly speaking, something in the division of labor between the hemispheres, in the different work they do. The term "ergotropic," as we have seen, is derived from the Greek *ergon*, "work" and *tropos*, "a turn, way, manner." It represents the autonomic nervous system in the mode of work, as a sympathetic subsystem, whereas the trophotropic system (from the Greek *trophē*, "food, nourishment") represents the autonomic nervous system in the mode of sustentation, as a parasympathetic subsystem responsible for producing a balance of functions and of chemical composition within an organism. This, too, is a kind of diffused work, less focused and mobilized, less intense than the ergotropic functions. But where does "play" play a part in this model? One seldom sees much mention of play in connection with brain neurophysiology. Yet play, as we have seen in the previous essay, is a kind of dialectical dancing partner of ritual and ethologists give play behavior equal weight with ritualization. D'Aquili and Laughlin hardly mention the word.

The hemispheres clearly have their *work* to do, and the autonomic nervous system has its *work* to do. The one makes for social dramas, the other for social routines. Whether normally functioning or intensely stimulated, the components of the central nervous system seem to have clearly assigned, responsible, interdependent roles to perform. One might speculate that at the neurobiological level play might have something to do with the sensitization of neural structures of an interface type, like the limbic system at the core of the brain, which is known to be intimately associated with the expression of emotion, particularly with the experience of pleasure, pain, and anger. We will return to this later.

As I see it, play does not fit in anywhere particular; it is a transient and is recalcitrant to localization, to placement, to fixation—a joker in the neuroanthropological act. Johann Huizinga, and Karl Groos before him, dubbed it a free activity, but Huizinga, Roger Caillois, and many afterwards have commented on the enclosure of playing within frames of "arbitrary, imperative, and purposely tedious conventions" (Caillois 1977:189). Playfulness is a volatile, sometimes dangerously explosive essence, which cultural institutions seek to bottle or contain in the vials of games of competition, chance, and strength, in modes of simulation such as theater, and in controlled disorientation, from roller coasters to dervish dancing—Caillois' "ilinx" or vertigo. Play could be termed dangerous because it may subvert the left-right hemispheric regular switching involved in maintaining social order. Most definitions of play involve notions of disengagement, of free-wheeling, of being out of mesh with the serious, "bread-and-butter," let alone "life-and-death," processes of production, social control, "getting and spending," and raising the next generation. The neuronic energies of play, as it were, lightly skim over the cerebral cortices, sampling rather than partaking of the capacities and functions of the various areas of the brain. As Don Handelman and Gregory Bateson have written that is possibly why play can provide a metalanguage (since to be "meta" is to be both beyond and between) and emit metamessages about so many and varied human propensities, and thus provide, as Handelman has said, "a very wide *range* of commentary on the social order" (Handelman 1977:189). Play can be everywhere and nowhere, imitate anything, yet be identified with nothing. Play is "transcendent" (to use Edward Norbeck's term), though only just so, brushing the surfaces of more specialized neural organizations rather than existing apart from them or looking down from a godlike height on them. Play is the supreme *bricoleur* of frail transient constructions, like a caddis worm's case or a magpie's nest in nature. Its metamessages are composed of a potpourri of apparently incongruous elements: products of both hemispheres are juxtaposed and intermingled. Passages of seemingly wholly rational thought jostle in a Joycean or surrealist manner with passages filleted of all syntactical connectedness. Yet, although "spinning loose" as it were, the wheel of play reveals to us (as Mihaly Csikszentmihalyi has argued [Csikszentmihalyi:1975]) the possibility of changing our goals and, therefore, the restructuring of what our culture states to be reality.

You may have guessed that play is, for me, a liminal or liminoid mode, essentially interstitial, betwixt-and-between all standard taxonomic nodes, essentially "elusive"—a term derived from the Latin *ex* for "away" plus *ludere*, "to play"; hence the Latin verb *eludere* acquired the sense of "to take away from someone at play," thus "to cheat" or "to deceive." As such play cannot be pinned down by formulations of left-hemisphere thinking—such as we all must use in keeping with the rhetorical conventions of academic discourse. Play is neither ritual action nor meditation, nor is it merely vegetative, nor is it just "having fun"; it also has a good deal of ergotropic and agonistic aggressivity in its odd-jobbing, *bricolage* style. As

Roger Abrahams has remarked, it makes fun of people, things, ideas, ideologies, institutions, and structures; it is partly a mocker as well as a mimic and a tease, arousing hope, desire, or curiosity without always giving satisfaction (Abrahams:pers. comm.). It is as much a reflexive interrupter as an inciter of what Csikszentmihalyi has described as flow states. Like many Trickster figures in myths (or should these be "antimyths," if myths are dominantly left-hemisphere speculations about causality?) play can deceive, betray, beguile, delude (another derivation of *ludere* "to play"), dupe, hoodwink, bamboozle, and gull—as that category of players known as "cardsharps" well know! Actually, Walter Skeat derives the English verb "play" itself from the Anglo-Saxon *plegian*, "to strike or clap"; the Anglo-Saxon noun *plega* means not only "a game, sport," but also, commonly, "a fight, battle" (here again with ergotropic implications).

Play, as stated earlier, draws its materials from all aspects of experience, both from the interior milieu and the external environment. Yet, as Handelman writes, it has no instrumental potency; it is, we might put it, a "shadow warrior," or *Kagemusha*; (see Akira Kurasawa's film, *Kagemusha*). For this very reason, its range of metacommunication is great; nothing human escapes it. Still, in its own oxymoronic style it has a dangerous harmlessness, for it has no fear. Its lightness and fleetingness protect it. It has the powers of the weak, an infantine audacity in the face of the strong. To ban play is, in fact, to massacre the innocents. If man is a neotenic species, play is perhaps his most appropriate mode of performance.

More than that, it is clear, as Konner points out, play is educative. The most intelligent and long-lived mammals have developed it most fully—the primates, the cetacea, and the terrestrial and aquatic carnivores. "It serves the functions of exercise, of learning about the environment and conspecifics, and, in some species, of sharpening or even acquiring fundamental subsistence and social skills." Opportunity for observation of a task in the frame of "play" while or before trying to do it has been "shown to improve the rate of learning it in a number of mammals in experimental settings" (Konner 1982:246–47). Play, then, is probably related to the higher cerebral centers—not forgetting its connection also with arousal and pleasure—particularly in rough and tumble games, where the limbic system is clearly engaged. Yet serious violence is usually controlled objectively and culturally by rules and subjectively by inhibitory mechanisms of perhaps a different type from the Freudian superego or ego-defense mechanisms, although perhaps play does defend consciousness from some of the more dangerous unconscious drives.

Finally, play, like other liminal phenomena, is in the subjunctive mood. What does this mean? The subjunctive designates a verb form or set of forms used in English to express a contingent or hypothetical action. A contingent action is one that may occur but that is not likely or intended.

Subjunctivity is possibility. It refers to what may or might be. It is also concerned with supposition, conjecture, and assumption, with the domain of "as-if" rather than "as-is." (Hence, there must be a good deal of left-hemispheric activity in play, linguistic, and conceptual activity, but done for its own sweet sake.) "As-is" refers to the world of what culture recognizes as factuality, the world of cause and effect, expressed in the "indicative mood"—which indicates that the denoted act or condition is an objective fact. This is *par excellence* the world of the left cerebral hemisphere. The world of the right hemisphere is, nevertheless, not identical with the world of play either, for its gestalt grasp of things holds for it in the sense of a higher reality, beyond speculation or supposition. Play is a light-winged, light-fingered skeptic, a Puck between the day world of Theseus and the night world of Oberon, putting into question the cherished assumptions of both hemispheres, both worlds. There is no sanctity in play; it is irreverent and is protected in the world of power struggles by its apparent irrelevance and clown's garb. It is almost as though the limbic system were itself endowed with higher intelligence, in a kind of carnivalesque reversal of the indicative situation.

However, since play deals with the whole gamut of experience both contemporary and stored in culture, it can be said perhaps to play a similar role in the social construction of reality as mutation and variation in organic evolution. Its flickering knowledge of all experience possible to the nervous system and its detachment from that system's localizations enables it to perform the liminal function of ludic recombination of familiar elements in unfamiliar and often quite arbitrary patterns. Yet it may happen that a light, play-begotten pattern for living or social structuring, once thought whimsical, under conditions of extreme social change may prove an adaptive, "indicative mood" design for living. Here early theories that play arises from excess energy have renewed relevance. Part of that surplus fabricates ludic critiques of presentness, of the status quo, undermining it by parody, satire, irony, slapstick; part of it subverts past legitimacies and structures; part of it is mortgaged to the future in the form of a store of possible cultural and social structures, ranging from the bizarre and ludicrous to the utopian and idealistic, one of which may root in a future reality, allowing the serious dialectic of left- and right-hemispherical functions to propel individuals and groups of individuals from earth to heaven and heaven to earth within a new indicative mood frame. But it was the slippery Trickster who enabled them to do it, and he/she modestly, in Jacques Derrida's ludic words, "erases the trace."

The experiments of James Olds and Peter Milner, at the California Institute of Technology from 1953 onwards, on stimulating by implanted electrodes the hypothalamus of the brains of rats, including the parts radiating from the hypothalamus like spokes (neural pathways to the olfactory and limbic systems, the septal areas, amygdala, etc.), seem to have a bearing on the pleasures of play, but I have not followed up this avenue of inquiry (Olds 1976).

Further Questions on the Brain: Religion, Archetypes, and Dreaming

By indirections we seek out directions. This long digression on hemispherical lateralization, play, and cultural subjunctivity brings me back to some of Burhoe's questions that have been vexing me. How does this picture of brain functioning and of the central nervous system accord with distinctive features of the varied religious systems that have survived to this point in time and exerted paradigmatic influence on major societies and cultures? Here we could profitably compare Eastern and Western religions and their variations. Can some be described as emphasizing in their cosmologies, theologies, rituals, meditative techniques, pilgrimages, and so on, right-hemispherical properties or left-hemispherical dominance? Do some emphasize rituals while others stress modes of meditation and contemplation as their central processes of worship? Again how does this picture fit with descriptions of the varieties of religious experience that have been noted by William James and his successors? Would it be a fruitful enterprise to foster experimental work on the varied genetic and experiential structurings of human brains which might throw light on aspects of religious experience and motivation? We will take a brief look later in this essay at some interesting guesswork by Jungians in relation to this problem. Conversely, can we illuminate, through cross-cultural comparison, the capacity of culturally shaped systems of ritual, symbols, myths, and rational structures to produce viable types of religious experience in the genetically varied population of brains? Here much more detailed descriptive work in the study of different kinds of ritual in a single religious system, as well as cross cultural and transhistorical studies of ritual systems is imperative. So many questions; so few answers. But we can only do fruitful research if we first ask the right questions.

Naturally, the findings of neurophysiologists have provoked many speculations from members of other disciplines not directly concerned with the brain and its workings. The notion of the triune brain propounded by MacLean, for instance, has encouraged Jungian psychologists to claim that a neurological basis has been found for the collective unconscious and its archetypes. One Jungian, Anthony Stevens, has been impressed by the work of P. Flor-Henry and of G. E. Schwartz, R. J. Davidson, and F. Maer (Flor-Henry 1976; Schwartz, Davidson, and Maer

1975). The latter showed that human emotional responses are dependent on neuronal pathways linking the limbic system of the midbrain (the old mammalian brain) with parietal and frontal areas of the right hemisphere. Flor-Henry found that this whole complicated right-hemispheric/limbic affectional system is under the surveillance and control of the left, I repeat, of the *left* frontal cortex. This lends additional testimony to the view that the left hemisphere (via the corpus callosum or the large cable of nerve fibers which connect the two cerebral hemispheres, functioning to transmit information between the hemispheres and to coordinate their activities) can repress or inhibit the activities, especially the emotionally toned activities (which are the vital concern of psychiatrists), of the right. In my discussion of the possible neuronal base of play, you will recall, I guessed at a connection between the midbrain and human upper brain. If Flor-Henry is correct in supposing a left-hemisphere inhibiting effect, might not the propensity to play result from a temporary relaxation of the inhibitory effect, perhaps through the focused cultural means of framing and arousal?

All this leads Stevens to speculate rather interestingly about the relationship of various psychical processes recognized by depth psychology to what is known about the neurophysiology of the brain. His views also bear on the questions I have been raising about the possible nature of religion as at once a supergenetic and a superindividual agency developed from the coadaptation or integration of two semiautonomous systems. These are, in Burhoe's terms, first, basic genetic information and its biological expression, particularly in the lower levels of the brain, whose genetic programs are not so very different from those in protohuman hominids, and, second, the specifically human generation of a living sociocultural system where the learning powers of the upper brain radically modify the common human gene pool, resulting in enormous cultural and phenotypical variation, that is, variation in manifest characteristics. Stevens argues, "While it may well be that psychic processes belonging to the personal 'Freudian' unconscious proceed in the right hemisphere, it seems probable that Jung was right when he guessed that the archetypal systems, if they could be given a local habitation and a name, must have their neuronal substrate located in the phylogenetically much older parts of the brain" (Stevens 1982:265 – 66).

For those who are unfamiliar with Jungian terminology, archetypes (according to Stevens's definition) are "innate neuropsychic centers possessing the capacity to initiate, control, and mediate the common behavioral characteristics and typical experiences of all human beings irrespective of cultural differences" (Stevens 1982:296). Jung himself, who rejected the view that humankind was a blank slate or a *tabula rasa* on which experience was prenatally (that is, experience begins in the womb, and communication between Mother and child correlates with the development of neuronal pathways in the fetal brain [see Treuarthan 1947]) and postnatally inscribed, held that our species is *born* with numerous predispositions for perceiving, feeling, behaving, and conceptualizing in particular ways. As he put it:

> There is no human experience, nor would experience be possible at all without the intervention of a subjective aptitude. What is this subjective aptitude? Ultimately it consists of an innate psychic structure which allows man to have experiences of this kind. Thus the whole nature of the human male presupposes woman, both physically and spiritually. His system is tuned in to woman from the start, just as it is prepared for a quite definite world where there is water, light, air, salt, carbohydrates, etc. The form of the world into which he is born is already inborn in him as a virtual image. Likewise parents, wife, children, birth, and death are inborn in him as virtual images, as psychic aptitudes. These *a priori* categories have by nature a collective character; they are images of parents, wife, and children in general, and are not individual predestinations. [This is perhaps Jung's clearest formulation of what he means by archetypes.] We must therefore think of these images as lacking in solid content, hence as unconscious. They only acquire solidity, influence, and eventual consciousness in the encounter with empirical facts which touch the unconscious aptitude and quicken it to life. They are, in a sense, the deposits of all our ancestral experiences, but they are not the experiences themselves" (Jung 1972:para. 300).

Archetypes manifest themselves subjectively in such things as dreams, fantasies, writing, poetry, painting and objectively in such collective representations as myths, rituals, and cultural symbols—and in many other modalities. Jung speaks of the Family archetype, the Feminine archetype, the God archetype, the Hero archetype, the Mother archetype, the Masculine archetype, the Wise Old Man archetype, using capital letters to distinguish them from the identically named roles occupied by actual, historical individuals.

Stevens thinks it is impossible to locate any of the archetypes in any precise neurological fashion. Each must have "an extremely complex and widely ramifying neurological substrate involving millions of neurones in the brain stem and limbic system (the instinctive or biological pole) and *both* cerebral hemispheres (the psychic or spiritual pole)" (Stevens 1982:266). However, E. Rossi, another Jungian psychologist, argues that it is the right hemisphere which principally processes archetypal components, since, "Jung's concepts of archetype, collective unconscious, and symbol are more closely associated with the use of the imagery, gestalt, and visuospatial characteristics of right hemispheric functioning" (Stevens

1982:266). Rossi also insists that, although the archetype is an imprint or pattern—perhaps a "trace"—which exists independently of the conscious ego, it constantly comes under left hemispheric processing in the form of words, concepts, and language. But when this happens the archetypes, he writes, "take their color from the individual consciousness in which they happen to appear" (Stevens 1982:266). Thus they are, so to speak, superficially denatured and clothed in the vestments provided by individual memory and cultural conditioning.

It is because of the difficulty of translating right-hemispherical processes into the logical, verbal formulations of the left brain that some emissions into ego consciousness of archetypal images are perceived as numinous, awesome and mysterious, or uncanny, preternaturally strange. They seem to be clad in primordial authority undetermined by anything known or learned. Henry and Stephens consider that both hemispheres are able to suppress communication from the limbic system (Henry and Stephens 1977). We have seen how the left hemisphere may inhibit communication from the right. Henry and Stephens believe that psychic health and personality integration depend as much on the maintenance of open communication between limbic system and cortex as on interhemispheric communication. They suggest that the neurophysiological function of dreaming is to facilitate integration of processes occurring in the limbic system with those of the cerebral hemisphere. This would fit well with Jung's views as well as with the French sleep expert Michel Jouvet's findings that the low voltage, high frequency EEG waves characteristic of dreaming sleep originate in the brain stem and spread upward through the midbrain to the cortex—perhaps bringing information from various levels of the unconscious (Jouvet 1975). Perhaps dreams, like the ritual symbols I have analyzed, are laminated, accreting semantic layers, as they move from brain stem through limbic system to the right hemisphere before final processing or editing by left-hemispheric processes.

The Composite Brain and the Bipolar Symbol

These findings are interesting when related to my fieldwork among the Ndembu, a matrilineal society of northwest Zambia, during the 1950s. I discovered that what I called dominant or pivotal symbols in their ritual processes were not only possessors of multiple meanings but also had the property of polarization. For example, a tree which exuded a milky white latex was the dominant symbol of the girls' puberty ritual (the novice was laid under a consecrated "milk tree" and wrapped in a blanket, where she had to lie motionless throughout a whole long day while initiated women danced around her and the tree). The whole milk tree site, almost *mise-en-scène* was called *ifwilu*, which means "place-of-dying," for it was there that she died from her childhood. At this point she was separated from her own mother, who took a minimal part in the ritual. But the milk tree (*mudyi*) was intimately connected with motherhood. I pieced together its many meanings from talking to many informants during many performances at which my wife and I were present, and have written about this research in several books, including *The Forest of Symbols* and *The Drums of Affliction* (Turner 1967 and 1968). Briefly, the milk tree was said to "be" (more than merely to "represent") mother's milk, lactation, breasts, and nubility, at what could be called the physiological or orectic pole of its meaning. "Orectic" is a term used by philosophers, and was formerly quite popular among psychologists, meaning "of or characterized by appetite or desire."

But the milk tree also "was" the matrilineage of the girl novice; it was where "the ancestress slept, where they initiated her and another ancestress and then another down to the grandmother and the mother and ourselves the children. It is a place where our tribe (*muchidi*) began—and also the men in just the same way" (Turner 1968). Thus it was more than a particular matrilineage; it was the principle of matriliny itself. It was even the whole Ndembu nation, one of whose distinctive features was its matrilineal organization. At some episodes of the long complex ritual, the milk tree was also said to stand for women and for womanhood. Another meaning, indexical rather than iconic, represented the milk tree as the relationship between the novice and her own mother in that place and at that time. It indicated that the relationship would be transformed by the performative action, since the daughter was no longer a dependent child but would become, like her mother, a married woman after the ritual seclusion and the coming-out rites were over and was potentially a mother herself. I called this more abstract set of meanings the normative or ideological pole, since it referred to principles of social organization, social categories, and values.

The milk tree also has other denotations and connotations, but it has struck me recently that these layers of meaning might well relate to what is being discovered about the functions of the brain. The orectic pole, referring to physical mothering and lactation, and charged with desire—the novice's desire to be fully a woman, the desire of the mature women to add a recruit to their number, the desire of a lineage for replenishment, the future bridegroom's desire for the novice (represented by the insertion of an arrow presented by the bridegroom into the ground among the roots of the milk tree) and many other modalities of desire—the orectic pole, then, surely has some connection with the functions of the limbic system, the old mammalian brain. This system MacLean calls the visceral brain because of its close connections to control centers for drive and emotion.

Structures in the limbic system are believed to be the sites of action of many psychotropic drugs, including antipsychotic tranquilizers (e.g., thorazine) and hallucinogens (e.g., LSD). In the ritual itself, with its powerful drumming and insurgent singing in which the women lampoon and deride the men, we observe ways of arousing the ergotropic system and the left-hemispheric functions of critical linear thought. We can also see a triggering of the right-hemispheric apprehensions of pattern and holism by finally including the men in the ritual action and making them part of a scenario in which the novice is borne off to a newly made seclusion hut on the margin of the village, where she will undergo liminal instruction by female elders for many months, before "coming out" in a ritual which is also the precursor of her marriage.

Clearly, too, the normative pole of meaning including the references to matriliny, womanhood, tribal unity and continuity, and the mother-child bond, has connections with upper brain activities involving both hemispheres. One might speculate that the Jungian archetype of the Great Mother and the difficulty, resolved among the Ndembu by prolonged and sometimes painful initiation ritual, of separation from the archetypal power of the Great Mother are in some way connected with the milk tree symbolism and with the ritual behavior associated with it. It is interesting to me that a dominant symbol—every ritual system has several of them—should replicate in its structural and semantic make-up what are coming to be seen as key neurological features of the brain and central nervous system.

Conclusion

Does the new work on the brain further our species' self-understanding? Clearly an extreme ethological view of human society as rigidly genetically determined is as uninformative as an extreme behaviorist view of the human brain as a *tabula rasa* written on by experience. According to the extreme ecologists, we are "innately aggressive, acquisitive, nationalistic, capitalistic, and destructive" (Rose 1976:351). Some of them announce our doom by overcrowding or urge the space race as a means of channelling aggressiveness. Some even give veiled approval to limited war or natural population control by drought, famine, or plague, as the means of securing ecological balance. While B. F. Skinner would modify and adapt us by environmental manipulation, reminding me irresistibly of H. G. Wells's *First Men on the Moon* in which the Selenites (the original Moonies), an insect species, were quite literally shaped by biological and psychological techniques to perform the labor appropriate to their caste, some ethologists would argue that our genetics damn us, despite our intelligence and will to survive. Regnarøkr, not Walden II, will be the end of history. Hence the vogue for doom talk about such inevitabilities as ecocide, population explosion, and innate aggressiveness. Surely, a middle path is possible. Cannot we see those modalities of human perception and conceptualization, the lower brain and the upper brain, the archaic and recent systems of innervation as having been for at least several millions of years in active mutual confrontation?

It seems to me that religion may be partly the product of humanity's intuitions of its dual interiority and the fruitful creative Spirit generated by the interplay of the gene pool, as the Ancient of Days, and the upper brain, as Logos, to use the intuitive language of one historical religion, Christianity. The Filioque principle (the Spirit proceeding from the Father *and* the Son), Western Christians might say! Since culture is in one sense, to paraphrase Wilhelm Dilthey, objectivated and crystallized mentality (*Geist*), it may well be that some cultures reinforce one or another semiautonomous cerebral system at the expense of others through education and other modes of conditioning. This results in conflict between them or repression of one by another, instead of free interplay and mutual support—what is sometimes called love.

As you can see, I have been asking questions and making guesses in this paper rather than coming up with answers. My career focus mostly has been on the ritual process, a cultural phenomenon, more than on brain neuroanatomy and neurophysiology. But I am at least half convinced that there can be genuine dialogue between neurology and culturology, since both take into account the capacity of the upper brain for adaptability, resilience, learning, and symbolizing, in ways perhaps neglected by the ethologists *pur sang*, who seem to stop short in their thinking about ritualization at the more obviously genetically programmed behaviors of the lower brain. It is to the dialectic, and even contradiction at times, between the various semiautonomous systems of the developed and archaic structures of innervation, particularly those of the human brain, that we should look for the formulation of testable hypotheses about the ritual process and its role as performing noetic functions in ways peculiar to itself, as a *sui generis* mode of knowing.

Let me conclude by reassuring those who may have obtained the impression that all I am saying is that ritual is nothing but the structure and functioning of the brain writ large, or that I am reducing ritual to cerebral neurology, that I am really speaking of a global population of brains inhabiting an entire world of inanimate and animate entities, a population whose members are incessantly communicating with one another through every physical and mental instrumentality. But if one considers the geology, so to speak, of the human brain and nervous system, we see represented in its strata—each layer still vitally alive—not dead like stone, the numerous pasts and presents of our planet. Like Walt Whitman, we "embrace multitudes." And even our reptilian and paleomammalian brains are human, linked in infinitely complex ways to the conditionable upper brain and kindling it with their powers. Each of us is a microcosm, related in the deepest ways to the whole life-history of that lovely deep blue globe swirled over with the white whorls first photographed by Edwin Aldrin and Neil Armstrong from their primitive space chariot, the work nevertheless of many collaborating human brains. The meaning of that living macrocosm may not only be found deep within us but also played from one mind to another as history goes on—with ever finer tuning—by the most sensitive and eloquent instrument of Gaea the Earth-spirit—the cerebral organ.

12

The New Neurosociology

In the course of writing these essays, as you have seen, I fell under the spell of the recent exploding research on brain neuroanatomy and neurophysiology and became interested in their implications for the study of ritual. I will go on to discuss theories and theorists of myth, to relate myth to ritual, and finally to link both to that set of concepts I have developed over the years under the general label of social drama. I am postulating that there are human universals in brain and nervous system, that total neuronic apparatus so sensitively responsive to the immediate situation we find ourselves in, so ready to be inscribed with the engrams of growing experience, and yet in its archaic parts and functions on such a short genetic leash, uniting and opposing ethological ritualization and cultural ritual in a dance of circumstance. Here I would go part of the way with the Gallo-structuralists such as Lévi-Strauss but deny what some would call their "left-hemispheric imperialism," as we shall see. There are other brains within the brain than the "dominant hemispheric." And I will also postulate, moving from neurology to culturology, that there are certain modes of human behavior, social dramas, found in all historical periods and in all societies at a given time, which are isolable, divisible into clearly marked phases, and can be shown to be the dynamic matrices, not only of ritual in the simpler societies, but of theater in societies of greater scale and complexity, and indeed of many other genres of cultural performance.

I dissented from Edmund Leach's definition of ritual as merely a "communication code," or as merely "potent in itself in terms of the cultural conventions of the actors but *not* potent in a rational-technical sense." I took the view that "potency" may have much to do with the subjective states of those involved in it, and there may be a great deal of sense in those definitions which take into full account not only habits, conventions, and rationality—though these are obviously important—but also the willing, desiring, feeling, affect, and intentionality of those engaged in ritual processes. I also mentioned E. d'Aquili and C. Laughlin's suggestion that the linkage of certain areas in the parietal and frontal regions of the left cerebral hemisphere, more specifically the inferior parietal lobule, the anterior convexity of the frontal lobes and their reciprocal connections, might be described as "the causal operator." What they are saying, in effect, is that human beings are "programmed" or "wired" to seek causes for any significant, more or less isolable "strip of behavior" or sequence of events, be it in nature, culture, or the self, such as Aristotle's First Mover and First Cause, and so forth. From this, they argue, arises the "birth of the gods" and the postulation of invisible or supernatural causes, God, deities, spirits, demons, witchcraft, or impersonal "power," to account for effects whose physical causes at a given epoch cannot be determined by rational or pragmatic or scientific means. Societies generate cosmogonic myths which state authoritatively how the known classified universe came into existence and what its first and final causes are. As d'Aquili and Laughlin (1972:161) put the matter: "Man has a drive, [termed by Roy Rappoport, "the cognitive imperative"] to organize unexplained external stimuli into some coherent cognitive matrix. This matrix generally takes the form of myth in nonindustrial societies and a blend of science and myth in western industrial societies." But myths sometimes *expose* paradoxes without sufficiently explaining them to anyone's rational satisfaction.

The point I wish to make here is the rather simple one that rituals are not, in general, simply the direct conversion of mythic narratives into bodily action and dramatic dialogue, though these narratives may be ingredients of a complex ritual process. Rituals, in a sense, *oppose* myths, in those cultures where both cultural genres are well developed, for there are cultures with *both* elaborately developed, others with much of one and little of the other, and others still with poor development of both. Rituals *oppose* myths because they posit an existential solution to problems which the left hemisphere, which is a substrate for much more than the causal operator (for example, linguistic ability, conceptualization, the perception of linear and temporal order, the perception of antinomies) finds itself intellectually unable to resolve. Here a distinction should, perhaps, be drawn between the *liturgies* of the historical, universalizing religions, in their "high culture," "Great Tradition" modalities, and the *rituals* of nonindustrial, "folk" or "little tradition" religions. Liturgies, despite their literal Greek meaning of "public services to the gods," from *leos, laos,* "people" plus *ergon*, "work," have indeed tended to be the translation into modes of symbolic action, if not of the myths, at any rate of the doctrines and dogmas logically and hence left-hemispherically derived from creation stories and foundation narratives of the deeds and words of founders, prophets, disciples, and first disseminators of major religions. They are often elitist, literate constructions translated into what, from the viewpoint of religious leaders, may represent "appropriate" symbolic actions. In other words, many liturgical actions lie under the sway of left-brain "imperialism," as some perhaps over-enthusiastic converts to right-brain "creativity" have called it. Not all liturgical actions, of course, may be so characterized because the ritual process tends to "come up from below," in the gestures, litanies, music, dramatic episodes, gospel singing, and chantings that perfuse and sometimes creatively undermine attempts to convert doctrines into doings.

Yet myths, especially creation and origin myths, should not be considered entirely as the products of left-hemispherical thinking, clothed in right hemispherical imagery, the implicit position of the earlier structuralists. As all now know, the great French anthropologist Claude Lévi-Strauss opposes the notion, put forward in particular by Lévy-Bruhl, but shared to some extent by Max Muller, Ernst Cassirer, and Henri Frankfort, that the human capacity for thinking has evolved from (even replaced) a "prelogical" or "subjective," or as Lévy-Bruhl would have said, "primitive" mentality, to a rational, objective, modern one, grounded in reality-testing and scientific experiment. Lévi-Strauss, and here I would go along with him, argues, that *primitives* and *civilisés* alike, think "naturally" in the same way. Universal human thought, *pensée sauvage*, thus replaces the evolutionist doctrine of progress from *mentalité primitive* to *mentalité civilisée*. The content of a culture's knowledge depends, of course, on the degree of technological and scientific development, but, so Lévi-Strauss argues, the "savage" mental structure which can be disengaged from the palpable integument of what often seem to us, in the West, bizarre modes of symbolic representation—as in myth—is identical with our own Western mental structure. As Leach once put it, the same digital logic is responsible for Telstar, the communication satellites, and the cosmogonic myths of the Australian aborigines. We share with primitive humankind, Lévi-Strauss holds, the same mental habits of thinking in terms of binary discriminations or oppositions; like them, too, we have rules governing the combination, segregation, mediation, and transformation of relationships and ideas. Thus we can find in the myths of Australian aborigines or ancient Sumerians the same types of binary thinking and its mediation that underlie computer construction and programming. The main difference between the paleo-Hegelian myth-making aborigine and the modern scientist, according to Lévi-Strauss, is that unconscious process in the former is conscious in the latter, and is applied by the scientist to different subject-matter, in his case to the material world. This position prompted Paul Ricoeur to characterize Lévi-Strauss's position as "Kantianism without a transcendential subject." Others have spoken in this connection of a "Kantian unconscious," that is, a "categorical, combinatory unconscious." Ricoeur argues that, unlike Kant's notion of mind, the structural unconscious is "a categorical system without reference to a thinking subject." Perhaps the subject is, as Leach has suggested, a generalized *esprit humaine*. Yet, in a sense, both Lévy-Bruhl and Lévi-Strauss are correct. Here we may revert once more to work on the neuroanatomy of the brain. Ever since Sperry did his Nobel Prize-winning research on commissurotomy, the split-brain operation which severs all direct connections between the two hemispheres of the forebrain, as pointed out in an earlier essay, there has been a growing flood of research on the functions of the left and right cerebral hemispheres, and, indeed, on the relationship between components of the archaic brain (brain stem and limbic system) and the developed human upper brain. Previous to this research, it was thought that the right hemisphere was unspecialized and subordinated to what was called the "dominant" left (in most right-handed and even in about half of left-handed individuals). But, as Barbara Lex (1972:125) puts it: "Ample evidence, carefully garnered from study of normal individuals, as well as of patients in whom the cerebral hemispheres have been surgically disconnected by transection of the intermediary neural structures (the corpus callosum and anterior commissure), documents the existence of two distinct modes of thought. Bogen summarizes the impact of these new findings: 'Our present recognition is that the hemispheres are not as much "major" or "minor" as that they are complementary, and that each hemisphere is capable of thinking on its own, in its own way.' " Many tests have shown that while the left hemisphere is better at using language and making logical deductions, the right hemisphere is better at perceptual and construction tasks, such as map-reading, block design, and picture-comprehension. The right is also better at holistic or configurational perception, such as one uses when recognizing a face (certain lesions in the right hemisphere lead to the condition known as prosopagnosia, inability to recognize faces, Greek *prósopon*), which may, however, merely be the sign of a genetic difficulty in making fine discriminations. The right can synthesize fragmentary sensory information into complete percepts, recognizable sensations received by the mind through the senses. The left brain is much more adept at analyzing and breaking down information into temporal sequences. Computers tend to be modeled almost exclusively on left hemispherical properties, it would seem. So far the other brain regions have not been replicated. Can we anticipate a computer with a complex limbic system? The Russian neurophysiologist Luria contrasted the left hemisphere's *sequential* processing with the *simultaneous* perceptual processing of the right. Some researchers mark the difference by calling those who operate under the dominant influence of the left brain "divergent" thinkers—whose ranks would include those who stress specific details and how things differ from one another—botanical taxonomists, for example. There is some clinical evidence that the "obsessional" or "compulsive" type of personality, nose down to detail, could be associated with hypertrophy of left hemispheric activity. The right-hemispherically dominant types, to the contrary, tend to seek out universal characteristics, common denominators, underlying the immense phenomenological richness of nature and culture. Obviously, in normal human beings both sides continuously collaborate, but these emphases are in the long run palpable and visible in accurate biographies. Thinking is thus not solely a function of the left-hemisphere, but is, to paraphrase D. H. Lawrence, "a brain in its wholeness wholly attending."

Musical appreciation, which calls on Gestalt perception rather than logical analysis—except, notoriously in the case of musicologists—is linked with the right hemisphere. There should be added here Arthur Deikman's notion that the left is the "active" hemisphere, the right the "receptive." The left "does," the right "is"; the former is energetic and purposive, the latter "witnesses." There is clearly a danger here of falling into the left hemisphere's own favorite trap of organizing the attributes of the hemispheres in terms of binary opposites, pluses and minuses. It seems to be more the case that different qualities of awareness are to be associated with the left and right brains. Some researchers have described these in computer terminology (which, again, to my mind denatures the difference) as *left-brain digital codification*, that is discursive, verbal, and logical processes, as against right-brain *analogic codification*, that is, nondiscursive, nonverbal and eidetic, designating visual images that are unusually vivid. Joseph E. Bogen (1969) previously quoted, approves of the formulation and writes: "Where *propositional* thought, that is, thought containing expressions in which the predicate affirms or denies something about the subject, is typically lateralized to one hemisphere, the other hemisphere evidently specializes in a different mode of thought which may be called appositional." Appositional means literally "put side by side," but Bogen prefers to leave its meaning vague. He says that since much of the right hemisphere is still *terra incognita*, the full meaning of "appositional" will only emerge as we gain further understanding of its capacities through experiment. He says the distinction seems to be, crudely and metaphorically, like that between the "head" and the "heart," which as Pascal observed, "has its reasons whereof reason is ignorant" (*la coeur a ses raisons que la raison ne connait pas*).

Back, then, to myth and the opposition between Lévy-Bruhl and Lévi-Strauss. Modern cerebral neuroanatomy suggests that both are correct and that it is not a question of the evolutionary development of a logical from a prelogical mode of thinking. Rather, Lévy-Bruhl, in his analysis of myth, seizes on what we now know to be right-hemispherical contributions to this genre, "mystical participation" among actors, symbols, and the like. Lévi-Strauss, on the other hand, asserts that the binary logic of myth (even though embedded in unconscious processes) is of the same type as that of modern science and is as rigorously applied. He may reduce, in one respect, diachrony to synchrony, but the underlying logic in myth, he would hold, proceeds in a linear and logical, and not in a Gestalt holistic, manner. It is this left-hemispheric reductionism (or "imperialism") which perhaps provoked from Mary Douglas the sweetly malicious comment: "It seems that whenever anthropologists apply structural analysis to myth they extract not only a different but a lesser meaning" (1975:166). She is perhaps suggesting here that what Bogen called the "appositional" richness of the right-hemispherical contribution to this narrative has been "commissurotomized," denuding it of its creative potential. She saw more of this potential in Augustine's "antitypical" interpretation, where he saw Noah's being mocked as a prefiguration of the mockery of Jesus after the scourging at the pillar by the Roman soldiers.

On the other hand, Lévy-Bruhl was quite put out when he received a rapturous letter from the Belgian poet Émile Verhaeren, whose work had included a profound critique of urbanized man caught up in the toils of *les villes tentaculaires*, the "tentacular towns." Verhaeren had just read *La Mentalité Primitive*, supposedly a positivistic analysis of primitive humankind's emotional, personal understanding of the world and its supernatural causes, thus an "earlier stage" in the evolution of consciousness. "You have shown me, master, just how we poets of modernity grasp the world," cried the ecstatic poet. Clearly, *this* mode of consciousness was still alive, not surpassed! To a major extent this was right-brain thinking, though inevitably transformed into left-brain sequences of words and empowered by sources deep in the archaic brain. Putting it simplistically, Lévi-Strauss's left hemispheric approach does not replace but complements Lévy-Bruhl's right hemispheric approach to myth and the mentality or thinking behind it.

This brings me to the depth psychologists, who, in their explanations of myth—which we have to relate cross-culturally to ritual, even when in any given society one or the other is attenuated, even virtually absent—regard the unconscious "psyche" or "mind" (terms now returning, apparently, to favor) as the supreme source of mythic symbols and their drive to cultural and public expression. Their stance is the opposite of those we have been considering, which rooted myth in cognitive attempts to explain humankind's insoluble dilemmas as each culture construes them: Why death? Why evil? Why multiplicity *and* unity? Why *not* immortality? Why man *and* woman? Why (the question in Lévi-Strauss's classical analysis of the Oedipus myth) does the human race originate from the earth as the ancient Greeks supposed (the notion of chthonic origin) and yet clearly is the result of human reproduction, as experience demonstrates? Do we originate from One or Two? True to his Durkheimian background, as Leach has written, Lévi-Strauss sees myth as "thinking itself" in men and women rather than being thought by individual men and women and then socially disseminated. A sort of over-consciousness, an over-mind, an *esprit humaine* is posited, language personified and hominiform.

The depth psychologists invert the source of myth, making of it an emergence from the unconscious of psychological needs and wishes pictured and played out in the bizarre, often incestuous, murderous, and cannibalistic deeds of the cosmogonic gods and society structuring culture heroes. Nevertheless they, too, posit a transpersonal, yet oddly hominiform entity, of a universal character, a sort of "underworld" *esprit humaine*, as the supreme author or architect of the mythic in all cultures. As the poet Rilke wrote, "Speak not of this one nor of that—It's Orpheus when there's song"—one poet in all poets, rising from the underworld. Freud, as we know, in his topographical model, assumed that there is in all humans an "unconscious" which is at once a source of innate drives (e.g., the longing for immortality—as in Nietzsche's phrase "*Alle Lust Will Ewigheit*") and a repository of experiences and feelings repressed into the unconscious, often from earliest infancy. The conscious ego is that part of the psyche, derived phylogenetically from the unconscious, which experiences the outside world through the senses, organizes the thought processes rationally, and governs actions. Normally it is unaware of the desires and conflicts present in the unconscious, due to a set of unconscious defense mechanisms which protect it from the upwelling of painful or anxious feelings associated with the repressed material. However, in addition to neurotic and psychotic symptoms, there are three major ways in which the unconscious drives are disguised and allowed some measure of conscious expression. These are dreaming, daydreaming, and the making of myths. It is of the essence of Freud's position that these masked and cloaked desires are to be regarded as "illusions," and that religion should be included among such illusions—as witness his book, *The Future of an Illusion,* which is for him the future of religion, and his characterization of myths as "the fairy tales of religion." He drew a parallel between the psychoanalytic therapeutic process in which the patient is assisted by the analyst to discriminate between real and fantasied happenings, and thereby to develop a strong healthy ego attuned to the environment and no longer browbeaten by the superego, the largely unconscious enforcer of unnaturally rigid moral standards, and the historical process of secularization through science which will "see through" all mythic guises by tracing their real source in the panhuman unconscious. In a way, his position complements that of Lévi-Strauss: Freud's affirms the need for the emergence and liberation of a strong rational ego from unconscious constraints and now able to cope with inner and outer stresses and strains; Lévi-Strauss's affirms the existence of such a rational consciousness *beneath* the apparently fanciful outward trappings of myth. Both, in their own ways, represent left hemispheric hegemony, if not imperialism, and would deny real value to the creative aspects of right hemispheric functioning.

As I mentioned earlier, Jung is a depth psychologist whose views seem, on the whole, partly consonant with the new neurological discoveries, and have in fact recently received some reinforcement from them; ironically, since it was Freud who began his career as a neurologist, and indeed coined the term *agnosia* to refer to any failure in the recognition of objects, whether at the earlier stage of form perception or the subsequent association of percepts to meaning. Like Freud, Jung insisted that myths are powerful expressions of the unconscious and preconscious psyche, just as dreams and daydreams are. But he made a further distinction, repudiated by Freud's followers, between the "personal unconscious," which he equated with Freud's unconscious, and the "collective unconscious," which all human beings share regardless of culture, ethnicity, gender, and time. Modern Jungians, like Anthony Stevens, E. Rossi, and J. P. Henry, speculate that the personal Freudian unconscious is mainly lodged in the processes of the right hemisphere, while the neuronal substrate of the Jungian collective unconscious they would locate in the phylogenetically much older parts of the brain, the brain stem and limbic system.

However, the Jungian archetypes, those genetically transmitted active, living dispositions, that perform and continually influence our thoughts and feelings and actions, though welling up from the archaic reptilian and paleomammalian brain segments, obviously have each a complex and widely ramifying neurological substrate, connecting the lower brains with the cerebral hemispheres (see Stevens 1982:262–67). Since they emerge as *imagery* in dreams and myths, it is possible that they are processed by the right hemisphere, but since they can also emerge in the form of words, concepts, and language, they do not escape the influence of the left hemisphere. Henry and Stephens (1977) conclude from their survey of neurophysiological evidence that not only can the left hemisphere inhibit communication from the right, but also that both hemispheres may be capable of suppressing communications from the limbic system which is concerned with emotionally toned activities. Jungian therapy sees its task as integrating and balancing the different mental systems, whose cerebral substrates the neurologists are beginning to discover. The emergence of archetypes, especially the mandala symbol, in dreams and art therapy, plays a major role in the maturation process of patients, known as "individuation." Thus Jung did not take the view that dream and myth symbols disguise repressed material, but that the collective unconscious is the repository of life-giving and unifying archetypal symbols— "symbols" because they clothe what are essentially "protoplasmic patterns" in imagery and ideas supplied by the upper brain and gleaned from the ego's experience in his/her natural and cultural environment.

How far is it true that the upper cortex is the seat of programs mainly structured by culture through the transmission of linguistic and other symbol systems to modify the expression of genetic programs? And how far do these higher symbols (of myth and ritual) derive their meaning and force for action from their association with earlier-established neural levels of animal nature? The conflicts among the scholars I have listed concerning whether myth is rational or irrational in character or whether it is located in conscious or unconscious thinking must surely yield to the new findings of the neurobiologists who are attempting to answer these and similar questions. Research now shows that we have in effect four semiautonomous centers, the extremely archaic brain stem, the limbic system, and the left and right hemispheres. The first two are on a tight genetic leash, the last two on a longer leash. It would appear that all goes well if the four are in harmony.

Somehow, I am irresistibly reminded of William Blake's *Prophetic Books*, in which the four brains seem to correspond to some extent with his "Four Zoas," "forms of life," whom he calls Urizen, Los, Luvah, and Tharmas. Urizen, who is the reasoning power, has strongly left-hemispheric attributes; Los, "the Eternal Prophet," the creative power, has right hemispherical attributes, despite the fact that he is sometimes equated with time, and his wife or "Emanation" Enitharmon, with space; Luvah, the erotic and passionate Zoa, the "King of Love," but who is also identified at times with "red Orc," "the King of Rage," and who is less distinctly human than the first two, has limbic system characteristics. Before the Fall, Luvah is the cupbearer of the Eternals, serving among them "the wine of eternity" (Blake 1965, *The Four Zoas* [1797]:385). Afterwards he becomes Love's "contrary," the "spiritual Hate from which springs Sexual Love" (Blake 1965, *Jerusalem* [1804]:201). While Tharmas, "Lord of the Waters," in "the World of Tharmas, where in ceaseless torrents His billows roll, where monsters wander in the foamy paths" (*The Four Zoas*:315)—sometimes called the "Parent power, darkening in the West" (*The Four Zoas*:297), and associated with the sense of touch—seems to represent the primordial element from which all life arises, the "stream of motion" associated by some neurologists, for example, Paul MacLean, with the brain stem's functions. Tharmas is also called "father of worms & clay" (*The Four Zoas*:325), terms that seem to link him with elementary forms. In Blake's personal myth, the Fall is an extraterrestrial event, which occurs when the Zoas become involved in a kind of power struggle, and each is displaced from or voluntarily renounces his proper function, claiming that of another. Disorder reigns; harmony is lost. In particular Urizen, the ratiocinating and regulative power, who, according to Blake, should be essentially the articulator and orderer of the productions of the others, tries to be their master and submit all to "the stony Law" which judges without mercy or love and rests on moral condemnation and punishment—superego characteristics which some researchers associate also with the left hemisphere. The original balance, the paradisial state, is destroyed and each Zoa follows his own selfish interests, with the possible exception of Los, who retains in some measure even after the Fall the "Human Form Divine" and continues to be associated with artistic creativity. When the Zoas are creatively coactive they appear, as Blake says, "as One Man" (sometimes personified as "Albion"), the archetypal Man, similar to the Adam Kadmon of the Kabbalists, although from another perspective they appear as an infinite multitude. Humankind is both One and Many, depending, as, Blake might say, "On the Organ that beholds it." In the state Blake calls Forgiveness ("Mutual Forgiveness of each Vice . . . Such are the Gates of Paradise"), a state that involves self-sacrifice through love rather than sacrifice of others as victims to perpetuate the "Stony Law" (which began to operate when the pristine operant unity broke down), the original unity of the Zoas is restored, and the long sleep of Albion, "the Sleeper on the Rock of Ages," is ended. Los emerges at the end of Blake's *Jerusalem* as a kind of Messiah-figure, identified with Jesus as Blake saw him, the archetypal "artist": "& Albion knew that it was the Lord the Universal Humanity, and Albion saw his Form/A Man. & they conversed as Man with Man, in Ages of Eternity./And the Divine Appearance was the likeness & similitude of Los" (Blake 1965, *Jerusalem* [1804]:253), as though humanity will ultimately be redeemed through art which, of course, was Blake's own calling, both as painter, poet, and engraver. But at that ultimate moment when, as he puts it, "Generation is swallowed up in Regeneration," he also places Science—no longer self-isolated from human life—represented by Newton, Bacon, and Locke, in one triumphal chariot equal to the one in which he has placed Milton, Shakespeare, and Chaucer, representing Art, the two together exemplifying Forgiveness and the restoration of human wholeness or perfection (*Jerusalem*:254). If Blake's vision is a sort of "projection" from the interiority of the cerebro-nervous system, this would suggest that the ideal state is one of perfect, uninhibited communion and communication between the four "brains" as characterized by Paul MacLean.

Blake's vision is curiously akin here to Jung's. Jung distinguished between the *Self* and the *Ego*. By *Self* he meant the entire archetypal system of the unconscious; it was for him a concept vital for understanding *individuation*, the process of personality development which leads to the fullest possible actualization of the *Self* in a given individual. As Jung puts it: "Individuation means becoming a single, homogenous being, and, in so far as 'individuality' embraces our innermost, last, and incomparable uniqueness, it also implies becoming one's own self, self realization" (Jung 1953 – 78: vol. 7, para. 266). Jung's Self is like Blake's Four Zoas in harmony. He defines it thus: "The Self is not only the center but also the whole circumference which embraces both conscious and unconscious; it is the center of this totality, just as the Ego is the center of the conscious mind" (Jung 1953 – 78: vol. 12, para. 44). Stevens considers the Self to be the psychic aspect of the *genome*, which is the complete genetic constitution of an organism, the entire genetic programming characterising the species. Rossi, Galin, and others locate *ego*-consciousness in the left hemisphere. But this may be a reflection of the left-hemispheric imperialism written into Western culture. Consciousness is surely not located in a specific area of the cerebrum, but is a complex process dependent on a network of multitudinous neuronal structures, some hierarchically arranged, others not. Roger Sperry concludes that consciousness is a property of brain circuitry and brain chemistry working as a whole. That is why it may be somewhat misleading to talk of "reptilian" and "mammalian" brains. Since all the major brain components are intricately interconnected, together they make up the *human* brain, thus even the brain stem and limbic system are "humanized," "made over" to the human condition (just as Blake personified each of the four Zoas), tinctured and invested with what comes to them and is taken from them by the higher centers. Consciousness and unconsciousness then are dynamic systems in constant interaction, whose events occur in both hemispheres, but in the West culture has come to decree that dominance should be assigned to the left hemisphere's "structuring" properties. So the dictatorship of Blake's Urizen over the other Zoas may represent the cultural reinforcement of a natural propensity, not a pure fact of nature. Blake's slogan "Art against Empire" may have been part of his attempt to restore the balance, like his emphasis on the equality of painting and drawing with written text, in his work.

Both Jung and Blake see wholeness as something to be achieved. It is to be achieved by an acceptance of the *inter*dependence of all the neuropsychic centers. Somehow human beings seem to have power to inhibit or resist the flow of consciousness and affect through all the systems. Hence the depth psychologists' notion of the Superego, which according to Freud represents the inner moral authority or ethical complex which monitors individual behavior so as to make it acceptable first to the parents and later to society. Perhaps the superego too has a phylogenetic foundation, despite its sensitivity to culture that is mediated initially through parental training and example.

For Jung, the individuation process was a lifelong struggle between the perceived needs of the conscious Ego and the movement towards manifestation or actualization of the Self, the total psychical being, where culturotype and genotype interact, seeking authentic symbiosis. The Ego, like Blake's Urizen, is not the master, but the son and servant or administrator of the Self. As Jung puts it: "The Self, like the unconscious, is an *a priori* existent out of which the Ego evolves. It is . . . an unconscious prefiguration of the Ego" (Jung 1953–78: vol. 11, para. 391). The Ego, in fact, is, according to Jung, a sort of projection of the Self into time, space, history, and culture, and its job is to facilitate the later, full emergence of the Self (or in Blake's term the Identity), the process Jung calls "individuation." As Jung also describes the relationship, "The Ego stands to the Self as the moved to the mover, or as object to subject, because the determining factors which radiate out from the Self surround the Ego on all sides and are therefore *supra*ordinate to it" (Jung 1953–78: vol. 11, para. 391). The Ego, however, is very often recalcitrant, unwilling to accept its function as servitor and resists unconsciously the sequential unfolding of the Self. Ego-lessness is not at *all* Ego's aim. The penalty of Ego-ness is inner impoverishment, since the conscious Ego cuts itself off from the unconscious replenishment it needs for its own fulfilment. Indeed, as several religions tell us, one must die to live more fully, one must lose one's life to save it (here "die to Ego to live as Self," or rather, to have Ego mirror Self fully). This Ego-death is painful, seeming to be a sacrifice of one's own individuality, certainly a relinquishment of power in the material sense over other egos, and an abandonment of possessions. It requires openness where there was once repression and secrecy. The upper and lower brain, the cultured and the archaic, the left and right, the masculine and feminine within (to change the terms of discourse) must freely communicate. The Many inside us must be One, in harmony (a word derived from the Greek *harmos*, "a fitting"), if we are to be one with the many outside us. This, I believe, is the psychogenic, even the neurogenic basis for that mode of human interrelatedness I have sometimes called *communitas*, an undifferentiated, egalitarian, direct, extant, nonrational, existential relationship which may arise spontaneously among human beings, but may frequently also be found in the liminal periods of ritual, or in nonritual types of liminal situations such as voyages, and training and summer camps.

These considerations lead me to see myth in somewhat a different light from that provided by d'Aquili and Laughlin, who tend to stress myth as the expression of conceptual models through the medium of language. [These models account for relations in what they term the *zone of uncertainty*, defined as "the range of disparity between man's ability to experience effects and his inability to isolate causes."] Myths certainly use language, but I should emphasize that anyone who has seen a myth told in its village or folk context will confirm that many nonverbal codes are used in the telling, gestures, mimicry, singing, drawing in the audience as a chorus, sometimes making pictures in the sand to illustrate the narrative; in brief, myth-telling is a subgenre of *ritual* performance, engaging the emotions of the group as well as their minds. Myths, too, are performances, as Dennis and Barbara Tedlock and Peter Seitel are demonstrating in their descriptive and analytical studies, not texts divorced from ritual or social action. Indeed, the Greek term *mythos* (μύθos), means "Anything delivered by word of mouth; a speech in the public assembly; a tale, story, narrative," from the verb *mytheomai* (μυθέομαι), meaning "I say, speak, or recount." Clearly, an audience is required, and I would guess, a verbally responsive one.

In a curious way, in myth, the human brain does more than merely reveal its cognitive structures; rather it allegorizes its own *e pluribus unum* character, as in the personalized Blake version, but even more so in the great collective representations which set forth the origins of things in major cultures and religions. Human beings grow from, embody, represent, and transcend the other terrene forms, inanimate and animate, which preceded them and in multitudinous instances continue to live with them, in various relationships ranging from indifference, through competition, to symbiosis. Each of these forms of life or protolife, which we have been or virtually been, has inscribed itself ineradicably and phylogenetically in our central nervous system, particularly in our complex and multiple brain. Terra's planetary unfolding re-unfolds in us, or, reversibly, folds itself manifoldly in the convolutions of the neo-cortex as we learn about our planet and ourselves "being there" on it. Do not be deceived by our transience as individuals; the aeons that have made us seek to be replayed in our lives. *Tempi* are irrelevant; it is the *pattern* of unfolding that matters. Here that mysterious thing, the will, seems to be able to accept or retard the Self's thrust to manifestation in the human sphere of culture and communication through language, despite external pressures or internal repressions, or, indeed, favorable circumstances. Myth is the whole brain, recent and archaic, playing or performing itself to itself, using the costumes, props, and masks of particular cultures, the products of social experience in specific habitats, but revealing the contours of its own topography and the traces of its own intersecting movements. It is as fully charged with limbic emotions, and with what may be the transcendent function—the reconciliation of opposed processes—performed by the cerebral commissure, that is, the "*limen*" or threshold between the hemispheres, in itself the very symbol of transition and the transcendence of previous states (at the very least a transformative bridge); it is as fully charged with the interplay of language, imagery, and music across that bridge from the left and right halves of the upper brain, as it is with cognitive structures or charters validating extant social structures (as Malinowski proposed). Walt Whitman wrote: "I embrace multitudes" and his "I" seems not to have been Jung's concept of Ego but of Self. In the same way, the brain is a multitude, reducible perhaps to a foursome, of which the dominant left hemisphere is like Blake's Urizen: only a part, though a most important part. If myth is a kind of brain map, in all honesty it cannot show the contraries in it as logically reconciled, in terms of left brain understandings. All it can do is to reveal logical paradox, and to indicate that left-brain consciousness may represent the loss of an ancient harmony, but, in compensation, may prove a live factor in the creation of a new harmony, to be achieved, not necessarily through cognition or logic, but through the mutual forgiveness of difference, even through rejoicing in difference. What is probably necessary here is a left-brain humility, not left-brain pride. Reason should not, of course, be subordinated to feeling, left brain to right, upper to lower, but the fully operational brain must learn to reason feelingly and feel reasonably.

And now, back to ritual, and from yet another angle. If myth can to some degree be considered a highly colored map of brain neuroanatomy, ritual may perhaps be thought of, however crudely, as given its momentum by brain neurophysiology. Ritual is powered by the different brain components and the body they nourish and are nourished by, in dynamic interaction, stimulated by the brains and bodies of other conspecifics. Interaction is here raised, so to speak, to a higher power, a meta-interaction or, as Silverstein would suggest, a meta-praxis, a way of doing which comments upon and assigns meaning to other human ways of doing. As I mentioned in my previous essay, d'Aquili and Laughlin (1979:177) argue that ritual is often performed (situationally) "to resolve problems posed by myth to the analytical verbalizing consciousness." This is because "like all other animals man attempts to master the environmental situation by means of motor behavior, in this case ritual, a mode going back into his phylogenetic past and involving repetitive motor, visual, and auditory driving stimuli, kinetic rhythms, repeated prayers, mantras, and chanting which strongly activate the ergotropic system." This, in turn, activates the trophotropic system. Eventually both cerebral hemispheres are aroused, producing, under favorable conditions, brief ecstatic states where "logical paradoxes or the awareness of polar opposites as presented in myth appear simultaneously both as antinomies *and* as a unified whole" (p. 176). Motoric awareness of unity, both in the immediate social situation and of the nature of things, exists without anxiety side by side with a sharpened intellectual apprehension of the contradictions in experience: life and death, nature and culture, animate and inanimate, Yin and Yang, one and many, two and one, and so on in a long list. The problems are not resolved, as in cold blood, at the cognitive left-hemispheric level, but directly in that nonverbal noetic mode known as "ritual knowledge."

Epilogue

Are There Universals of Performance in Myth, Ritual, and Drama?

In this final essay I will discuss what I think is a characteristic developmental relationship from ritual to theater, and I will lay out the relationship of both to social drama. The figures in this chapter express schematically some of these connections. I have argued that every major socioeconomic formation has its dominant form of cultural-esthetic "mirror" in which it achieves a certain degree of self-reflexivity. Nonindustrial societies tend to stress immediate context-sensitive ritual; industrial pre-electronic societies tend to stress theater, which assigns meaning to macroprocesses—economic, political, or generalized familial problems—but remains insensitive to localized, particularized contexts. Yet both ritual and theater crucially involve liminal events and processes and have an important aspect of social metacommentary. In many field situations I have observed in markedly different cultures, in my experience of Western social life, and in numerous historical documents, I have clearly seen a community's movement through time taking a shape which is obviously "dramatic." It has a proto-esthetic form in its unfolding—a generic form like the general mammalian condition that we still have with us throughout all the global radiation of specific mammalian forms to fill special niches. As detailed in earlier essays, in the first stage, Breach, a person or subgroup breaks a rule deliberately or by inward compulsion, in a public setting. In the stage of Crisis, conflicts between individuals, sections, and factions follow the original breach, revealing hidden clashes of character, interest, and ambition. These mount towards a crisis of the group's unity and its very continuity unless rapidly sealed off by redressive public action, consensually undertaken by the group's leaders, elders, or guardians. Redressive action is often ritualized, and may be undertaken in the name of law or religion. Judicial processes stress reason and evidence, religious processes emphasize ethical problems, hidden malice operating through witchcraft, or ancestral wrath against breaches or tabu or the impiety of the living towards the dead. If a social drama runs its full course, the outcome (or "consummation," as the philosopher John Dewey might have called it)—the fourth stage in my model—may be either (a) the restoration of peace and "normality" among the participants, or (b) social recognition of irremediable or irreversible breach or schism. Of course, this mode, like all models, is subject to manifold manipulations. For example, redressive action may fail, in which case there is *reversion* to the phase of crisis. If law and/or religious values have lost their cultural efficacy, endemic continuous factionalism may infect public life for long periods. Or redressive failure in a local community may lead to appeal to a higher court at a more inclusive level of social organization—village to district to province to nation. Or the *ancien régime* may be rejected altogether and revolution ensue. There may a "transvaluation of values."

In that case the group itself may be radically restructured, including its redressive machinery. Culture obviously affects such aspects as the style and tempo of the social drama. Some cultures seek to retard the outbreak of open crisis by elaborate rules of etiquette. Others admit the use of organized ritualized violence (almost in the ethological sense) in crisis or redress, in such forms as the holmgang (island single-combat) of the Icelanders, the stick-fights of the Nuba of the Sudan, and the reciprocal head-hunting expeditions of the Ilongot hill peoples of Luzon in the Philippines. Simmel, Coser, Gluckman and others have pointed out how conflict, if brought under gradual control, stopping short of massacre and war, may actually enhance a group's "consciousness of kind," may enhance and revive its self-image. For conflict forces the antagonists to diagnose its source, and in so doing, to become fully aware of the principles that bond them beyond and above the issues that have temporarily divided them. As Durkheim said long ago, law needs crime, religion needs sin, to be fully dynamic systems, since without "doing," without the social friction that fires consciousness and self-consciousness, social life would be passive, even inert. These considerations, I think, led Barbara Myerhoff (1978:22) to distinguish "definitional ceremonies" as a kind of collective "autobiography," a means by which a group creates its identity by telling

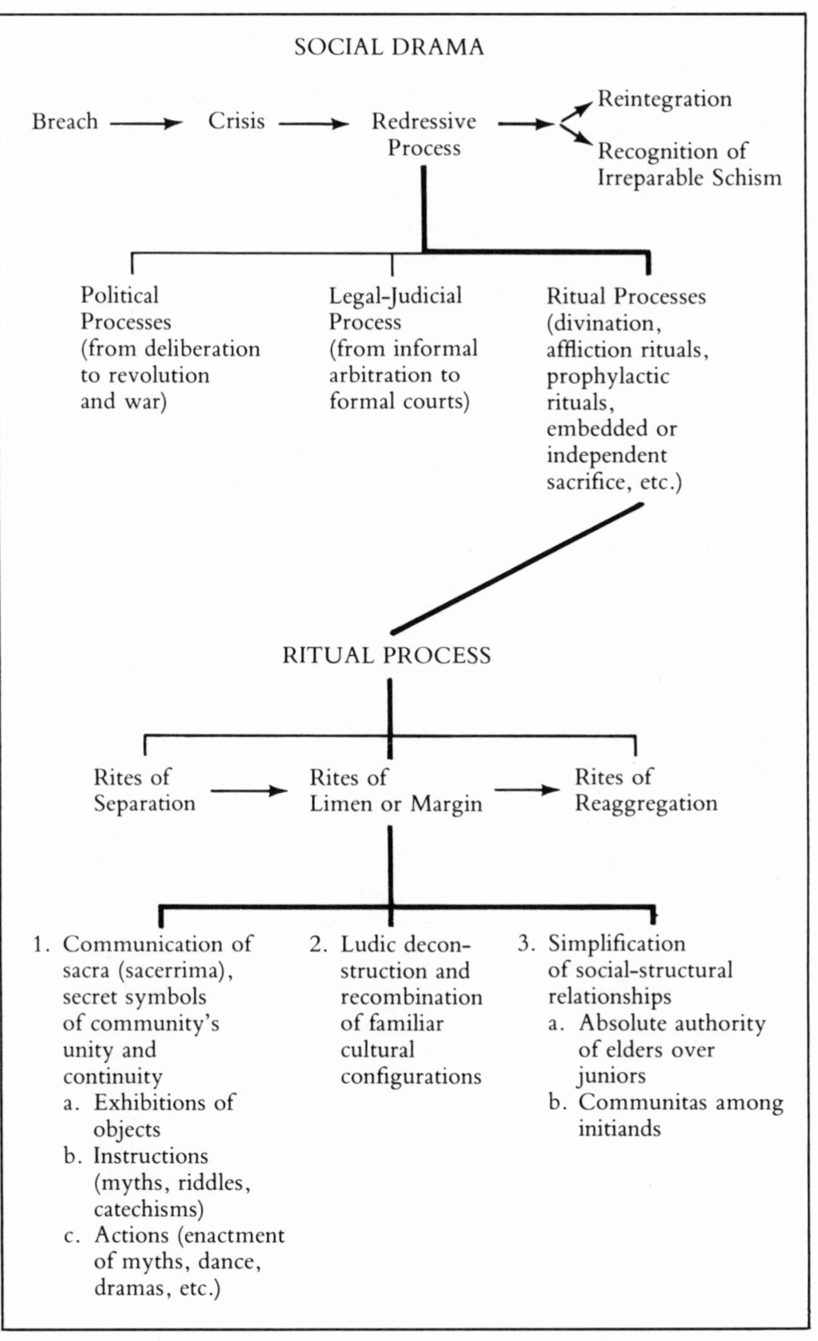

Fig. 3. The relationship between social drama and ritual process.

itself a story about itself, in the course of which it brings to life "its Definite and Determinate Identity" (to cite William Blake). Here, meaning, in Wilhelm Dilthey's sense, is engendered by marrying present problems of the living present to a rich ethnic past, which is then infused into the "doings and undergoings" (to quote John Dewey) of the local community. Some social dramas may be more "definitional" than others, it is true, but most social dramas contain, if only implicitly, some means of *public reflexivity* in their redressive processes. For by their activation groups take stock of their own current situation: the nature and strength of their social ties, the power of their symbols, the effectiveness of their legal and moral controls, the sacredness and soundness of their religious traditions, and so forth. And this is the point I would make here: the world of theater, as we know it both in Asia and America, and the immense variety of theatrical sub-genres derive not from imitation, conscious or unconscious, of the processual form of the complete or "satiated" social drama—breach, crisis, redress, reintegration, or schism—but specifically from its third phase, the one I call redress, especially from redress as *ritual* process, rather than *judicial, political*, or military process, important as these are for the study of political or revolutionary action. Redressive rituals include divination into the hidden causes of misfortune, personal and social conflict, and illness (all of which in tribal societies are intimately interconnected and thought to be caused by the invisible action of spirits, deities, witches, and sorcerers); they include curative ritual (which may often involve episodes of spirit-possession, shamanic trance mediumship, and trance states among the patients who are subjects of ritual); and initiatory rites connected with these "rituals of affliction." Moreover, many of those rites that we call "life-crisis ceremonies," particularly those of puberty, marriage, and death, themselves indicate a major, if not altogether unexpected breach in the orderly, customary running of group life, after which many relationships among its members must change drastically, involving much potential and even actual conflict and competition (for rights of inheritance and succession to office, for women, over the amount of bridewealth, over clan or lineage allegiance). Life-crisis rituals (and seasonal rituals, too, for that matter) may be called "prophylactic," while rituals of affliction are "therapeutic." Life-crisis rituals portray and symbolically resolve archetypal conflicts in abstraction from the milling, teeming social life which characteristically and periodically throws up such conflicts. Society is, therefore, better equipped to deal with them concretely, having portrayed them abstractly.

All these "third-phase" or "first-phase" (if we are talking about life-crises) ritual processes contain within themselves what I have in several writings called a liminal phase, which provides a stage (and I used this term advisedly when thinking about theater) for unique structures of experience (a translation of Dilthey's *Erlebnisse* "living-through"), in milieus detached from mundane life and characterized by the presence of ambiguous ideas, monstrous images, sacred symbols, ordeals, humiliations, esoteric and paradoxical instructions, the emergence of "symbolic types" represented by maskers and clowns, gender reversals, anonymity, and many other phenomena and processes which I have elsewhere described as liminal. The limen, or threshold, a term I took from van Gennep's second of three stages in rites of passage, is a no-man's-land betwixt-and-between the structural past and the structural future as anticipated by the society's normative control of biological development. It is ritualized in many ways, but very often symbols expressive of ambiguous identity are found cross-culturally: androgynes, at once male and female, theriomorphic figures, at once animals and men or women, angels, mermaids, centaurs, human-headed lions, and so forth, monstrous combinations of elements drawn from nature *and* culture. Some symbols represent both birth *and* death, womb *and* tomb, such as caverns or camps secluded from everyday eyes. I sometimes talk about the liminal phase being dominantly in the "subjunctive mood" of culture, the mood of maybe, might-be, as-if, hypothesis, fantasy, conjecture, desire, depending on which of the trinity, cognition, affect, and conation (thought, feeling, or intention) is situationally dominant. We might say, in terms of brain neurobiology, that here right-hemispheric and archaic brain functions are very much in evidence and probably culturally triggered by ritual action. "Ordinary" day-to-day life is in the indicative mood, where we expect the invariant operation of cause-and-effect, of rationality and commonsense. Liminality can perhaps be described as a fructile chaos, a fertile nothingness, a storehouse of possibilities, not by any means a random assemblage but a striving after new forms and structure, a gestation process, a fetation of modes appropriate to and anticipating postliminal existence. It is what goes on in nature in the fertilized egg, in the chrysalis, and even more richly and complexly in their cultural homologues.

Theater is one of the many inheritors of that great multifaceted system of preindustrial ritual which embraces ideas and images of cosmos and chaos, interdigitates clowns and their foolery with gods and their solemnity, and uses all the sensory codes, to produce symphonies in more than music: the intertwining of dance, body languages of many kinds, song, chant, architectural forms (temples, amphitheaters), incense, burnt offerings, ritualized feasting and drinking, painting, body painting, body marking of many kinds, including circumcision and scarification, the application of lotions and drinking of potions, the enacting of mythic and heroic plots drawn from oral traditions. And so much more. Rapid advances in the scale and complexity of society, particularly after industrialization, have passed this unified liminal configuration through the

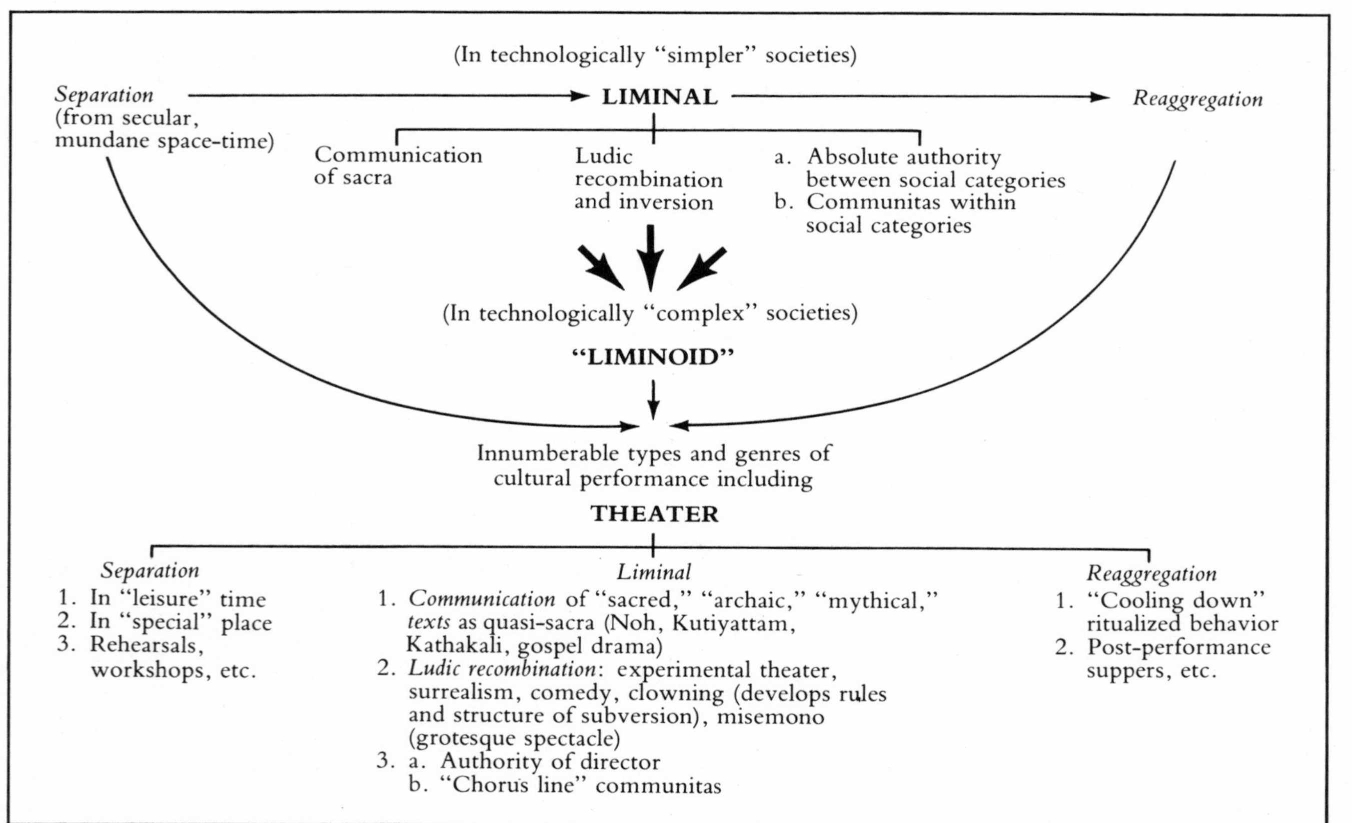

Fig. 4. The evolution of cultural genres of performance: from "Liminal" to "Liminoid."

analytical prism of the division of labor, with its specialization and professionalization, reducing each of these sensory domains to a set of entertainment genres flourishing in the leisure time of society, no longer in a central, driving place. The pronounced numinous supernatural character of archaic ritual has been greatly attenuated.

Nevertheless, there are today signs that the amputated specialized genres are seeking to rejoin and to recover something of the numinosity lost in their *sparagmos*, their dismemberment. Truly, as John Dewey has argued, the aesthetic form of theater is inherent in sociocultural life itself, in what I call "social drama" and Kenneth Burke calls "dramas of living," but the reflexive and therapeutic character of *theater*, as essentially a child of the redressive phase of social drama, has to draw on power sources often inhibited or at least constrained in the cultural life of society's "indicative" mood. The deliberate creation of a detached, still almost-sacred liminal space, allows a search for such sources. One source of this excessive "meta-" power is, clearly, the liberated and disciplined body itself, with its many untapped resources for pleasure, pain, and expression. Here, the experimental theater of Jerzy Grotowski, the Becks, Joe Chaikin, Richard Schechner, Peter Brook, Tadashi Suzuki, and Squat Theater in New York City has its growing importance. Another source draws on unconscious processes, such as may be released in trance foreshadowed by some of Antonin Artaud's theories. This is akin to what I have often seen in Africa, where thin, ill-nourished old ladies, with only occasional naps, dance, sing, and perform ritual activities for two or three days and nights together. I think that a rise in the level of social arousal, however produced, is capable of unlocking energy sources in individual participants. Then there is the work we have been considering on the neurobiology of the brain, summarized in *The Spectrum of Ritual* (d'Aquili et al. 1979:146), which, among other things, shows how the "driving techniques of ritual (including sonic driving by, for example, percussion instruments) facilitate right hemisphere dominance, resulting in Gestalt, timeless nonverbal experiences, differentiated and unique when compared with left hemisphere functioning or hemisphere alternation" (Lex 1979:125). Conferences devoted to the neural substrate of mental and emotional phenomena in ritual and the role of ritual in human adaptation may help to throw further light on the organic and neurological correlates of ritual behaviors.

My argument has been that what I would like to call the anthropology of experience (abolishing the sharp distinction between the classical study of culture and sociobiology) finds in certain recurrent forms of social experience (notably social dramas) sources of aesthetic form, including stage drama and dance. But ritual and its progeny, the performance arts among them, derive from the subjunctive, liminal, reflexive, exploratory heart of the social drama, its third, redressive phase, where the contents of group experiences (*Erlebnisse*) are replicated, dismembered, remembered, refashioned, and mutely or vocally made meaningful (even when, as so often in declining cultures, the meaning is that there is no meaning as in some Existentialist theater). True theater is experience of "heightened vitality," to quote John Dewey again (McDermott 1981:540). True theater "at its height signifies complete interpenetration of self and the world of objects and events." When this happens in a performance, there may be produced in audience and actors alike what d'Aquili and Laughlin (1979:177) call in reference both to ritual and meditation a "brief ecstatic state and sense of union (often lasting only a few seconds) and may often be described as no more than a shiver running down the back at a certain point." A sense of harmony with the universe is made evident, and the whole planet is felt to be communitas. This shiver has to be won, achieved, though, to be a consummation, after working through a tangle of conflicts and disharmonies. Theater best of all exemplifies Thomas Hardy's dictum: "If a way to the better there be, it exacts a full look at the worst." Ritual or theatrical transformation can scarcely occur otherwise. Problems and obstacles (the "crisis" stage of social dramas) challenge our brain neurobiology into full arousal, and culture supplies that aroused activity with a store of preserved social experiences which can be "heated up" to supply the current hunger for meaning with reliable nutrients.

I have had to defend myself against such trenchant critics as my former teachers Sir Raymond Firth and the late Max Gluckman, who accused me of unwarrantably introducing a model drawn from literature (they did not say Western literature, but clearly they had the Aristotelian model of tragedy in mind) to throw light on *spontaneous* social processes, which are not authored or set in conventions, but arise from clashes of interest or incompatible social structural principles in the give and take of everyday life in a social group. Recently, I have taken heart from an article by Clifford Geertz, "Blurred Genres: The Refiguration of Social Thought," which not only suggests "that analogies drawn from the humanities are coming to play the kind of role in sociological understanding that analogies drawn from the crafts and technology have long played in physical understanding" (Geertz 1980a:196), but also gives qualified approval to the "drama analogy for social life" (Geertz 1980a:172). Geertz numbers me among "proponents of the ritual theory of drama"—as against "the *symbolic action* approach" to drama which stresses "the affinities of theater and rhetoric—drama as persuasion, the platform as stage" (Geertz 1980a:172), associated with Kenneth Burke and developed by Erving Goffman. He writes: "For Turner, social dramas occur 'on all levels of social organization from state to family.' They arise out of conflict situations—a village falls into factions, a husband beats a wife, a region rises against the state—and proceed to their denouements through publicly performed conventionalized behavior. As the conflict swells to crisis and the excited fluidity of heightened emotion, where people feel at once more enclosed in a common mood and loosened from their moorings [a good description of "ergotropic" behavior], ritualized forms of authority—litigation, feud, sacrifice, prayer—are invoked to contain it and render it orderly [trophotropic response]. If they succeed, the breach is healed and the status quo, or something resembling it, is restored; if they do not, it is accepted as incapable of remedy and things fall apart into various sorts of unhappy endings: migrations, divorces, or murders in the cathedral. With differing degrees of strictness and detail, Turner and his followers have applied this schema to tribal passage rites, curing ceremonies, and judicial processes; to Mexican insurrections, Icelandic sagas, and Thomas Becket's difficulties with Henry II; to picaresque narrative, millenarian movements, Caribbean carnivals, and Indian peyote hunts; and to the political upheaval of the Sixties. A form for all seasons."

The last comment arises from Geertz's insistence in several of his writings that the social drama approach focuses too narrowly on "the *general* movement of things" (italics added) and neglects the multifarious cultural contents, the symbol systems which embody the ethos and eidos, the sentiments and values of *specific* cultures. He suggests that what he calls the "text analogy" (Geertz 1980:175) can remedy this, that is, textual analysis attends to "how the inscription of action is brought about, what its vehicles are and how they work, and on what the fixation of meaning from the flow of events—history from what happened, thought from thinking, culture from behavior—implies for sociological interpretation. To see social institutions, social customs, social changes as in some sense 'readable' is to alter our whole sense of what such interpretation is towards modes of thought rather more familiar to the translator, the exegete, or the iconographer than to the test giver, the factor analyst, or the pollster" (Geertz 1980a:175 – 76). The inscriptions may be usefully subjected to structural analysis; but, in a sense, and often, they are like the shucked off husks of living process, tiderows left by the receding sea, useful signs, indicators, markers, pointers, readings, crystallizations. But their vitality has gone elsewhere—it is found in the *drama* process.

One answer I could make to Geertz would be simply to reiterate certain features of the social drama approach. He mentions "ritualized forms of authority—litigation, feud, sacrifice, prayer" that are used "to contain (crisis) and to render it orderly." Such forms may crystallize any culture's uniqueness; they are forms for particular seasons. They dominate the third stage of the social drama which can compass immense variabilities. For my part I have, indeed, often treated the ritual and juridical symbol systems of the Ndembu of Western Zambia as text analogues. But I have tried to locate these texts in *context* of *performance*, rather than to construe them from the first into abstract, dominantly cognitive systems. However, Geertz does, in fact, concede that many anthropologists today, including himself, use both textual and dramatistic approaches, according to problem and context. His book entitled *Negara* (1980b), on the drama of kingship in Bali, exemplifies his dual approach. Some of these misunderstandings and apparent contradictions can be resolved if we examine the relationship between the two modes of acting—in "real life" and "on stage"—as components of a dynamic system of interdependence between social dramas and cultural performances. Both dramatistic and textual analogies then fall into place.

Richard Schechner and I represented this relationship as a bisected figure eight laid on its side (see Fig. 5). The two semicircles above the horizontal dividing line represent the manifest, visible public realm. The left loop or circlet represents social drama, which could be divided into its four main phases: breach, crisis, redress, positive or negative denouement. The right loop represents a genre of cultural performance—in this case, a stage of "aesthetic" drama (though it would be better to say the total repertoire of types of cultural performance possessed by a society). Notice that the *manifest* social drama feeds into the latent realm of stage drama; its characteristic form in a given culture, at a given time and place, unconsciously, or perhaps preconsciously, influences not only the form but also the content of the stage drama of which it is the active or "magic" mirror. The stage drama, when it is meant to do more than entertain—though entertainment is always one of its vital aims—is a metacommentary,

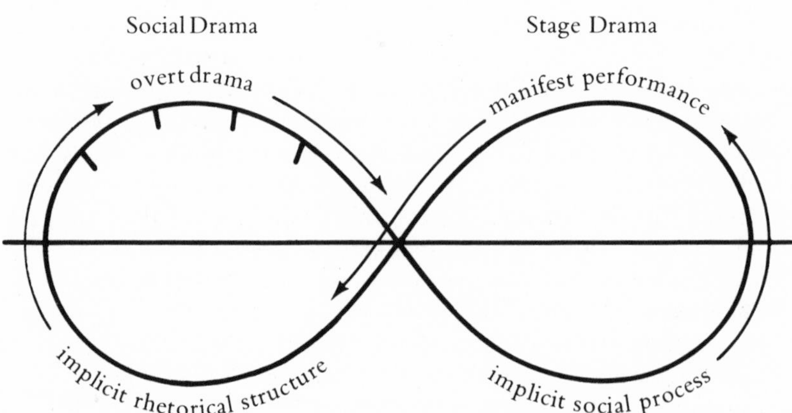

Fig. 5. The interrelationship of social drama and stage drama.

explicit or implicit, witting or unwitting, on the major social dramas of its social context (wars, revolutions, scandals, institutional changes). Not only that, but its message and its rhetoric feed back into the *latent* processual structure of the social drama and partly account for its ready ritualization. Life itself now becomes a mirror held up to art, and the living now *perform* their lives, for the protagonists of a social drama, a "drama of living," have been equipped by aesthetic drama with some of their most salient opinions, imageries, tropes, and ideological perspectives. Neither mutual mirroring, life by art, art by life, is exact, for each is not a planar mirror but a matricial mirror; at each exchange something new is added and something old is lost or discarded. Human beings learn through experience, though all too often they repress painful experience, and perhaps the deepest experience is through drama; not through social drama, or stage drama (or its equivalent) alone, but in the circulatory or oscillatory process of their mutual and incessant modification.

If one were to guess at origins, my conjecture would be that the genres of cultural performance, whether tribal rituals or TV specials, are not, as I have said, simply imitations of the overt form of the completed social drama. They are germinated in its *third*, redressive phase, the reflexive phase, the phase where society pulls meaning from that tangle of action, and, therefore, these performances are infinitely varied, like the result of passing light through a prism. The alternative versions of meaning that complex societies produce are innumerable. Within societies there are different classes, ethnicities, regions, neighborhoods, and people of different ages and sexes, and they each produce versions which try painfully to assign meaning to the particular crisis pattern of their own society. Each performance becomes a record, a means of explanation.

Finally, it should be noted that the interrelation of social drama to stage drama is not in an endless, cyclical, repetitive pattern; it is a spiraling one. The spiraling process is responsive to inventions and the changes in the mode of production in the given society. Individuals can make an enormous impact on the sensibility and understanding of members of society. Philosophers feed their work into the spiraling process; poets feed poems into it; politicians feed their acts into it; and so on. Thus the result is not an endless cyclical repetitive pattern or a stable cosmology. The cosmology has always been destabilized, and society has always had to make efforts, through both social dramas and esthetic dramas, to restabilize and actually *produce* cosmos.

PART FOUR

Reference Material

Bibliography

Andersson, Theodore

1964 *The Problems of Icelandic Saga Origins*. New Haven and London: Yale University Press.

1967 *The Icelandic Saga: An Analytical Reading*. Cambridge: Cambridge University Press.

Arent, Margaret A.

1964 *The Laxdaela Saga: Its Structural Patterns*. Seattle: University of Washington Press.

Barfield, Owen

1962 "Poetic Diction and Legal Fiction." In *The Importance of Language*. Ed. Max Black, pp. 51–71. Englewood Cliffs, New Jersey: Prentice-Hall.

Bateson, Gregory

1972 *Steps to an Ecology of Mind*. New York: Ballantine.

Bedseman, Bernard

1970 *The Dynamics of Drama*. New York: Knopf.

Belmont, Nicole

1944 *Arnold van Gennep: The Creator of French Ethnography*. Chicago: Chicago University Press.

Benamou, Michel, and C. Caramello, eds.

1977 *Performance in Postmodern Culture*. Madison, Wisconsin: Coda.

Bennett, K. A., R. H. Osborne, and R. J. Miller

1975 "Biocultural Ecology." In *Annual Review of Anthropology*. Ed. B. Siegel et al., pp. 163–81. Palo Alto: Annual Reviews.

Bento, Dilson

1979 *Malungo: Decodificação da Umbanda*. Rio de Janeiro: Civilização Brasileira.

Blake, William

1965 *The Poetry and Prose of William Blake*, ed. David V. Erdman. Garden City, New York: Doubleday. *Jerusalem* first published in 1804, *The Four Zoas* in 1797.

Bogen, Joseph E.

1969 "The Other Side of the Brain: An Appositional Mind." *Bulletin of the Los Angeles Neurological Societies* 34:135 – 62.

Brown, D. E.

1974 "Corporations." *Current Anthropology* 15,1:29 – 52.

Brown, J.

1977 *Mind, Brain, and Consciousness*. New York: Academic Press.

Brown, Richard H., and Stanford M. Lyman, eds.

1978 *Structure, Consciousness, and History*. Cambridge: Cambridge University Press.

Burhoe, Ralph Wendell, with Robert L. Moore, and Philip J. Hefner

1983 Introduction. Symposium on *Ritual in Human Adaptation*. *Zygon*, vol. 18, no. 3 (September): 209 – 19.

Caillois, Roger

1979 *Man, Play, and Games*. New York: Schoken.

Chappell, E. D., and C. S. Coon

1942 *Principles of Anthropology*. New York: Henry Holt.

Cohen, Abner

1974 *Two-Dimensional Man: An Essay on the Anthropology of Power and Symbolism in Complex Society*. London: Routledge and Kegan Paul.

Collier, J. F.

1975 "Legal Processes." In *Annual Review of Anthropology*. Ed. B. Siegel et al., pp. 121 – 43. Palo Alto: Annual Reviews.

Collingwood, R. G.

1977 *The Idea of History*. London: Oxford University Press. First published 1946.

Crapanzano, Vincent

1980 *Tuhami: Portrait of a Moroccan*. Chicago: Chicago University Press.

Csikszentmihalyi, Mihali

1974 *Beyond Boredom and Anxiety*. San Francisco: Jossey-Bass.

d'Aquili, E., C. D. Laughlin, Jr., and John McManus, eds.

1979 *The Spectrum of Ritual*. New York: Columbia University Press.

Deutsch, Karl

1966 *The Nerves of Government*. New York: Free Press.

Dilthey, Wilhelm

1914-1974 *Gesammelte Schriften*. Vols. 1 – 12, Stuttgart: Teubner; and Göttingen: Vandenhoeck and Ruprecht. Vols. 13 – 17, Göttingen: Vandenhoeck and Ruprecht.

1957 *Dilthey's Philosophy of Existence*. Trans. W. Kluback and M. Weinbaum. New York: Bookman. First published 1931.

1959 "The Understanding of Other Persons and Their Life Expressions." In *Theories of History: Readings in Classical and Contemporary Sources*, ed. P. Gardiner, pp. 213 – 25. New York: Free Press.

1961 *Pattern and Meaning in History: Thoughts on History and Society*. Ed. H. P. Rickman. New York: Harper Torchbooks.

1976 *Selected Writings*. Trans. and Ed. H. P. Rickman. Cambridge: Cambridge University Press. First published 1914 – 1936.

Douglas, Mary

1975 *Implicit Meanings*. London: Routledge and Kegan Paul.

Drekmeier, Charles

1962 *Kingship and Community in Early India*. Stanford: Stanford University Press.

Dumazedier, J.

1962 *Le loisir et la ville*. Paris: Seuil.

Easton, David

1959 "Political Anthropology." In *Biennial Review of Anthropology*. Ed. B. Siegel, pp. 210 – 62. Stanford: Stanford University Press.

Elwin, Verrier

1955 *The Religion of an Indian Tribe*. London: Cumberlege.

Emery, Stephen A., and William T. Emery

1969 *The Essence of Philosophy*. New York: AMS Press.

Emmet, Dorothy

1958 *Function, Purpose, and Powers*. London: Macmillan & Co.

Epstein, A. L.

1967 "The Case Method in the Field of Law." In The *Craft of Social Anthropology*. Ed. A. L. Epstein, pp. 205 – 30. London: Tavistock.

Evans-Pritchard, E. E.

1949 *The Sanusi of Cyrenaica*. Oxford: Clarendon.

1950 "Social Anthropology: Past and Present." *Man* 50:118 – 24.

1961 *Anthropology and History*. Manchester: Manchester University Press.

1963 *Essays on Social Anthropology*. London: Faber & Faber.

Fallers, Lloyd

1965 "Political Anthropology in Africa." In *New Directions in Anthropology*. London: Tavistock.

Filmer, P., M. Phillipson, D. Silverman, and D. Walsh

1972 "Sociology and the Social World." In *New Directions in Sociological Theory*, pp. 15 – 35. London: Collier-Macmillan.

Firth, Raymond

1957 "A Note on Descent Groups in Polynesia." *Man* 57:4 – 8.

1964 *Essays on Social Organization and Values*. London: Athlone.

1973 *Symbols, Public and Private*. Ithaca: Cornell University Press.

Firth, Raymond (*cont.*)

1975 "Appraisal of Modern Social Anthropology." In *Annual Review of Anthropology*. Ed. B. Siegel et al., pp. 1–25. Palo Alto: Annual Reviews.

Flor-Henry, P.

1976 "Lateralized Temporal-Limbic Dysfunction and Psychopathology." *Annals of the New York Academy of Science* 380:777–97.

Fortes, Meyer

1966 "Religious Premisses and Logical Technique in Divinatory Ritual." In *A Discussion on Ritualization of Behaviour in Animals and Man*, organized by Julian Huxley. *Philosophical Transactions of the Royal Society of London*, Series B, vol. 251, Biological Sciences, pp. 409–22. London: Royal Society of London.

Fortes, Meyer, and E. E. Evans-Pritchard, eds.

1940 *African Political Systems*. London: Oxford University Press for the International African Institute.

Fox, Robin

1973 *Encounter with Anthropology*. New York: Harcourt Brace Jovanovitch.

Freud, Sigmund

1922 *Collected Papers*. London: Hogarth.

Gardiner, Patrick

1959 *Theories of History: Readings in Classical and Contemporary Sources*. New York: Free Press.

Gardner, Howard

1975 *The Shattered Mind*. New York: Vintage.

Gebser, Jean

1973 *Ursprung und Gegenwart*, 3 vols. Munich: Deutsche Taschenbuch Verlag. First published 1949–1952.

Geertz, Clifford

1980a "Blurred Genres: The Refiguration of Social Thought," *American Scholar* (Spring):165–79.

1980b *Negara: The Theatre State in Nineteenth-Century Bali*. Princeton, New Jersey: Princeton University Press.

Gellhorn, E., and W. F. Kiely

1972 "Mystical States of Consciousness: Neurophysiological and Clinical Aspects." *Journal of Mental and Nervous Diseases* 154:399–405.

Gennep, Arnold van

1937 *Manuel de folklore français contemporain*. Paris: Picard.

1960 *The Rites of Passage*. London: Routledge and Kegan Paul. First published 1909.

Gluckman, Max

1954 "Political Institutions." In *Institutions of Primitive Society*. Ed. E. E. Evans-Pritchard. Oxford: Blackwell.

1955a *The Judicial Process among the Barotse of Northern Rhodesia.* Manchester: Manchester University Press.
1955b *Custom and Conflict in Africa.* Oxford: Blackwell; Glencoe, Illinois: Free Press.
1958 *Analysis of a Social Situation in Modern Zululand.* Rhodes-Livingstone Paper No. 28. Manchester: Manchester University Press.
1963 *Order and Rebellion in Tribal Africa.* London: Cohen and West; Glencoe, Illinois: Free Press.
1965 *Politics, Law, and Ritual in Tribal Society.* Oxford: Blackwell.
1962 ———, Ed. *Essays in the Ritual of Social Relations.* Manchester: Manchester University Press.

Gluckman, Max, and Ely Devons, eds.
1964 *Introduction to Closed Systems and Open Minds: The Limits of Naivety in Social Anthropology.* Edinburgh: Oliver and Boyd.

Gordon, E. V.
1927 *Introduction to Old Norse.* London: Oxford University Press.

Grenell, R. G., and S. Gabay, eds.
1976 *Biological Foundations of Psychiatry*, vol. 1. New York: Raven.

Grimes, Ronald
1976 "Ritual Studies: Two Models." *Religious Studies Review* 2 (4):13–25.
1982 *Beginnings in Ritual Studies.* Washington, D.C.: University Press of America.

Gumplowicz, L.
1963 *Outlines of Sociology.* Ed. I. L. Horowitz. New York: Whitman. First published 1833.

Gudmundsson, Bardi
1958 *Höfundur Njalu.* Reykjavik: Bokautgafa Menningarsjods.

Hallberg, Peter
1962 *The Icelandic Saga.* Lincoln, Nebraska: University of Nebraska Press.

Handelman, Don
1977 "Play and Ritual: Complementary Frames of Metacommunication." In *It's a Funny Thing, Humour.* Ed. A. J. Chapman and H. Foot, pp. 185–92. London: Pergamon.

Henry, J. P., and P. M. Stephens
1977 *Stress, Health, and the Social Environment.* New York: Springer-Verlag.

Hermannsson, Halldor
1930 Introductory Essay to *The Book of the Icelanders (Íslendingabók)* by Ari Thorgilsson. Ithaca, NY.: Cornell University Press.

Hess, W. R.
1925 *On the Relationship Between Psychic and Vegetative Functions.* Zurich: Schwabe.

Heusler, Andreas
1941 *Die Altgermanische Dichtung*. Potsdam: Athenaion.

Hinde, Robert, ed.
1972 *Non-Verbal Communication*. Cambridge: Cambridge University Press.

Hockett, Charles
1960 "Logical Considerations in the Study of Animal Communication." In *Animal Sounds and Communication*. Ed. W. E. Lanyon and W. N. Tavolga, pp. 392–430. Washington: American Institute for the Biological Sciences.

Hodges, Herbert
1952 *The Philosophy of Wilhelm Dilthey*. London: Routledge and Kegan Paul.

Hoebel, E. A.
1954 *The Law of Primitive Man: A Study in Comparative Legal Dynamics*. Cambridge: Harvard University Press.

Hügel, Friedrich von
1912 *Eternal Life: A Study of Its Implications and Applications*. Edinburgh: T. and T. Clark.

Huizinga, J.
1955 *Homo Ludens*. Boston: Beacon. First published 1938.

Huxley, Julian, ed.
1966 Introduction to *A Discussion on Ritualization of Behaviour in Animals and Man. Philosophical Transactions of the Royal Society of London*, Series B, vol. 251, Biological Sciences, pp. 249–71. London: Royal Society of London.

Ivins, Jr., William R.
1975 *On the Rationalization of Sight: With an Examination of Three Renaissance Texts on Perspective*. New York: Da Capo.

James, W.
1918 *Principles of Psychology*. New York: Henry Holt. First published 1890.

Jameson, Frederick, trans.
1972 "The Rise of Hermeneutics" by William Dilthey. *New Literary History* vol. 3, no. 2 (Winter).

Jouvet, Michel
1975 "The Function of Dreaming: A Neurophysiologist's Point of View." In *Handbook of Psychobiology*. Ed. M. S. Gazzaniga and C. Blakemore, pp. 499–527. New York: Academic Press.

Jung, Carl
1953–1978 *Collected Works*, vols. 7, 11, and 12. Ed. M. Fordham and G. Adler. London: Routledge and Kegan Paul.

Junod, Henri
1962 *The Life of a South African Tribe*, New Hyde Park, New York: University Books. First published 1912–1913.

Ker, W. P.
1967 *Epic and Romance*. New York: Dover. First published 1908.

Kimball, Solon T.
1960 *Introduction*. In English translation of *Les Rites de Passage*, by Arnold van Gennep, v – xviii. London: Routledge and Kegan Paul.
1968 "Arnold van Gennep." In *International Encyclopedia of the Social Sciences*, vol. 6, pp. 113 – 14. New York: Macmillan Co. and Free Press.

Kluback, William
1956 *Wilhelm Dilthey's Philosophy of History*. New York: Columbia University Press.

Kluback, William, and Martin Weinbaum, trans.
1978 *Dilthey's Philosophy of Existence*. Originally Bookman Associates. [1957]Reprinted by Westport, Conn.: Greenwood Press.

Konner, Melvin
1982 *The Tangled Wing: Biological Constraints on the Human Spirit*. New York: Holt, Rinehart, and Winston.

Kroeber, A. L.
1935 "History and Science in Anthropology." *American Anthropologist* 37 (4), October – December:538 – 69.

Kuhn, Thomas
1962 *The Structure of Scientific Revolutions*. Chicago: Chicago University Press.

Kuper, Hilda
1947 *An African Aristocracy*. London: Oxford University Press for the International African Institute.

Leach, Edmund R.
1966 "Ritualization in Man in Relation to Conceptual and Social Development." In *A Discussion on Ritualization of Behaviour in Animals and Man*, organized by Julian Huxley. *Philosophical Transactions of the Royal Society of London*, Series B, vol. 251, Biological Sciences, pp. 403 – 8. London: Royal Society of London.
1972 "The Influence of Cultural Context on Non-Verbal Communication in Man." In *Non-Verbal Communication*. Ed. Robert A. Hinde, pp. 315 – 47. Cambridge: Cambridge University Press.

Legesse, Asmoron
1973 *Gada: Three Approaches to the Study of African Society*. London: Collier-Macmillan.

Levine, Donald
1965 *Wax and Gold: Tradition and Innovation in Ethiopian Culture*. Chicago: Chicago University Press.

Lévi-Strauss, Claude
1955 *Triste Tropique*. New York: Atheneum.
1963a *Structural Anthropology*. New York: Anchor Books.

Lévi-Strauss, Claude *(cont.)*
1963b *The Savage Mind*. Chicago: Chicago University Press.
1964 *Mythologiques: le crut et le cuit*. Paris: Plon.
1967 *The Scope of Anthropology*. London: Cape.

Levy, M. J.
1952 *The Structure of Society*. Princeton, N.J.: Princeton University Press.

Levy, Reuben
1967 Prologue to his translation of *The Epic of the Kings: Shah-nama, The National Epic of Persia*. London: Routledge and Kegan Paul.

Lévy-Bruhl, Lucien
1923 *Primitive Mentality*. New York: Macmillan Co. First published as *La mentalité primitive* 1922.

Lewin, Kurt
1951 *Field Theory in Social Science*. Ed. D. Cartwright. New York: Harper.

Lewis, I. M.
1968 *History and Social Anthropology*, ASA Monograph 7. London: Tavistock.

Lex, Barbara
1979 "Neurobiology of Ritual Trance." In *The Spectrum of Ritual*. Ed. E. d'Aquili et al., pp. 117–51. New York: Columbia University Press.

Liddell, H. G. and Robert Scott, eds.
1975 *An Intermediate Greek-English Lexicon*. Oxford: Clarendon.

Lord, Albert
1960 *The Singer of Tales*. Cambridge: Harvard University Press.

Lyons, J.
1972 "Human Language." In *Non-Verbal Communication*. Ed. Robert A. Hinde, pp. 49–85. Cambridge: Cambridge University Press.

McDermott, J. J., ed.
1981 *The Philosophy of John Dewey*. Chicago: Chicago University Press.

MacKay, D. M.
1972 "Formal Analysis of Communicative Processes." In *Non-Verbal Communication*. Ed. Robert A. Hinde, pp. 3–25. Cambridge: Cambridge University Press.

MacLean, Paul D.
1949 "Psychosomatic Disease and the 'Visceral Brain': Recent Developments Bearing on the Papez Theory of Emotion." *Psychosomatic Medicine* 11:338–53.
1973 "A Triune Concept of Brain and Behavior." In *The Hinks Memorial Lectures*. Ed. T. Boag and D. Campbell, pp. 6–66. Toronto: Toronto University Press.

1975 "On the Evolution of Three Mentalities." *Man-Environment Systems* 5.

1976 "Sensory and Perceptive Factors in Emotional Functions of the Triune Brain." In *Biological Foundations of Psychiatry*, vol. 1. Ed. R. G. Grenell and S. Gabay, pp. 177–98. New York: Raven.

1982 "Evolution of the Psychencephalon." *Zygon* 17 (June):187–211.

McNeill, William H.

1963 *The Rise of the West*. New York: Mentor.

Makkreel, R. A.

1979 *Dilthey: Philosopher of the Human Studies*. Princeton, New Jersey: Princeton University Press.

Mandell, Arnold J.

1980 "Towards a Psychobiology of Transcendence." In *The Psychobiology of Consciousness*. Ed. J. M. Davidson and J. R. Davidson. New York: Plenum.

Middleton, John

1960 *Lugbara Religion*. London: Oxford University Press.

Misch, Georg

1957 Introduction to *Gesammelte Schriften* by Wilhelm Dilthey, vol. 5. Stuttgart: Teubner; Göttingen: Vandenhoeck and Ruprecht.

Mitchell, J. Clyde

1955 *The Yao Village*. Manchester: Manchester University Press.

Moore, Sally Falk

1975 Epilogue in *Symbol and Politics in Communal Ideology*. Ed. Sally Falk Moore and Barbara Myerhoff, pp. 210–38. Ithaca: Cornell University Press.

1978 *Law as Process*. London: Routledge and Kegan Paul.

Moore, Sally Falk, and Barbara Myerhoff, eds.

1977 *Secular Ritual*. Amsterdam: Van Gorcum.

Morgan, Lewis Henry

1871 *Systems of Consanguinity and Affinity in the Human Family*. Washington, D.C.: Smithsonian Institution.

Murdock, G. P.

1949 *Social Structure*. New York: Macmillan Co.

Murphy, R. F.

1971 *The Dialectics of Social Life*. New York: Basic Books.

Myerhoff, Barbara

1978 *Number Our Days*. New York: Dutton.

Myerhoff, Barbara, and Sally Falk Moore, eds.

1977 *Secular Ritual*. Amsterdam: Van Gorcum.

Nadel, S. F.

1954 *Nupe Religion*. London: Routledge and Kegan Paul.

Nauta, Walle

1971 "The Problem of the Frontal Lobe: A Reinterpretation." *Journal of Psychiatric Research* 8:167–87.

Njal's Saga
1900 Trans. George W. Dasent as *The Story of Burnt Njal*. London: Grant Richards. Written in the thirteenth century.

Nordal, Sigurdur
1953 "Sagalitteraturen." In *Litteratur-Historie B. Norge og Island*, Nordisk Kultur, 8B. Stockholm: Bonnier.

Old, James
1976 "Behavioral Studies of Hypothalamic Functions." In *Biological Foundations of Psychiatry*, vol. 1. Ed. R. Grenell and S. Gabay. New York: Raven.

Olney, James
1972 *Metaphors of Self*. Princeton, N.J.: Princeton University Press.

Olsen, B. M.
1911 "Om Gunnlaugs Saga Ormstungu." D. Kgl. Danske Vidensk. Selsk. Skrifter 7, Roekke, Hist. og Fil. Afd. II, part i, pp. 1–54.

Palmer, Richard
1977 "Towards a Postmodern Hermeneutics of Performance." In *Performance in Postmodern Culture*. Ed. Michel Benamou, pp. 19–32. Madison, Wisconsin: University of Wisconsin Press.

Pálsson, Herman, and Paul Edwards, trans.
1973 *Eyrbyggya Saga*. Edinburgh: Southside.

Peltason, J. W.
1969 "Judicial Process." In *International Encyclopedia of the Social Sciences*, vol. 8, pp. 283–91. New York: Macmillan and Free Press.

Plog, Fred T.
1975 "Systems Theory in Archeological Research." In *Annual Review of Anthropology*. Ed. B. Siegel et al., pp. 207–23. Palo Alto: Annual Reviews.

Radcliffe-Brown, A. R., and Daryll Forde, eds.
1950 *African Systems of Kinship and Marriage*. London: Oxford University Press.

Richmond, Farley
1980 "The Rites of Passage and Kutiyattam, the Sanskrit Theater of Kerala." In *The Communication of Ideas*. New Delhi: Concept.

Richmond, Farley, and Yasmin Richmond
1980 "The Multiple Dimensions of Time and Space in Kutiyattam, the Sanskrit Theater of Kerala." Paper delivered at the 9th Annual Conference on South Asia, Madison, Wisconsin, 7–9 November.

Rickman, H. P.
1961 *Pattern and Meaning in History: Thoughts on History and Society*. New York: Harper Torchbooks.
1976 ———, trans. and ed. *W. Dilthey: Selected Writings*. Cambridge: Cambridge University Press.

Ricoeur, Paul
1963 "Symbole et temporalité." *Archivie di filosophia* 1–2:5–41.

Roheim, Geza
1978 *The Origin and Function of Culture*. New York: Johnson Reprint Corporation. First published 1943.

Rose, Stephen
1976 *The Conscious Brain*. New York: Vintage.

Rossi, E.
1977 "The Cerebral Hemispheres in Analytical Psychology." *Journal of Analytical Psychology* 22:32–51.

Sapir, Edward
1930–1935 "Symbols." In *Encyclopedia of the Social Sciences*, XIV. New York: Macmillan.

Schechner, Richard
1977 *Essays on Performance Theory*. New York: Drama Books.

Scholte, Bob
1973 "The Structural Anthropology of Claude Lévi-Strauss." In *Handbook of Social and Cultural Anthropology*. Ed. J. J. Honigmann, pp. 637–716. Chicago: Rand McNally.

Schutz, A.
1962 *Collected Papers*, vol. 1. The Hague: Nijhoff.

Schwartz, G. E., R. J. Davidson, and F. Maer
1975 "Right Hemisphere Lateralization for Emotion in the Human Brain: Interaction with Cognition." *Science* 190:286–88.

Schwartz, Theodore
1978 "Where is the Culture?" In *The Making of Psychological Anthropology*. Ed. George Spindler, pp. 419–41. Berkeley: University of California Press.

Simmel, Georg
1950 *The Sociology of Georg Simmel*, trans. K. W. Wolff. Glencoe: Free Press.

Singer, Milton, ed.
1966 *An Anthropologist Looks at History*. Berkeley and Los Angeles: University of California Press.

Spindler, George, ed.
1978 *The Making of Psychological Anthropology*. Berkeley: University of California Press.

Spiro, Melford
1978 "Culture and Human Nature." In *The Making of Psychological Anthropology*. Ed. George Spindler, pp. 331–60. Berkeley: University of California Press.

Srinivas, M. N.
1952 *Religion and Society among the Coorgs of South India*. Oxford: Clarendon.

Steiner, George
1962 *Homer: A Collection of Critical Essays*. Englewood Cliffs, New Jersey: Prentice-Hall.

Stevens, Anthony
1982 *Archetypes: A Natural History of the Self*. New York: Morrow.

Sturla Thordarson
1970 *Sturlunga Saga*. Tran. Julia H. McGrew. New York: Twayne. Written in the thirteenth century.

Sveinsson, Einar O.
1953 *The Age of the Sturlungs: Icelandic Civilization in the Thirteenth Century*. Ithaca, N.Y.: Cornell University Press.

Swartz, Marc, ed.
1968 *Local-Level Politics*. Chicago: Aldine.

Swartz, Marc, Victor Turner, and Arthur Tuden, eds.
1966 *Political Anthropology*. Chicago: Aldine.

Trevarthen, Colwyn
1974 "Cerebral Embryology and the Split Brain." In *Hemispheric Disconnection and Cerebral Function*. Ed. M. Kinsbourne and W. L. Smith, pp. 208 – 36. Springfield, Ill.: Charles C. Thomas.

Turner, Victor
1957 *Schism and Continuity in an African Society: A Study of Ndembu Village Life*. Manchester: Manchester University Press.
1962 "Three Symbols of *Passage* in Ndembu Circumcision Ritual: An Interpretation." In *Essays on the Ritual of Social Relations*. Ed. M. Gluckman, pp. 124 – 73. Manchester: Manchester University Press.
1964 "Betwixt and Between: The Liminal Period in Rites of Passage." In *Proceedings of the American Ethnological Society for 1964*, pp. 4 – 20. Seattle: University of Washington Press.
1967 *The Forest of Symbols: Aspects of Ndembu Ritual*. Ithaca, N.Y.: Cornell University Press.
1968 *The Drums of Affliction: A Study of Religious Processes among the Ndembu of Zambia*. Oxford: Clarendon.
1969 *The Ritual Process: Structure and Anti-Structure*. Chicago: Aldine.
1974 *Dramas, Fields, and Metaphors: Symbolic Action in Human Society*. Ithaca, N.Y.: Cornell University Press.
1975a *Revelation and Divination in Ndembu Ritual*. Ithaca, N.Y.: Cornell University Press.
1975b "Symbolic Studies." In *Annual Review of Anthropology*. Ed. B. Siegel et al., pp. 145 – 61. Palo Alto: Annual Reviews.
1977 "Frame, Flow, and Reflection: Ritual Drama as Public Liminality." In *Performance in Postmodern Culture*. Ed. Michel Benamou and C. Caramello, pp., 33 – 55. Madison, Wisconsin: Coda.

1982 *From Ritual to Theatre*. New York: Performing Arts Journal Publications.

Turville-Petre, E. O. G.
1953 *Origins of Icelandic Literature*. Oxford: Clarendon.

Ullendorf, Edward
1960 *The Ethiopians*. London: Oxford University Press.

Vansina, Jan
1965 *Oral Tradition*. Chicago: Aldine.

Van Velsen, Jaap
1964 *The Politics of Kinship*. Manchester: Manchester University Press.
1967 "The Extended-Case Method and Situational Analysis." In *The Craft of Social Anthropology*. Ed. A. L. Epstein, pp. 129–49. London: Tavistock.

Vayda, A. P., and B. J. McCay
1975 "New Directions in Ecology and Ecological Anthropology." In *Annual Review of Anthropology*. Ed. B. Siegel et al., pp. 293–305. Palo Alto: Annual Reviews.

Veblen, Thorstein, trans.
1925 *The Laxdaela Saga*. New York: B. W. Huebsch.

Velho, Yvonne Maggie Alves
1975 *Guerra de Orixá: Um Estudo de Ritual e Conflito, War of Gods: A Study of Ritual and Conflict*. Rio de Janeiro: Zahar Editores.

Vigfusson, Gudbrand
1879 *Sturlunga Saga*. Oxford: Clarendon.

Vigfusson, Gudbrand, and F. York Powell
1905 *Origines Islandicae*, 2 vols. Oxford: Clarendon.

Wax, Rosalie
1969 *Magic, Fate, and History: The Changing Ethos of the Vikings*. Lawrence, Kansas: Coronado Press.

Whiting, J. W., and I. L. Child
1953 *Child Training and Personality: A Cross-Cultural Study*. New Haven: Yale University Press.

Williams, Robin
1968 "The Concept of Values." In *International Encyclopedia of the Social Sciences*, vol. 16, pp. 283–86. New York: Macmillan and Free Press.

Wilson, Monica
1957 *Good Company*. London: Oxford University Press for the International Institute.

Wilson, Godfrey, and Monica Wilson
1945 *Analysis of Social Change*. Cambridge: Cambridge University Press.

Young, Frank W.
1965 *Initiation Ceremonies: A Cross-Cultural Study of Status Dramatization*. Indianapolis: Bobbs-Merrill.
Zuesse, Evan M.
1979 *Ritual Cosmos*. Athens, Ohio: Ohio University Press.

Index